Java®
Programming

for the absolute beginner

Check the Web for Updates

To check for updates or corrections relevant to this book and/or CD-ROM visit our updates page on the Web at **http://www.prima-tech.com/support**.

Send Us Your Comments

To comment on this book or any other PRIMA TECH title, visit our reader response page on the Web at **http://www.prima-tech.com/comments**.

How to Order

For information on quantity discounts, contact the publisher: Prima Publishing, P.O. Box 1260BK, Rocklin, CA 95677-1260; (916) 787-7000. On your letterhead, include information concerning the intended use of the books and the number of books you want to purchase. For individual orders, turn to the back of this book for more information.

Java® Programming

for the absolute beginner

Joseph P. Russell

A Division of Prima Publishing

Prima Publishing and colophon are registered trademarks of Prima Communications, Inc. PRIMA TECH is a trademark of Prima Communications, Inc., Roseville, California 95661.

Java, Forte, NetBeans and all trademarks and logos based on Java, Forte and NetBeans are trademarks or registered trademarks of Sun Microsystems, Inc. in the U.S. and other countries. Internet Explorer is a registered trademark of Microsoft Corporation in the United States and/or other countries. Netscape is a registered trademark of Netscape Communications Corporation in the U.S. and other countries.

Important: Prima Publishing cannot provide software support. Please contact the appropriate software manufacturer's technical support line or Web site for assistance.

Prima Publishing and the author have attempted throughout this book to distinguish proprietary trademarks from descriptive terms by following the capitalization style used by the manufacturer.

Information contained in this book has been obtained by Prima Publishing from sources believed to be reliable. However, because of the possibility of human or mechanical error by our sources, Prima Publishing, or others, the Publisher does not guarantee the accuracy, adequacy, or completeness of any information and is not responsible for any errors or omissions or the results obtained from use of such information. Readers should be particularly aware of the fact that the Internet is an ever-changing entity. Some facts may have changed since this book went to press.

ISBN: 0-7615-3522-5

Library of Congress Catalog Card Number: 2001-091380

Printed in Canada

00 01 02 03 04 WC 10 9 8 7 6 5 4 3

Publisher:
Stacy L. Hiquet

Managing Editor:
Sandy Doell

Acquisitions Editor:
Melody Layne

Project Editor:
Kezia Endsley

Technical Reviewer:
Michelle Jones

Copy Editor:
Kezia Endsley

Associate Marketing Manager:
Heather Buzzingham

Interior Layout:
William Hartman

Cover Design:
Prima Design Team

Indexer:
Sharon Shock

Proofreader:
Jenny Davidson

This book is dedicated to
Brianne, Tyler, and to the
rest of my family, past,
present, and future.

You all make life on this great
big ball of dung worth living.

Acknowledgments

I would like to thank my parents, Joe and Joan, for cheering me on and helping me out with Brianne and Tyler while I was working on this book. Thanks also to Brianne and Tyler for keeping me happy while I wasn't. Thanks also to my sister Roseanne, for putting me on the right career path. I love all of you.

I'd also like to thank Kezia Endsley for doing a great editing job and rewording my babble so that it actually makes sense.

Thanks to Melody Layne for finding me and bringing me in to work in this project. Thanks also to Michelle Jones, Jenny Davidson, and everyone else that was a part of this project.

About the Author

Joseph P. Russell is a development programmer for Meditech, a major medical information systems software and service company, developing software for their client/server financial products. He is a Sun certified programmer for the Java 2 platform. He is also a contributing writer for eastcoastgames.com (**http://www.eastcoastgames.com**). He is a graduate from Rhode Island College where he majored in computer science. He also worked as a Web developer for their Web site (**http://www.ric.edu**). It was during his college years that he acquired a passion for Web development and decided to learn Java and JavaScript. After graduating, he worked as a Web developer/programmer for Progressive Systems Technology, a company that provides Progress database consulting and develops applications for commercial Internet based companies.

In his spare time, he enjoys game programming, painting, and playing his electric bass guitar. He is a father of two beautiful children, a girl and a boy, and he loves being a family man. You can visit his home page at **http://members.home.net/j.p.russell** or e-mail him at **j.p.russell@home.com**.

Contents at a Glance

Contents

CHAPTER 2
Variables, Data Types, and Simple I/O
25

CHAPTER 3
The Fortune Teller: Random Numbers, Conditionals, and Arrays
55

CHAPTER 4
Using Loops and Exception Handling
93

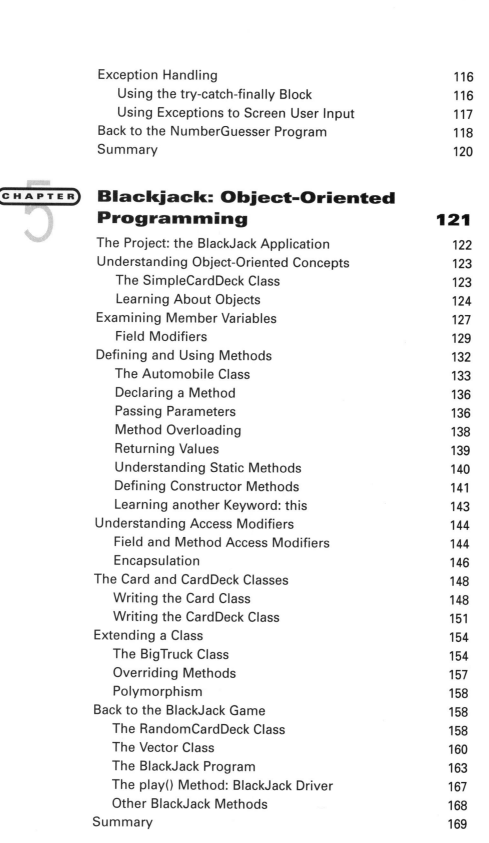

CHAPTER 5

Blackjack: Object-Oriented Programming   121

Creating a GUI Using the Abstract Windowing Toolkit 171

Advanced GUI: Layout Managers and Event Handling 221

CHAPTER 8 — Writing Applets 277

CHAPTER 9   The Graphics Class: Drawing Shapes, Images, and Text   313

CHAPTER 10   Animation, Sounds, and Threads   353

Custom Event Handling and File I/O 377

Introduction

Hello and welcome to *Java Programming for the Absolute Beginner*. You probably already have a good understanding of how to use your computer. These days it's hard to find someone who doesn't, given the importance of computers in today's world. Learning to control your computer intimately is what will separate you from the pack! By reading this book, you learn how to accomplish just that through the magic of programming.

There is a world of difference between using a computer and controlling its operations. When I was a kid, I didn't merely play with my toys. I found more enjoyment in taking them apart to see how they worked from the inside out. Similarly, when I started playing computer games in elementary school, I wasn't happy with just playing them. Sure, the games were fun, but I wanted to see how they worked.

I found the source code to one of the games we were allowed to play in the school library, so I changed a few things. Needless to say, the game no longer worked and I was banned from using the computer, but my interest in programming was sparked that very day.

This book thoroughly covers basic programming concepts using the Java programming language. You apply these concepts through programming games that are not only challenging and rewarding to create, but are fun to play! In addition, you can apply your knowledge to change the game programs to work the way you want them to, just as I did when I started programming. Even better than that, you can program your own games from the ground up.

Java has infinitely more uses in the real world than game development. The purpose of this book is not to teach game development. I use game programs as fun examples that demonstrate programming concepts that you can apply to any kind of Java programming solution.

Many companies use Java because of its *platform independence*. Another use of Java is to create applets for Internet solutions. Internet companies, such as online stores, can use Java to create user interfaces that online shoppers can use to purchase their goods. They can also use server-side Java programs to keep their databases up to date as their products are being purchased. Knowledge of Java is a great asset to any programmer, especially given the Internet's importance in today's business world.

Another goal of this book is to demonstrate programming skills in such a way that allows you to apply these skills when writing other Java programs or when learning new languages. I believe that you will find this approach to learning programming through the use of game examples very comfortable. The examples are fun to program, and at the same time, demonstrate important programming skills that you can use to write different types of programs.

Who Should Read This Book?

I do not assume that you have any programming experience. If you do have some programming experience, but have little to no experience with Java, you will also benefit from reading this book and learning Java at a beginner's level. If you have already read another book on Java or have taken even an intro Java course, this book is not for you.

You should have a good graphics editor and sound editor. In addition, you will need Sun's Java 1.3 SDK (software development kit) and documentation, which you can find at **http://java.sun.com/j2se/1.3/docs.html**. All the other requirements are included on the accompanying CD-ROM. You will need a text editor such as Notepad or a Java IDE (Integrated Development Environment) such as NetBeans so that you can write and edit your Java programs. There is a link to the home page of NetBeans on the CD-ROM in the "Web Links" section. This book does not explain how to use the IDE. The instructions for writing and compiling your programs assume you are using a text editor. You will also need recent versions of Web browsers such as Netscape 6 and Internet Explorer 5, or later versions, to run the applets. (Internet Explorer 5.5 is included on the CD-ROM.)

How to Use This Book

Learning a programming language such as Java is a process. First, you need to learn the basic skills, and then you build upon them to learn the more involved skills. If you have no experience with programming or are new to the Java language, I urge you to read the chapters in order. Just about all of the chapters in this book build upon concepts covered in earlier chapters. The first five chapters lay the groundwork by covering basic syntax, variables, arrays, loops, conditionals, and object-oriented programming concepts. If you feel adventurous and want to skip around, you should at least read the these chapters in order.

If you already have some experience with Java, you may be able to skim through Chapters 1 through 5 quickly, or possibly skip ahead to the chapters that follow them to learn more advanced Java programming right away.

At the beginning of each chapter, you are presented with a complete program. This program encompasses all the major topics covered within that chapter. It allows you to see what you'll accomplish by reading the chapter. You should consider these programs your projects for the chapters, or your goals to achieve by the time you are finished reading the chapters.

Next, you learn each of the topics covered in the chapter, one at a time, and write a program for each of the new skills that you learn. Finally, you put these concepts together to build the project you see at the beginning of the chapter. Each of the smaller examples are straightforward and to the point so that you will quickly learn the concepts and not be confused by too much unnecessary code.

It is important that you actually get your hands dirty and program the examples yourself. The best way to get a good feel for Java, or any other language, is not from simply reading a book. You need to work hands-on. Not only that, you should feel free to put your own spin on each of the examples and experiment on your own. If you don't feel like saying "Hello, world!" in Chapter 1, and instead, feel like saying "Ciao, Il Mondo!", go ahead. If you have an idea of how to improve or expand upon the examples, you should do so. Experiment and have fun!

Added Advice to Make You a Pro

Throughout the book, certain conventions are used to enhance your reading experience:

- **Hints**: These are programming notes that give you more insight into a particular topic.
- **Traps**: There are certain areas in the Java language that are prone to common mistakes. I point them out to you by using these traps.
- **Tricks**: These are programming tips that you can use to make writing code easier or to make your programs run more efficiently.
- **In the Real World**: These sidebars explain how the topics you are learning and the simple programs you are writing can be used in the real world.
- **Key terms**: Each time you come across a new term, it is italicized and explained carefully.
- **Challenges**: At the end of each chapter, you will find some exercises that challenge you to use the skills you have learned up to that point. The code

for these challenges is not found in the book or on the CD-ROM. They are for you to program on your own and will help you get a better feel for Java. Don't think of these as test questions. They are there to help you learn by encouraging you to think for yourself.

What's on the CD-ROM?

On the book's CD-ROM, you'll find the following helpful utilities and programs:

- Sun's SDK 1.3.1 for Windows, Solaris, and Linux
- All the source code and class files from the book, organized by chapter
- The GIMP image editor
- Cool Edit Pro sound editor demo
- Microsoft Internet Explorer 5.5
- Winzip 8.0

See Appendix A for instructions on how to install and use it.

CHAPTER 1

Getting Started

With this chapter, you begin to become familiar with the Java programming language and learn how to apply your knowledge to create Java applications and applets. Java *applications* are stand-alone programs that run on your system's operating system. Java *applets* are programs that run within a Web browser as part of a Web page. For example, if you do a search for "Java Games" on **http://www.yahoo.com**, you will see a list of links to games that were written as applets that you can play online within your Web browser. Everything you need to know in order to create your first simple application and applet can be found within the pages of this chapter. I cover all the basics here: from installing Sun's Java Software Development Kit (SDK 1.3), to writing your first set of programs, to compiling and running them. Make sure that you read this chapter carefully. By reading the information it contains, you form a base of knowledge that you will call upon in the later chapters. Specifically, in this chapter, you:

- **Learn what Java is**

- **Install the Java Software Development Kit (SDK 1.3)**

- **Write your first Java application**

- **Learn Java syntax basics**

- **Write your first Java applet**

The Project: the *HelloWeb* Applet

The HelloWeb applet runs within your Web browser. It simply displays a message, "Hello, World Wide Web!" In Figure 1.1, you can see what this applet looks like when it runs.

FIGURE 1.1

This is the HelloWeb applet as it appears while running in Internet Explorer 5. The darker rectangle displaying "Hello, World Wide Web!" is the applet's area.

By the end of this chapter, you will be able to create this `HelloWeb` applet. More importantly, you will understand all the concepts behind it and will be able to create similar programs of your own. This simple applet displays some text within a Java-enabled Web browser.

At this point, you might not consider this applet a big deal because all it does is display a message. Although it isn't very useful in that you don't need to write a Java program to display text in an HTML document, it is a big step for anyone starting out with Java. It isn't simply the output that is important. By the time you produce this applet, you will understand how to write a Java program, how to compile it, and how to include it in an HTML document. You will be well on your way to learning the more complicated aspects of the Java programming language. In this book, the most significant concepts are the first that you learn. After you have the basics down, you can consider yourself a Java programmer who is able to take on more challenging Java concepts. So learning how to create this simple applet really is a big deal if you think about it.

What Is Java?

The fact that you are reading this book suggests that you have at least heard of Java and have a basic idea how it is used. Sun Microsystems began developing Java behind closed doors in 1991. It wasn't revealed to the public until 1995, when Sun announced the language and Netscape announced Web browser support. Java is a relatively new and exciting technology. Interestingly enough, it was initially developed as a solution for household appliances. From there it has evolved into a fully functional programming language. What makes Java so special? Well, Java can be integrated directly into a Web page as an applet, making the Internet

---

HOW DID JAVA GET ITS NAME?

When you think of other programming languages' names, such as BASIC, FOR-TRAN, COBOL, C, C++, and PASCAL, the name Java doesn't really fit in. The name itself is interesting enough to garner curiosity. So just how did Java get its name? The original name for Java was intended to be "OAK", but they couldn't use that name because it was already taken (by Oak Technologies). Other names floating around were "Silk" and "DNA". Apparently, the name "Java" was ultimately picked because it gave the Web a "jolt" and Sun wanted to avoid names that sounded nerdy. Java certainly does its part in making the Internet the interactive, dynamic, not to mention fun, technology that it is. You can read more about this at http://www.javaworld.com/javaworld/jw-10-1996/jw-10-javaname.fullquote.html.

a much more dynamic and interesting place to gather information, do business, or just have fun! In fact, it is more than likely that this dynamic aspect of Java is what initially sparked your interest, as it did mine. Java can do much more than that, as you will see, and it continues to grow and evolve.

Java Is a Programming Language

Granted, the title of this book is *Java Programming for the Absolute Beginner*, so I'm sure that you understand that Java is a programming language. Still, it is beneficial to understand exactly what a programming language is and what a programming language should be able to do. A *program* is a structured series of instructions that directs a computer to perform specific operations. A computer is a machine. It does not have any intelligence of its own. It needs to be controlled; much like a car must be driven. A car cannot drive itself, with the fictional exception of Kit, the beloved star of the '80s hit television program *Knight Rider*. A driver is needed to operate, or control, the car.

Similarly, a computer program controls a computer's operation. A *programming language* contains a vocabulary that allows a programmer to communicate a series of instructions to a computer in a form that the computer can understand and obey. Without programs, a computer is as useless as a car without a driver. In this way, Java is a fully functional programming language, more easily compared to C, C++, or Visual Basic in its capabilities than it is to JavaScript, VBScript, or HTML, which might be surprising to anyone who considers Java only an Internet development tool.

More specifically, Java is a high-level programming language. A *high-level programming language* uses instructions that more closely resemble a written language (such as English) than machine language. On the other end, machine language, in which groups of ones and zeros represent instructions that are interpreted by the computer directly, is cryptic, and difficult to interpret, unless you are a computer. High-level languages are much easier to understand. In fact, without ever formally learning the Java language, you can probably randomly flip to any program listing in this book, read a line of code, and make a pretty good guess as to what that line of code does.

Java Is Platform Independent

One of the most appealing aspects of Java is its platform independence. Java is *platform independent* because you can run Java programs on any operating system without having to rewrite or recompile them for each system. This is a significant advantage, particularly when developing applets or applications that are downloaded from the Internet and that need to run on many different systems.

Java runs independently of any specific hardware architecture or operating system. In other programming languages, it is common for a programmer to make references to operating system-dependent APIs within his or her code. An *API* is an application programming interface containing predefined functions that make it easier for programmers to perform tasks. Operating system-dependent APIs are closely associated to the operation system and will not work on other operating systems. In other words, Windows has its own set of APIs that differ from Mac's APIs and both of these operating systems have different API sets than Linux. If you want to run a program on a different operating system, you need to rewrite it. With other such languages, even if there are no platform-dependent references, you might need to recompile the program before it will run on a different operating system.

 Although it is possible to make references to platform-dependent APIs in Java code, it is considered bad practice. In doing so, you strip away your program's advantage of being platform independent. There are almost always alternatives, so it is worth the effort to do a bit more research so that your programs retain their platform independence.

How is this platform independence possible, you ask? The answer lies in the way operating systems interpret Java. No matter what system you are programming for, the source code you write will be the same. *Source code* is a listing of the program code, as it appears when the programmer writes it. When you *compile* the source code, or translate it into a form that the computer can interpret, it becomes Java byte code. *Java byte code* is a compiled Java program that is readily interpreted by the Java run-time environment (JRE). Each operating system has its own JRE, which is essentially a Java interpreter, also known as the Java virtual machine, or Java VM for short, running on it. The JRE interprets Java byte code and instructs the operating system it resides on as to which operations to perform. Figure 1.2 shows how all this works.

Java Is Object-Oriented

You and I live in a world full of objects—books, cars, tables, chairs, remote controls, televisions, and so on. Although this is not a new concept in life, it is a fairly new concept in computer programming. You see, most of the older programming languages are procedure-oriented. A *procedure-oriented* program follows a logically ordered set of instructions to perform a specific task. For example, let's say you're going to a *Metallica* concert. The band is performing at a place you've never been to, so you have to call ahead to get directions. The person on the other end of the phone will tell you things like "Get on the highway and go South to exit 22." And "Turn left at the light." The point is that he or she will give you a specific,

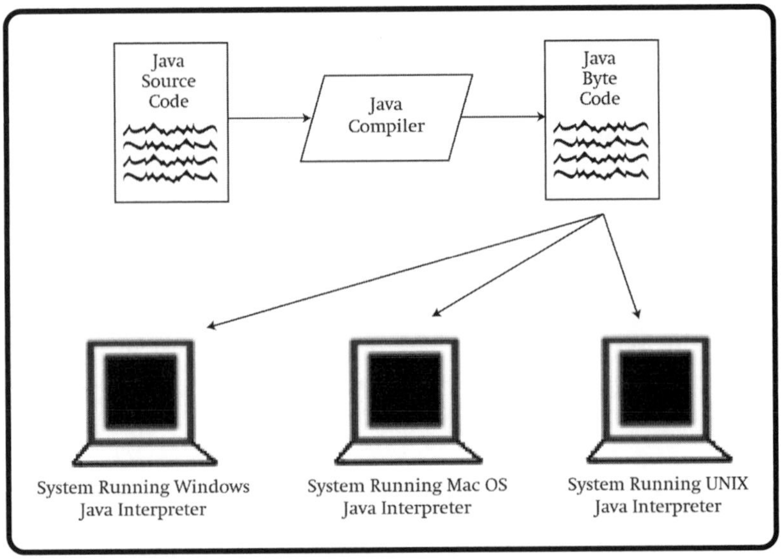

FIGURE 1.2

Java source code
is compiled into
Java byte code,
which can be
interpreted by any
system running a
Java interpreter.

ordered, set of directions for you to follow to get from point A to point B. This is basically how procedural programming languages are structured.

Object-oriented programming (OOP) languages, on the other hand, have the added capability to encapsulate sets of characteristics and functions into what are called *classes*. Instances of these classes are called *objects*.

As an analogy, consider a ball as a basic class of objects. A ball is spherical, can have a specific color, can be solid or hollow, large or small, and it can have many other characteristics. What can you do with a ball? You can throw it, bounce it, hit it with a bat, or kick it, depending on what kind of ball it is. You can consider "ball" to be a class of objects in which every ball is defined to have the same set of characteristics. Pick up any ball, any specific ball at all. That ball belongs within the class ball and has all the basic characteristics and uses that every other ball in the universe has. It is a specific instance of a ball.

From a programming perspective, a class is programming code that defines attributes and functions used to describe objects. Say you wanted to add an OK button in a user interface so that users can click it to perform some task. How convenient it would be for you to be able to write code that basically translates to something similar to "Get a button that says OK, and when a user clicks it, do the following things." By using object-oriented programming, you can do just that. You need to write code that describes what a button is and can do only once. Then you can reuse that code by referring to a button object in your code. Even simpler than that, if someone else already "described" what a button is, you can use that code by calling some object in your code a button. Object-oriented programming is covered in detail in Chapter 5, "Blackjack: Object-Oriented Programming."

Why Learn Java?

There are so many programming languages to choose from. Why should you learn Java? Undoubtedly you have at least a passing interest in Java to have read this far into Chapter 1. There are many reasons why learning Java is a good thing. If you are learning your first programming language, Java is a good choice. I feel that Java, being an object-oriented programming language, is intuitive. You understand how to use real objects in everyday life, so it isn't a big stretch for you to grasp the object-oriented nature of Java. It is a high-level programming language, so you can learn and understand the code pretty easily. Java has a wide range of uses, from creating stand-alone applications that run on your computer to creating applets for Internet solutions. Java is exciting. It has a solid future, so whether you are just expanding your knowledge or furthering your career, there are many benefits to learning Java.

Java Is Relatively Easy to Learn

If you already know C or C++, learning Java won't prove too difficult for you. Java was designed to be syntactically similar to C-type languages. C++ can be used for object-oriented programming. It can also be used as a strictly procedural language, but if you already understand C++ OOP concepts, learning Java will be a breeze. On the other side of things, if you don't know the first thing about programming, it might be difficult to get started in learning basic programming concepts, but don't throw in the towel just yet. This book is geared toward beginners and does not assume that you have any programming experience. Java's design makes it easier to learn than other programming languages, because it was initially designed to be small and simple.

As you know, Java is a high-level programming language that resembles human language more closely than machine language. Learning to program a high-level programming language is much easier than learning a low-level programming language. Choosing an object-oriented language as a first language is also a good idea. The concepts behind object-oriented programming are intuitive. After you learn one programming language, you find that learning other programming languages is much easier because you already know concepts that apply across all programming languages. Therefore, why not start with a language that is intuitive and easy to learn? This is why Java is a good choice.

Java Works Everywhere

You learned earlier that Java is platform independent. You can be sure that no matter which operating system you have, it will be able to run your Java programs as long as it has a Java interpreter installed on it. This is beneficial while you are learning Java because it means that your code will be portable. You can save your programs to a disk and run them on a different system, such as Mac OS or Windows. You can work from the same disk without having to tailor your code for either system. Even after you've learned Java you can develop software for a wide range of users and not be forced to develop multiple versions of your software for multiple operating systems.

Installing and Setting Up the Java SDK

I know that you're anxious to get started and write some Java, but you need to make sure that you set up your system correctly first. If you already have the Java SDK (Software Development Kit) installed and working, you can skip this section. These instructions are for installing the Java Software Development Kit on a system running Windows.

 Be sure to download the latest version of the SDK/JDK from Sun's Web site at **http://java.sun.com/j2se/1.3/docs.html**. There, you will also find loads of Java resources and information.

Windows (Win32) Installation and Setup

Win32 includes Windows 95/98/Me and Windows NT/2000. Follow these instructions if you are running any of these operating systems.

1. Run the SDK installer program. The file `j2sdk-1_3_1-win.exe` is the installer program. It can be found on the CD-ROM at the path `D:\SDK\j2sdk-1_3_1-win.exe`, assuming your CD-ROM drive letter is D. If you install JDK in the default directory, a folder named `jdk1.3.1` will be created on your C drive.

2. Update the `PATH` variable. The `PATH` variable tells your system which directories to look in when running commands or .EXE files. Setting the `PATH` variable allows you to easily compile and run your Java programs from any directory. Before you do this, you need to verify where your SDK's bin folder is. If you used the default installation directory, the path is C:\jdk1.3.1\bin. If you installed to a different directory, you need to find the jdk1.3.1 directory, which will contain the bin directory.

For Windows NT/2000, follow these steps next:

1. Start the Control Panel. You can find the control panel by clicking the Start menu and looking under Settings. Select the System icon, Environment, and look for "Path" in the User Variables and System Variables.

2. Append the path to the right side of your PATH variable in your bin directory. Directories are separated by semicolons (;). Click OK.

For Windows 95/98/Me, follow these steps instead:

1. Locate your autoexec.bat file by clicking the Start menu and choosing Run. Type in **sysedit** and click OK. Find the window titled AUTOEXEC.BAT and click it.

2. Look for the PATH statement (if you don't have one, you can add it). Append the path of your bin directory to the right side of the PATH statement. Use a semicolon (;) to separate it from the other paths. A typical PATH will look like this:

```
SET PATH=C:\WINDOWS;C:\WINDOWS\COMMAND;C:\JDK1.3.1\BIN
```

Next, follow these steps regardless of your Windows version:

1. Check your CLASSPATH variable. You might need to set it. To determine this, start up your MS-DOS Prompt window (Start menu -> Programs -> MS-DOS Prompt). At the command prompt, type set. If CLASSPATH does not appear, you can skip this step. If it does appear, you might need to modify it. This is done in exactly the same way you updated your PATH variable. If your CLASSPATH variable includes the current directory, represented by a dot (.), you can leave it as it is. If not, then you need to add it in by appending ;. (semicolon, dot) to the right side of the variable. You can also choose to remove the CLASSPATH variable altogether if no other application uses it. If you are upgrading from a previous version of Java, which required the variable to be set, you can just remove it, as this version of Java will run fine without it.

2. You can run the autoexec.bat file to update your system variables or you can just reboot your computer. Now you are all set and ready to use the SDK! You can run this by opening your MS-DOS prompt window as described in Step 1. Your autoexec.bat file should be on your C: drive outside of any directory. Type **C:** at the command prompt to make sure you are on the C: drive, then type **CD** to get to the root directory (exit all directories). Your command prompt should now look like this:

```
C:\>
```

Just type autoexec at this prompt to make it run. However, this will only update your environment variables for the current MS-DOS session. You will need to reboot your computer to set these variables globally.

Solaris Installation

Follow these instructions for installing the SDK on Solaris SPARC or Solaris x86 (Intel) platforms.

1. Copy the self-extracting binary to the directory where you want the SDK to be installed. You can find it on the CD-ROM in the /SDK/ directory. Use the j2sdk-1_3_1-solsparc.sh file for SPARC or j2sdk-1_3_1-solx86.sh for the Intel platform.

2. Make sure that the execute permissions are set by using the following commands.

   For SPARC:
   ```
   chmod +x j2sdk-1_3_1-solsparc.sh
   ```

   For Intel:
   ```
   chmod +x j2sdk-1_3_1-solx86.sh
   ```

3. Run the SDK self-extracting binary. This will create a subdirectory called j2sdk1_3_1.

Linux Installation

The CD-ROM provides two installation options. You can install the SDK using the self-extracting binary file or the RPM file.

Follow these instructions if you are using the self-extracting binary file:

1. Copy the self-extracting binary file to the directory in which you want to install the SDK. The file can be found on the CD-ROM in the /SDK/ directory. The file is named j2sdk-1_3_1-linux-i386.bin.

2. Run the installer by using the following commands in the directory where you copied the self-extracting binary to:
   ```
   chmod a+x j2sdk-1_3_1-linux-i386.bin
   ./j2sdk-1_3_1-linux-i386.bin
   ```

Follow these instructions if you are using the RPM file to install the SDK in package form:

1. Copy the installer program into the directory where you want to install the SDK. On the CD-ROM, you can find this file in the /SDK/ directory. The filename is j2sdk-1_3_1-linux-i386-rpm.bin.

2. Run the installer by using the following commands from the directory which you copied the installer file to:
   ```
   chmod a+x j2sdk-1_3_1-linux-i386-rpm.bin
   ./j2sdk-1_3_1-linux-i386-rpm.bin
   ```

   This will create a file named jdk-1.3.1.i386.rpm in the current directory.

3. Become root by using the `su` command.

4. Use the `rpm` command to install the packages into the newly created `/usr/java/jdk1.3.1 directory`.

5. Add the `/usr/java/jdk1.3.1/bin` directory to your `PATH` environment variable by using this command:

```
export PATH=/usr/java/jdk1.3.1/bin:$PATH
```

TRICK These installation instructions refer to directory paths you use to find the installation files on the CD-ROM. You can also find these files by navigating the CD-ROM HTML documents in your Web browser, if your CD-ROM is auto-run enabled. It should automatically run when you insert the CD. If not, you can run it manually by opening the `start_here.html` file in your browser. After you accept the license agreement, click on the Java SDK button and then click on the appropriate installer file, depending on your operating system. You can also follow the link to get more information and installation instructions from Sun's Web site at **http://java.sun.com/j2se/1.3/.**

WAR STORY

One of the reasons I decided to include such an extensive explanation of how to get your system set up to run Java in Chapter 1 rather than in the Introduction was because of the difficulty I had getting started. My first Java book was good, but it didn't go over how to get set up. I installed the JDK 1.02 software on my PC, but I was still unable to get the first application to compile or run. I tried everything. I wasn't sure if I had my `PATH` or `CLASSPATH` variables set up correctly. I tried rebooting in DOS mode. That didn't work. No matter what I set my `PATH` and `CLASSPATH` variables to, I was still unable to compile anything. My problem ended up being that I was editing the autoexec.bat file but the variables weren't actually being updated. The best way to accomplish this is to reboot your system after you edit the autoexec.bat file. You know that you're all set if you can compile your applications without compiler errors to the effect that either `java` is a bad command or that there is a problem finding some of the classes.

Writing Your First Application

The best way to learn Java is to jump right into it. In this section, you write a stand-alone application that can run on any system that has a Java interpreter. You write the source code, learn how to compile it, and then run it. Keep in mind as you do this that you will be coming back to it and analyzing it afterward, so don't worry if you don't get it right away. In fact, you probably won't understand it until I go over with you what you did.

Hello, World!

This application is as basic as it gets. It is the typical first program used in programming books for many different languages. Basically, the HelloWorld application demonstrates how to code a simple Java program by printing a message to the screen. Take a look at the source code:

```
/*
 * Hello World
 * The classic first program
 */

public class HelloWorld {

  public static void main(String args[]) {
    System.out.println("Hello, world!");
  }

}
```

All that you need to do to write your first Java application is to copy this source code into the text editor of your choice (I used Notepad). To do this, create a file named HelloWorld.java and type this source code in the file. This file, as well as all the other source code, is available on the CD-ROM; however, for your own benefit, I urge you to actually type the source code yourself. You get a better feel for the language that way. After you finish typing this code, save the file.

TRAP When you save the source code, the filename is important. It must be named HelloWorld.java. The filename is case-sensitive, which means that uppercase letters are differentiated from lowercase letters. Your program will not run if you name it incorrectly. Even the names helloWorld.java or helloworld.java will cause the program to fail.

Compiling the Program

After you saved the HelloWorld source code, you need to compile it before it will run. The command instructing the JDK to compile your code is javac. First, open your command prompt window, such as Windows' MS-DOS prompt. Make sure you are in the directory (folder) that contains your HelloWorld.java source file. If you are unfamiliar with navigating your directory structure from a command prompt environment, here's a brief explanation of the cd command. You use the cd command to change directories in DOS. If you want to enter a subdirectory of the directory you are currently in, you type:

```
cd subdir
```

where *subdir* is the name of the subdirectory you want to enter. The command prompt by default indicates where you currently are in your directory structure. For instance, if you are in a directory named `superdir` that is on the `C:` drive and is not itself in any other directory, your command prompt looks like this:

```
C:\superdir>
```

And if you then typed `cd subdir`, your command prompt would look like this:

```
C:\superdir\subdir>
```

To back out of a directory, type `cd..` at the command prompt. To get out of all directories and back to the root directory, type `cd\`. UNIX works similar to this except the slash is a forward slash (/) instead of a backslash (\).

Next, at your operating system's command prompt (such as the DOS prompt), type:

```
javac HelloWorld.java
```

HINT

If you are using a **Macintosh** to compile your source file, drag and drop your source file on to the Java Compiler icon.

Make sure that you are in the proper directory and that you have the Java Developer's Kit (JDK) installed. Figure 1.3 demonstrates a successful compile, whereas Figure 1.4 demonstrates the importance of naming your file correctly. If you are having trouble with this step and you are sure that JDK is installed, make sure that you have copied the HelloWorld source code exactly and that your file is named HelloWorld.java.

TRICK

If you are having difficulty compiling your source code, you can copy the HelloWorld.java source file from the CD to your computer. Then you should be able to compile and run it.

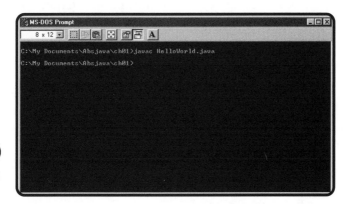

FIGURE 1.3

This is a successful compile.

FIGURE 1.4

Naming your source code file correctly is important.

What happens when you *compile* Java programs? Your source code is translated into what is known as *Java byte code*. The file extension for Java byte code is .class. After you've compiled HelloWorld.java, you should see a new file named `Hello-World.class` created by the Java compiler in the same directory as the source code file. The Java interpreter, referred to as the *Java Runtime Environment* or JRE, is able to read this byte code and interpret it in such a way that your computer will know what operations it needs to perform for your application.

Recall that Java is a system-independent programming language. This means that you need to compile the program only once and it can run on any system that has a Java interpreter installed on it. Each operating system has its own system-dependent Java interpreter that is able to interpret the same Java byte code into machine language specific to the computer running the program. Java is known as the "Write once, run anywhere" language. Simply put, this means you can write and compile your code on whatever computer you want to and your program will run on any other computer.

Running the Application

Now that you have written and compiled your program, how do you see the product of your efforts? To run the program from Windows, type the following at your command prompt:

```
java HelloWorld
```

If you're a Mac user, double-click on your new `HelloWorld.class` file. The Java Runner application will then prompt you for any arguments (you don't need any just yet). It will then display the output, "Hello, world!" in a pop-up window titled *stdout*, short for standard output.

After you do that, your Java interpreter will kick into action and you should see something similar to what is shown in Figure 1.5. Congratulations! You've just completed your first Java program!

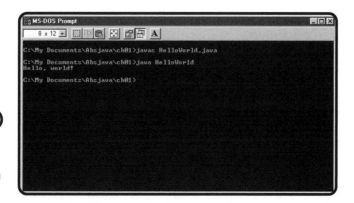

FIGURE 1.5

This is what your
first application
looks like when you
run it.

TRAP It is a common beginner's mistake to misuse the `javac` compile command and `java` run command. Keep in mind that when compiling your source code, the full filename is required, including the .java extension, but when using the `java` command to run the program, the filename minus the .class extension is used.

When you run your application, you call the JRE to process your compiled program code and perform the actions you describe therein. The JRE is system-dependent. It interprets system-independent byte code and tells your specific system which operations to perform.

Learning Java Syntax Basics

You've written your first Java program. Now you need to step back and take a closer look at what you did. First, I explain the rules to writing Java source code. The set of rules you must follow when writing program code are referred to as Java *syntax*. You can think of syntax as grammar for programming.

You will continue to learn Java syntax throughout this book. For now, I explain only the basic syntax used in your HelloWorld source code. After you have learned the basics of Java syntax, it becomes easier to learn new features of the Java programming language because the syntax remains consistent and is therefore intuitive. At the beginning of the code, notice the forward slash followed by an asterisk and some text. This is one way to add comments to your code. More on that later.

```
/*
 * Hello World
 * The classic first program
 */
```

HINT The compiler ignores white space, or blank lines, in between Java statements. White space in Java, unlike languages such as **COBOL** or **FORTRAN**, has no effect on the functionality of the program. (Note, however, that Java doesn't ignore all carriage returns. You can't split a line right in the middle with a carriage return.)

The next line of code is a blank line, which as you might imagine, does nothing. Following that is the beginning of your program class definition:

```
public class HelloWorld {
```

You must define a class in every Java program. Basically, a *class* is a group of functions and characteristics in Java code that can be reused. The `public` keyword, used as a modifier that describes other classes' access to this class, is not required, but it is a good idea to use it anyway. This way you will start off with good coding habits. It is not necessary at this point to fully understand the `public` keyword. Although you see it in every program in this book, it is not essential to understand until you learn object-oriented programming in Chapter 5. The same goes for the `class` keyword. It is used to identify `HelloWorld` as a class. The open brace denotes the beginning of the contents of your class definition and the corresponding closing brace (the last line of the program) denotes the end of the class definition. To sum it up, this line of code starts a Java program called `HelloWorld`, and all the code within the braces makes up its guts.

 Keywords are reserved words used in Java to perform specific functions. They cannot be used for anything else such as naming classes, variables, or methods.

The next line of code starts the `main()` method definition.

```
public static void main(String args[]) {
```

Methods are groups of statements that are executed by your computer when instructed to do so. You learn about methods in Chapter 5. For now, it is important that you know that the `main()` method actually drives Java applications. It is the first place the Java VM looks when you run your application. The group of statements within this method, collectively called a *block statement*, is defined within its own set of braces. Within the braces of this method, you define a list of steps you want the computer to do when running your program.

The one statement inside the `main()` method, which is your next line of code, instructs your computer to say hello to the world.

```
System.out.println("Hello, world!");
```

This is actually a call to a method that handles your system's standard output. It prints one line to the screen and adds a carriage return. You can refer to the Java API documentation for classes `System` and `PrintStream` for more detailed information about how standard output works. Inside the parentheses, within quotes, is what your system outputs to the users. All single statements end with a semi-colon ;. Figure 1.6 shows you how the compiler will complain if you forget to put the semicolon at the end of this line.

FIGURE 1.6

Oops! I better put that semicolon back and recompile before the book is released!

The last two lines of code are the closing braces for the main() method and the HelloWorld class definition, respectively. These closing braces end the blocks started with their corresponding open braces. Braces are important. If you look back at the full code list, it is easier for you to understand their significance. The first open brace right after the HelloWorld class name doesn't close until the last line of the program. Everything within these braces is encompassed within the HelloWorld class, including entire the main() method and the statement it contains.

TRAP Don't forget to close all your braces! If you're trying to compile a large source file and you've forgotten a closing brace or two, it can be a nightmare to debug.

TRICK To make it easier to remember to close your braces and also for the purposes of readability, you should follow certain source code formatting conventions. Each time a new brace is opened, indent all the contained statements a couple of spaces. Close the brace on a line of its own, using the same number of spaces to indent as the line of code containing the open brace. This will simplify the debugging process.

Including Comments

Adding comments to your code is not required, although it is definitely a good practice. Comments help you or anyone reading your code understand what your program does. This can greatly facilitate the debugging process. You will be able to read your comments later and remember what the different components of

your procedure are. Comments also help when you go back and add new functionality to your code because you will be less likely to be confused by what you
had previously done. There are two basic types of comments in Java—single-line
comments and multi-line comments. If you just want to make a note about a particular line of code, you usually precede that line of code with a single-line comment as shown here:

```
//The following line of code prints a message using standard output
System.out.println("Hello, World!");
```

Single-line comments start with double slashes //. This tells the compiler to dis-
regard the following line of code. After the double slashes, you can type anything
you want to on that single line and the compiler will ignore it.

TRICK **Single line comments are also commonly used to temporarily disable a line of
code during the debugging process. Simply add the double slashes at the beginning of the line of code to make the compiler skip the line. You typically do this if
you want to test a modified version of the commented line or if you need to see
how the program runs without executing that particular statement. This way, you
don't have to delete it and you can replace the statement simply by removing the
double slashes.**

Sometimes you might want to write a comment that spans more than one line
of code. You can precede each line with double slashes if you choose to, but Java
allows you to accomplish this more easily. Simply start your comment with a
slash followed by an asterisk: /*. You can type anything you want to after this,
including carriage returns. To end this comment, all you need to do is type */.

```
/* I just started a comment
I can type whatever I want to now and the compiler will ignore it.
So let It be written
So let It be done
I'm sent here by the chosen one
so let It be written
so let It be done
to kill the first born pharaoh son
I'm creeping death
from Metallica's song, Creeping Death
I guess I'll end this comment now */
```

Everything in between the start and end of this comment is considered free text.
This means you can type anything you want to within them. If you take another
look at the HelloWorld source code, you will notice that I used a multi-line comment. I typed the name of the HelloWorld program and then followed with several more lines. I preceded every line with an asterisk. You don't have to do this.
I only did it to make the comments stand out more. Feel free to develop your own
style of commenting your code, but keep in mind that you or someone else

might need to refer to the source code, so try to make your comments easy to understand.

 HINT There is actually another form of multi-line commenting used in Java. It has the added capability to be converted into HTML documentation using the javadoc utility included with the JDK.

The *main()* Method

When running a Java application, the main() method is the first thing the interpreter looks to. It acts as a starting point for your program and continues to drive it until it completes. Every Java application requires a main() method or it will not run. In this section, I point out what you should understand about it because you'll be using it often. In fact, you use it in every application you write.

The main() method always looks just like it did when you programmed the HelloWorld application.

```
public static void main(string args[]) {
```

Let's take a closer look at the parts of the main() method:

- The public and static keywords are used in object-oriented programming. Simplified, public makes this method accessible from other classes and static ensures that there is only one reference to this method used by every instance of this program (class). Static methods are also referred to as class methods, because they refer to the class and not specific instances of the class. This is a difficult concept to understand at this point. You can simply gloss over it for now.

- The void keyword means that this method does not return any value when it is completed.

- main is the name of the method, it accepts a parameter—String args[]. Specifically, it is an array (list) of command-line arguments. As is the case with all methods, the parameters must always appear within the parentheses that follow the method name.

- Within the curly braces of the main() method, you list all the operations you want your application to perform. I stated earlier that every Java application requires a main() method; however, it is possible to write a Java source code file without defining a main() method. It will not be considered an application, though, and it won't run if you use the java command on it. Now your head might be spinning at this point. Don't let all this make you forget what I stated earlier. The main() method is simply the driver for your application.

Writing Your First Applet

Applets differ from stand-alone applications in that they must be run within a Java-enabled browser and they don't require a main() method. In this section, you write an applet, learn how to incorporate it into an HTML document, run it within your browser and also by using the appletviewer utility, which is built into the JDK. The appletviewer utility allows you to run applets from the command prompt, outside of your browser. Applets are covered in greater detail in Chapter 8, "Writing Applets." At this point, your goals are to understand what an applet is, to learn how to create a simple one, and to understand how an applet differs from an application.

Back to the *HelloWeb* Applet!

Remember the project introduced at the beginning of this chapter? In this section, you actually learn to create the HelloWeb applet. This applet performs a task similar to that of the HelloWorld application, but it runs within a Web browser instead of as a stand-alone application. Applets add a great deal of life to Web documents. If you include an applet in a Web document and publish it on the Internet, anyone can browse to it and run your program without having to explicitly download it. In the real world, you can play Java games online. The source code, although only one statement longer than the HelloWorld application, is a bit more complex. Now, you will create this applet.

```
/*
 * HelloWeb
 * A very basic Applet
 */

import java.awt.Graphics;

public class HelloWeb extends java.applet.Applet {

  public void paint(Graphics g) {
    g.drawString("Hello, World Wide Web!", 10, 50);
  }

}
```

Copy or type this source code into your text editor and name the file Hello-Web.java. Even though this is an applet, you compile it exactly the same way as you do applications. Just use the javac command. After it's compiled, your applet is still not ready to run. Figure 1.7 shows what will happen if you try to run this as an application, further emphasizing the fact that all applications must define a main() method.

There is no `main()` method, so it cannot be run as an application.

Writing the HTML

In order to run the applet, you need to write an HTML document and include the applet within it. You don't need to know much about HTML for the purposes of this book. You write only the bare essentials in the HTML document and include the applet. This is the listing for the HTML document:

```
<html>
<head>
<title>HelloWeb Applet</title>
</head>

<body>
<h1 align=center>HelloWeb Applet</h1>
<center>
<applet name="HelloWeb" code="HelloWeb.class"
        width=250 height=100></applet>
</center>
</body>

</html>
```

Copy or type this HTML code into your text editor and save it as `helloweb.html` in the same directory as your applet. The name is not all that important but the .html extension is.

Running the Applet

After you have created the HTML file, you are ready to run your applet. You can do this in one of two ways. First, you can use the `appletviewer` tool by typing the following at the command prompt:

```
appletviewer helloweb.html
```

Figure 1.8 shows what the appletviewer window looks like while running the HelloWeb applet.

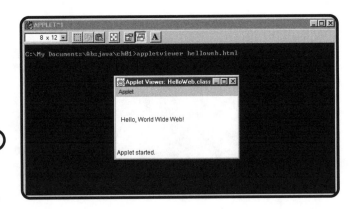

FIGURE 1.8

Using the
appletviewer to
view your applet.

Next you can double-click your helloweb.html icon to run the applet in your browser.

Congratulations! You've just written and run your first Java applet. If your applet is running fine using appletviewer, but you can't get it to run inside your browser, you should make sure that you have the latest Java plug-in.

I will quickly explain the new syntax that appears in this applet's source code. First, there is the import statement:

```
import java.awt.Graphics;
```

This code *imports* the Graphics class. By importing classes, you tell the JRE where to look for the class definition so you can use it in your code. Your applet uses the Graphics class, so you must import it. Your applet also uses the extends keyword:

```
public class HelloWeb extends java.applet.Applet {
```

You can see that it is part of your class definition statement. This is what actually makes your program an applet. *Extending* a class, such as the Applet class, is a way of reusing the functionality of another class that has already been defined and gives you the capability to extend its characteristics and capabilities. When one class extends another, it is referred to as a *subclass* and the class it extends is called its *super class*. This is one of the benefits of object-oriented programming. One last thing to understand is the way you instructed your applet to print a message.

```
Public void paint(Graphics g) {
  g.drawString("Hello, World, Wide, Web!", 10, 50);
}
```

The pre-existing `Applet` class already defines a `paint()` method. Here you override it to do what you want it to do. You tell the `Graphics` class to draw the string `"Hello, World Wide Web!"` inside of your applet with `g.drawString()`. The numbers that follow your string in your parameter list are the x, y coordinates describing where to paint the string. You'll learn more about this in Chapter 8.

Summary

You accomplished a lot in this chapter. You learned that Java is a platform-independent, object-oriented programming language that you can use to write applications and applets. You installed the Software Development Kit and set it up, giving your system the capability to compile and run Java programs. You wrote your first application, learned how to use the `javac` command to compile it and the `java` command to run it. After you successfully ran the HelloWorld application, you looked back and examined your code. You learned the basics of Java syntax. You also wrote your first applet and learned the basic differences between applications and applets. You learned how to include an applet within an HTML document. Finally, you learned how to run an applet by using the `appletviewer` utility and also how to run it in your browser. You are ready to take on some new challenges. In the next chapter you learn about variables, data types, mathematical operations, and how to accept simple user input.

CHALLENGES

1. Write a Java application that prints your first name to standard output.

2. Rewrite your Java application from challenge #1 to print your last name to standard output without deleting any lines by commenting out the line you don't need and adding the one that you do.

3. Write a Java application that prints two separate lines to standard output by repeating the System.out.println() statement using a different sentence.

4. Write an applet that displays your name and run it with both the appletviewer utility and with your browser.

CHAPTER

2

Variables, Data Types, and Simple I/O

In this chapter, you learn how to use variables, data types, and standard input/output to create an interactive application. You start by learning what variables are and what they are used for. Then you learn what the primitive data types are and how they are assigned to variables. After you understand variables, you learn how to work with numbers and use mathematical operations. After that you learn about strings and how to accept simple user input. Finally, you put all this knowledge together and build an application that uses standard output, accepts user input, and works with strings and numbers. In this chapter, you will

- Learn to use data types

- Declare and name variables

- Work with numbers

- Get simple user input

- Parse strings to numbers and other String class operations

- Accept command-line arguments

The Project: the *NameGame* Application

You'll use the concepts introduced in this chapter to create this interactive application. It is interactive because it allows users to enter input. It then processes this input and issues output. Figure 2.1 shows how this application appears when you run it.

In this simple game, the program prompts the user for a first name. Next, the program responds to the user and asks a last name. The program then proceeds to manipulate the name and show off to the user. In fact, it demonstrates, however basically, most of the concepts behind what an application should be able to do. It provides a user interface, which prompts the user for some information, allows the user to enter this information, processes the information, and outputs the information in a new form for the user to ingest. These basic functions are present in any useful application and are the keys to learning any programming language.

Variables and Data Types

In this section you learn what variables and data types are and how Java uses them. *Variables* are basically containers that hold specific types of data. Oddly enough, these specific types of data, such as integers, floating-point numbers, and bytes, are called *data types*. The data contained by the variable can vary (that's why it's called a variable), but the data type cannot change. Variables are used to temporarily store pieces of data that the program makes use of. Think of a folder. A folder holds documents. A person can use the folder by reading the information that it holds. This person can also take the document out and put a new one in it that can be used later. In this analogy, the folder acts as the variable, documents act as the data type, and the information in the documents acts as the data.

Learning Primitive Data Types

A variable must have a data type. A variable's data type can be a reference data type or a primitive data type. *Primitive data types* are built into the system. They are not objects. They are specific values that can easily be stored by a computer using a specific amount of memory. If you declare a variable to be of a specific primitive data type, that variable will always hold a value that is of that data type. For example, if you specify variable n to be an int type, n will always hold an integer. Reference data type variables—used for class, interface, and array references—don't actually contain the object data. Instead, they hold a reference to the data. In other words, they tell the computer where to find the object's data in memory. Unlike other languages, primitive data types in Java are system-independent because Java specifies their size and format. There are eight primitive data types. They are listed in Table 2.1.

The four integer types (byte, short, int, and long) can be positive, negative, or zero. The same is true for the two floating-point types (float and double). The char type can hold one Unicode character (for example: a, b, c, A, B, C, 7, &, *, and ~). Unicode is a character set that provides a unique number for every character. The boolean type can hold only the values true or false. After you have declared a variable to be of a certain type, it can only hold that specific type of data.

TABLE 2.1 PRIMITIVE DATA TYPES

Keyword	Description	Size
byte	Byte-size integer	8-bit
short	Short integer	16-bit
int	Integer	32-bit
long	Long integer	64-bit
char	Single character	16-bit
float	Single-precision floating point	32-bit
double	Double-precision floating point	64-bit
boolean	True or false	1-bit

HINT

The primitive data type you use depends upon what the purpose of the variable will be. For example, if you wanted to store highly precise scientific calculations, you would probably want to use a `double`. If you were using an integer to store the day of the month, the possible values should only be 1-31, so you could use a byte to minimize memory use. The range of possible byte values is -128-127.

Understanding Literals

Literals are used to indicate specific data values. Basically, what you type is what you get. If you type a 1, Java interprets that to mean the integer value 1. If you type a B, Java determines that to be the character value B. If you type the string "Obi-wan Kenobi", the value of that string literal will be "Obi-Wan Kenobi". You've used literals before. In the HelloWorld application, the string "Hello, World!" is a literal.

You can assign literal values to variables, which you will do in the next section. Literals have specific data types. Typing the number 27, for example, implies that you are specifying a literal of type `int`. However, if you were to assign this to, say, a `double`, it would be treated as a `double`. Table 2.2 shows different types of number literals the way that you express them in Java syntax.

TABLE 2.2 LITERAL DATA TYPES

Literal	Data Type
27	int
033	int (octal representation when preceded by 0)
0x1b	int (hexadecimal representation when preceded by 0x)
27L	long
27.0	double
27.0D	double
27.0e3	double (27.0 × 10^3, or 27,000.0)
27.0F	float
'B'	char
true	boolean
false	boolean
null	null object reference

Because Java considers integer literals, such as 27 to be an int, if you want it to be considered a long, you have to explicitly indicate that. The way to do this is by adding the letter L at the end of the number. Simply type 27L.

You can use lowercase letters when specifying data types for literals. For example, you can use the lowercase letter l to specify a long, but you can see how it can be confused with the number 1. 27l can be mistaken for 271 quite easily. To avoid this situation, it is good practice to use uppercase letters. (This is a small exception to the fact that Java is case-sensitive in most cases.)

There is also another way to do this by casting the int to a long. *Casting* data types is expressing a value of a data type in terms of a different data type, such as expressing the int 1 as the float 1.0. The way you can explicitly cast data types is by typing the data type in parentheses in front of the number, like this:

```
(long) 27
```

This number can also be expressed as a byte, short, float, or double by either casting it in a manner similar to the example or for a float or double, you can type 27F for a float or 27D for a double. You can also cast a value that is already stored by a variable. For example, if x holds an integer value, but you need to express it as a double, you can do it by casting it to a float:

```
(float) x
```

This operation doesn't actually change the data type of x from int to float. Instead, it gets the value that is stored in x and expresses it as a float type; x is still an int, though. You use casting operations inside of mathematical operations or for assigning the value of a variable to another variable that is declared to be a different type. So, if y is a float and x is an int, the following assignment (you'll learn about assignments shortly) is legal:

```
y = (float) x;
```

This next one is not legal and will cause a compiler error:

```
y = x;
```

Using Character Escape Codes

Literals can also be strings of characters. This is the case in the HelloWorld application. The string literal you used in that procedure is "Hello, World!", which, as you can see is expressed within double quotation marks. I will go over strings in more detail later on in this chapter. There are some characters that will cause problems in your code if typed explicitly, such as the carriage return or double quotation mark. Typing these directly into your code where you want them to print is problematic and would most likely cause compiler errors. For example, consider the following:

```
System.out.println("Some people call me "Joey".");
```

You can see how a programmer might mistakenly use this code if he or she were trying to make the output of the program be:

```
Some people call me "Joey".
```

However, this is not the correct way to accomplish this. The compiler is not intelligent. Granted, it's a marvelous work on Sun's part, but it can't just guess what the programmer means. The compiler sees that the programmer has opened a quote and it sees the next double quotation mark as the closing quotation mark. In the preceding example, after the compiler reads the quotation mark before the name Joey, it doesn't know what to do; so it issues you error messages. Figure 2.2 demonstrates that this confuses the compiler.

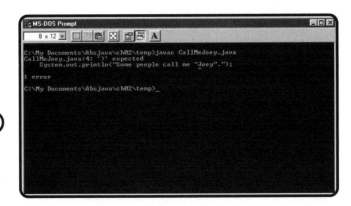

FIGURE 2.2

The compiler doesn't like those misplaced double quotation marks.

There is a way to express double quotation marks to the compiler in a way that it can understand. This is by using character escape codes. Character escape codes begin with a backslash and follow with a code that the compiler will understand. You type the escape codes directly into your code where you want the character it represents to appear. You can refer to Table 2.3 to learn these escape codes. The previous example can be successfully coded by typing the following:

```
System.out.println("Some people call me \"Joey\".");
```

HINT The newline character (\n) and carriage return character (\r) can be a bit confusing. Both of these characters represent new lines. Different operating systems and word processors use these characters differently. For example, DOS uses both a carriage return and a newline character, whereas the Mac uses only the carriage return and UNIX uses only the newline character.

TABLE 2.3 CHARACTER ESCAPE CODES	
Escape Code	**Interpretation**
\'	Single quotation mark
\"	Double quotation mark
\b	Backspace
\f	Form feed (page break)
\n	Newline character
\r	Carriage return
\t	Tab

Naming Variables

There are specific syntax rules that you must follow when naming variables. The compiler needs to know when you are referring to variables and doesn't want to mix them up with anything else. That's why these rules are in place. Java variable names can start with letters, underscores (_), or dollar signs ($). They cannot start with a number or the compiler will assume it is a number literal. Any characters that follow the first character can be any letter, number, underscore, or dollar sign. None of the following characters can be used when naming variables: #%&'()*+,-./:;<=>?@[\]^`{|}~.

Aside from these rules there are some naming conventions you should stick to so that your code is readable. Variable names typically start with a lowercase letter. Subsequent letters are lowercase unless they start a new "word," such as `myNumber`, `numSeconds`, or `costPerUnit`. It is also a good idea to choose a name that is descriptive of the data it holds. It makes readability so much better. Keep all this in mind when naming your variables.

Declaring and Assigning Values to Variables

In this section, you will learn about declaring variables and assigning values to them in more detail. *Declaring* a variable is creating a variable by specifying its name and data type. For example if you wanted to declare a variable that will be used to hold integers, you could do it by typing the following:

```
int myNumber;
```

This declares a variable of type `int` named `myNumber`. Note that the syntax for declaring a variable is the data type followed by the name of the variable. If you typed the previous example in your code, the variable `myNumber` becomes a container that is able to hold integers. It does not contain any value until it is assigned. *Assigning* a value to a variable is making the variable hold specific data. A variable remains unusable until it contains data. If the compiler is able to see that a variable might not be *initialized*, or assigned its initial value, it gives you an error message. Now that you have declared your variable, you can assign the literal 27 to it by typing the following:

```
MyNumber = 27;
```

This puts the integer 27 into the variable `myNumber`. Note that the syntax for this is the variable name followed by the assignment operator (the equals sign =), followed by the value being assigned to the variable. Anytime the code refers to `myNumber`, it will find its contents to be 27 until the variable is reassigned a new value. It can be reassigned different values as many times as you want, but it must always contain an integer. The following snippet of code demonstrates that a variable can be assigned different values:

```
myNumber = 1;
// The value of myNumber is now 1.
myNumber = 4;
// The value of myNumber is now 4.
```

Expressions to the right of the assignment operator don't necessarily have to be literals. You can assign the value of one variable to another variable. For example, assume `myNumber` and `myOtherNumber` are both integers and `myNumber` already has its value. The following line assigns the value stored in `myOtherNumber` to the `myNumber` variable.

```
MyNumber = myOtherNumber;
```

You can declare and assign the initial value to a variable on one single line if you choose to do so. To declare the `myNumber` variable and assign it the number 27 on only one line, you type:

```
int myNumber = 27;
```

This line declares an `int` variable called `myNumber` and assigns it the value 27 all on one single line. This can be useful if you know what the initial value of your variable will be. Variables inherently can contain any value specific to the data type, so you should never assume the value of a variable when writing your programs. It might be okay to assume the value of a variable after you have just assigned it a value, but that is not a good practice. You should always treat a variable in such a way that you might not know its contents. You should only assume what the data type of the variable is. If you need to use a specific value in your program, just use a literal.

You can also declare multiple variables on a single line:

```
double a, b, c = 2.28, d, e = 1.11;
```

The previous line declares five `double` variables named a, b, c, d, and e. When declaring multiple variables on a single line of code, the data type appears to the left of the variable list just as if it were one variable. The variable names, separated by commas, are listed to the right of the data type. You should also notice that I assigned values to two of the variables (c and e). Now is a good time to put your knowledge of variables to use. From this point forward I assume that you already know how to write, compile, and run your Java applications, so here is the source code to the `VariableDemo` application:

```
/*
 * VariableDemo
 * Demonstrates the declaration and assignment of variables
 */

public class VariableDemo {

  public static void main(String args[]) {
    //Declare an int
    int myNumber;

    //Assign a value
    myNumber = 43;

    //Print out the value of the variable
    System.out.println("myNumber = " + myNumber);

    //Do other stuff with variables
    double myDouble = 4.0;
    char c1 = '?';
    boolean happy = true, sad = false;
    int myOtherNumber = myNumber;

    System.out.println("myDouble = " + myDouble);
    System.out.println("c1 = " + c1);
    System.out.println("happy = " + happy);
    System.out.println("sad = " + sad);
    System.out.println("myOtherNumber = " + myOtherNumber);
  }

}
```

This application demonstrates the use of variables—naming, declaring, and assigning values to them. Feel free to write, rewrite, and modify this program until you get a good feel for working with variables. There is some syntax in this program that you might be unfamiliar with. When you print the value of your variables, you used the `System.out.println()` method in a slightly different way than before:

```
System.out.println("myNumber = " + myNumber);
```

This line prints `"myNumber = 43"` when you run the program as it is listed previously. This appends the value of `myNumber` to the string literal `"myNumber = "` and prints the result. You learn more about string operations in the "Strings and String Operations" section later in this chapter. Figure 2.3 shows the output.

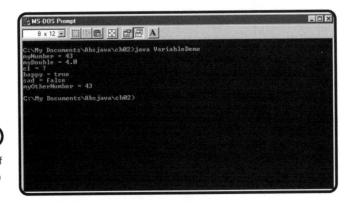

FIGURE 2.3

This is the output of the `VariableDemo` application.

Working with Numbers

In this section, you learn how Java handles numbers. You learn how to use mathematical operations on numerical variables. I also go over operator precedence and you write an application that applies these concepts.

The *TipAdder* Program

Now you will write a program that calculates a 15 percent tip to give to your waiter or waitress after a nice meal, assuming he or she wasn't rude of course. Here is a listing of the source code:

```
/*
 * TipAdder
 * Demonstrates simple floating point math and importance of precision
 */
```

```
public class TipAdder {
   public static void main(String args[]) {
      float meal = 22.50F;
      float tip = 0.15F * meal;
      float total = meal + tip;

      System.out.println("The meal costs $" + meal);
      System.out.println("The 15% tip is $" + tip);
      System.out.println("The total bill is $" + total);
   }

}
```

This program performs mathematical operations on floating-point numbers. Based on what you've learned so far, this application should not be difficult to understand. The only new concept introduced here is the use of mathematical operations. The following line declares the variable meal and assigns it the initial value 22.50. Remember that the letter F specifies the literal 22.50F to be a float:

```
float meal = 22.50F;
```

On the next line, tip is declared to be a float and is immediately assigned its intended value–15% of the cost of the meal:

```
float tip = 0.15F * meal;
```

This mathematical operation multiplies the literal 15.0F by the value stored in the meal variable. The result of this operation is stored in the tip variable.

The next line of code calculates the total cost of your dining experience by adding tip to meal and storing the result in total. After that, the application proceeds to issue messages to the user indicating the cost of the meal, the tip amount, and the result of its total meal cost calculation. Figure 2.4 shows what a run of this application looks like:

FIGURE 2.4

The TipAdder application in action.

There are different mathematical operations for addition, subtraction, multiplication and division. There is also a modulus operation, which calculates the value of the remainder after a division operation. Table 2.4 introduces how these mathematical operators are used on integers and Table 2.5 shows how they affect real numbers.

HINT The modulus operator works by dividing the number on the left side by the number on the right side evenly and giving the remainder. An example of this is 5 % 2. The result of this operation is 1. 2 goes into 5 two times with 1 left over. This modulus operator works similarly on real numbers except the result is not necessarily an integer. An example of this is 9.9 % 4.5. The result of this operation is 0.9. Why? Because 4.5 goes into 9.9 two times evenly with 0.9 left over.

TABLE 2.4 MATHEMATICAL OPERATORS: INTEGER MATH

Operator	Description	Example	Result
+	Addition	5 + 2	7
-	Subtraction	5 - 2	3
*	Multiplication	5 * 2	10
/	Division	5 / 2	2
%	Modulus (division remainder)	5 % 2	1

TABLE 2.5 MATHEMATICAL OPERATORS: FLOATING POINT MATH

Operator	Description	Example	Result
+	Addition	9.9 + 4.5	14.4
-	Subtraction	9.9 - 4.5	5.4
*	Multiplication	9.9 * 4.5	44.55
/	Division	9.9 / 4.5	2.2
%	Modulus (division remainder)	9.9 % 4.5	0.9

TRAP Computers cannot precisely store real numbers (`floats` and `doubles`). The more precision you give to a real number, such as using a `double` instead of a `float`, the more precise the computer's calculations will be. Note that the tip calculation is slightly off in the TipAdder application. It multiplies `0.15 * 22.50` and determines the result to be `3.3750002` instead of `3.375`, which is what you expect. Keep this in mind when using real numbers in your Java programs.

Operator Precedence

Operator precedence determines the order in which operations are applied to numbers. In general, multiplication (*), division (/), and modulus (%) have precedence over addition (+) and subtraction (-). This means that multiplication, division, and modulus operations are evaluated before addition and subtraction. When operator precedence is the same, operations occur from left to right. Take the following line of code for example:

```
int x = 10 - 4 +  14 / 2;
```

The value of x after this assignment is not 10. It would be if it evaluated strictly left to right. 10 - 4 = 6; 6 + 14 = 20; 20 / 2 = 10. Because the division operator is evaluated first, the value of this expression is 13. (10 - 4 + 7 = 13). There is a way to force operator precedence using parentheses (like in Algebra). The operations within parentheses have precedence. The value of y after the following assignment is 10:

```
int y = (10 - 4 + 14) / 2;
```

Write and run the following program that demonstrates how parentheses affect arithmetic operations (check out the result in Figure 2.5):

```
/*
 * ParenMath
 * Demonstrates the effect of parentheses on
 * mathematical operations.
 */

public class ParenMath {

  public static void main(String args[]) {
    //The value of a will be 13 (the parentheses make no difference here)
    int a = (10 - 4) + 14 / 2;
    System.out.println("(10 - 4) + 14 / 2 = " + a);
```

```
//The value of b will be 1.
//The addition happens first because of the parentheses
//Next the division and then the subtraction.
int b = 10 - (4 + 14) / 2;
System.out.println("10 - (4 + 14) / 2 = " + b);

//The value of c will be -1
int c = 10 - (4 + 14 / 2);
System.out.println("10 - (4 + 14 / 2) = " + c);
    }

}
```

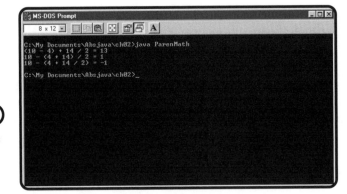

Getting Simple User Input

Thus far, the programs you have written have been one-sided in that they perform specific tasks and do not accept any user input. Every time you run these
programs the output is exactly the same, making them all but useless in the eyes
of a user after the first few times they are run. How can you make procedures
more dynamic? By adding the functionality to accept and use user input. Anytime the user runs the application, he or she can enter different input, causing
the program to have the capability to have different output each time it is run.
Because programmers write programs in the real world to be useful to users, this
almost always means that the programs provide some interface that accepts user
input. The program then processes that input and spits out the result. Accepting
command-line input is a simple way to allow users to interact with your programs. In this section, you will learn how to accept and incorporate user input
into your Java programs. What follows is a listing of the HelloUser application:

```
/*
 * HelloUser
 * Demonstrates simple I/O
 */

import java.io.*;
public class HelloUser {
  public static void main(String args[]) {
    String name;
    BufferedReader reader;

    reader = new BufferedReader(new InputStreamReader(System.in));
    System.out.print("\nWhat is your name? ");
    try {
      name = reader.readLine();
      System.out.println("Hello, " + name + "!");
    }
    catch (IOException ioe) {
      System.out.println("I/O Exception Occurred");
    }
  }

}
```

As you can see in Figure 2.6, the program prints a message asking for the user's name. After that the cursor blinks awaiting user input. In Figure 2.7 you see that the user entered her name, "Roseanne" and the application read it in and then printed "Hello, Roseanne!"

FIGURE 2.6

The user is prompted for his or her name, which is accepted through standard input.

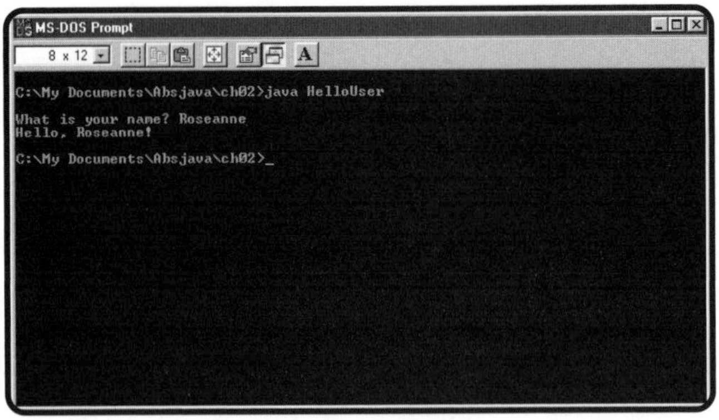

FIGURE 2.7

The program says hello to the user after she enters her name.

Using the *BufferedReader* Class

Unfortunately, getting simple user input is not very straightforward. One might think it would make sense that the syntax for reading a line would be as simple as writing a line of output. However, this is not the case. As you know, writing standard output can be done like this:

```
System.out.println("Shampoo is better!");
```

So, it would be natural to think reading input could be done like this:

```
System.in.readln();
```

But it is not that simple. First you must import the java.io package, which provides functionality for system input and output:

```
import java.io.*;
```

A *package* is a group of complimentary classes that work together to provide a larger scale of functionality. This is the second Java program you've written that uses the import statement. In the HelloWeb applet from Chapter 1, you imported the java.awt.Graphics class, which is part of the java.awt package. The difference here is that you use an asterisk to signify that you might be interested in all the classes that the java.io package groups together. Basically, you are importing the java.io package here to give your program the capability to call upon the I/O functionality. Specifically, it allows you to use the BufferedReader and Input-StreamReader classes in your program. At this point, you don't need to understand anything about these classes except that InputStreamReader reads the user's input and BufferedReader buffers the input to make it work more efficiently.

You can think of a buffer as sort of a middle man. I hear the Corleone family had a lot of buffers. When reading data in, a program has to make a system call, which can take a relatively long time (in computer-processing terms). To make up for this, the buffering trick is used. Instead of making a system call each time you need a piece of data, the buffer temporarily stores a chunk of data before you ask for it using only one system call. The buffer is then used to get data for subsequent requests because accessing memory is much faster than using a bunch of system calls.

Inside the main() method, you declared two variables:

```
String name;
BufferedReader reader;
```

Neither of them is a primitive data type. They are both instances of classes. The name variable is declared to be a String, giving it the capability to hold strings, which are covered in the next section, and reader is declared to be a BufferedReader, giving it the functionality to buffer input. The next line basically specifies reader to be a standard input buffer:

```
reader = new BufferedReader(new InputStreamReader(System.in));
```

HINT In this program you used a slightly different approach to printing a line of output. You used the System.out.print() method instead of the System.out.println() method. What's the difference? The System.out.println() method prints a message to the screen and then adds a carriage return to the end of it. The System.out.print() method does not add a carriage return to the end of the output line. As you see in Figures 2.6 and 2.7, the computer prompts the user for his or her name and the user types the name on the same line as the prompt. It is also important to note that you used a newline character escape code \n within the string passed to System.out.print() method. This moves the cursor down one line before printing the message.

After you have instantiated the BufferedReader object, which you have stored in the reader variable, it can be used to accept user input. This line of code is what prompts the user.

```
name = reader.readLine();
```

Confused? That's okay if you are. The important thing here is that you learn the syntax for accepting user input. Bear with me, this concept, as well as others, become clearer later on. You'll use this method of obtaining simple user input in these early chapters to create command prompt-based games until you learn graphic user interface (GUI) programming later.

Handling the Exceptions

Although exception handling is covered in more detail later in this book, I feel that I should explain the basics of it here because you are required to handle exceptions in this application. *Exceptions* are encountered when code does not work as it is expected to. Exception handling is used to plan a course of action in the event your code does not work as you expect it to. Here is an analogy to help you digest this concept. You have to go to work or school every normal weekday, right? Well, what if there is a blizzard or a tornado and you cannot go to work? In this analogy, the blizzard or tornado is the exception because it is an abnormality. The way this exception is handled is that you end up staying home from work.

Java requires that exceptions be handled in certain situations. In the HelloUser application, you are required to handle an IOException (input/output exception). What if you never actually get the user's input here? This would be an exception and you would not be able to incorporate the user's name in the program's output. In the case of this application, you issue an error message, indicating that an exception was encountered. You do not say "Hello" to the user—you can't because you were not able to retrieve the user's name.

You handled exceptions in the HelloUser application by using the try...catch structure. Any code, such as reading user input that might cause an exception, is placed within the try block, or "clause". Remember that a block is one or more statements enclosed within a set of curly braces:

```
try {
      name = reader.readLine();
      System.out.println("Hello, " + name + "!");
}
```

Here, you are trying to read user input and use it in a standard output line. What if it doesn't work? That's what the catch clause is for:

```
catch (IOException ioe) {
      System.out.println("I/O Exception Occurred");
}
```

If the code within the try clause does not work as it is expected to—there is an IOException— the code within the catch clause is executed. In this case the error message "I/O Exception Occurred" is printed to standard output to let the users know that a problem was encountered. In the real world, you try to handle exceptions as gracefully as you can. When detecting exceptions, you should try to handle them in a way so that your program uses default values instead of halting abruptly, but in some instances, your program just can't continue due to some error that you can't provide a work-around for. In these cases, you should at the very least, try to generate meaningful error messages so that users can use them to resolve any possible problems on their end.

The Math Game

In this section you incorporate much of what you've learned so far into a single application. After you write and compile this application, you can actually use it as a tool to remind yourself how arithmetic operators work in Java. Here is a listing of the source code for `MathGame.java`:

```java
/*
 * MathGame
 * Demonstrates integer math using arithmetic operators
 */

import java.io.*;
public class MathGame {
  public static void main(String args[]) {
    int num1, num2;
    BufferedReader reader;

    reader = new BufferedReader(new InputStreamReader(System.in));
    try {
      System.out.print("\nFirst Number: ");
      num1 = Integer.parseInt(reader.readLine());
      System.out.print("Second Number: ");
      num2 = Integer.parseInt(reader.readLine());
      reader.close();
    }
    // Simple Exception Handling
    catch (IOException ioe) {
      System.out.println("I/O Error Occurred, using 1...");
      num1 = num2 = 1;
    }
    catch (NumberFormatException nfe) {
      System.out.println("Number format incorrect, using 1...");
      num1 = num2 = 1;
    }

    //Avoid this pitfall e.g. 1 + 1 = 11:
    //System.out.println(num1 + " + " + num2 + " = " + num1 + num2);
    System.out.println(num1 + " + " + num2 + " = " + (num1 + num2));
    System.out.println(num1 + " - " + num2 + " = " + (num1 - num2));
    System.out.println(num1 + " * " + num2 + " = " + (num1 * num2));
    System.out.println(num1 + " / " + num2 + " = " + (num1 / num2));
    System.out.println(num1 + " % " + num2 + " = " + (num1 % num2));
  }
}
```

As shown in Figure 2.8, this program prompts the user for two integers and then performs arithmetic operations on them. It displays the results of these operations to the user. It's not exactly a game, unless math is fun for you, but you get the point.

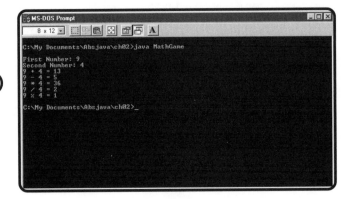

FIGURE 2.8

The MathGame application demonstrates mathematical operations applied to integers.

Parsing Strings to Numbers

Most of the code in the MathGame application should already be familiar to you. The code that is new to you is the code that parses a string value into an integer value:

```
Integer.parseInt(reader.readLine());
```

Parsing, just like casting, is changing the data type of the value of a variable or literal. The BufferedReader.readLine() method accepts the users input in string form. You cannot assign strings to int variables or perform mathematical operations on them, so you must first convert them to numbers. For instance, you can't do this:

```
int myNumber = "8";
```

An int variable can only store a valid int value, but in the line above "8" is expressed as a String literal, not an int. Because you need to accept user input here in string form, you need a way to parse the String input to an int. Integer.parseInt() does this. It is a method defined within the Integer class. It accepts a String argument and returns the int value of that string. For example if the String literal "8" is passed to this method, it returns the int 8. Here are some useful methods for converting strings to numbers:

Byte.parseByte(String s)	Converts a string to a byte.
Short.parseShort(String s)	Converts a string to a short.
Integer.parseInt(String s)	Converts a string to an int.
Long.parseLong(String s)	Converts a string to a long.

```
Float.parseFloat(String s)     Converts a string to a float.
Double.parseDouble(String s)   Converts a string to a double.
```

TRAP The string passed to a method that parses it to another data type must be a valid representation of that data type. For example, if you tried to parse the String "one" to an integer using Integer.parseInt(), it would cause a NumberFormatException, however, it is not required that you handle this exception, although you do in the MathGame application by simply using the int 1 if user input isn't obtained. If you don't handle the NumberFormatException, your program will crash if the user types a value that cannot be parsed to an int.

The *TipCalculator* Application

Here is another program for you to take a look at. It uses concepts of the Math-Game and TipAdder applications. It prompts the user for the price of the meal, converts the String value of the user's input into a double and then calculates the tip and displays the information to the user. Take a look at the source code:

```java
/*
 * TipCalculator
 * Parses user input and does floating point math
 */

import java.io.*;
public class TipCalculator {
  public static void main(String args[]) {
    String costResponse;
    double meal, tip, total;
    BufferedReader reader;

    reader = new BufferedReader(new InputStreamReader(System.in));
    System.out.print("\nHow much was the meal? ");
    try {
      costResponse = reader.readLine();
      // Note: we are not handling NumberFormatException
      meal = Double.parseDouble(costResponse);
      tip = meal * 0.15;
      total = meal + tip;
      System.out.println("The meal costs $" + meal);
      System.out.println("The 15% tip is $" + tip);
      System.out.println("The total is $" + total);
      reader.close();
    }
```

```
catch (IOException ioe) {
    System.out.println("I/O Exception Occurred");
  }
 }

}
```

Figure 2.9 shows the output of this program. Notice that this calculation is more precise than in the TipAdder program. That's because you used doubles instead of floats. Oh, one more thing, you didn't handle any of the exceptions. Figure 2.10 shows what happens when you don't get the double value you expect.

FIGURE 2.9

The output of the TipCalculator application.

FIGURE 2.10

Oops, my program crashed! I didn't type a valid double value.

Accepting Command-Line Arguments

As mentioned in Chapter 1, it is possible to pass command-line arguments to your application. *Command-line arguments* are parameters that are passed to the program when it is initially started up. This is done, as you'd imagine, from the

> **IN THE REAL WORLD**
>
> Command-line arguments are used for a number of different purposes in the real world. They are used as parameters that affect the way the program runs. Command-line arguments can exist to allow the user certain options while running your program. One other major use of command-line arguments from a programmer's standpoint is to aid in debugging or testing your code. You can use a command-line argument to set some sort of debug-mode parameter. With this debug mode set, you can debug your code by giving yourself special options that would not normally be available. For example, say you are a video game programmer. You need to test a particular game level, but it is a particularly difficult level for you to get through or would be time consuming. You can use a command-line argument that gives you access to any position in any level of the game you're programming, so you can just test the parts you need to.

command prompt. You pass parameters to an application by using the following syntax when running the application:

```
java ApplicationName command_line_arguments
```

When using a Macintosh, you will be prompted for any command-line arguments when you run your application. Command-line arguments are passed to the `main()` method as its only parameter: `String args[]`. It is an array (list) of parameters, so you can handle it like any other array. You learn about arrays in the next chapter. For now, you can just write the following application to give yourself a basic idea of how Java can accept and use command-line arguments.

```
/*
 * HelloArg
 * Uses command-line arguments
 */

public class HelloArg {
  public static void main(String args[]) {
    System.out.println("Hello, " + args[0] + "!");
  }

}
```

As you can see in Figure 2.11, I ran this procedure three times using different command-line arguments causing the application to issue different output. By the way, I wouldn't make the last guy angry, you wouldn't like him very much if he gets angry.

```
MS-DOS Prompt                                                    _ □ X
8 x 12 ▼  □ □ □  ⊠ ⊠  □ □  A
C:\My Documents\Abs java\ch02>java HelloArg Neo
Hello, Neo!
C:\My Documents\Abs java\ch02>java HelloArg Dr. Banner
Hello, Dr.!
C:\My Documents\Abs java\ch02>java HelloArg "Dr. Banner"
Hello, Dr. Banner!
C:\My Documents\Abs java\ch02>_
```

FIGURE 2.11

Passing command-
line arguments to
the HelloArg
application.

TRAP Arguments are separated by spaces. Make sure that if an argument needs to
include spaces, you surround the argument with double quotation marks.
Otherwise, it will be broken into multiple arguments and your application will
not run as you intended it to.

Strings and String Operations

A *string* is a sentence, or a succession of characters strung together. You already
used strings in every program you've written to this point (remember "Hello,
world!" and "\nFirst number: "). Now you learn about strings in more detail.
You learn about the String class, and its operations and methods.

The *String* Class

A string is not a primitive data type. It is a class of its own. The String class
includes methods for examining and operating on its individual characters. It
also has methods for searching strings, for comparing them, *concatenating* them
(appending one string to another), for extracting *substrings* (smaller segments of
strings) and for converting alphabetical characters from uppercase to lowercase
(or visa versa). It also has methods for converting other data types into string
values.

Java treats all string literals as String objects. String literals are always surrounded by quotation marks. That's how Java knows they're strings and not variable names or some other Java code. An *object* is an instance of a particular class.
Any operations that you can perform with String objects stored in variables can
also be performed with String literals. Here is an example using the
String.charAt() method. This method will return the char at a particular index
of the String. The *index* of a string is a number that represents a character's position within the string, starting with 0. To put it another way, the index of the

first character in a `String` is 0, the index of the second character is 1, the next index is 2 and so on until the last character in the string. The index of the last character is one less than the total length of the `String`.

```
//Create a String Object
String str = "Cranberry";
//the next two lines of code do basically the same thing
char strChar = str.charAt(4);
char cranChar = "Cranberry".charAt(4);
```

Both variables `strChar` and `cranChar` will have the value b because that is the value of the `char` at index 4 (the fifth letter of `Cranberry`).

Notice that in this program and in some other programs you've written that you used the + operator to "add" strings together. This operator works differently when used on strings. Adding substrings together to form larger strings is called *concatenation*. It's a pretty big word for something so simple, isn't it? An example of this is as follows:

```
String dogsName = "Mario " + "Don Cagnolino";
```

The value `"Mario Don Cagnolino"` is assigned to the `dogsName` variable. Note that I put a space after `"Mario"` in the first substring. If I didn't do that, the value would have been `"MarioDon Cagnolino"`. In the real world, concatenation is used to build strings from multiple sources, just like you did in the `HelloArg` program. You concatenated the string literal, `"Hello, "` with the string value stored in `args[0]`, and then concatenated the exclamation point. `args[0]` can be any string, so you add it to the hard-coded literal that you always want to print, `"Hello, "` to build the string you want to print. FYI: the term hard-coded refers to values directly written into program code that don't depend on any run-time value.

String Methods

The final project in this chapter uses `String` methods to manipulate the user's name. The `String` method includes quite a few useful methods used to operate on strings or to parse other data types to strings. Table 2.6 describes some of the useful methods defined within the `String` class.

Getting Back to the Name Game

The `NameGame` application introduced at the beginning of this chapter uses some `String` methods to play around with the user's name. Now that you're almost at the end of the chapter and have already learned so much about the Java language,

TABLE 2.6   SOME STRING CLASS METHODS

Method	Description
char charAt(int *index*)	Returns the character at the specified index.
String concat(String *str*)	Concatenates this string with another and returns the result.
Boolean endsWith(String *str*)	Tests whether this string ends with the suffix *str*.
boolean equals(String *str*)	Compares this string to another and returns true if they're equal.
boolean equalsIgnoreCase(String *str*)	Tests whether this string equals *str*, ignoring case.
int indexOf(char *c*)	Returns the integer index of char *c* at its first occurrence.
int indexOf(char *c*, int *n*)	Returns the first index of *c* starting at index *n*.
int indexOf(String *str*)	Returns the index of the first occurrence of *str*.
int indexOf(String *str*, int *n*)	Returns the index of the first occurrence of *str* starting at index *n*.
int length()	Returns the length (number of characters) of this string.
String replace(char *c1*, char *c2*)	Replaces all occurrences of *c1* with *c2* and returns the result.
String substring(int *n1*, int *n2*)	Returns the substring of this string between index *n1* and *n2*.
String toLowerCase()	Converts all letters in this string to lowercase.
String toUpperCase()	Converts all letters in this string to uppercase.
String valueOf()	Converts the argument to a string. There are versions of this method that accept boolean, char, double, float, int, and long data types.

you should be able to understand the source code. Try writing this application and running it:

```
/*
 * NameGame
 * Joseph P Russell
 * Demonstrates Simple I/O and String Methods
 */
```

```java
import java.io.*;
public class NameGame {
  public static void main(String args[]) {
    String firstName = "";
    String lastName = "";
    String fullName;
    String initials;
    int numLetters;
    BufferedReader reader;

    reader = new BufferedReader(new InputStreamReader(System.in));
    System.out.print("What is your first name? ");
    try {
      firstName = reader.readLine();
    }
    catch (IOException ioe) {
      System.out.println("I/O Exception Occurred");
    }

    System.out.println("That's a nice name, " + firstName + "!");
    System.out.println("I'll shout it! " + firstName.toUpperCase() + "!");
    System.out.print("OK, what's your last name? ");
    try {
      lastName = reader.readLine();
    }
    catch (IOException ioe) {
      System.out.println("I/O Exception Occurred");
    }
    fullName = firstName;
    //alternative to using the '+' operator
    fullName = fullName.concat(" ").concat(lastName);
    System.out.println("Oh, so your full name is " + fullName + ".");
    System.out.println("Or sometimes listed "
      + lastName + ", " + firstName + ".");
    initials = firstName.charAt(0) + "." + lastName.charAt(0) + ".";
    System.out.println("Your initials are " + initials);
    numLetters = firstName.length() + lastName.length();
    System.out.println("Did you know there are "
      + numLetters + " letters in your name?");
    System.out.println("Bye!");
  }
}
```

When you run this program it should look similar to Figure 2.1. Try running this program using different names to see how this program's output can be different each time. Here's an explanation of how this program works. Variables firstName and lastName are strings that are used to hold the user's first and last names. They are initialized to the null string (""). You must do this because accepting user input can possibly cause an exception. If it does, these strings will remain uninitialized and the compiler checks for this and forces you to initialize it outside of the try block before you access these variables' values. fullName is a string that holds the user's full name, initials holds the user's initials, and numLetters is an int that holds the number of letters in the user's name. The last variable reader is a BufferedReader that is used to accept the user's input.

When the program starts, it prints "What is your first name?". Remember, you use the System.out.print() method so that you can accept user input on the same line as the prompt because it doesn't append a newline character to the end of the string. Next, you use the reader object to read in the user's first name and print some output using the name the user entered. You use the String.toUpperCase() method to convert the name to uppercase:

```
System.out.println("I'll shout it! " + firstName.toUpperCase() + "!");
```

Next, you prompt for and accept the user's last name. Now that you have the first and last name, you can use them to build the full name. The lines of code that do this deserve an explanation:

```
fullName = firstName;
fullName = fullName.concat(" ").concat(lastName);
```

First, you assign the first name to fullName. Then you concatenate a space and the last name. Here I wanted to demonstrate how you can use the string returned by the String.concat() method to call a string method. fullName.concat(" ") returns the string value of the first name with a space appended to the end of it. This value is returned as a string object, so you can use it to call string methods. Here you did this by using a dot right after the first method call and then called the String.concat() method again to append the last name. You can also write it this way to make it more readable, it does the same thing:

```
FullName = firstName.concat(" " + lastName);
```

You get the user's initials using the firstName.charAt(0) and lastName.charAt(0). To count the number of letters in the user's name, you added firstName.length() to lastName.length(). Remember that this method returns the total number of characters in the string, but the character index starts at 0. This means that if you wanted to get the last character in the user's full name, you do it this way: fullName.charAt(fullName.length() - 1).

Summary

You have learned a lot in this chapter. You learned how to write a Java application and a simple Java applet. You learned about variables and data types and how to use them in your applications. You also learned how to obtain simple user input and how to create interactive applications. You learned how to handle numerical values in Java and perform arithmetic operations on them. You were also introduced to some more advanced topics such as event handling and object-oriented programming. Don't worry if you don't understand it all yet. It's a lot to absorb. You will continue to build upon what you already know about Java in the chapters to come. In the next chapter, you learn how to generate random numbers and conditional statements, and to work with arrays.

CHALLENGES

1. Write an application that calculates a 5% tax for any given price and displays the total cost.

2. Write an application that prints the multiplication table for integers 1 through 12.

3. Write an application that accepts a number from the user and prints its multiplication table values (multiply it by 1 through 12 and print the results).

4. Write an application that reads in a user's sentence of unknown, possibly mixed upper- and lowercase letters, capitalizes the first letter of the sentence, makes all other letters lowercase, and makes sure there is a period at the end.

5. Write an application that searches for your first name in a string and replaces it with your last name.

3

The Fortune Teller: Random Numbers, Conditionals, and Arrays

So far, all the programs in this book have been predictable. Every time they run, they do exactly the same thing. They vary only based on user input or command-line arguments. How cool would it be to be able to write a program so that even you can't predict its output each time you run it? In this chapter you learn how to generate random numbers and use them to add a level of unpredictability to your programs. You will use random numbers in real-world projects to create games that have replay value, as they run differently each time you play them. You also learn to dynamically branch the flow of your programs based on certain conditions that you can test for. You learn about arrays and understand how to use them in your Java programs.

Arrays are used in real-world programming to collect data of a single type together in a list. For example, say you're writing a retail cash register program. You would want to keep track of the purchase item prices separately so you could print them all out as individual lines on the receipt. It would be ridiculous to have an instance variable for each item, right? Instead, you could store all of the prices in a list by using a `double` type array. Once you have the list of prices, you can list them individually and total them up at the end, using just one variable name. At the end of the chapter, you put these topics together in one single project. In this chapter, you will

- Generate random numbers using `Math.random()` and `java.util.Random`

- Use the `if` statement

- Use the `switch` statement

- Use the ternary operator (`?  :`)

- Declare, initialize, and iterate arrays

The Project: the Fortune Teller

The final project of this chapter is the `FortuneTeller` application. You can see the final project in Figure 3.1.

FIGURE 3.1

The Great Randini predicts tomorrow.

When you run this application, your fortune is read for tomorrow. Each time you run it, you'll see a different fortune. The exact output is not predictable. Maybe the Great Randini can predict it, but unless you're psychic, you cannot. It is impossible for you to create this application using only the techniques you learned in the first two chapters, so read on young padawan!

Generating Random Numbers

In this section, you learn about the Math class and how you can use it to generate random numbers. You also take a look at other ways to use the Math class to call upon mathematical functions. Another class that you learn about is the Random class. You learn how to use this class as an alternative way to generate random numbers.

The *NumberMaker* Application

The NumberMaker application demonstrates how to generate a random double and assign that value to a variable. It's very straightforward to program. Here is a listing of the source code:

```
/*
 * NumberMaker
 * Generates random numbers
 */

public class NumberMaker {

  public static void main(String args[]) {
    double randNum = Math.random();
    System.out.println("Random Number: " + randNum);
  }

}
```

There is one line here that you should be unfamiliar with:

```
double randNum = Math.random()
```

In this line, you declare randNum as a double and assign a random number to it. You do this by calling the Math.random() method, which returns a random number (as a double). The values range from 0.0 (inclusive) to 1.0 (exclusive). *Inclusive* means that the lower limit, 0.0, is included as a possible value, whereas *exclusive* means that 1.0, as the upper limit, is only a cap and is not a possible value. Another way to state this is that the range of possible values are all the values that are greater than or equal to 0.0 and less than 1.0. This program just spits out the random number and doesn't really have any use for it except to show how to generate random numbers. Run it a few times, as in the example in Figure 3.2. Your output should be different each time, as was mine.

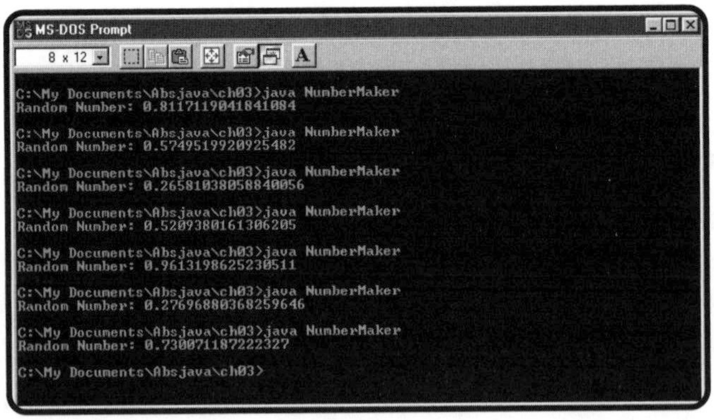

FIGURE 3.2

The NumberMaker displays random numbers generated by the Math.random() method.

The *java.util.Random* Class

Another way that you can generate random numbers is by using the Random class in the java.util package. The Random class offers different methods for different data types. Specifically, it can generate random booleans, doubles, floats, ints, and longs. Refer to Table 3.1 for a list of these methods.

TABLE 3.1 SOME JAVA.UTIL.RANDOM METHODS

Method	Description
boolean nextBoolean()	Randomly returns either true or false boolean values.
double nextDouble()	Returns a random double value ranging from 0.0 (inclusive) to 1.0 (exclusive).
float nextFloat()	Returns a random float value ranging from 0.0 (inclusive) to 1.0 (exclusive).
int nextInt()	Returns a random int value (all 232 values are possible).
int nextInt(int *n*)	Returns a random int value ranging from 0 (inclusive) to *n* (exclusive).
long nextLong()	Returns a random long value (all 264 values are possible).

In order to call one of the methods in Table 3.1, you need to create a new Random object first, and then use that object to call the desired method. The Number-MakerUtil application demonstrates how this is done. Take a look at the source code:

```
/*
 * NumberMakerUtil
 * Uses java.util.Random to generate random numbers
 */
```

```java
import java.util.Random;

public class NumberMakerUtil {

  public static void main(String args[]) {
    Random rand = new Random();

    System.out.println("Random Integers:");
    System.out.println(rand.nextInt() + ", "
                         + rand.nextInt() + ", "
                         + rand.nextInt());

    int iLimit = 11;
    System.out.println("\nRandom Integers between 0 and 10:");
    System.out.println(rand.nextInt(iLimit) + ", "
                         + rand.nextInt(iLimit) + ", "
                         + rand.nextInt(iLimit));

    System.out.println("\nRandom Floats:");
    System.out.println(rand.nextFloat() + ", "
                         + rand.nextFloat() + ", "
                         + rand.nextFloat());

    System.out.println("\nRandom Booleans:");
    System.out.println(rand.nextBoolean() + ", "
                         + rand.nextBoolean() + ", "
                         + rand.nextBoolean());

  }

}
```

The output of the `NumberMakerUtil` program is displayed in Figure 3.3.

FIGURE 3.3

This is the output of the `NumberMakerUtil` program. It generates random numbers and `boolean` values by using the `java.util.Random` class.

In the source code, you do the following things. First, you create a `Random` object:

```java
Random rand = new Random();
```

This makes rand an instance of the Random class and you use it to generate random values. Now that you have created rand, you can call the methods defined in the Random class. In this code:

```
int iLimit = 11;
    System.out.println("\nRandom Integers between 0 and 10:");
    System.out.println(rand.nextInt(iLimit) + ", "
                        + rand.nextInt(iLimit) + ", "
                        + rand.nextInt(iLimit));
```

You declare iLimit to be an int whose value is 11. Then you make calls to the nextInt(int n) method to generate random numbers from 0 to 10. The range is from 0 to 10, as you remember, because 11 is the upper limit and is not a possible value. In this program, you also use some other methods shown in Table 3.2.

HINT When you call the Math.random() method, you get the same result as if you created a Random object and made a call to the Random.nextDouble() method. In fact, when you call the Math.random() method, it creates a Random object and calls its nextDouble() method. That Random object is used thereafter in subsequent calls to Math.random().

The Random class actually generates pseudorandom numbers. *pseudorandom* numbers are generated in a completely nonrandom way, but in a way that simulates randomness. The way Random methods do this is by taking a seed, an initial value (basically), and via some specific algorithm, generates other values based on the seed. An *algorithm* is a finite number of problem-solving steps (a solution to a specific problem or a way to get from point A to point B). Every Random object has a seed that it feeds through its randomization algorithm. This method can create all possible values with equal frequency given any seed. The values occur in order, but given infinite number of passes through the algorithm, all values are possible.

If you don't specify Random's seed (you can, by the way), it is initialized by the value of the system clock in milliseconds. The system clock is your computer's interpretation of the current time. Because the algorithm is not random, you'd come to the conclusion that one specific seed will generate a non-randomly ordered list of numbers. You'd be right and now you know why Random's methods start with "next...". Furthermore, you would be willing to bet your paycheck that if two Random objects use the same seed, they both generate the same list of pseudorandom numbers. You would double your money because that's exactly the case. Take a look at the AmIRandom program, which demonstrates the concept of the seed and pseudorandom numbers.

```
/*
 * AmIRandom
 * Demonstrates the concept of a seed and pseudorandom numbers
 */
```

```java
import java.util.Random;

public class AmIRandom {

   public static void main(String args[]) {
     //don't specify a seed
     Random rand1 = new Random();

     //the number in parentheses is the seed
     Random rand2 = new Random(12345);

     //Or you can do it this way by using setSeed
     Random rand3 = new Random();
     rand3.setSeed(12345);

     System.out.println("\nrand1's random numbers:");
     System.out.println(rand1.nextInt() + " "
                        + rand1.nextInt() + " "
                        + rand1.nextInt());

     System.out.println("\nrand2's random numbers:");
     System.out.println(rand2.nextInt() + " "
                        + rand2.nextInt() + " "
                        + rand2.nextInt());

     System.out.println("\nrand3's random numbers:");
     System.out.println(rand3.nextInt() + " "
                        + rand3.nextInt() + " "
                        + rand3.nextInt());

   }

}
```

There are three Random objects, rand1, rand2, and rand3. You don't specify rand1's seed, so the system clock is checked. But, you did set the seed for rand2 and rand3 to 12345. You set rand1's seed by putting that number in as a parameter when creating the Random object.

```java
Random rand2 = new Random(12345);
```

You set rand3's seed after it was already assigned its Random object by using the setSeed() method:

```java
rand3.setSeed(12345);
```

As you can see in Figure 3.4, rand1's random numbers vary each time you run the program, but rand2's and rand3's numbers are invariably 1553932502, -2090749135, and -287790814.

Now that you know two ways to generate randomization, you might be wondering which one you should use. Some programmers opt to use Math.random() for its simplicity. When you use that method, you don't have to explicitly create a

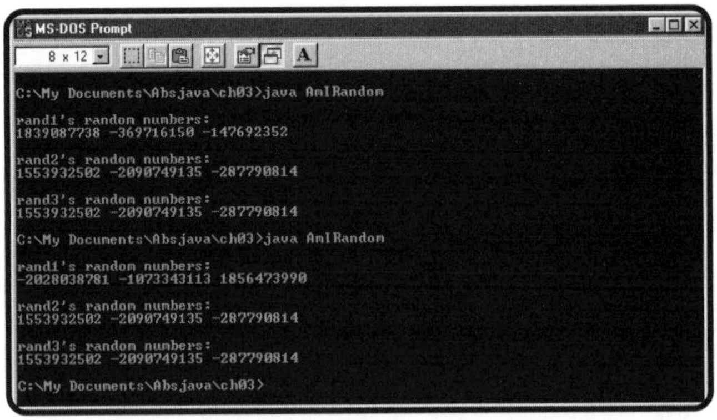

FIGURE 3.4

This is the output of the AmIRandom application. rand2 and rand3 will always generate the same output.

Random object yourself. On the other hand, I find it easier to use the Random class in programs that need a specific type and range of random data. You can use Math.random() to generate ranges of random integers, longs, or whatever, but you have to parse the double values and perform mathematical operations.

IN THE REAL WORLD

In the real world, one use for random numbers is to create the element of surprise in video games. Games such as Tetris, Solitaire, and Minesweeper wouldn't be any fun if every time you played it, the same thing happened. Eventually, you'd memorize it all and it wouldn't be a game anymore, it would be monotonous. You would always know where the mines are, or where the aces are, or what the next hundred or so Tetris blocks would be. You'd have to put the games aside and actually get some work done. How boring!

The *Math* Class

You used the Math.random() method to generate random numbers. Now you learn more about the Math class. The Math class defines methods for performing basic mathematical operations such as calculating absolute values, exponents, logarithms, square roots, and trigonometric functions. Table 3.2 lists some of these methods. Note that not all versions of a particular method are listed. For example, there are versions of Math.abs() that accept data types: int, long, float, and double. Refer to the Math class in the Java documentation for more detailed information.

The MathClassTest application shows how to use some of these methods and by comparing the source code to the output, as shown in Figure 3.5, you'll get a better idea of what these methods do:

TABLE 3.2   MATH CLASS METHODS

Math Method	Description
Math.abs(int *n*)	Absolute value (*n* or 0-*n*, whichever is greater)
Math.acos(double *d*)	Arc cosine of *d*
Math.asin(double *d*)	Arc sine of *d*
Math.atan(double *d*)	Arc tangent of *d*
Math.ceil(double *d*)	Ceiling (smallest value not less than *d* that is an integer)
Math.cos(double *d*)	Cosine of *d*
Math.exp(double *d*)	(e^d, where e=2.718...)
Math.floor(double *d*)	Floor (highest value not greater than *d* that is an integer)
Math.log(double *d*)	Natural logarithm of *d*
Math.pow(double *a*, double *b*)	a^b
Math.random()	Generates a random number between 0.0 and 1.0
Math.round(float *f*)	Rounds *f* to the nearest int value
Math.round(double *d*)	Rounds *d* to the nearest long value
Math.sin(double *d*)	Sine of *d*
Math.sqrt(double *d*)	Square root of *d*
Math.tan(double *d*)	Tangent of *d*
Math.toDegrees(double *d*)	Converts *d* (in radians) to degrees
Math.toRadians(double *d*)	Converts *d* (in degrees) to radians

FIGURE 3.5

The MathClassTest application output.

```
/*
 * MathClassTest
 * Demonstrates use of Math class methods
 */

public class MathClassTest {

    public static void main(String args[]) {
        double d = -123.456;

        System.out.println("My number is: " + d);
        System.out.println("The absolute value is: " + Math.abs(d));
        System.out.println("The ceiling is: " + Math.ceil(d));
        System.out.println("The floor is: " + Math.floor(d));
        System.out.println("Rounded off, it is: " + Math.round(d));

        System.out.println("The square root of 100 is " + Math.sqrt(100));
        System.out.println("3^2 is: " + Math.pow(3, 2));
    }

}
```

Controlling the Random Number Range

You know how to use `Math.random()` to generate random `double` values ranging from 0.0 to 1.0. You also know how to use the `java.util.Random` class to generate random numbers. You can use it to generate all possible `int` and `long` values, as well as `float`s and `double`s ranging from 0.0 to 1.0. You also know how to have limited control of random `int` values using the `Random.nextInt(int n)` method, which gives you a range from 0 to (n-1). This section covers how to generate random numbers that fit within a specific range.

IN THE REAL WORLD

In the real world, you will write your code in such a way that it acts differently based on what the value of a random number is. Using the Tetris game example again, there are only seven differently shaped blocks that can possibly fall into the play area. In this instance, you only need to handle seven possibilities, so you only need a random number that only can be one of seven values, such as 0 through 6.

Getting Values Larger Than 1

When you use `Math.random()`, the largest value you can get is less than 1.0. To get values larger than 1, you multiply the value returned by `Math.random()` by the number you want to have as the upper limit of random numbers. For example:

```
double d = Math.random() * 45.0;
```

In this line of code, d is assigned a random value ranging from 0.0 (inclusive) to 45.0 (exclusive). You can do the same thing when using `Random` methods with random floating point numbers. Okay, so now you can get a range of numbers, but the lower limit has to be 0.0.

Specifying a Range

If you needed to get a more specific range, say from 32.0 to 212.0, you could do it this way:

```
double d = Math.random() * 180 + 32;
```

The d variable is assigned a random value from 32.0 (inclusive) to 212.0 (exclusive). Here's how it works. As you know, `Math.random()` returns some random value between 0.0 and 1.0. This value is multiplied by 180 because 212.0 - 32.0 = 180.0. The difference between the lower and upper limit ranges from 0.0 to 180.0. When 32 is added to that value, the range becomes 32.0 to 212.0, just like you needed.

If you need a range of integers; for example, from 1 to 10 inclusive, you do it this way:

```
int n = (int) (Math.random() * 10 + 1);
```

This code assigns a random `int` ranging from 1 to 10 inclusive. `Math.random()` generates a random number from 0.0 to 1.0; the range is multiplied by 10 and becomes 0.0 to 10.0. Add 1 to that and now it ranges from 1.0 to 11.0. Remember that the upper limit is not a possible value. The lowest possible value is 1.0 and the highest possible value is essentially 10.99999... When you cast this positive value to an `int`, it has the same effect as using `Math.floor()` because it is *truncated* (the fractional portion is ignored).

The Dice Roller

Want to write a program using random numbers that actually does something meaningful? The `DiceRoller` application simulates rolling dice. When you run it, it displays two dice with randomly generated face values. Here is a source listing of `DiceRoller.java`:

```
/*
 * DiceRoller
 * Simulates rolling of die using random
 * values between 1 and 6 (inclusive).
 * Two methods of random number generation are used.
 */

import java.util.Random;

public class DiceRoller {

  public static void main(String args[]) {
    double rand;
    Random random = new Random();
    int die1;
    int die2;

    System.out.println("Rolling dice...");

    // Get random double using Math.random()
    rand = Math.random();

    // get a value between 0.0 (inclusive) and 6 (exclusive)
    rand = rand * 6;

    // cast it to an integer and add 1
    // to get an int between 1 and 6 (inclusive)
    die1 = (int) (rand + 1);

    // Get random int between 0 and 5 (inclusive) and add 1
    // using java.util.Random
    die2 = random.nextInt(6) + 1;

    System.out.println("You rolled: ["
                        + die1 + "][" + die2 + "]");
  }

}
```

The rand variable is a double value that holds the random value returned by Math.random(). random is a Random object, and die1 and die2 are integers that represent the face value of a set of dice. You take the two approaches to generating random numbers that you've learned to produce this effect. Figure 3.6 shows the output.

When this program generates the value for die1, it calls the Math.random() method. It uses the algorithm described in the previous section for generating the specific range of 1 to 6. The program uses three separate lines to generate the random number to make the steps in the process clear, but it can all be done with one statement like this:

```
die1 = (int) (Math.random() * 6 + 1);
```

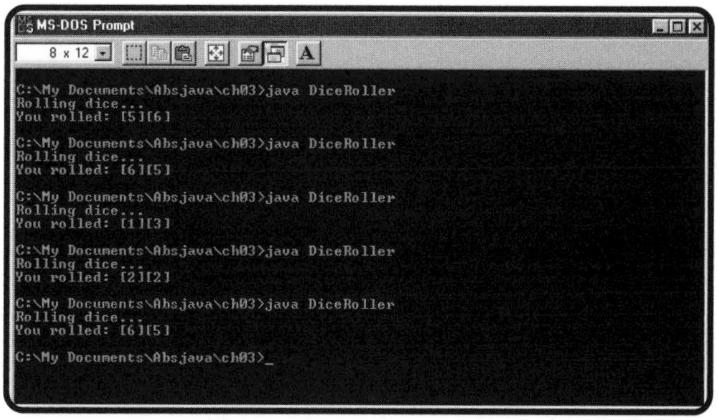

FIGURE 3.6

The DiceRoller application is a simulation of rolling dice.

The program demonstrates how to generate this range using the java.util. Random class. The die2 variable gets its value this way. The call to the Random. nextInt(int n) method returns a random integer between 0 and 5 inclusive, so you just need to add 1 to shift that range to where you need it to be.

The *if* Statement

Wouldn't it be great if you could conditionally direct the flow of your program based on certain conditions? You can do this by using conditional statements. *Conditional statements* test for certain conditions and execute or skip statements based on the results. For example, you can generate a random number and have the program print "Even" only when the random number is even:

```
if (myRandomNumber % 2 == 0){
    System.out.println("Even");
}
```

The expression within the parentheses is the condition. If the condition is true, the System.out.println("Even") statement is executed. This particular if statement prints "Even" only when myRandomNumber is even. Recall that % is the modulus operator, so any number that is evenly divided by two (the remainder is 0) is even. The equality operator == results in the boolean value of true or false. When used with numbers or expressions that evaluate to numbers, the value will be true only when the number on the left side is equal to the number on the right side. The syntax for the if statement is as follows:

```
if (condition) {
    ...
    java statements;
    ...
}
```

The if keyword is followed by a condition within parentheses. The statements that execute if the condition is true are placed within the braces. Recall that a group of statements within a set of braces is collectively called a *block statement.* The braces are optional if you need to execute only one statement. Figure 3.7 shows the flow of a conditional statement. You can see that if the condition is true, the flow of the program is directed toward executing some Java statement or statements. These statements are not executed if the condition is false.

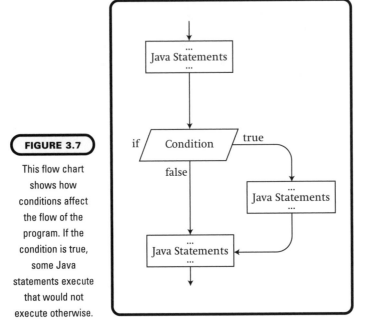

FIGURE 3.7

This flow chart shows how conditions affect the flow of the program. If the condition is true, some Java statements execute that would not execute otherwise.

Conditions and Conditional Operators

Conditions evaluate to either `true` or `false`. A condition can be expressed as a `boolean` literal, `boolean` variable, or any method or expression that evaluates to a `boolean` value. In this section you learn about conditions and conditional operators. *Conditional operators* are used in conditional expressions to test for certain states of the operands. There are conditional operators used for comparison, for testing equality, and there are also conditional-AND and conditional-OR operators that are used to form compound conditions by grouping conditions together.

The four numerical comparison operators (<, <=, >, >=), also called relational operators, are used for comparing numerical data. The type of each of the operands must evaluate to a primitive numerical type, such as `int`, `long`, `float`, or `double`. The operand on the left side of the operator is compared to the operand on the right side of the operator and returns a Boolean value corresponding to whether the comparison holds true. Table 3.3 lists these operators, including descriptions. Note that in this table, both x and y can be any numerical data type.

TABLE 3.3   NUMERICAL COMPARISON OPERATORS

Operator	Syntax	Description
<	x < y	Result is true if x is *less than* y; otherwise, it is false.
<=	x <= y	Result is true if x is *less than or equal to* y; otherwise, it is false.
>	x > y	Result is true if x is *greater than* y; otherwise, it is false.
>=	x >= y	Result is true if x is *greater than or equal to* y; otherwise, it is false.

Some examples of how these operators work are as follows: 1 < 2 is true because one is less than two. If it were written 2 < 1, the result would be false because 2 is not less than one. 1 < 1 is false because one is not less than one, however both 1 <= 1 and 1 >= 1 are true because one is equal to one. You can use the equality operator (==) to test for strict equality. This operation results in true only when the operands on either side are exactly equal.

TRICK

Remember that floating-point numbers cannot be stored precisely by a computer? This is important to remember when comparing these values in conditional statements. We all can figure out on paper that 22.5 × 0.15 is 3.375, **but the comparison** 22.5F * 0.15F == 3.375F **is false. This calculation in Java actually results in** 3.3750002, **which is not exactly equal to** 0.375. **This is a precision error. When comparing floating-point numbers, you can avoid this problem by comparing values to acceptable ranges. For example, instead of testing that the value is exactly equal to** 3.375, **you can test that it is greater than** 0.3749 **and less than** 0.3751. **Of course, the acceptable range will vary depending on how accurate the value must be.**

You can also test for inequality by using the not-equal-to operator (!=). This operation will return true if the operands on either side are not equal to each other. It is the opposite of the equality operator. These operators are used not only for numerical data types, but are also used to compare Boolean values and objects. When comparing Boolean values, the equality operator will return true if both values are equal. For example, true == true is true and false == false is also true. Otherwise, the equality operator is false. The inequality operator will result true if the Boolean values are different, such as when one is false and one is true. Keep in mind for future chapters that when objects are tested for equality in this way, they are equal only when both operands, usually variables holding objects, reference the exact same object. That is, technically speaking, they must both point to (reference) the same memory location. This is true when one object exists, but two separate variables reference it.

TRAP The equality and inequality operators evaluate from left to right. Okay, so what? Do you think the expression 2 == 2 == 2 evaluates to true or false? Upon first glance, you would probably say "true" because two equals two equals two, but that is not the case. It causes a compiler error. Take a closer look and you can see why. You know that the equality operator results in a boolean value. You also know that it evaluates from left to right. This expression evaluates to (2 == 2) == 2. The left side of this expression is (2 == 2). This evaluates to true, so you are left with the expression true == 2. The data types of the two operands are incomparable; thus the compiler will generate errors.

The exclamation point character in Java is called the *logical compliment operator* or simply "not". It must be followed by a Boolean or an expression that results in a Boolean value, or the compiler will yell at you. It reverses the Boolean value that follows it. For example, !true, which is read "not true", is false and !false is true. Further, !(1 < 2) is false and !(2 < 1) is true.

The conditional-AND (&&) operator operates on Boolean operands and results in a boolean value. Both sides of this operand must be true (such as true && true) for the result to be true. Any other combination of true and false values will result in a false. It makes sense. If I am a man AND I have children, I am a father. Both conditions must be true here. I can be a man, but not have any kids, or I can have kids, but not be a man, or I can be a woman and be childless too. In all these cases, I would not be a father.

The conditional-OR operator (||) also must have Boolean operands. At least one of the operands must be true for the result to be true; only false || false results in false. If you want to see that new R-rated movie, you must be over 17 or you must be accompanied by an adult. One or the other (or both) will do fine, but if you don't meet either of the two conditions, you can't see the movie (unless you bribe the guy at the ticket stand).

HINT This conditional-AND operator has a short-circuit property. When you use the conditional-AND operator, the JRE evaluates the left side first. If the left side is false, it ignores the right side. If the left side is false, it doesn't matter what is on the right side, the operation will evaluate to false. This is useful to know because you can avoid run-time errors this way. For example, if you were testing whether the second character of a string, str, was 'b', but you were unsure of its length, you could do it this way:

```
if (str.length() > 1 && str.charAt(1) == 'b') …
```

Attempting to access the character at index 1 would cause a run-time error if the string is not more than one character long, but here you won't have to worry about it because `str.charAt(1)` isn't evaluated by the JRE at all if `str.length()` is not greater than 1. This works similarly with the conditional-OR operator except if the left side is true, the right side is ignored and the result is true. The right side is evaluated only when the left side is false.

 TRICK

All these conditional operators ultimately result in Boolean values. You can actually assign the values of these operations to Boolean variables. For example:

```
boolean xEqualsY = (x == y);
```

The Boolean variable `xEqualsY` stores true or false, depending on how the conditional expression `x == y` evaluates.

Using Boolean Logical Operators

There are some other operators that work similar to the conditional-AND and conditional-OR operators. They can get confusing, because they have other uses too, but it is important that I explain them here so you can at least reference what they do when you see them in someone else's code. If your brain is full right now or you just feel like skipping this part, feel free to, because these operators are only explained here and are not used in the rest of the book. You can always come back to this part if you need to reference this information when you start moving on to more advanced Java programming. These operators are called either *Boolean logical operators* or *integer bitwise operators*, depending on what type of operands they are operating on.

If the operands are Boolean types, these operators are Boolean logical operators. The *logical-AND* operator (&) (note there is a single ampersand, unlike the conditional-AND, which uses a double ampersand) works almost exactly the same as the conditional-AND operator. It results in true only if both sides are true. The difference is that both operands are evaluated always, even if the left side is false. The logical-OR operator (|) works exactly the same as the conditional-OR operator except that both sides are evaluated even if the left side is true. The logical-XOR (exclusive OR) operator (^) works similar to the logical-OR operator except that the operands must be different—one must be true and one must be false—for the result to be true. The result of `true ^ true` is false unlike the conditional-OR operator. Table 3.4 summarizes these concepts.

When both operands are integer types, these operators are integer bitwise operators. They work at the binary level, you know, ones and zeros. This concept is not important in terms of the concepts defined in this book, so I won't spend too much time on them here. Basically, computers store information in memory using a series of bits that are either on, represented as ones or off, represented as zeros. The ones can be considered true and the zeros can be considered false.

TABLE 3.4 AND AND OR OPERATORS

Operator	Description	Examples	Results
&&	Conditional-AND	false && false	false
		false && true	false
		true && false	false
		true && true	true
||	Conditional-OR	false || false	false
		false || true	true
		true || false	true
		true || true	true
&	Logical-AND	false & false	false
		false & true	false
		true & false	false
		true & true	true
|	Logical-OR	false | false	false
		false | true	true
		true | false	true
		true | true	true
^	Logical-XOR	false ^ false	false
		false ^ true	true
		true ^ false	true
		true ^ true	false

Note: Logical-AND and OR operators always evaluate both operands, but conditional-AND and OR operators only evaluate the right side if it is necessary to determine the overall value of the expression.

These operators operate on binary values this way. The binary number 1010 is essentially true false true false.

When a bitwise operator operates on two binary values, such as 1010 and 1100 (`true true false false`), they are compared digit by digit (technically bit by bit). The first bit of the left side operand is compared to the left side of the right side operand, the second bit of the left side operand is compared to the second bit of the right side operand, and so on. The bitwise operations work on this example as follows:

```
1010 & 1100      1000
1010 | 1100      1110
1010 ^ 1100      0110
```

There is one more operator that you need to learn, simply called the *conditional*, or *ternary* operator. The conditional operator (? :) uses the Boolean value of one expression to decide which of the two other expressions should be evaluated. The syntax is as follows:

```
condition ? expression1 : expression2;
```

The syntax is the condition followed by a question mark (?), and then the expression to be evaluated if the condition is true followed by a colon (:), and finally the expression to be evaluated if the condition is false. Here is an example:

```
String s = x < y ? "x is less than y" : "x is not less than y";
```

String s is assigned "x is less than y" only when x < y; otherwise, it is assigned "x is not less than y". The condition is x < y and the expressions are "x is less than y" and "x is not less than y". The condition and two expressions make up the three parts of the ternary operator. Ternary literally means consisting of three units or components.

The *LowTemp* Program

The LowTemp program demonstrates the use of the if statement and conditional statements. It generates a random number and interprets it as a temperature in degrees Fahrenheit. If the temperature is determined to be low, by using an if statement and a numerical relational operator, a message is displayed: "You should bring a coat." You should write this program and run it a few times to see how the conditional statement works. Here is a listing of the source code for LowTemp.java:

```
/*
 * LowTemp
 * Uses the if statement to display a message
 * that depends on whether or not the random
 * temperature is low. Also demonstrates how
 * to get a random number within a specific range.
 */

import java.util.Random;

public class LowTemp {

  public static void main(String args[]) {
    int min = -40;
    int max = 120;
    int diff = max - min;
```

```
    int temp;
    Random rand = new Random();

    temp = rand.nextInt(diff + 1) + min;
    System.out.println("The temperature is " + temp +"F.");

    if (temp < 50) {
       System.out.println("You should bring a coat.");
    }
  }

}
```

Figure 3.8 demonstrates how the if statement prints the message "You should bring a coat." only when the condition temp < 50 evaluates to true. Feel free to play around with the conditions and also the random number generator to suit your own tastes and to better understand the concepts of this chapter.

FIGURE 3.8

The LowTemp
program
conditionally prints
a message using
the if statement.

The *if-else* Statement

The if statement alone only allows you to conditionally execute a statement or a set of statements. If the conditional expression results true, the program executes the statements contained within the brackets of the if statement. The program executes any statements that follow the if unconditionally. For example, consider this snippet of code:

```
if (noShoes || noShirt) {
  service = false;
  System.out.println("No service!");
}
System.out.println("service = " + service);
```

For the purposes of this example, assume that noShoes, noShirt, and service are all Boolean variables. If either noShoes or noShirt is false, the program sets the variable service to false and prints "No service!". There is no alternative set of code to execute. Next, the program prints the value of service, which will be false if the noShoes || noShirt condition holds true. If the condition is false, it is possible that service has not been initialized and will cause a run-time error.

Suppose you want to do something differently if the condition fails than what you do when it is true. If noShoes or noShirt is true, you want to set service to false and print "No Service!", or else you want to set service to true and print "At your service!". That is what the if-else statement is used for. Figure 3.9 shows a flowchart of the if-else structure. You can compare it to Figure 3.7. The difference is that there is a choice of two sets of statements that the program executes depending on whether the condition is true or false.

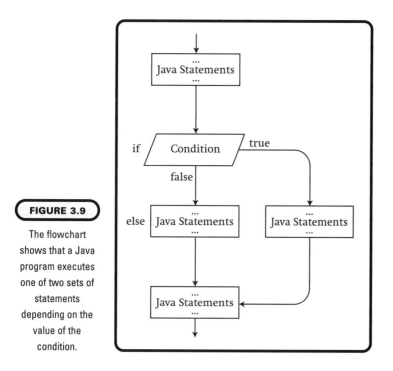

FIGURE 3.9

The flowchart shows that a Java program executes one of two sets of statements depending on the value of the condition.

The if-else structure allows for execution of a conditional choice of two statements, executing one or the other but not both. The syntax is as follows:

```
if (condition) {
  java_statements_for_true_condition;
}
else {
  java_statements_for_false_condition;
}
```

If the condition is true, the program executes the statements represented here by java_statements_for_true_condition. If the condition is false, the statements represented by java_statements_for_false_condition are executed. There can never exist a case where the program executes both statements. If you are using the `else` structure, you must place the `else` keyword directly after the corresponding `if` statement. If you do not, you get a compiler error to the effect "else without if" and you are forced to fix your code to get it to compile correctly. Getting back to the `"No shoes, no shirt, no service"` example—I rewrote it so it uses the `if-else` structure to get the desired results:

```
if (noShoes || noShirt) {
   service = false;
   System.out.println("No service!");
}
else {
   service = true;
   System.out.println("At your service!");
}
System.out.println("service = " + service);
```

Here's another quick example that uses the `if-else` structure to print `"even"` if the `int x` is even or else print `"odd"`:

```
if (x % 2 == 0) {
   System.out.println("even");
}
else {
   System.out.println("odd");
}
```

HINT

Notice that in the "No shoes, no shirt, no service" examples I use the condition:

```
if (noShoes || noShirt)
```

Because the condition is working on Boolean variables, this has the same effect as the following code:

```
if ( (noShoes == true) || (noShirt == true) )
```

Because all conditional expressions evaluate to a Boolean value, Boolean variables can be used directly in any place within a conditional statement where a conditional expression can be used.

You can also use the `not` operator in conjunction with a Boolean variable, which comes in handy to eliminate an `else` from an `if-else` statement. Here's an example. Say you have a `boolean` variable, `done`, which indicates whether a calculation has already been performed. If it is already done, you don't need to do it again. This is how you would write the code without using the `not` operator:

```
if (done) {
   //don't need to do anything anymore
}
else {
   //You need to do it here
}
```

Using the not operator, you can eliminate the else from this code because you have to handle the situation only when the calculation is not done:

```
if (!done) {
  //You need to do it here
}
```

The *HighOrLowTemp* Program

The HighOrLowTemp program expands upon the LowTemp program explored earlier in this chapter. The LowTemp program is limited in that it only prints a message "You should bring a coat" if the random temperature is cold (below 50 degrees Fahrenheit). The HighOrLowTemp program uses the if-else statement to print the same message if the temperature is cold. In addition, if the temperature is not cold, it will print a different message: "You don't need a coat." The source code for HighOrLowTemp.java is as follows:

```
/*
 * HighOrLowTemp
 * Demonstrates the if - else structure.
 */

import java.util.Random;

public class HighOrLowTemp {

  public static void main(String args[]) {
    int min = -40;
    int max = 120;
    int diff = max - min;
    int temp;
    Random rand = new Random();

    temp = rand.nextInt(diff + 1) + min;
    System.out.println("The temperature is " + temp +"F.");

    if (temp < 50) {
      System.out.println("You should bring a coat.");
    }
    else {
      System.out.println("You don't need a coat.");
    }
  }

}
```

This program is essentially the same as LowTemp except for the use of the else structure. Figure 3.10 demonstrates the output. Note that only one of the two messages prints at one time.

FIGURE 3.10

This is several runs of the HighOrLowTemp program.

Nesting *if-else* Structures

So far, you are able to conditionally execute one of two statements based on a single condition. Sometimes you need to have more than two branches in the flow of your program based on a set of related conditions. This is possible in Java. You know that in the if-else structure, the statement (any valid Java statement) that the program executes if the condition is false follows the else keyword. The key here is *any valid Java statement*—including another conditional statement. These types of structures are called *nested if-else statements*. Take a look at the syntax:

```
if (condition1) {
  java_statements_for_true_condition1;
}
else if (condition2) {
  java_statements_for_true_condition2;
}
else {
  java_statements_for_false_conditions;
}
```

If *condition1* is true, the program executes *java_statements_for_true_condition1*. If *condition1* is false, *condition2* is tested. You do this by immediately following the else keyword with another if conditional statement. If *condition2* is true, the program executes *java_statements_for_true_condition2*. Finally, if neither condition is true the *java_statements_for_false_conditions* are executed. Take a look at this quick example, and then move on to the next section where you use apply this concept in an actual program:

```
if (name == "Joseph") {
  System.out.println(name + " is my first name.");
}
else if (name == "Russell") {
  System.out.println(name + " is my last name.");
}
else {
  System.out.println(name + " is not my name.");
}
```

Assume that name is a string holding some person's name. This snippet of code indicates that the name is my first name if it is "Joseph", else if it is "Russell", the code indicates that it is my last name. If it is neither my first name nor my last name, the code indicates that it is not my name.

The *ManyTemps* Program

The ManyTemps program demonstrates the use of the nested if-else structure. It prints a different message depending on the range of the randomly generated temperature.

```
/*
 * ManyTemps
 * Demonstrates if-else nesting structure.
 */

import java.util.Random;

public class ManyTemps {

  public static void main(String args[]) {
    int min = -40;
    int max = 120;
    int diff = max - min;
    int temp;
    Random rand = new Random();

    temp = rand.nextInt(diff + 1) + min;
    System.out.println("The temperature is " + temp +"F.");

    if (temp < -20) {
      System.out.println("It's DANGEROUSLY FREEZING! Stay home.");
    }
    else if (temp <  0) {
      System.out.println("It's extremely cold! Bundle up tight.");
    }
    else if (temp < 33) {
      System.out.println("It's cold enough to snow.");
    }
    else if (temp < 50) {
      System.out.println("You should bring a coat.");
    }
    else if (temp < 70) {
      System.out.println("It's nice and brisk.");
    }
    else if (temp < 90) {
      System.out.println("It's warm outside.");
    }
    else if (temp < 100) {
      System.out.println("It's hot. Stay in the shade.");
    }
```

```
    else {
        System.out.println("I hope you have an air conditioner!");
    }
  }

}
```

There are a couple of things to explain here. One thing is that you can nest as many if-else statements as you need to. Another thing worth mentioning is with the way that these if conditions are nested here, you can assume the value of the conditions that are evaluated in previous if conditions within the same nested structure. The first condition temp < -20 assumes nothing about temp except that it can be less than -20. The next condition temp < 0 assumes that the temperature is not less than -20 because if it were, the program would never get to this point. So if the condition temp < 0 evaluates to true, the program rightfully assumes the temperature ranges somewhere between -20 and -1. This is why, although temp is random, the final else statement can assume that the temperature is not less than 100 and can safely mention the air conditioner. Figure 3.11 displays the output of several runs of this program.

FIGURE 3.11

The ManyTemps program conditionally prints one of eight messages.

Indentation and Syntax Conventions

As you can see in all the examples using the if statement, for the sake of readability, I tend to use the following spacing and syntax conventions for if-else structures. Other people might have their own style. I follow the if keyword with a space, and then I type the condition within the parentheses. Within the condition, I use spaces between operands and operators. I also tend to use parentheses, even when technically not necessary, within the conditional expression if the evaluation order could possibly be confusing later.

After the condition, I use a space and then open the brace for the block statement that executes if the condition is true. As you read later chapters, you notice that

I don't always use braces. If there is only one simple statement that follows the condition, I tend to omit the brace; however, in nested if-else statements, or any other if statements that might be confusing, I use them. I indent lines within the braces two or three spaces, so they will be quickly identifiable as being part of the block statement. I always close braces on lines of their own and use the same indentation I used with the line with the opening brace.

You can develop your own style of spacing and indentation, but keep in mind that in the real world, your company might have its own conventions that it requires all of its programmers to follow. In any case, keeping all of its code consistently formatted makes it so much more readable when working with other programmers' code.

Using the *switch* Statement

Programmers commonly find themselves in situations where they need to test the value of an expression against some set of values. If the expression is not equal to the first value, test it against the second value. If the expression is not equal to the second value, test it against the third one, and so on. You can accomplish this with an if-else structure, but there is an alternative, neater, way to do it. Consider printing a text description of a number, n, that can range from one through five. Using the if-else structure, you do it this way:

```
if (n == 1) {
  System.out.println("one");
}
else if (n == 2) {
  System.out.println("two");
}
else if (n == 3) {
  System.out.println("three");
}
else if (n == 4) {
  System.out.println("four");
}
else if (n == 5) {
  System.out.println("five");
}
else {
  System.out.println("some other number");
}
```

You can see how many times I needed to repeat the n variable. You can probably also imagine how confusing this structure would be if I were testing for even more different values or if n wasn't just a variable, but a complex expression that would need to be repeated in each condition. Take a look at how I write this using the switch statement:

```
switch (n) {
  case 1:
    System.out.println("one");
    break;
  case 2:
    System.out.println("two");
    break;
  case 3:
    System.out.println("three");
    break;
  case 4:
    System.out.println("four");
    break;
  case 5:
    System.out.println("five");
    break;
  default:
    System.out.prinln("some other number");
}
```

You can immediately see that I only have to reference the n variable once in this switch block. The syntax for the switch conditional statement is as follows:

```
switch (expression) {
  case value1:
    statements_for_value1;
    break;
case value2:
    statements_for_value2;
    break;
case value3:
    statements_for_value3;
    break;
default:
    statements_for_any_other_value;
}
```

The switch keyword is followed by an expression in parentheses. The type of this expression must evaluate to char, byte, short, or int. If it doesn't, you get a compile-time error. After the expression, you open the block using the brace. Following that is the case keyword, and then the value to compare the expression to and a colon. After the colon, place any statements to be executed if the expression is equal to the value that follows this particular case. After that, you use the break keyword to exit the switch statement. The default keyword, which is optional, is used to define statements that execute if the expression doesn't equal any of the case values.

TRICK The switch block is useful if you need to perform one action for multiple values. Take the following switch block that prints a message for multiples of 10 as an example:

```
switch (n) {
  case 1:
  case 2:
  case 5:
  case 10:
    System.out.println(n + " is a multiple of 10.");
    break;
  default:
    System.out.println(n + " is not a multiple of 10.");
}
```

The cases in which n is a multiple of 10 do not have any statements in them (although they can), most importantly though, they don't use the break statement. This allows the appropriate message to print for values 1, 2, 5, or 10.

WAR STORY

When switch statements were fairly new to me I kept forgetting to use the break statements and I was getting some weird results. If you don't use the break statements where you need to, the flow of the switch block moves into the next case statement and executes whatever other statements it finds there. I was baffled by what was going on. I was working with random numbers, but my results weren't random. Of course, I automatically assumed that there was some problem with the way my code was generating random numbers. I wasted a lot of time before I finally realized what my mistake was. If you get into the habit of always using if structures and hardly ever using switch, like I once did, try not to forget about the break statements when you actually do use a switch block.

The *FuzzyDice* Program

This program uses the switch conditional structure to print the face value of one die. The face value of the die is generated randomly and the program tests it for values being equal to one of the face values of a six-sided die: 1 through 6. Here is the source code listing for FuzzyDice.java:

```
/*
 * FuzzyDice
 * Demonstrates use of the switch structure
 */

import java.util.Random;

public class FuzzyDice {
```

```
public static void main(String args[]) {
  Random random = new Random();
  int die;
  String s;

  System.out.println("Rolling die...");

  die = random.nextInt(6) + 1;

  s = "\n -------";
  switch (die) {
    case 1:
      s = s + "\n|         |";
      s = s + "\n|    *    |";
      s = s + "\n|         |";
      break;
    case 2:
      s = s + "\n|       * |";
      s = s + "\n|         |";
      s = s + "\n| *       |";
      break;
    case 3:
      s = s + "\n|       * |";
      s = s + "\n|    *    |";
      s = s + "\n| *       |";
      break;
    case 4:
      s = s + "\n| *    * |";
      s = s + "\n|         |";
      s = s + "\n| *    * |";
      break;
    case 5:
      s = s + "\n| *    * |";
      s = s + "\n|    *    |";
      s = s + "\n| *    * |";
      break;
    case 6:
      s = s + "\n| *    * |";
      s = s + "\n| *    * |";
      s = s + "\n| *    * |";
      break;
    default:
      //should never get here
      s = s + "\n|         |";
      s = s + "\n|         |";
      s = s + "\n|         |";
  }

  s = s + "\n -------";

  System.out.println(s);
  }

}
```

die is a random integer ranging inclusively from 1 through 6. The switch block uses the die variable as its expression. The program tests the value and conditionally builds a string that represents a "drawing" of the face of the die based on its value. If the program generates the random number correctly, it will never reach the default statements that build a string that represents a blank die face. Figure 3.12 demonstrates a couple of runs of this program.

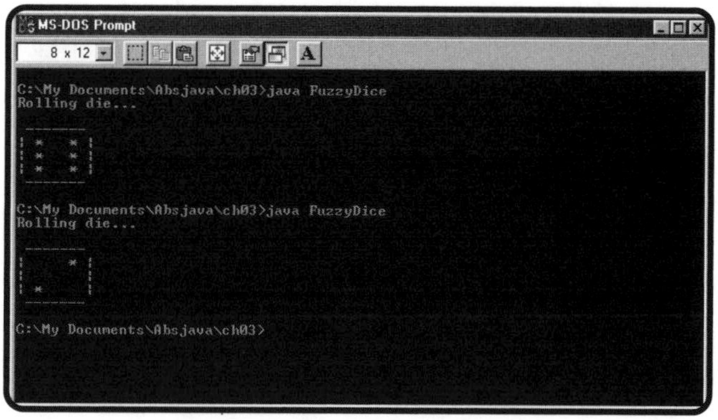

FIGURE 3.12

The FuzzyDice program randomly creates pictures of the face of a die.

Understanding Arrays

An *array* is a list of primitive data type values or objects. It is a way to store collections of items of the same data type under one variable name. Arrays are actually objects themselves and can be treated as such. You've already worked with arrays somewhat in Chapter 2 when you learned about accepting command-line arguments. Recall that the single parameter accepted by an application's main() method is an array of strings. Now you learn about arrays in more detail. To create an array, you need to declare it, assign it an array object, and then you can assign actual values within the array.

Declaring an Array

When declaring an array, you need to specify the data type that the array will maintain in its list. You need to give it a variable name and specify it as being an array by using square brackets ([]). Here are a few examples of declaring arrays:

```
int sillyNumbers[];
double mealPrices[];
Object objectList[];
boolean testAnswers[];
```

You can use the brackets where they are used previously, or you can optionally use the brackets after the data type. When I declare arrays, I do it this way:

```
int[] sillyNumbers;
double[] mealPrices;
Object[] objectList;
boolean[] testAnswers;
```

After you declare an array variable, you need to assign an array object to it before you can start using it. You do this by using the new keyword like you do when creating any new object. You have to specify the *array length*, which is its size, or more specifically, the number of items it can hold—its capacity. You define the length of an array within the square brackets of the array object you are creating. The following examples assign array objects to the arrays declared previously:

```
sillyNumbers = new int[10];
mealPrices = new double[18];
objectList = new Object[3];
testAnswers = new boolean[100];
```

After these array objects are created, sillyNumbers is an array able to hold 10 integers, mealPrices is an array able to hold 18 doubles, objectList is an array able to hold 3 objects, and testAnswers is an array able to hold 100 Booleans.

Assigning Values to and Accessing Array Elements

After you declare an array and assign an array object to it, you can assign values to the array *elements*. Array elements are the individual values stored under specific *subscripts* of the array. Array subscripts are integers that represent an item's position within the array. An array subscript is also called an array index. The element's subscript is specified within square brackets that follow the array's name. Here are some examples to clear things up:

```
sillyNumbers[0] = 3000;
sillyNumbers[9] = 1;
```

The first line assigns 3000 to the first element of the sillyNumbers array. The first element of an array is always indexed by 0. The second line assigns the integer 1 to the array's last element. Note that the subscript of the last element of an array is equal to one less than the array's total length because the subscripts start at 0, not 1.

You can also declare an array, assign an array object, and assign values to the array's elements on one line. The following line declares an array of strings, family. Using braces and specifying the elements' values, in order, separated by commas initializes the elements of the array. The length of family is 5 because it is initialized using 5 strings:

```
String[] family = {"Vito", "Santino", "Michael", "Fredo", "Connie"};
```

After initializing this array, `family[0]` is `"Vito"`, `family[1]` is `"Santino"`, and so on. Let's get rid of `"Fredo"` because he sleeps with the fishes:

```
family[3] = null;
```

Okay, that's taken care of. You can access elements that are already stored in the array by using its subscript, just like when you assign its value. When you access an array element, you can treat it like any other variable of the same type. For example:

```
System.out.println("Don " + family[0] + " Corleone");
```

This line prints `"Don Vito Corleone"`.

You can get the length of an array by using the syntax: *arrayName.length*. Remember that the last subscript of an array is one less than its length. If you attempt to access an element of an array by using a subscript that is out of the array's bounds (by using a number that is not a subscript of the array, usually greater than the last subscript), you get a run-time error, as shown in Figure 3.13. The `ArrayOOB` program demonstrates this. The source code listing for `Array-OOB.java` is listed here:

```
/*
 * ArrayOOB
 * Demonstrates what happens when an array index
 * is out of bounds.
 */

public class ArrayOOB {

  public static void main(String args[]) {
    //declare an array of length 10
    int[] arr = new int[10];

    //incorrect attempt to access its last value
    System.out.println("Last value: " + arr[10]);
```

FIGURE 3.13

This program causes an `ArrayIndexOutOf BoundsException` and crashes.

```
    //program will crash before it gets here
    System.out.println("Is anyone alive out there?");
  }

}
```

Multidimensional Arrays

In Java, *multidimensional arrays* are actually arrays of arrays, or a list of lists. Multidimensional arrays use sets of square brackets—one for each dimension of the array. Here's a quick example:

```
Int[][] table = new int[12][12];
```

This declares a multidimensional array of twelve by twelve integers. table[0] stores an array of twelve integers, table[1] stores another array of twelve integers, and so on. It can be simpler to think of two-dimensional arrays as having rows and columns.

The *ArrayTest* Program

The ArrayTest program (shown in Figure 3.14) demonstrates how to declare, create, and assign elements to arrays. Write this program and run it, and then compare the output to the source code to get a good feel for how arrays work in Java. Don't be afraid to be adventurous and create your own arrays here. The source code for ArrayTest.java is as follows:

```
/*
 * ArrayTest
 * Demonstrates the use of arrays
 */

public class ArrayTest {

  public static void main(String args[]) {
    //declare a char array
    char[] arr1;

    //create the array with length 3
    arr1 = new char[3];

    //give it some values
    arr1[0] = 'a';
    arr1[1] = 'b';
    arr1[2] = 'c';
```

```
//output its length, first value and last value
System.out.println("The length of arr1 is " + arr1.length);
System.out.println("Its first value is " + arr1[0]);
System.out.println("Its last value is "
                    + arr1[arr1.length - 1]);

//declare a double array of length 4
double[] arr2 = new double[4];
System.out.println("The length of arr2 is " + arr2.length);

System.out.println("Its values are:");
System.out.println(arr2[0] + ", " + arr2[1] + ", "
                    + arr2[2] + ", " + arr2[3]);

arr2[0] = 3.0;
arr2[1] = 5.0;
arr2[2] = arr2[1] + arr2[0];
arr2[3] = arr2[1] - arr2[0];

System.out.println("Now Its values are:");
System.out.println(arr2[0] + ", " + arr2[1] + ", "
                    + arr2[2] + ", " + arr2[3]);

//declare an array and initialize its values
int[] arr3 = { 1, 4, 26, 0, 97, 75, 11, 28, 27, 3};
System.out.println("The length of arr3 is " + arr3.length);

System.out.println("Its values are:");
System.out.println(arr3[0] + ", " + arr3[1] + ", "
                    + arr3[2] + ", " + arr3[3] + ", "
                    + arr3[4] + ", " + arr3[5] + ", "
                    + arr3[6] + ", " + arr3[7] + ", "
                    + arr3[8] + ", " + arr3[9]);

    }

}
```

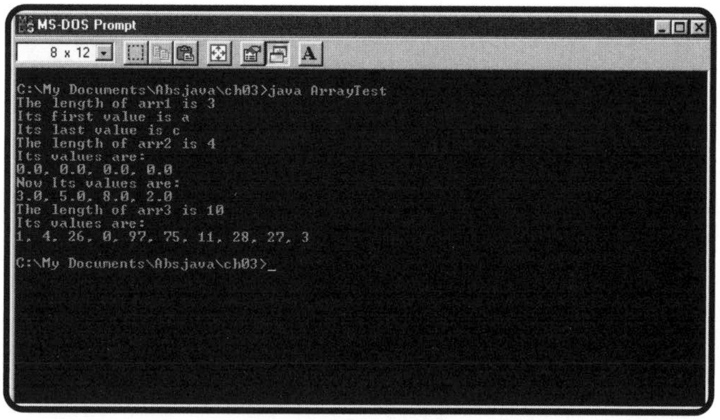

FIGURE 3.14

The ArrayTest
program works with
arrays.

Back to the Fortune Teller

The FortuneTeller program that was introduced at the beginning of this chapter is listed here. At this point, you should be able to understand all the code within this program. It creates a *Random* object randini to generate random numbers. Then it builds an array of Strings called fortunes that represent the possible fortunes. It sets the int fortuneIndex to be a random number that can be used as an index of the fortune array.

Then it generates a random number ranging from 0 through 6, which is used to represent one of the seven days of the week. This random number is generated within the expression of the switch statement. Depending on the value of the random number, the day String variable is set to one of the days of the week. Finally, the output is generated using these randomly and conditionally generated String values. Here is the full listing of FortuneTeller.java:

```
/*
 * FortuneTeller
 * A game that predicts the future.
 * Demonstrates the usefulness of random numbers, arrays,
 * and conditionals in creating dynamic programs.
 */

import java.util.Random;

public class FortuneTeller {

    public static void main(String args[]) {
        Random randini = new Random();
        int fortuneIndex;
        String day;
        String[] fortunes = { "The world is going to end :-(.",
            "You will have a HORRIBLE day!",
            "You will stub your toe.",
            "You will find a shiny new nickel.",
            "You will talk to someone who has bad breath.",
            "You will get a hug from someone you love.",
            "You will remember that day for the rest of your life!",
            "You will get an unexpected phone call.",
            "Nothing significant will happen.",
            "You will bump into someone you haven't seen in a while.",
            "You will be publicly humiliated.",
            "You will find forty dollars.",
            "The stars will appear in the sky.",
            "The proper authorities will discover your secret.",
            "You will be mistaken for a god by a small country.",
            "You will win the lottery!",
            "You will change your name to \"Bob\" and move to Alaska.",
            "You will discover first hand that Bigfoot is real.",
            "You will succeed at everything you do.",
            "You will learn something new.",
```

```
          "Your friends will treat you to lunch.",
          "You will meet someone famous.",
          "You will be very bored.",
          "You will hear your new favorite song.",
          "Tomorrow... is too difficult to predict" };

      System.out.println("\nYou have awakened the Great Randini...");

      fortuneIndex = randini.nextInt(fortunes.length);

      switch (randini.nextInt(7) % 7) {
        case 0:
          day = "Sunday";
          break;
        case 1:
          day = "Monday";
          break;
        case 2:
          day = "Tuesday";
          break;
        case 3:
          day = "Wednesday";
          break;
        case 4:
          day = "Thursday";
          break;
        case 5:
          day = "Friday";
          break;
        case 6:
          day = "Saturday";
          break;
        default:
          day = "Tomorrow";
      }

      System.out.println("I, the Great Randini, know all!");
      System.out.println("I see that on " + day);
      System.out.println("\n" + fortunes[fortuneIndex]);
      System.out.println("\nNow, I must sleep...");
  }

}
```

Summary

In this chapter, you learned about random numbers and how to generate them two ways in Java. You learned how to control the random number range, and to convert non-integer values to integers. You also learned how to create other types of random values. You learned about the Math class and how to use the methods it contains to perform mathematical functions. You learned about the if statement and conditional expressions and how to nest `if-else` statements to create multiple branches that conditionally affect the flow of your programs. You also learned about the `switch` conditional statement. Last, but certainly not least, you learned about arrays. In the next chapter, you learn all about loops.

CHALLENGES

1. Modify the `MathGame` program from Chapter 2 to operate on random integers instead of hard-coded ones.

2. Write a program that simulates randomly pulling a card from a deck of cards. You can use numbers or characters to represent the face values and strings to represent the suits.

3. Write a program that generates a random number ranging from 1 through 3 and print "one", "two", or "three" accordingly. Do this first using `if`, and then rewrite it using `switch`.

4. Write a program that builds an array of any type or size that you choose and prints the values of the first element, the last element, and the length of the array.

4

Using Loops and Exception Handling

In this chapter, you learn how to create repeating blocks of Java code called *loops*. You learn how to use the for loop to repeat a section of code a set number of iterations. You learn how to increment and decrement a variable to count the number of times your code is repeated and how to stop the loop after it has iterated a set number of times. You also learn how to use the while loop to loop an indeterminate number of times based on some condition that must be met before the loop terminates. The do-while loop, which is similar to the while loop, is another subject you learn in this chapter. Exception handling, which you learned a bit about in previous chapters, is explained here in more detail. You'll put these concepts together in this chapter's project, the NumberGuesser program. In this chapter, you will

- Understand the for loop

- Use the while loop

- Include the do loop

- Include exception handling in your code

The Project: The *NumberGuesser*

In this application, users are prompted to guess a number between one and one hundred. They get as many guesses as they need. This demonstrates how loops are used to repeat a block of code an indeterminate number of times. The users are continually prompted until they guess the correct number. The loop terminates when the users guess correctly. As you can see in Figure 4.1, the user guesses 50 first. The program hints that its number is higher so that the user isn't stuck all day, randomly picking numbers between one and one hundred. The user guesses again, this time 75. Now, the program indicates that the number is lower than 75. Ultimately the user responds correctly and the program terminates, telling the user how many times it took to guess the correct number.

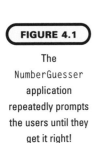

FIGURE 4.1

The NumberGuesser application repeatedly prompts the users until they get it right!

Counting Forward with Loops

This section explains how to make a loop repeat itself a set number of times by counting how many times it has repeated and stopping it after it has repeated the number of times you require it to. A repeating block of code is called a *loop*. This is the same term used when you set your music tape or CD player to continuously play both sides of the tape until you press the Stop button. Or when you download a video from the Internet and set it to loop so you can watch it over and over again. Each time through the loop is said to be an *iteration*. In real-world programs, you use a lot of loops. You use loops to perform the same action on multiple data. For example, you might write a payroll program that loops on all of a company's employees and cuts them a check. Instead of writing code to handle all of the employees separately, you write code that cuts a check and then put it in a loop that accounts for all of the employees. You learn all about loops in this section. More specifically, in this section, you learn about the `for` loop and the ++ (increment) operator.

The *Racer* Program

Here is your first program that uses loops. Although the actual code in this application is not overwhelmingly difficult, it is not that straightforward either. This program is not much more than a loop. It prints `Go!` before the loop starts, iterates through the loop 10 times, and then prints `Finish!` after the loop terminates. While inside the loop, it prints the number of laps (iterations) through the loop. Write this application and run it. Take notice of how quickly the program runs. The source for `Racer.java` is as follows:

```
/*
 * Racer
 * Demonstrates the for loop
 */

public class Racer {

  public static void main(String args[]) {
    System.out.println("GO!");

    for (int lap=1; lap <=10; lap++) {
      System.out.println("Completed " + lap + " laps.");
    }

    System.out.println("Finish!");
  }
}
```

Figure 4.2 shows the output of this application. The `lap` variable is incremented by one each time through the loop and printed as the number of laps. I describe the inner workings of the `for` loop in the next section.

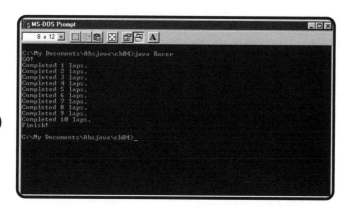

FIGURE 4.2

The `Racer` application counts 10 laps, and then terminates.

The *for* Loop

The `for` loop is typically used to reiterate a block of code a set number of times. You use this loop, as opposed to the `while` loop you learn later on in this chapter, when you are using some method of counting the number of iterations and stopping the loop based on this count. The `for` loop comes in handy when looping on arrays. As you know, arrays are lists of related data. A lot of times you need to loop on an array to do something to all of its elements. For example, you might have an array of bank transactions that need to be posted to an account. You can write a loop to iterate through all of the transactions to do this.

Typically, although not always, you declare a variable specific to this loop instead of declaring one outside of the loop structure, which can get confusing sometimes. The basic syntax of the `for` loop is:

```
for (initial_value; condition; increment) {
    statements;
}
```

The `for` keyword is followed by parentheses containing three parts. Here, *initial_value* is the expression that starts (initializes) the loop, usually by giving the variable that counts the number of iterations some initial value to start with. For example, in the `Racer` program, you used `int lap=1;` to initialize the `lap` variable with the value 1.

When the value of *condition* is `true`, the loop will continue to iterate. The loop will terminate once the condition becomes `false`. In the `Racer` program, you used the condition `lap <=10;`. As long as `lap` was less than or equal to 10, the loop continued to repeat. The *increment* variable changes the value of the variable, usually by adding one, to count the number of times through the loop, so that eventually the condition will evaluate to `false`. In the `Racer` program, you used the increment `lap++`, which as described next, adds one to the `lap` variable. The *statements;* are evaluated repeatedly for each iteration of the loop until the loop finally terminates.

Taking a closer look at `Racer`, notice that the initial value of the `lap` variable is the first value that is printed to the screen. This is always the case with `for` loops. First, the initialization takes place. Next the condition is evaluated. If the value is `false`, the statements within the loop, referred to collectively as the *loop body,* are not executed. If the condition evaluates to `true` then the statements are executed. After the loop body is evaluated, the iteration takes place, and the condition is checked again. If the condition is `true`, the loop executes again. This continues until the condition becomes `false`. At the most basic level, the `for` loop in the `Racer` program initializes the variable `lap` to 1, and then prints the value and increments it and prints it again. It continues to do this until the condition `lap <= 10` is no longer `true`.

The Increment (++) Operator

You used the ++ operator in the Racer program, but I haven't explained it in detail yet. This operator, known as the *increment operator*, adds one to the variable it follows. It is shorthand for adding one to a variable and assigning the result to the original variable:

```
//These two lines of code do the same thing - add one to x
x = x + 1;
x++;
```

To be more specific, this operator, as it is used here, is called the *postfix increment operator,* because it is placed after the variable. The type of the variable used (x in the example) must be numerical (yes, that means floating point too, unlike C or C++). If the type is not numerical, you get a compiler error.

The ++ operator can also be used in front of the variable. In this case, the operator is referred to as the *prefix increment operator.*

```
//These three lines of code do the same thing - add one to x
x = x + 1;
x++;
++x;
```

Whether used in a prefix increment expression or a postfix increment expression, the variable is incremented by one. However, there is a difference between prefix and postfix. The postfix increment is evaluated *after* any assignments or operations are performed, whereas the prefix increment is evaluated *before* any assignments or operations are performed. For example, the following code fragment results in the value 2 being assigned to y:

```
int y, x = 1;
y = ++x;
```

because x is incremented before y gets its value. The following code fragment, on the other hand, results in the value 1 being assigned to y:

```
int y, x = 1;
y = x++;
```

because x is incremented after y gets its value. In both cases, x ends up having the value 2.

The following program demonstrates this fact:

```
/*
 * PrePost
 * Demonstrates the difference between prefix
 * and postfix increment expressions.
 */

public class PrePost {
```

```
public static void main(String args[]) {
   int x = 0, y = 0, a = 0, b = 0;
   System.out.println("y and x both = 0");
   y = x++;
   System.out.println("The expression y = x++ "
                      + "results in y = " + y
                      + " and x = " + x);
   System.out.println("a and b both = 0");
   b = ++a;
   System.out.println("The expression b = ++a "
                      + "results in b = " + b
                      + " and a = " + a);

}
}
```

The output of this program is displayed in Figure 4.3. Note that the variable y is assigned the value 0, which is the value of x before it is incremented because that is the value of the postfix increment expression. On the other hand, the value of the b variable is 1, which is the value of a after it is incremented. Although this type of distinction might seem trivial to you at the moment, it is an important concept for you to understand.

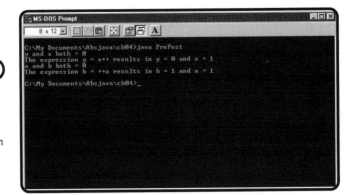

FIGURE 4.3

The PrePost application demonstrates the difference between prefix and postfix increment operations.

Skipping Values

In the previous section, you learned about the increment operator ++. As you know, this operator causes the operand to be incremented by one. What if you wanted to skip values while incrementing your variable in the loop? You can write a loop that counts in increments of five like this:

```
for (int i=5; i<=100; i = i + 5) {
   System.out.print(i + ", ");
}
```

The output of this program is 5, 10, 15, 20, 25, 30, 35, 40, 45, 50, 55, 60, 65, 70, 75, 80, 85, 90, 95, 100. There is a niftier way to do this, described in the next section.

IN THE REAL WORLD

In the real world, skipping values is useful. You might have an array that stores sets of data. For example, you can write an array that stores item numbers and inventory counts, called `inventory[]`. In this array, `inventory[0]` stores the first item number and `inventory[1]` stores the quantity of that item in your inventory. Following this pattern, all even indices store item numbers and any given odd index stores the quantity of the item that precedes it in the array. If you wanted to initialize your inventory to zero, you would only want to affect the odd numbers (to set the quantities all to zero).

The *CountByFive* Program

The CountByFive program (shown in Figure 4.4) uses the *compound increment assignment operator* to increment the i variable by five after each iteration of the loop. A compound assignment operator combines an arithmetic operation and an assignment in one operator. Take a look at the source code and the output:

```
/*
 * CountByFive
 * Demonstrates skipping values when incrementing numbers
 * in a loop using the += operator
 */

public class CountByFive {

  public static void main(String args[]) {
    for (int i=5; i <= 100; i+=5) {
      System.out.print(i);
      if (i < 100) System.out.print(", ");
    }
  }
}
```

FIGURE 4.4

The CountByFive program counts to one hundred in increments of five.

Using Compound Assignment Operators

The += operator used in the CountByFive program is one of the compound assignment operators. You can see some others in Table 4.1. As described earlier, compound assignment operations combine an arithmetic operation with an assignment operation. The syntax for compound assignment operations is:

```
variable op= expression;
```

Where *variable* is a variable of some primitive type, *op* is a mathematical operator, and *expression* is an expression that evaluates to some value that can be cast to the primitive type of the variable. Consider the example:

```
int x = 1;
x += 5;
```

The result of x becomes 6. It is initialized to 1, and then 5 is added to it. Also consider this less intuitive example:

```
int x = 1;
x += 5.9;
```

The result of x at the end of this operation is still 6. Performing a compound assignment operation implies a cast of the right-side expression to the data type of the variable. In this example, 5.9 is cast (converted to) the integer 5 before it is added to x. I mentioned that the variable must be of some primitive type. There is an exception to this rule, but only specifically for the += operator. The variable might also be a string. When the left operand is a string, the right-side operand can be of any type. The following example uses the increment assignment operator on a String variable.

```
String s = "";
    s += 1;
    s += ", ";
    s += 2;
    s += ',';
    s += " buckle my shoe";
```

The value of s becomes "1, 2, buckle my shoe". Here the code initializes s to the empty String "", and then each subsequent operation appends the right-side operand to s.

HINT

There are also compound assignment operators: &=, |=, and ^= in Java for Boolean logical operations, as well as <<=, >>=, and <<<= for bit shift operations. These operations are out of the scope of this book. For more information about them, follow this URL: **http://java.sun.com/docs/ books/jls/second_edition/html/j.title.doc.html**.

TABLE 4.1 COMPOUND ASSIGNMENT OPERATORS

Operator	Description	Example	Same Result as
+=	Increment assignment operator	x += 5;	x = x + 5;
-=	Decrement assignment operator	x -= 5;	x = x - 5;
*=	Multiplication assignment operator	x *= 5;	x = x * 5;
/=	Division assignment operator	x /= 5;	x = x / 5;
%=	Modulus assignment operator	x %= 5;	x = x % 5;

Counting Backwards

So far, every for loop you've encountered counts forwards, but you can also write a for loop in such a way that it counts backwards. You might want to do this in your Java programs in order to perform quicker array searches. For example, if you had an array of String objects sorted alphabetically and you needed to loop through your array to see whether the word "zebra" was stored there, you would probably want to start searching from the last entry and work your way backwards since that word would be toward the end of the array. It would take longer, especially if you had a huge array, to start from the beginning and loop through to the end. You initialize the variable used to keep track of the loop's iterations to some higher value than the *sentinel* value, and then decrement it after each iteration through the loop until the sentinel value is reached. A sentinel, much like the squid-like sentinel killing machines from *The Matrix*, is used to kill. It kills a loop (stops it from repeating). Actually, the term sentinel is better used to describe a situation in which you are looking for some exact value (the sentinel value) before exiting the loop, but some programmers prefer to use it more loosely to mean whatever condition causes the loop to terminate. The CountDown program (shown in Figure 4.5) uses a for loop to count backwards:

```
/*
 * CountDown
 * Demonstrates how to make a for loop count backwards
 * by using the -- operator
 */

public class CountDown {

  public static void main(String args[]) {
    System.out.println("Countdown:");
    System.out.print("T-");
```

```
    for (int t=10; t > 0; t--) {
      System.out.print(t + " ");
    }
    System.out.println("\nBLASTOFF!");
  }

}
```

FIGURE 4.5

The CountDown
program uses a
for loop to count
backwards.

Making a *for* Loop Count Backwards

In the CountDown program, you wrote a for loop that counts backwards from 10.
In order to accomplish this, you initialize the t variable to the value 10. Remember that in a for loop, the initial value of the loop variable is the value it contains
during the first iteration of the loop, which is why the first time t is printed, its
value is 10. You want this loop to terminate when t reaches zero, so you use the
condition t > 0. Although t is greater than zero, this loop will continue to iterate. Each time through the loop you decrement t by one. You do this by using the
decrement operator ---. This operator works very similarly to the increment operator you learned about earlier except that it subtracts one from the operand
instead of adding one.

```
//These three lines of code do the same thing - subtract one from x
x = x - 1;
x--;
--x;
```

The same prefix and postfix rules apply to the decrement operator. If the prefix
decrement operator is used in an assignment (such as y = --x;), y will be
assigned the value of x before it is decremented by one. If the postfix operator is
used (such as y = x--;), y will be assigned the value of x after it is decremented
by one.

Nested *for* Loops

You can put any valid Java code within a for loop. That includes another loop. If you place one loop inside another loop, the inner loop is called a *nested loop*. For each iteration of the outer loop, the inner loop is executed as well. The flow of the code works as follows. The interpreter enters the outer for loop. The code for the outer loop initializes a variable and enters the body of the loop if the value of the condition is true. Then within the body of the outer loop, another loop exists. The interpreter enters that loop, which initializes its own variable and the code enters the body of this loop if its condition is true. This inner loop will continue to iterate until its condition evaluates to false. Then, ultimately, the control will return to the outer loop, which will continuously cause subsequent calls to the inner loop until its own condition evaluates to false. You use nested loops to iterate through multidimensional arrays. Confused? This next example will help.

```
/*
 * NestedLoops
 * Demonstrates the use of nested for loops
 */

public class NestedLoops {

  public static void main(String args[]) {
    for (int i=0; i < 3; i++) {
      for (int j=0; j < 3; j++) {
        System.out.println("[i][j] = [" + i + "][" + j + "]");
      }
    }
  }

}
```

The NestedLoops program, as described most basically, counts to 3 three times. The loop's variables, i for the outer loop and j for the inner loop, are incremented after each iteration of their respective loops. As you can see in the output of this program in Figure 4.6, the i variable in the outer loop is initialized to zero. Then the inner loop's j variable is initialized to zero. This fact is illustrated in the first line of output. Then, j is incremented by one, so j = 1. Because the condition of the inner loop, j < 3 is still true, the body of the inner loop is executed again. The second line of output shows that i is still zero and j is now one. The inner loop continues to iterate until j is no longer less than three. At this point, control is returned to the outer loop. i is incremented by one, and because i is still less than three, the inner loop is entered once again. The j variable is again initialized to zero and the inner loop iterates again until j is not less than three. Then i is incremented again. And the list goes on.

FIGURE 4.6

The NestedLoops
program
demonstrates
nesting loops.

Another example of nesting loops is the MultiplicationTable program. It uses nested for loops to print the multiplication table you might remember from the inside cover of your elementary school math book or notebook. Here is a listing of MultiplicationTable.java:

```
/*
 * MultiplicationTable
 * Prints the multiplication table using nested loops
 */

public class MultiplicationTable {

  public static void main(String args[]) {
    for (int i=1; i <=12; i++) {
      System.out.print('\n');
      for (int j=1; j <= 12; j++) {
        System.out.print((i * j + "     ").substring(0, 5));
      }
    }
  }

}
```

The i variable of the outer loop counts from 1 to 12 and so does the j variable of the inner loop. Inside the outer loop, before getting to the inner loop, it prints a new line character \n. The inner loop prints all the output on a single line, so that is why the new line is printed right before it. The line that produces the output in the inner loop, as follows,

```
System.out.print((I * j + "     ").substring(0, 5));
```

first takes i * j and appends four spaces to it (i * j + "   "), which creates a string. As you learned in Chapter 2, "Variables, Data Types, and Simple I/O," the String method called substring()returns a piece of a string starting with the first index argument up to the string index that is one less than the second argument.

In this program, the first argument is 0 and the second argument is 5. The reason you append spaces and then take a substring of the result is so that all the columns line up. Doing it this way ensures that every time data is printed, it is the same string length. The output is shown in Figure 4.7.

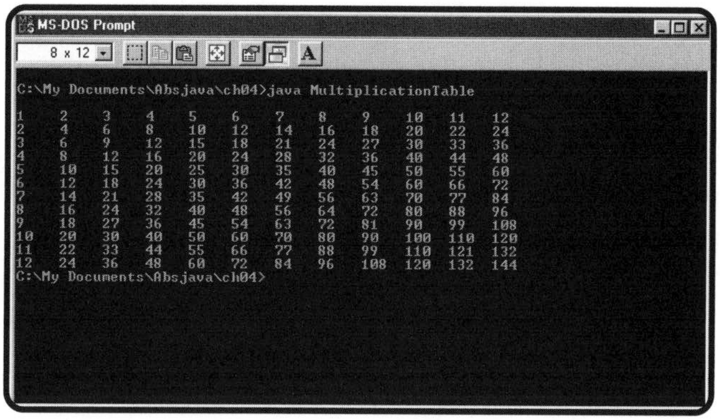

FIGURE 4.7

The Multiplication-Table program prints the multiplication table.

Looping on Arrays

As you know, arrays store their multiple elements by indexing them by integer subscripts. To get all the values inside an array individually, you have to reference them all by the integer subscript. For instance, if you want to print all the elements of a small array, you can do it like this:

```
char[] myArray = { 'a', 'b', 'c'};
System.out.println(myArray[0]);
System.out.println(myArray[1]);
System.out.println(myArray[2]);
```

IN THE REAL WORLD

In the real world, just about all programs loop on some data, especially database applications. A program might read in some data source, a file perhaps, and then temporarily store that data in an array. Then the program will loop on that data, either searching for a particular entry to modify, or to modify all them in some way. Writing the data back to the file might occur in a separate loop. Another program might be written to create a report on this data. It will loop on it to read it in and possibly loop on it again to resort the temporary structure to suit the particular report's sorting preferences. It might filter out some records, add up subtotals and grand totals, all in the same loop before printing the actual output. Typically, a programmer is working with a great deal of data, and loops perform operations on it all.

What if you had a huge array, though? You wouldn't want to do it this way. You can stick the array inside a loop that does all this work for you. The previous action would better be implemented in a `for` loop like so:

```
char[] myArray = { 'a', 'b', 'c' };
for (int i = 0; i < myArray.length; i++) {
  System.out.println(myArray[i]);
}
```

Looping on Multidimensional Arrays

So far in this chapter, you have learned how to nest `for` loops and how to use `for` loops to loop on arrays. You just need to put these two concepts together to understand how to loop on multidimensional arrays. Take a two-dimensional array for example. Assume `my2Darray` is a two-dimensional array that is already initialized. This is how you loop on its contents:

```
for (int i = 0; i < my2Darray.length; i++) {
  for (int j = 0; j < my2Darray[i].length; j++) {
    System.out.println(my2Darray[i][j]);
  }
}
```

A multidimensional array is an array of arrays. In the inner loop, where you check for the array length for the condition, you check the length of the array by referencing it this way: `my2Darray[i].length`. This refers to the length of the array contained within `my2Darray` at index `i`.

Got more than a two-dimensional array? No problem. Just nest another `for` loop. There is a one to one ratio of nested `for` loops and dimensions of the array. Here is an example of how to loop on a three-dimensional array:

```
for (int i = 0; i < my3Darray.length; i++) {
  for (int j = 0; j < my3Darray[i].length; j++) {
    for (int k = 0; k < my3Darray[i][j].length; k++) {
      System.out.println(my3Darray[i][j][k]);
    }
  }
}
```

The *MultiplicationArray* Program

The `MultiplicationArray` program declares a multidimensional array of `int`s, called `mTable`. Its dimensions are twelve by twelve (twelve arrays, each of length twelve). First, the program generates the contents of the array within a nested `for` loop. This loop is a bit different than the previous examples. The loops don't start with their variables equal to zero; they start at one because the program builds the multiplication table based on integers one through twelve and doesn't include zero. As a result, the subscripts have to be referenced by subtracting one:

```
for (int i=1; i <=12; i++) {
  for (int j=1; j <= 12; j++) {
    mTable[i - 1][j - 1] = i * j;
  }
}
```

So mTable[0][0] is 1 * 1, mTable[1][1] is 2 * 2, mTable[4][6] is 4 * 7, and so on. After the program builds the array, it prints it similarly to the way that the MultiplicationTable program did. As you can see in the output shown in Figure 4.8, the output is exactly the same as in MultiplicationTable. Here is the full source code listing for MultiplicationArray.java:

```
/*
 * MultiplicationArray
 * Prints the multiplication table using nested loops
 * to loop on a multidimensional array
 */

public class MultiplicationArray {

  public static void main(String args[]) {
    int[][] mTable = new int[12][12];

    //nested loop to build the array
    for (int i=1; i <=12; i++) {
      for (int j=1; j <= 12; j++) {
        mTable[i - 1][j - 1] = i * j;
      }
    }

    //nested loop to print the array
    for (int i=0; i < mTable.length; i++) {
      System.out.print('\n');
      for (int j=0; j < mTable[i].length; j++) {
        System.out.print((mTable[i][j] + "     ").substring(0, 5));
      }
    }
  }
}
```

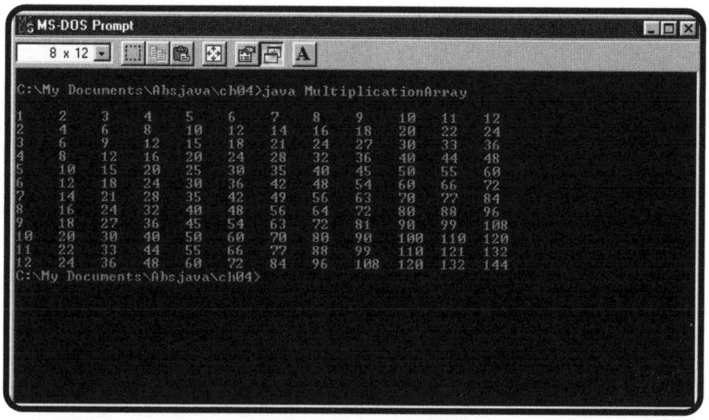

FIGURE 4.8

You're using nested loops to print multidimensional arrays!

Using the *while* Loop

You use the for loop when you know how many times you need to loop or are counting something. You use the while loop when you don't know how many times you need to loop. Such as when you are performing searches within an array. You don't know which index holds your desired value, so you continue to search for it until you find it. In other words, while you haven't found the right value yet, keep looking for it. A while loop takes one condition that evaluates to either true or false and the loop continues to iterate as long as the condition is true. Unlike the for loop, there is no initialization or incrementing. The syntax for the while loop is as follows:

```
while (condition) {
  statements;
}
```

The while keyword is followed by a condition within parentheses, and then a block statement. All the statements within the braces execute each time the loop iterates. The loop terminates once the condition evaluates to false. If the condition is initially false, the loop's statements are not executed. The WookiPiNub program demonstrates how a while loop is used. The source code for WookiPiNub is:

```
/*
 * WookiPiNub
 * Demonstrates use of the while loop in looping
 * an indeterminate number of times
 */

public class WookiPiNub {

  public static void main(String args[]) {
    String[] allTheWrongPlaces = {"Divorce Court",
                                  "Mars",
                                  "Transylvania",
                                  "Antarctica",
                                  "Love",
                                  "Hell, MI",
                                  "Oz"};
    boolean found = false;
    int place = 0;

    //looking for love in allTheWrongPlaces
    System.out.println("Looking for Love...");
    while (!found) {
      found = allTheWrongPlaces[place] == "Love";
      if (!found) {
        System.out.println("Not at index " + place);
        place++;
      }
```

```
        else {
          System.out.println("I found Love at index " + place);
        }
      }
    }
  }

}
```

The allTheWrongPlaces variable is a String array initialized with some values. The Boolean variable, found, is declared and initialized to false. The while loop's condition is !found (not found), so although the found Boolean variable's value is false, the loop will continue to iterate. This is why you initialize it to false; so the loop will iterate at least once. Inside the loop, there is the assignment statement:

```
found = allTheWrongPlaces[place] == "Love";
```

The value of allTheWrongPlaces[place] == "Love" is a Boolean value because of the equality operator ==. When it evaluates to true, the loop will no longer iterate. You want to continue looping only until you find what you're looking for, "Love". place is the int variable that stores the index of the allTheWrongPlaces array while searching for the "Love" string.

TRAP

I purposely wrote the while loop in the WookiPiNub program so that you could improve upon it. Specifically, I'm talking about the condition !found. found will only be true when there an entry in the allTheWrongPlaces array that is "Love". Luckily, in this case, I initialized the array with that value right before the loop, but what if the loop is modified in such a way that it is impossible to know whether a "Love" entry exists? If it doesn't, eventually the place variable is going to be out of the index range for the allTheWrongPlaces array. If that happens, an ArrayIndexOutOfBoundsException will occur and the program will crash. A better condition would be

```
while (!found && place < allTheWrongPlaces.length) { … }
```

This way, although "Love" will never be found, the program won't crash either.

Although "Love" is not found, the loop prints the fact that it could not find it at the current index of allTheWrongPlaces. When it finally does find it, the loop prints that fact and specifies what index it found it at. The output shown in Figure 4.9 shows that the loop could not find "Love" until it got to index 4.

The *do-while* Loop

The do-while loop is similar to the while loop, except it's backwards. The statements of the loop come before the condition, so no matter what, the loop will iterate at least once. A typical real-world use of the do-while loop is accepting

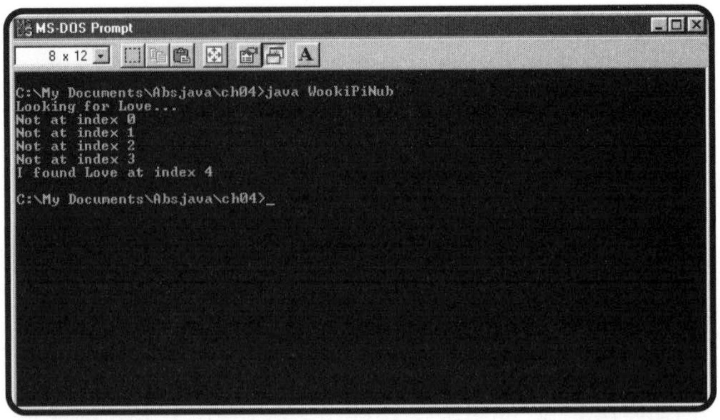

FIGURE 4.9

Looking for "Love"
in allThe-
WrongPlaces
inside a while
loop.

user input. First you print a message that prompts the user, such as "Item number:", for example. Then you accept user input. You definitely want to print the prompt message at least once and then repeat it while the user continues to enter data. After the loop iterates once, the condition is checked. As long as the condition remains true, the loop will continue to iterate. After it becomes false, the loop will terminate. The do keyword is used. After do, the block statement for the loop is written. After the block statement, the while keyword is used, followed by the condition for the loop. The syntax for this is as follows:

```java
do {
    statements;
}
while (condition);
```

The control of the code first enters the do block statement and executes them. After that, the code looks at the while condition. As long as the condition is not false, the statements in the do block statement will repeatedly execute. The JokeTeller program demonstrates this. Here is the source code for JokeTeller.java:

```java
/*
 * JokeTeller
 * Demonstrates use of the do-while loop
 */

import java.io.*;

public class JokeTeller {

    public static void main(String args[]) {
        BufferedReader reader;
        String answer = "TO GET TO THE OTHER SIDE";
        String response;
        boolean correct;

        reader = new BufferedReader(new InputStreamReader(System.in));
```

```
  try {
    do {
      System.out.println("Why did the chicken cross the road?");
      response = reader.readLine();
      if (!response.equalsIgnoreCase(answer)) {
        correct = false;
        System.out.println("Sorry, try again.");
      }
      else {
        correct = true;
        System.out.println("That's it!");
      }
    }
    while (!correct);
  } catch (IOException ioe) {}
 }
}
```

In this application, the oldest joke in the book is told. Why did the chicken cross the road?. The program then prompts the users for the answer. If the users do not answer correctly, To get to the other side, the program will repeat the question. This continues until the users get the answer correct. As you can see in the output in Figure 4.10, the user answers incorrectly two times before answering correctly.

The correct variable stores the Boolean value that is the expression of the do loop. You don't have to initialize this variable before the loop, as you would have had to in a while loop, where the condition is evaluated before the statements of the loop are executed. Note that the program uses the equalsIgnoreCase() String method so that the users can enter the answer in any mixture of upper- or lowercase letters. The value returned by this method is a Boolean value, so you can use the method call as the condition of your loop. If the user's response is not to get to the other side, correct is assigned false and the loop will reiterate. If it is equal, correct will be assigned true and the loop will terminate because the condition !correct is true.

FIGURE 4.10

The JokeTeller program loops until the users get it right.

Preventing Endless Loops

As you've seen, loops continue to iterate until the condition that causes the loop to continue becomes false. If the condition never becomes false, the loop will continue forever. This is known as an *endless* or *infinite loop* and is definitely something you want to avoid. Here's an example of an obvious infinite loop:

```
while (true) {
   System.out.print("true");
}
```

This loop is obviously infinite because in order for the while loop to terminate, the condition must be false and because the true literal can never be false, the loop will never terminate. If you stick this code in a main() method and run the program, you can see that it repeatedly prints the word "true" and never stops. In the real world, though, it is never this obvious. Here is an example of an infinite for loop. Although it is not difficult to notice (especially in a section of a book called "Preventing Endless Loops"), it is less obvious than the previous example:

```
for (int i = 0; i < 100; i--) {
   System.out.print(i);
}
```

In this loop, the i variable is initialized to 0. The loop continues as long as i is less than 100. The problem here is the way that the i variable is updated. It is decremented instead of incremented, so it keeps getting smaller. It will never not be less than 100, thus the loop will continue forever. When an infinite loop occurs, your program may just hang there and do nothing for a long period of time (like forever) or until you manually halt the program. From the MS-DOS prompt in Windows, for example, you can use Ctrl+C to halt a program that won't quit on its own.

To prevent infinite loops, make sure that at some point during the actual looping, the condition of the loop will ultimately be false. You need to make sure that any variables that make up a loop's condition are somehow modified during the looping. Not only that, but there must be a possibility for the condition to become false, or the loop will continue forever.

The *break* and *continue* Statements

The break statement transfers control out of an enclosing statement. In other words, it is used to break out of a loop explicitly. This means that it takes control out of a switch, while, do, or for statement. It must appear within a switch, while, do, or for statement or a compile-time error occurs. Here is an example:

```
while (true) {
  System.out.print("true");
  break;
}
System.out.println(" Out of Loop");
```

 HINT While debugging your programs, you will come across both compile-time errors and run-time errors. *Compile-time errors* are caught by the compiler. When you try to compile your program, it won't work. It will give you an error message indicating where you might have an error in your source code. *Run-time errors*, on the other hand, are not determinate at the point of compilation. They occur when your program encounters an error after it has already been compiled and is currently running.

At first glance this looks like an infinite loop, but it's not. The loop will iterate once because the condition is true, but the break statement takes it right out of the loop as soon as it is reached. The output of this is a single line "true Out of Loop".

A break statement followed by a label identifier works a bit differently. It does not have to be enclosed within a switch, while, do, or for statement. Instead, it must be enclosed by a labeled statement with the identifier as its label or you will get a compile-time error. The syntax for this is the label identifier for the labeled statement followed by a colon (:), and then an open brace followed by the statements that make up the labeled statement:

```
label: {
  statements;
  break label;
  moreStatements;
}
```

The *label* identifier follows the break keyword. This causes control to break out of the indicated labeled statement. In this case, *moreStatements* will never be reached. This actually causes a compile-time error because the compiler is smart enough to notice code that will never be reached in this type of situation and yells at you. For you to be able to compile your code, it must be possible for the break statement to not be reached. You can accomplish this by using a conditional statement. It is up to you, however, to write a valid condition, the compiler doesn't care whether the condition always evaluates to true, as in this example:

```
boolean b = true;
abc: {
  System.out.println("in abc");
  def: {
    System.out.println("in def");
```

```
    ghi: {
        System.out.println("in ghi");
        if (b) break ghi;
        System.out.println("still in ghi");
      }
      System.out.println("out ghi");
    }
  System.out.println("out def");
}
System.out.println("out abc");
```

The output of this is:

```
in abc
in def
in ghi
out ghi
out def
out abc
```

The break ghi statement breaks out of the ghi labeled statement, moving control back to the immediately enclosing structure, which happens to be the def labeled statement. If the break statement was break def instead, the output would be:

```
in abc
in def
in ghi
out def
out abc
```

because control breaks out of the def labeled statement, thus also breaking out of the ghi labeled statement. out ghi doesn't get printed because control never reaches the code that causes this to happen.

A continue statement must occur within an iteration statement such as a for, while, or do. What this does is indicate that the loop should attempt to iterate again. A quick and dirty simple example:

```
boolean b = true;
while (b) {
  if (b) continue;
  System.out.println("never gets here");
}
```

The continue statement doesn't break completely out of the loop. Instead it causes the loop to stop where it is and loop again from the beginning. The condition for the loop (the continuation point) is checked again and if it is true, the loop iterates again. The previous example is an endless loop.

The `continue` statement can also be followed by a label identifier to transfer control to the continuation point of a specific enclosing loop. Here is an example:

```
boolean b = true;
outerLoop: do {
  while(b) {
    System.out.println("loop");
    if (b) continue outerLoop;
    System.out.println("never get here");
  }
  System.out.println("never get here either");
}
while (!b);
```

Here, the outermost loop, do, itself is labeled `outerLoop`. Inside the inner `while` loop, the `continue  outerLoop` statement causes control to check the do loop's `while` condition `!b`, which evaluates to `false`, so the loop terminates. The output here is a single line `loop`. The two attempts to print more are never reached.

How about a practical example to help you understand this better? The `while` loop in the `WookiPiNub` program can be rewritten this way and would work exactly the same as in the original program:

```
System.out.println("Looking for Love...");
looking: while (!found) {
  found = allTheWrongPlaces[place] == "Love";
  if (!found) {
    System.out.println("Not at index " + place);
    place++;
    continue looking;
  }
  System.out.println("I found Love at index " + place);
}
```

The `while` loop is labeled "looking". If "Love" is not found at `allTheWrong-Places[place]`, that fact is printed, `place` is incremented, and then the `continue looking` statement causes the loop to stop there and iterate again from the beginning. Because of this, the statement that prints that "Love" is found is skipped and doesn't need to be in an `else` statement, as it was before.

HINT

If the `break` and `continue` statements just seem confusing to you, you don't need to worry about them. It is possible never to use them. Whether you do use them is part of your own programming style. Some programmers feel that using `break` and `continue` causes unnecessary confusion and makes it harder to trace the flow of the program because it jumps around from one place to another. Conditional statements can be used just as effectively and are arguably easier to trace.

Exception Handling

Exception handling describes a way to handle certain situations, called exceptions, which would otherwise cause your program to crash. Exceptions can occur when errors are encountered. For example, the ArrayIndexOutOfBoundsException exception occurs when you try to reference an array element using an index that is out of the bounds of the array. Another example is the IOException, which can occur while reading simple user input (as one particular instance). Methods that *throw* exceptions probably almost always work, but in some instances might not. Using the array example again, a programmer probably has written solid code that doesn't try to access index entries that are out of the array's bounds, but it does happen sometimes. In this instance, an ArrayIndexOutOfBoundsException is thrown. *Throwing* an exception is what causes an exception to occur.

Methods that throw exceptions can be declared using the throws keyword. When you're writing a program, you might know of a situation where your code won't work right. For example, if you have code that expects a variable to refer to the number of widgets that can fit in a box, you don't expect to get any negative numbers. In this instance you might want to throw an exception—NegativeWidgetCountException, possibly, so that implementers of your code can handle that type of exception in their own way. In instances where these types of methods are called, the exceptions must be handled in a try-catch. The throw keyword throws the exception. You will understand this better after reading Chapter 5, "Blackjack: Object-Oriented Programming," which covers methods. The compiler does not force you to handle run-time exceptions (RunTimeException and its subclasses), such as an ArrayIndexOutOfBoundsException.

Using the *try-catch-finally* Block

You have used the try-catch block before. It wraps around code that might cause an exception so that you can handle the exception in such a way that your program doesn't crash. The syntax is as follows:

```
try {
  maybeException();
} catch (anExceptionThatMayOccur) {
  doSomethingAboutIt;
} catch (anotherExceptionThatMayOccur) {
  doSomethingAboutIt;
} finally {
  doSomethingThatHappensNoMatterWhat;
}
```

You write some operation that might cause an exception inside a try block. If an exception occurs and is caught, the program executes the statements within the catch block that specifies the exception that occurred. The finally keyword indicates a block of code that must execute regardless of whether an exception occurs. Here's an example of how you might prevent your program from crashing with an `ArrayIndexOutOfBoundsException` exception:

```
try {
  val = myArray[i];
} catch (ArrayIndexOutOfBoundsException aoob) {
  val = SOME_DEFAULT_VALUE;
}
```

In your code, you might be in a situation where the i index variable is not known and might be out of the `myArray` bounds. If you try to access the element with an index that is out of bounds, you get an `ArrayIndexOutOfBoundsException` exception. Because the code handles this situation, your program won't crash. In this example, you try to assign val the value of the element at index i. If there is no such index, you assign it `SOME_DEFAULT_VALUE`.

Using Exceptions to Screen User Input

If one thing is definitely unpredictable, it's user input! If you prompt the users to enter a number, they might make a mistake and enter "one". Although to you and I, "one" is a number, it can't be parsed by the `Integer.parseInt()` method. It causes a `NumberFormatException` exception to occur. The `InputChecker` program demonstrates how to make sure you get valid numbers from the users. Here is a source listing for `InputChecker.java`:

```
/*
 * InputChecker
 * Filters user input using exceptions and loops
 */

import java.io.*;

public class InputChecker {

  public static void main(String args[]) {
    BufferedReader reader;
    boolean gotValidNumber = false;
    int inputNumber = 0;
    reader = new BufferedReader(new InputStreamReader(System.in));

    do {
      System.out.print("Enter a number: ");
      try {
        inputNumber = Integer.parseInt(reader.readLine());
        gotValidNumber = true;
      } catch (NumberFormatException nfe) {
        System.out.println("That is not a valid integer.");
      } catch (IOException ioe) {}
    }
```

```
    while (!gotValidNumber);
    System.out.println("Your number is " + inputNumber);
  }
}
```

The variables are reader, a BufferedReader, gotValidNumber, a Boolean value that tracks whether you got a valid integer from the users, and inputNumber, an int used to store the user's input. In the try block, you try to read in the user's input, parse it to an int, and assign it to inputNumber. You put this in a try block so that you can handle exceptions that occur, a NumberFormatException, or an IOException. A NumberFormatException exception is thrown by the Integer.parseInt() method if its String argument is not a valid representation of an integer. If the users don't enter a valid number, you catch the NumberFormatException exception that is thrown and tell the users that they didn't enter a valid number. You initialized gotValidNumber to false. If a NumberFormatException is thrown, the assignment gotValidNumber = true is never reached, so the loop continues to iterate. When the users finally do enter a valid number, gotValidNumber becomes true, the loop terminates, and you print the user's number to show that you got a valid number. The output of this program is shown in Figure 4.11.

TRAP In the InputChecker program, you had to initialize the inputNumber variable because it is assigned in a try block that might never work. If you don't initialize the variable, you will get a compiler error. It will complain about the line where you print inputNumber. It will tell you that inputNumber might not be initialized.

FIGURE 4.11

The InputChecker program forces the users to enter a valid integer.

Back to the *NumberGuesser* Program

You've now learned everything you need to know to write the NumberGuesser program. It generates a random number, and then in a loop it continuously prompts the users for a number until they guess correctly. It also uses exception handling to make sure the users are entering valid numbers. Here is the source code listing for NumberGuesser.java:

```
/*
 * NumberGuesser
 * Picks a random number which the user must guess
 */

import java.io.*;
import java.util.Random;

public class NumberGuesser {

  public static void main(String args[]) {
    BufferedReader reader;
    Random rand = new Random();
    int myNumber = rand.nextInt(100) + 1;
    int guess = -1;
    boolean invalid;
    int nGuesses = 0;
    reader = new BufferedReader(new InputStreamReader(System.in));

    System.out.println("I'm thinking of a number between 1 and 100.");
    System.out.println("Can you guess what it is?");

    do {
      nGuesses++;
      System.out.print("Your guess: ");
      invalid = false;
      try {
        guess = Integer.parseInt(reader.readLine());
      } catch (IOException ioe) {
      } catch (NumberFormatException nfe) {
        System.out.println("That is not a valid Integer!");
        guess = -1;
        invalid = true;
      }
      if (guess >= 1 && guess <= 100) {
        if (guess == myNumber) {
          System.out.println("You guessed my number in "
                             + nGuesses + " guesses!");
        }
        else if (guess < myNumber) {
          System.out.println("My number is HIGHER.");
        }
        else {
          System.out.println("My number is LOWER.");
        }
      }
      else if (!invalid) {
        System.out.println("Remember, my number is between "
                           + "1 and 100.");
      }
    }
    while (guess != myNumber);
  }
}
```

You initialize reader, the BufferedReader used to read user input, rand, the Random object you use to generate random numbers, and guess, the user's guess. You also have the variable myNumber, the random number that the users have to guess. nGuesses counts the number of times it takes the users to guess the correct number. The boolean invalid variable tracks whether the user's input is a valid int.

In the do loop, you increment nGuesses, and prompt the users for a number. If the users don't enter a valid number, you set guess to -1 and invalid to true. The reason you set guess to -1 is because it must have some value when it gets to the if statements that follow. You set it out of the range of possible numbers, so you don't confuse your bogus value with an actual real value. The invalid variable eliminates the "Remember, my number is between 1 and 100." error message if the number isn't valid; the users will get the "That is not a valid integer!" error instead. The if-else structure determines whether the guess is correct, lower, higher, or out of range and tells the users in any of these cases. The while(guess != myNumber) loop condition keeps the loop iterating until the users guess the correct number. Try writing this program yourself. The output is similar to that shown in Figure 4.1.

Summary

In this chapter, you learned about loops and exception handling. You used for loops to count forwards and backwards. You used them to loop on arrays and nested for loops to loop on multidimensional arrays. You learned different ways to increment and decrement variables and how to skip values. You also learned about the while and do loops. You learned about exception handling and how to use it with loops to filter and get valid user input. In the next chapter, you learn all about object-oriented programming concepts and methods.

CHALLENGES

1. Write a for loop that counts from –100 to 100.

2. Write a program that allows the users to input an array's size, and then prompts the users for all the values to put in that array, and finally prints them all. Make sure you use exception handling to get valid user input.

3. Write a while loop that generates random numbers between 1 and 100 and stops looping after it generates the same number twice.

5

Blackjack: Object-Oriented Programming

Object-oriented programming, OOP for short, is central in learning Java. Java is a strictly object-oriented programming language. In every Java program you've written thus far, you had to define a class. A *class* is more or less a template for an object. It defines what an object is and how it behaves. An instance of a class is called an *object*. In this chapter, you learn all about object-oriented programming concepts. You create a good amount of class definitions and learn to create and use instances of these classes. Ultimately, at the end of this chapter, you use these skills to create a text-based blackjack game. Before you move on to the later chapters of this book, make sure you understand the concepts in this chapter. The rest of the book assumes you understand the object-oriented programming concepts described herein. Venture onward! The main issues covered in this chapter are as follows:

- **Work with objects**

- **Use member variables**

- **Learn about access modifiers**

- **Use methods**

- **Understand encapsulation**

The Project: the *BlackJack* Application

The project in this chapter is a simulation of a blackjack card game. If you're not familiar with blackjack, here's a brief explanation. The game consists of a dealer and at least one player. The game you create in this chapter will assume only one player. The goal of the game is to get a hand as close to 21 without going over. The dealer deals himself and the player two cards each. The dealer has one card face down and one face up, whereas the player has both cards face up. Each card has a specific point value. Cards 2 through 10 have the face value of the card regardless of suit. Picture (or face) cards (Jack, Queen, and King) all have point values of 10. The Ace is a special case. The value of an Ace can be one or eleven, depending on which is more beneficial.

The best possible hand, called a blackjack, consists of two cards totaling 21. This must be a 10-point card and an Ace. If either the dealer or the player has a blackjack, he or she instantly wins the hand, if they both have a blackjack, the game is a push (tie). Once the cards are dealt, the player has the option to hit (be dealt another card). The player's goal is to come as close to 21 without going over, so players must be careful when hitting. If the players go over 21, they bust and lose the hand. When the players want to leave their hand as is, they are said to *stand*. When the players stand, the dealer reveals the hidden card and always hits if his hand is 16 or lower and always stands if it is 17 or higher, even when it is lower than the player's score. If the players come closer to 21 than the dealer, they win. If they tie, again it is called a *push*. If the dealer is closer, the players lose. There are some more complicated rules that I didn't include in the game for simplicity's sake; these are the basic rules of blackjack.

The BlackJack application uses an instance of a class, RandomCardDeck, which defines basically what a deck of cards does. Because Java is a object-oriented programming language, BlackJack is a class itself. Towards the end of this chapter, you create these classes to develop the game. Figure 5.1 shows the output of a typical session of the game. String objects represent the cards. The last character represents the suit: C is for clubs, D is for diamonds, H is for hearts, and S is for spades. The dealer's hidden card is represented by the String ??.

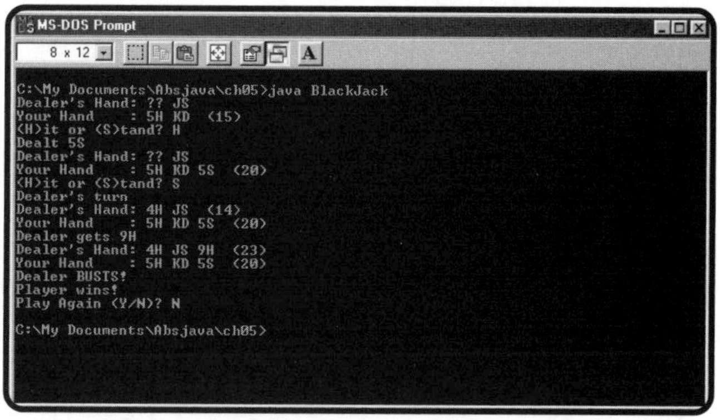

FIGURE 5.1

The player wins a hand of blackjack.

Understanding Object-Oriented Concepts

In this section, you create a simple class, SimpleCardDeck. You learn what instance variables and methods are and how they are part of class definitions. You also create an application that tests the SimpleCardDeck class, so you get a feel for how to create an object, access its members, and call its methods.

The *SimpleCardDeck* Class

The SimpleCardDeck class has a simple class definition. It is more or less just a demonstration of how to define a class. You've already defined classes in every Java program you've written, but you will notice a difference here: there is no main() method. This is because SimpleCardDeck is not an application; it's a class definition that needs to be instantiated for its functionality. Here is the listing of SimpleCardDeck.java:

```
/*
 * SimpleCardDeck
 * This class defines a simple deck of cards.
 */

public class SimpleCardDeck {

  //cards is a member variable
  String[] cards = {"2C", "3C", "4C", "5C", "6C", "7C", "8C",
                    "9C", "10C", "JC", "QC", "KC", "AC",
                    "2D", "3D", "4D", "5D", "6D", "7D", "8D",
```

```
                    "9D", "10D", "JD", "QD", "KD", "AD",
                    "2H", "3H", "4H", "5H", "6H", "7H", "8H",
                    "9H", "10H", "JH", "QH", "KH", "AH",
                    "2S", "3S", "4S", "5S", "6S", "7S", "8S",
                    "9S", "10S", "JS", "QS", "KS", "AS"};

  public void list() {
    for (int c=0; c < cards.length; c++) {
      System.out.print(cards[c] + " ");
    }
  }

}
```

Try creating this class and compiling it. If you try to run it by using the `java Sim-pleCardDeck` command, it won't work because there is no `main()` method. This further emphasizes the fact that this class is not an application. Go ahead and try it if you want to see what errors you will get.

You create the `SimpleCardDeck` class here by using the `class` keyword and the class name. Now at this point, you're used to defining the `main()` method. Instead you immediately declared `cards`, a string array. Because you declare this within the class definition (remember that the code within the curly braces is part of the class definition), it belongs to the `SimpleCardDeck` class. All `Simple-CardDeck` objects are instances of the `SimpleCardDeck` class and own their own `cards` variable.

Another part of the class definition here is the `list()` method. You learn more about methods shortly, but even though you don't know all about methods yet, you already have some familiarity with them. Creating the `list()` method is similar to creating the `main()` method. Similar to the `cards` member concept, this method is part of the class definition and is accessible to any `SimpleCardDeck` object. Basically, it just lists the contents of the object's `cards` array.

Learning About Objects

Object-oriented programming is one of the most important programming concepts you can learn. Put simply, object-oriented programming is a way to organize your programs so that they mimic the way things work in the real world. Objects in the real world are made up of smaller objects and interact with other objects. A ball, for example, is made up of a specific material that has its own properties and might be filled with air, or whatever. A person, another object, is made up of arms, legs, a head, and a torso, which are made up of skin, muscle, bone, which are made up of cells, and so on. The person can interact with the ball by throwing it or kicking it. These basic concepts are used to structure object-oriented programs.

For example, if you were programming a card game, which you are by the way, you write some sort of a class that defines a deck of cards and what can be done with it. Then in your game program, you create an instance of the class, a deck of cards object, and you can treat it like a deck of cards in your program. In turn, you can reuse that class in a different card game you write without needing to change the behavior of the card class. You only need to change the rules of the game, which resides in the game program itself.

You know how to build a class definition. Now you learn how to create an instance of a class and reference its variables and methods. You created the SimpleCardDeck class. Here you write the SimpleCardDeckTest application that will create a SimpleCardDeck object and test it. Here is the source code listing for SimpleCardDeckTest.java:

```
/*
 * SimpleCardDeckTest
 * Tests the use of the SimpleCardDeck class.
 */

public class SimpleCardDeckTest {

  public static void main(String args[]) {
    // create a new SimpleCardDeck object
    SimpleCardDeck deck = new SimpleCardDeck();

    // access its member variable "cards"
    System.out.println(deck.cards[0]);
    System.out.println(deck.cards[10]);
    System.out.println(deck.cards[51]);
    // etc...

    //Call its list() method
    deck.list();
  }

}
```

Ah, something more familiar, a class with just a main() method. It's the guts of main() that are interesting here. You declare and instantiate deck, a SimpleCard-Deck object in the line:

```
SimpleCardDeck deck = new SimpleCardDeck();
```

You've done this before with BufferedReader and Random objects. The Simple-CardDeck deck segment of the statement declares deck to be a SimpleCardDeck object. The = new SimpleCardDeck() segment of the statement passes deck a reference to a new SimpleCardDeck object, so at this point, deck contains a Simple-CardDeck object.

Now that you have a SimpleCardDeck object, you can access its cards variable. To access an object's variable (also called a *field*), you use dot notation to separate the object name from the field name (note that there are no spaces between the names):

```
objectName.fieldName
```

In the `SimpleCardDeckTest` program, you accessed the `cards` field and printed its contents:

```
System.out.println(deck.cards[0]);
```

You can't directly access the field without the reference to the object. The object owns the field and must be accessed using the dot notation. The `SimpleCard-DeckTest` program can declare its own `cards` variable, which is separate from deck's `cards` variable. You can see in the following code why dot notation is needed to specify which variable you are referencing:

```
SimpleCardDeck deck = new SimpleCardDeck();
int cards = 52;
//access my cards variable
System.out.println(cards);
//access deck's cards variable
System.out.println(deck.cards[0]);
```

You also use dot notation to call the `SimpleCardDeck`'s `list()` method. When you call this method, it executes the statements defined within the method's braces. The `list()` method simply loops through the `cards` array and lists all its contents. The syntax for calling an object's method is as follows:

```
objectInstance.instanceMethod(arguments);
```

The line that calls deck's `list()` method is as follows:

```
deck.list();
```

It has no arguments, but the parentheses are required anyway. They differentiate methods from variables. Figure 5.2 shows the output of the `SimpleCardDeckTest` program.

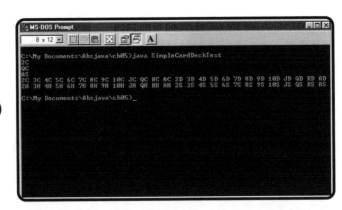

FIGURE 5.2

The `SimpleCard-DeckTest` application uses a `SimpleCardDeck` object.

Examining Member Variables

In Chapter 2, you learned how to declare and use local variables. *Local variables* are declared within a method and are accessible only within that method. More specifically, they are accessible only within the block statement you declare them in. Class member variables are declared within the outer-most braces of the class definition, and are accessible to the class as a whole. Member variables are declared in almost the same way as local variables; in fact, so far, the only difference is the location you declared them in.

Member variables can be either *instance variables* or *class variables*. Instance variables, such as `cards` variable from the `SimpleCardDeck` class, are owned by a particular instance of the class. In the `SimpleCardDeckTest` program, `deck` is an instance of `SimpleCardDeck` and owns its own `cards` variable. If a second `SimpleCardDeck` object (`deck2`) is declared, it has its own `cards` variable and can manipulate it independently of `deck`'s version of the same variable.

```
SimpleCardDeck deck2 = new SimpleCardDeck();
```

Class variables apply to the class and are not specific for each instance of the class. They are called *static* variables and I use the two terms interchangeably throughout the book. Oddly enough, the `static` keyword specifies that a variable is a class variable. The following `ChristmasLight` class definition declares an instance variable and a static variable.

```
/*
 * ChristmasLight
 * Demonstrates static variables
 */

public class ChristmasLight {
   //color is an instance variable
   String color;
   //isLit is a static variable
   static boolean isLit;
}
```

The `color` variable is an instance variable, so each `ChristmasLight` object can store a different value in its own `color` variable. On the other hand, the `isLit` variable is a class variable and will hold only one value that must be shared by all instances of the `ChristmasLight` object. Wanna test it out? Of course you do! After all you know that you won't remember any of this unless you do it for yourself, right? Here is the source listing for `ChristmasLightTest.java`:

```
/*
 * ChristmasLightTest
 * Shows the effect of changing a static variable's value
 */
```

```java
public class ChristmasLightTest {

  public static void main(String args[]) {
    ChristmasLight[] lights = { new ChristmasLight(),
                                new ChristmasLight(),
                                new ChristmasLight() };

    lights[0].color = "green";
    lights[1].color = "red";
    lights[2].color = "blue";

    //Can access a class variable without an instance
    ChristmasLight.isLit = true;

    //Or with an instance
    for (int i=0; i < lights.length; i++) {
      System.out.print("The " + lights[i].color + " light is ");
      if (!lights[i].isLit) System.out.print("not ");
      System.out.println("lit.");
    }

    System.out.println("\nThe red light goes out.\n");
    lights[1].isLit = false;

    //All instances are affected
    for (int i=0; i < lights.length; i++) {
      System.out.print("The " + lights[i].color + " light is ");
      if (!lights[i].isLit) System.out.print("not ");
      System.out.println("lit.");
    }
  }

}
```

As you can see in the output shown in Figure 5.3, all instances of the Christ-masLight class always share one value for their isLit variable.

FIGURE 5.3

One light goes out,
they all go out!

As you can see, there are two ways to access a static variable. You can access it without a specific instance of the class by using the class name:

```
ChristmasLight.isLit = false;
```

You can also access the variable using a specific instance:

```
lights[1].isLit = false;
```

 TRAP Although you can access static class variables by using a specific instance of the class, it makes your code hard to follow. Doing it that way, you can easily confuse the class variable with an instance variable. You could spend hours or even days debugging your code before you realize that, although you meant to change the state of only one of your instances, you were unintentionally changing them all. As a rule of thumb, always reference class variables through the class name.

Field Modifiers

Field modifiers are keywords that you place before variable names to specify the characteristics of the variables. For example, the `static` keyword you learned about in the previous section is a field modifier. Other field modifiers are `final`, used to declare constants, `volatile`, used for multithreading and covered in Chapter 10, "Animation, Sounds, and Threads," and `transient`, which is out of the scope of this book.

To declare a constant field, you use the `final` keyword and initialize its value. You can assign a value to a final variable only once. If you try to reassign a new value to a final variable that has already been assigned a value, you will get a compiler error. Conventionally, constant names are uppercase and separated by underscores _.

```
final int MY_CONSTANT = 10;
```

Declaring `MY_CONSTANT` to be final and assigning it the value 10 ensures that its value will always be 10. Constants are also typically declared to be class variables because they typically mean the same thing for all instances of the class. Take the following snippet of code for example:

```
public class Tricycle {
  String color;
  final static int NUM_WHEELS = 3;
}
```

I declared `NUM_WHEELS` to be a final static field and initialized its value to 3. An instance of `Tricycle` can be any color, but can never modify the number of wheels (otherwise it isn't a Tricycle, right?). You make reference to this constant like any other static field, but you can never change its contents:

```
System.out.println("There are " + Tricycle.NUM_WHEELS + " wheels.");
```

HINT

I stated that you create a constant simply by using the `final` keyword and initializing its value. That's fine and dandy when you're working with primitive data types, but what happens when your final variable contains an object? A final variable that references an object will always reference that particular object; however, performing operations on the object can change the state of that object. For example, if you create a final instance of the `Tricycle` example class:

`final Tricycle myTrike = new Tricycle();`

you can modify its `color` field as follows:

`mTrike.color = "red";`

but `myTrike`, which is a pointer to a `Tricycle` object, is final, so it must always point to the same instance. In other words, you can't do this:

`myTrike = new Tricycle();`

If you try something like this, the compiler will tell you that you "cannot assign a value to final variable `myTrike`."

The `Employee` class defines instance variables, class variables, and constants. The `EmployeeTest` program demonstrates the different behavior of these variables and emphasizes exactly what the field modifiers are used for. Here is the source code for `Employee.java`:

```
/*
 * Employee
 * This class demonstrates the use of member variables
 */

public class Employee {
  String name;
  int age;
  char sex;
  String position;
  double payRate;
  static int vacationDays;
  final static char MALE = 'M';
  final static char FEMALE = 'F';

  public void list() {
    System.out.println("Name: " + name);
    System.out.println("Age: " + age);
    System.out.println("Sex: " + sex);
    System.out.println("Position: " + position);
    System.out.println("Pay Rate: " + payRate);
    System.out.println("Vacation Days: " + vacationDays);
  }
}
```

In this class, the fields `name`, `age`, `sex`, `position`, and `payRate` are all instance variables. `vacationDays` is a class variable. It applies to all instances of `Employee`. You can think of `vacationDays` as being the number of vacation days per year an `Employee` gets as a benefit. `Employee.MALE` and `Employee.FEMALE` are class constants. The characters that represent these states never change. Here is the source code listing for `EmployeeTest.java`:

```
/*
 * EmployeeTest
 * Accesses and Employee object's variables
 */

public class EmployeeTest {

  public static void main(String args[]) {
    Employee jack = new Employee();
    jack.name = "Jack";
    jack.age = 26;
    jack.sex = Employee.MALE;
    jack.position = "Water Gopher";
    jack.payRate = 5.00;
    jack.vacationDays = 10;
    jack.list();

    Employee jill = new Employee();
    jill.name = "Jill";
    jill.age = 22;
    jill.sex = Employee.FEMALE;
    jill.position = "Assistant Water Gopher";
    jill.payRate = 4.75;
    //changes jack's vacationDays too.
    //static variables apply to all instances.
    jill.vacationDays = 11;
    jill.list();

    System.out.println("I am Jack's vacation days: "
      + jack.vacationDays);

    //static reference by class name
    Employee.vacationDays = 15;

    System.out.println("I am Jack's vacation days: "
      + jack.vacationDays);
    System.out.println("I am Jill's vacation days: "
      + jill.vacationDays);

  }
}
```

The first `Employee` object, `jack`, sets its instance variables. Take notice of how it sets its `sex` variable:

```
jack.sex = Employee.MALE;
```

`jack.sex` is not a constant, as you know, but is an instance variable. You know that it should logically only have one of two values, `M` or `F`, and that these values are stored in the constants, `Employee.MALE` and `Employee.FEMALE` respectively, so using these two constants is a safe way to assign appropriate values to the `jack.sex` variable.

I wanted to demonstrate a bit how class variables can easily be confused with instance variables when you don't follow the convention of preceding an instance variable with the class name instead of a particular instance of the class. If you didn't just see the `Employee` class, you would have no clue that `vacation-Days` was a class variable by looking at the line:

```
jack.vacationDays = 10;
```

In fact, you would almost definitely assume that it is an instance variable, especially if you are used to seeing these conventions, which in the real world, you would, ahem...most of the time...hopefully.

Next, you declare `jill` and happily set its instance variables to values that differ from `jack`'s, comfortable with the fact that `jack` remains unaffected. That is, until you mess with `jill`'s vacation days. `jill.vacationDays` is `jack.vacation-Days` is `Employee.vacationDays`. Changing the state of this variable in any one of these ways will be reflected when you reference the `vacationDays` variable in each of the other two ways. See for yourself in Figure 5.4.

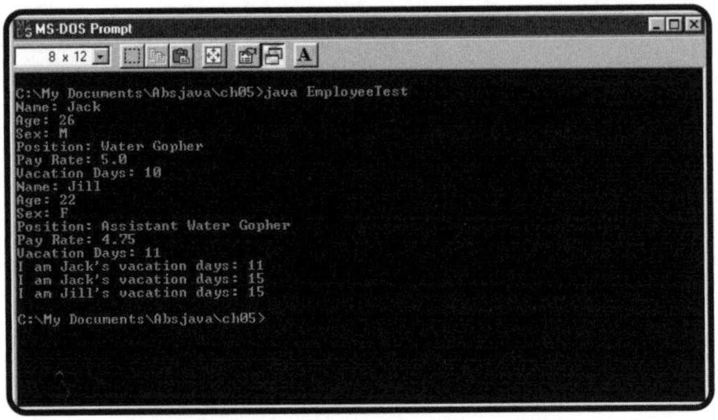

FIGURE 5.4

I am Jack's object-oriented bliss.

Defining and Using Methods

A *method* defines executable code that can be invoked (called), passing a fixed number of arguments. More simply, you can think of methods as lines of Java code that execute when you tell them to. You define methods in a separate section of your program and give it a name so that you can tell it to run from another method, such as `main`, by using the name you gave it. You have already created numerous methods, including `main()`. You have invoked methods such as `System.out.prinln()` and the `list()` method from both the `SimpleCardDeck` and `ChristmasLight` classes you created. In this section, I explain in greater detail what methods are, how to define them, and how to invoke them. I also explain how to return values from methods and how to pass them parameters.

The *Automobile* Class

The `Automobile` class defines some variables and also some methods. It has methods that return no value, methods that return values, methods that accept no parameters, and methods that accept different types of parameters. Here is the source code for `Automobile.java`:

```java
/*
 * Automobile
 * Defines a simple automobile class
 */

public class Automobile {

  public static final String DEFAULT_COLOR = "white";
  public String name;
  public boolean running;
  public String color;
  public int numMiles;

  public Automobile() {
    this(false, DEFAULT_COLOR, 0);
  }

  public Automobile(boolean running, String color, int numMiles) {
    this.running = running;
    this.color = color;
    this.numMiles = numMiles;
    name = null;
  }

  public void start() {
    if (running) {
      System.out.println("Can't start, already running.");
    }
    else {
      running = true;
      System.out.println("The automobile has been started.");
    }
  }

  public void shutOff() {
    if (!running) {
      System.out.println("Can't shut off, not running.");
    }
```

```
      else {
        running = false;
        System.out.println("The automobile has been shut off.");
      }
  }

  public String getColor() {
      return color;
  }

  public void setColor(String color) {
      this.color = color;
  }

  public void drive() {
      if (running) {
        numMiles += 10;
        System.out.println("You have driven 10 miles");
      }
      else {
        System.out.println("You need to start the automobile first.");
      }
  }

  public int getNumMiles() {
      return numMiles;
  }

  public String toString() {
      String str;
      str = "name = " + name
            + ", running = " + running
            + ", color = " + color
            + ", numMiles = " + numMiles;
      return str;
  }

}
```

Write it out and compile it, and then create the AutomobileTest class, listed next, which tests the Automobile class's methods by invoking them, passing in parameters, and accepting returned values. Then, move on to the next sections, which explain what's going on.

```
/*
 * AutomobileTest
 * Tests the Automobile class
 */

public class AutomobileTest {
```

```
public static void main(String args[]) {
  Automobile auto1 = new Automobile();
  System.out.println("Auto 1: " + auto1.toString());

  Automobile auto2 = new Automobile(true, "green", 37000);
  auto2.name = "INGRID";
  System.out.println("Auto 2: " + auto2.toString());

  System.out.println("Driving Auto 1...");
  auto1.drive();
  System.out.println("Driving Auto 2...");
  auto2.drive();

  System.out.println("Starting Auto 1...");
  auto1.start();
  System.out.println("Starting Auto 2...");
  auto2.start();

  System.out.println("Giving Auto 1 a paint job...");
  auto1.setColor("red");
  System.out.println("Auto 1 is now " + auto1.getColor());
  System.out.println("Renaming Auto 1...");
  auto1.name = "CHRISTINE";
  System.out.println("Auto 1 is named " + auto1.name);

  System.out.println("Shutting off Auto 2...");
  auto2.shutOff();
  System.out.println("Shutting off Auto 2 AGAIN...");
  auto2.shutOff();

  System.out.println("Auto 1: " + auto1.toString());
  System.out.println("Auto 2: " + auto2.toString());
  }

}
```

Figure 5.5 shows the output of the AutomobileTest program.

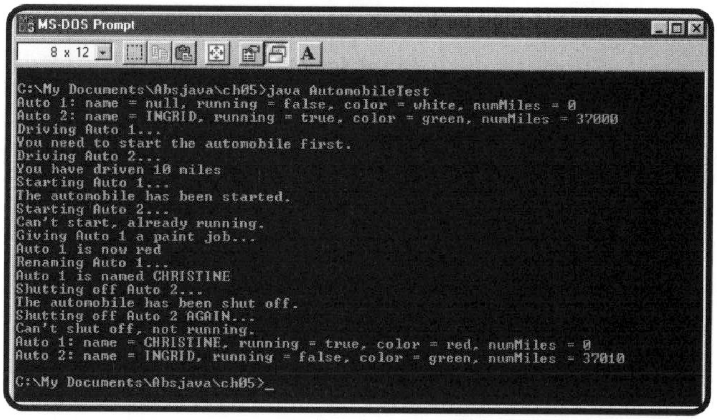

FIGURE 5.5

The AutomobileTest program tests the Automobile class.

Declaring a Method

In order to declare a method, you must define it within the class source file. The method declaration includes the *method signature*, which includes any modifiers, a return value, the method name, and the types and names of any arguments that are required to be passed in. The method body follows the method signature, which is a collection of statements that are executed when the method is invoked. The syntax for declaring a method is as follows:

```
method_modifiers return_value methodName(arguments) {
   method_body;
}
```

An example of this from the Automobile class is the setColor() method. It uses the public modifier to make the method accessible. It doesn't return any value, so it uses the void keyword to specify that fact. The name of the method is set-Color. It accepts a String argument. Within the method body, the argument is referenced by its name color, which is specified in the argument list. The argument list can consist of multiple arguments, separated by commas:

```
public void setColor(String color) {
    this.color = color;
  }
```

In order to invoke this method, first you create an Automobile object, and then you call the method like this:

```
Automobile car = new Automobile();
car.setColor("yellow");
```

Passing Parameters

You have seen that you need to specify the arguments that will be accepted by the method in the method declaration. When you call a method, you *must* pass in the same number and type of arguments (*note that argument and parameter are interchangeable terms*) as was defined in the method declaration, or you will get a compiler error. You can think of parameters as variable declarations that are assigned values by passing them in when you call the method.

```
public class Adder {
  public void add(int arg1, int arg2) {
    int result = arg1 + arg2;
    System.out.println(result);
  }
}
```

Now if you create an adder object and you call the add() method, you must pass in two integers.

```
adder.add(1, 2);
```

When you call the add() method in this way, arg1 gets the value 1 and arg2 gets the value 2. Inside of the method body, another variable, result, is declared. The lifetime of these variables exists only within the body of this method. When the method returns, these variables no longer have any values. Here you can see that the add() method accepts the two integer arguments, adds them, stores the result in result, and prints the value to the screen.

When you pass in a variable of some primitive data type, it is *passed by value*, meaning the value is passed in, not the reference to where the value of the variable is stored. Any operations to the argument do not affect the original variable that was passed in. Here is an example:

```java
public class Test {
  public void add(int a, int b) {
    a += b;
    System.out.println(a);
  }

  public static void main(String args[]) {
    Test t = new Test();
    int x = 1, y = 2;
    t.add(x, y);
    System.out.println(x);
  }
}
```

In the main() method, you declare variables int x = 1, y = 2, and then you pass their values to the add() method (t.add(x, y)). Even though the add() method reassigns a new value to its first argument, a, x remains unaffected when the method returns control back to main(). When you print the value of x, it is still 1.

When you pass in an object, its reference is passed in, rather than a copy of the object. Therefore, the variable within the method that is assigned the object references the same storage area as the original variable. Any operations performed on the object within the method will cause the original variable to reflect the same changes. Here is an example to demonstrate this point:

```java
public class Test {
  int x, y;

public static void main(String args[]) {
    Test t = new Test();
    t.x = 1;
    t.y = 2;
    t.add(t);
    System.out.println(t.x);
  }
```

```
public void add(Test tt) {
   tt.x += tt.y;
   System.out.println(tt.x);
}
}
```

Now the Test class defines two integer variables, x and y. In main(), you declare a Test object, t, and set t.x to 1 and t.y to 2. Next, you call the add() method, only this time, it accepts a Test object reference instead of two primitive data types as its argument. The reference to t is named tt within the method. You can see that it does the same thing as in the previous example. It adds up two variables' values and stores the result in the first variable.

The difference here is that these variables belong to the Test object, which is referenced by both t (outside the method) and tt (inside the method). When you reassign the tt.x variable, the value becomes 3, and is printed. When control returns to main(), the value of t.x will reflect this change and will be 3, too. It's like when you call the plumber to come and fix your toilet. You don't send him a clone of your toilet, you tell him where it is so he can work his magic and when he's done, your toilet is fixed. It's the same concept here, you tell the method where your object is and then it goes and operates on it, and when it's done, your object might have changed.

Method Overloading

Another important parameter-passing concept for you to learn is *method overloading*. When two methods have the same name, but have different types or numbers of arguments, the method is overloaded. Methods names are not unique, you can have two different methods with the same name that do two different things if their signatures are different. Consider these three methods:

```
//method accepts two int arguments
public void add(int a, int b) {
   a += b;
   System.out.println(a);
}

//method accepts three int arguments
public void add(int a, int b, int c) {
   a += b + c;
   System.out.println(a);
}

//method accepts two double arguments
public void add(double a, double b) {
   a += b;
   System.out.println(a);
}
```

They are all named add(), but they are three different methods. Obviously, because they are all named the same thing, they should do something similar. The first one adds the two int arguments and prints the result. The second one adds the three int arguments and prints the result, and the last one adds the two double arguments and prints the result. The one that is called depends on the number and type of arguments you pass in. The following snippet of code calls these three different methods:

```
add(1, 2);
add(1, 2, 3);
add(1.5, 2.5);
```

Returning Values

Sick of seeing the void keyword in front of every single method? As you know, when you declare a method using the void keyword, you are signifying that the method does not return any values. You can, however, return a value from a method. When a method *returns* a value, it passes it back to the invoker. A method returns a value by using the return keyword. The type of value returned is part of the method signature. For example, the following high() method accepts two int arguments and returns the value that is the higher of the two (or the second value if they are the same):

```
public int high(int a, int b) {
  int higher;
  if (a > b) higher = a;
  else higher = b;
  return higher;
}
```

Every method that returns a value must use the return keyword followed by a value, variable, or expression of the type specified in the method signature. In this example, the following line returns the value of the higher variable which is assigned the value of either a or b (the higher of the two):

```
return higher;
```

You can use a call to a method that returns a value in an assignment statement to capture the return value. Take the high() method as an example. To call this method and assign its value to the max variable, do this:

```
int max = higher(2, 4);
```

The high() method does its thing and then returns the value 4, which is assigned to the max variable.

There's a bit more to learn about the return keyword. It abruptly exits the method and returns control back to the method invoker, ignoring any statements that follow the return keyword within the method. You can rewrite the high() method example as follows:

```
public int high(int a, int b) {
  if (a > b) return a;
  return b;
}
```

Knowing this, you don't have to declare a local higher variable to temporarily store the return value. Notice that I didn't include an else? If the condition a > b evaluates true, return a; will be executed, taking control out of the method, never to reach the return b; statement. If it is false, return a; is never evaluated, bringing control to the return b; statement. You can also return from a method that does not return a value by using the return keyword not followed by an expression. For example, say the processOdd method example that follows is a method that prints only odd numbers that are passed to it.

```
public void processOdd(int oddNumber) {
  if (oddNumber % 2 == 0) return;

  ...
  doStuffWithOddNumbers;
  ...
}
```

If you know right off the bat that you don't want to process even numbers, but you don't want to stick the bulk of your method's statements inside of an if - else condition, you can just exit the method using the return statement.

Understanding Static Methods

Just like static variables, static methods do not operate on specific instances of the class, but apply to the class as a whole. A great example that demonstrates this concept is the String.valueOf(int) method. The signature for this method is as follows:

```
public static String valueOf(int i)
```

It returns the String representation of the integer argument passed to it. You don't need a specific instance of String to perform this task, so the method is a static method. You don't have to create a String object just to get a String representation of an int. To invoke this method, because it is a static method, you only need to reference the String class, the method name, and pass it an int:

```
int myIntValue = String.valueOf(5);
```

The main() method is a static method that is called by the Java interpreter when you run an application, but you can also explicitly call this method like any other static method. The MainTest program, listed next, calls the SimpleCardDeckTest's static main() method. As you can see in Figure 5.6, the same results shown in Figure 5.2 are output.

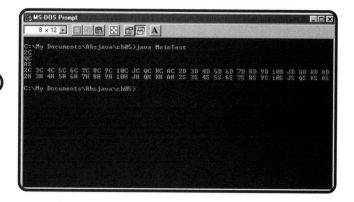

FIGURE 5.6

The `SimpleCard-DeckTest`'s `main()` method is directly called by the `MainTest` application.

```
/*
 * MainTest
 * Shows how main() can be treated like any other
 * static method.
 */

public class MainTest {
  public static void main(String args[]) {
    SimpleCardDeckTest.main(null);
  }
}
```

Defining Constructor Methods

Another type of method is the *constructor method*. Constructor methods initialize an object of a class when the class is instantiated. Constructor methods are similar to other methods except that they must have the same name as the class they are defined in and they never have a return type defined in their method signatures. Take a look at the `Automobile` class again. There are two different constructors, one that accepts no arguments, and another that accepts three: a Boolean, a string, and an `int`. The constructor is overloaded and the constructor that's called depends on the arguments that are passed to it:

```
public Automobile() {
    this(false, DEFAULT_COLOR, 0);
  }

  public Automobile(boolean running, String color, int numMiles) {
    this.running = running;
    this.color = color;
    this.numMiles = numMiles;
    name = null;
  }
```

Looking back at the `AutomobileTest` class, both of these constructors were called:

```
Automobile auto1 = new Automobile();
```

and...

```
Automobile auto2 = new Automobile(true, "green", 37000);
```

You've seen the new keyword before. Anytime you create a new object, you use the new keyword to allocate space in memory for the object and call its constructor. You've seen this syntax before, now you know what it means:

```
ClassName objectName = new ClassName();
```

The parentheses are there because it is actually making a call to the constructor method. You do not have to define a constructor for your class, although in most cases, you will. Defining constructors allows you to have more control over the initial state of your objects when they are created. If you don't define a constructor, an empty do-nothing constructor is created for you by the compiler, which accepts no arguments and doesn't have a method body.

HINT

When you create a new object using the new keyword, your system allocates memory to store the object and initializes its instance variables. Variables that hold objects are initialized to null, numbers are initialized to 0, Boolean values are initialized to false, and character values are initialized to \u0000. If you assign values to instance variables where they are declared (remember, instance variables are not declared in any method), the variables are assigned those values first. If your constructor reassigns values to the variables, they get those values when the object is created.

TRAP

If you do not define any constructor methods, you create a new object using this syntax:

```
MyClass objectName = new MyClass();
```

This is because the constructor, MyClass(), is created by the compiler. The compiler does this only if you don't define a constructor yourself. So if you do define at least one constructor that accepts any number of arguments, the compiler won't create the no-argument MyClass() constructor. For example, if you define a constructor with a signature similar to:

```
public MyClass(int myNumber)
```

but you don't explicitly define a constructor with no arguments, such as MyClass(), you can no longer create an object without passing in an int argument. In other words,

```
MyClass objectName = new MyClass();
```

will not work anymore, unless you define MyClass(), but the following construction will work:

```
MyClass objectName = new MyClass(1);
```

If at least one constructor method is defined in your Java source file and you try to compile it, you will get a compiler error if any of those methods call an undefined constructor method. This is why it's best to use constructor overloading. By overloading the constructor, the program can either pass in an `int` argument or choose to not pass in any arguments.

Learning another Keyword: *this*

Sometimes it is beneficial to be able to refer to the current object in the body of a method. The `this` keyword specifies the current instance of the class. Which instance? *This* one. Most of the time it is omitted, but you do need it to specify a variable as belonging to the instance of the class if there is another variable of the same name declared locally within the method. The `this` keyword can only be used in instance methods and constructors. It cannot be used in class (`static`) methods because they do not operate on specific instances of the class. Take the `setColor()` method from the `Automobile` class as an example.

```
public void setColor(String color) {
    this.color = color;
}
```

The `color` variable is declared locally in this method as its only parameter. A variable of the same name is also declared within the class definition as a member variable. The statement `color = color;` reassigns the local variable's value to itself. You need a way to specify that you are assigning the value of the parameter to the member variable. Using the `this` keyword makes it possible. The `this.color = color;` statement is like saying, "Take the parameter given and assign it to this instance's `color` variable." Don't forget, because this is an instance method, it must be called through an instance of the `Automobile` class. In the `AutomobileTest` program, the line:

```
auto1.setColor("red");
```

assigns the `auto1` `Automobile` object's `color` variable to `red`. `this` can also call a constructor. Again, you can look to the `Automobile` class for clarification. You see there are two constructors. As is typically done, the grunt work is done in one of the constructors, the one that accepts the most arguments. The constructor that does not accept any arguments simply calls the other constructor, using default values for the parameters, to do the work for it:

```
this(false, DEFAULT_COLOR, 0);
```

This statement calls the workhorse constructor, with the default values, `false`, the static variable `DEFAULT_COLOR`, and `0`. Then you can see in the `Automobile(boolean, String, int)` constructor, `this` specifies the current object's variables because the parameters are named the same as the instance variables. That's all I have to say about that...er, `this`.

Understanding Access Modifiers

As you know, objects interact with each other by referencing fields and methods of other objects. *Access modifiers* define accessibility of an object's fields and methods. The access modifiers are `public` (you've seen this one before), `protected`, and `private`.

Field and Method Access Modifiers

You can access public variables and methods anywhere. They are directly accessible from instance methods, which assume the current object if the `this` keyword is missing. If a public instance variable is referenced from a static method, it must be accessed through a specific instance of the class. Public member variables are also available from subclasses of the class they are defined in. You learn about subclasses a bit later in this chapter.

```
public class Foo {
  public int myNumber;
  public static int three = 3;

  public void myMethod() {
    //can access both fields here
    myNumber = three;
  }

  public static void main(String args[]) {
    Foo manChu = new Foo();

    // can't access myNumber without the actual manChu object
    // no-no: myNumber = three;
    // but CAN access three because it is static, the same for all instances
    manChu.myNumber = three;
    // - or - the same thing…
    manChu.myNumber = Foo.three;
  }4

}
```

Outside of the class definition itself, public variables and methods are accessible, given an instance of the class, within any other class that can reference the class itself. The following `FooTest` class references a `Foo` object's public `myNumber` variable, as well as `Foo`'s static `three` variable.

```
public class FooTest {
  public static void main(String args[]) {
    Foo manChu = new Foo();
    ManChu.myNumber = Foo.three;
  }
}
```

The protected keyword specifies that a variable or method is accessible only within a class definition or a subclass of the class it is defined in, or from other classes in the same package. Trying to access a protected from any other class will not work. The same goes for private variables and methods, except they are further restricted. private variables and methods are only accessible in the class file they are defined in—they are not accessible even to subclasses. A quick example of a compiler error you can get is shown in the AccessErrorTest application. First, here is a listing of AccessError.java:

```
/*
 * AccessError
 * Has a private method
 */

public class AccessError {

  public AccessError() {
    //Can access it from within this class
    getPrivateStuff();
  }

  private void getPrivateStuff() {
    System.out.println("private stuff");
  }

}
```

The method getPrivateStuff() in this class is declared private. It is called from its single constructor. You can write and compile this program without any errors because the private method is accessible anywhere in this class. Now, here is a listing of AccessErrorTest.java:

```
/*
 * AccessErrorTest
 * Demonstrates a method access error
 */

public class AccessErrorTest {

  public static void main(String args[]) {
    AccessError ae = new AccessError();
    //can't access private method here
    ae.getPrivateStuff();
  }

}
```

If you try to compile this program, you will get the compiler error message shown in Figure 5.7. AccessErrorTest is not AccessError and therefore does not have access to its getprivateStuff() method.

FIGURE 5.7

You can't access a
`private` member
or method from
outside of the class
definition.

Encapsulation

Why do access modifiers exist? Using access modifiers allows you to hide internal values and operations from the outside world, allowing for *encapsulation*. Encapsulation is one of the benefits of object-oriented programming. With encapsulation, types are accessed through their exposed, external values and operations and not by their internal implementations. This is beneficial because you can change the way your classes are implemented internally, but as long as you keep the external operations the same, you don't have to go back and fix the programs that use it. For an example of encapsulation, take a look at the PrimaryColor class:

```
/*
 * PrimaryColor
 * Demonstrates encapsulation and get and set conventions
 */
public class PrimaryColor {
  public final static String BLUE = "blue",
                             RED = "red",
                             YELLOW = "yellow",
                             DEFAULT = "yellow";

  private String color;

  public PrimaryColor(String c) {
    setColor(c);
  }

  public void setColor(String c) {
    if (c == BLUE || c == RED || c == YELLOW) {
      color = c;
    }
    else {
      color = DEFAULT;
    }
  }
```

```
  public String getColor() {
    return color;
  }

}
```

The `color` variable is declared to be `private`, which means it can't be referenced from outside of the class definition. However, access is granted to set its value through the `public setColor()` method or through the constructor, which actually just calls the `setColor` method. This allows you to filter the value before assigning it to your precious private variable. Remember, this is only a small example. What if there were other operations in this class that depended on the fact that the `color` variable was, `red`, `blue`, or `yellow`? What if your program crashed horribly when it was any other value or even `null`? You don't have to worry about this because of encapsulation. You filter the value and make sure a valid value is passed in. If it's not, you set it to some valid value yourself. The `PrimaryColorTest` application tests this encapsulation stuff:

```
/*
 * PrimaryColorTest
 * Demonstrates the concept of encapsulation in the
 * PrimaryColor class
 */

public class PrimaryColorTest {

  public static void main(String args[]) {
    PrimaryColor red = new PrimaryColor("red");
    System.out.println("red is " + red.getColor());

    PrimaryColor pink = new PrimaryColor("pink");
    System.out.println("pink is " + pink.getColor());

    PrimaryColor blue = new PrimaryColor(PrimaryColor.BLUE);
    System.out.println("blue is " + blue.getColor());
  }

}
```

The output of the `PrimaryColorTest` application is shown in Figure 5.8. The `PrimaryColorTest` application creates three `PrimaryColor` objects. The first one, `red`, is constructed using the parameter "red", which is fine, because `red` is a valid argument defined in the implementation of the `PrimaryColor` class.

The second one, `pink`, passes "pink" to the constructor. Well, `pink` isn't a valid argument, but that's okay too because you just need to set it to the default value `PrimaryColor.DEFAULT`, and there won't be any trouble down the line. You can see in the output that the `setColor()` method caught the fact that an invalid argument was sent and set it to the default value "yellow". The last object, `blue`,

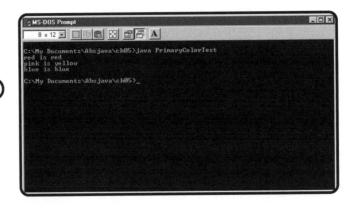

FIGURE 5.8

The Primary-
ColorTest
application
demonstrates the
concept of
encapsulation.

demonstrates a better, more typical way to write such an object creation. If a class constant is available to be passed in, it is typically used for readability's sake.

The *Card* and *CardDeck* Classes

Now that you understand many of the important concepts of object-oriented programming, you're ready to write the Card and CardDeck classes. Writing these classes reiterates what you have learned up to this point. They are also used in this chapter's final Blackjack game project.

Writing the *Card* Class

Way back in the SimpleCardDeck class, you represented a deck of cards as an integer of string values. In writing an actual card game, it helps to have a class that defines an individual card. That is what the Card class is for. Here, you define the Card class, and then you will define the CardDeck class that groups together a bunch of Cards. Not only will writing the Card class make it easier to write the BlackJack project, it will force you to go deeper into the world of OOP. Here is the full source code for Card.java:

```
/*
 * Card
 * A class that defines a playing card that you
 * find in any standard deck of cards.
 * Possible cards are 2, 3, 4, 5, 6, 7, 8, 9, 10,
 * and Jack, Queen, King, and Ace.
 * Possible suits are clubs, diamonds, hearts, and spades.
 */

public class Card {

    public static final int JACK = 11,
                            QUEEN = 12,
                            KING = 13,
```

```
                    ACE = 14,
                    MIN = 2,
                    MAX = 14;
/* faceValue is restricted from 2 to ACE (14)
   but actualValue can be any integer */
protected int faceValue;
protected int actualValue;
protected char suit;
protected boolean visible;

public Card(int fv, char s, boolean v) {
  this(fv, fv, s, v);
}

public Card(int fv, int av, char s, boolean v) {
  faceValue = (fv >= MIN && fv <= MAX) ? fv : 2;
  actualValue = av;
  if (s == 'C' || s == 'D' || s == 'H' || s == 'S') {
    suit = s;
  }
  else {
    suit = 'C';
  }
  visible = v;
}

public void setVisible(boolean v) {
  visible = v;
}

public boolean getVisible() {
  return visible;
}

public String toString() {
  if (!visible) {
    return "??";
  }
  String face;
  if (faceValue >= 2 && faceValue <=10) {
    face = String.valueOf(faceValue);
  }
  else {
    switch (faceValue) {
      case JACK:
        face = "J";
        break;
      case QUEEN:
        face = "Q";
        break;
      case KING:
        face = "K";
        break;
```

```
            case ACE:
                face = "A";
                break;
            default:
                face = "2";
        }
    }
    face += suit;
    return face;
}

public void setValue(int av) {
    actualValue = av;
}

public int getValue() {
    return actualValue;
}

public int getFaceValue() {
    return faceValue;
}

public static char[] getSuits() {
    char[] suits = { 'C', 'D', 'H', 'S' };
    return suits;
}

/* returns true if this card is a picture card
 * i.e. jack, queen, or king */
public boolean isPictureCard() {
    if (faceValue >= JACK && faceValue <= KING) {
        return true;
    }
    return false;
}

}
```

The Card class represents playing cards in terms of an actual value and a face value. The actual value, stored in actualValue, is intended to be some point value associated with the game the Card is used in. Its value is not restricted. The face value, stored in the faceValue variable, is the int value that represents the face value of the card. Valid values are restricted to either 2 through 10, for playing cards of the same face value, or 11 for a Jack, 12 for a Queen, 13 for a King, and 14 for an Ace. The Card class provides corresponding int constants to make this easier to implement: JACK, QUEEN, KING, and ACE. The suit variable is a char representation of four possible suits of a playing card: C for Clubs, D for Diamonds, H for Hearts, and S for Spades. The Boolean visible variable specifies whether a card is visible (whether it's face up or face down).

There are two constructors. One of them accepts a face value, a suit, and a visible flag as arguments. The other one accepts these arguments as well as an actual value argument. If the first constructor is used, the actualValue variable is just set to the same value as the faceValue variable. You can see constructor overloading and encapsulation at work here. The constructors ensure that no invalid values are set. Notice that all but the constants are protected. public methods exist to either get or set the values as needed.

Writing the *CardDeck* Class

The CardDeck class simulates a deck of cards by organizing a group of Card objects. It maintains this group of Card objects in a protected Card array and defines certain methods to allow operations to be performed on the deck. Here is the source code listing for CardDeck.java:

```
/*
 * CardDeck
 * Defines properties and operations of a deck of cards
 */

public class CardDeck {
  protected Card[] cards;
  protected int top;

  public CardDeck() {
    top = 0;
    char[] suits = Card.getSuits();
    //number of possible cards is number of suits * number of
    //possible values.
    int numValues = Card.MAX - Card.MIN + 1;
    cards = new Card[suits.length * numValues];
    int cIndex;

    for (int s=0; s < suits.length; s++) {
      for (int v=Card.MIN; v <= Card.MAX; v++) {
        cIndex = s * numValues + v - Card.MIN;
        cards[cIndex] = new Card(v, suits[s], true);
      }
    }
  }

  public Card getCard(int index) {
    return cards[index];
  }

  public void list() {
    for (int c=0; c < cards.length; c++) {
      System.out.print(cards[c].toString() + " ");
    }
  }
```

```
public int getTopIndex() {
   return top;
}

/* returns the card at top index and moves the index */
public Card deal() {
   Card dealt = cards[top];
   top ++;
   //if last card dealt, reset the top card
   if (top >= cards.length) reset();
   return dealt;
}

public void reset() {
   top = 0;
}

public int getNumCards() {
   return cards.length;
}

public int getNumCardsLeft() {
   return cards.length - top;
}

}
```

CardDeck's two member variables are cards and top. cards is an array of Card objects and top is the index of the cards array that represents the top card of the deck, initially 0. The constructor takes no arguments. It calls the static method Card.getSuits(), which returns a char array containing the valid suits. Then it calculates the number of possible face values by taking the Card.MAX constant, which represents the highest possible face value 14, subtracting the Card.MIN constant (2) from it and adding 1, resulting in 13. The number of suits times the number of face values produces the total number of cards, so this number initializes the cards array's size (to 52).

The nested for loops create every possible combination of face value and suit to create the 52 Card objects that it sticks in its cards array. Some of the methods are self-explanatory. Some are a bit more complicated. The deal() method returns the current top Card (the one stored in the array under the subscript top) and shifts the index of the array to reflect the next top Card. Also, if the last Card is dealt, the top index is reset to 0.

The CardDeckTest application tests the Card and CardDeck classes. It creates a CardDeck object, deck, and lists its contents using its list() method. It defines a Card object, card, and uses deck's deal() method to return the top Card and assign it to card. It does this twice and lists them to show that the next card is being dealt. Then it calls the deck object's reset() method to reset its top card, prints the top card's index and also the last card in the deck. Here is a listing of the source code. Take a look at Figure 5.9 for the output.

```
/*
 * CardDeckTest
 * Tests the CardDeck class.
 */

public class CardDeckTest {

  public static void main(String args[]) {
    CardDeck deck = new CardDeck();
    System.out.println("Deck Listing:");
    deck.list();
    Card card = deck.deal();
    System.out.println("Dealt " + card);
    card = deck.deal();
    System.out.println("Dealt " + card);
    System.out.println("Top index: " + deck.getTopIndex());
    deck.reset();
    System.out.println("Reset deck... Top index: "
                        + deck.getTopIndex());
    card = deck.deal();
    System.out.println("Dealt " + card);
    System.out.println("The last card is " +
      deck.getCard(deck.getNumCards() - 1));
  }

}
```

FIGURE 5.9

Card and CardDeck work together to simulate a deck of playing cards.

TRICK

Did you notice that, in the CardDeckTest application, I printed the value of the individually dealt cards merely by using the object name in the System.out.println() method?

```
System.out.println("Dealt " + card);
```

I didn't call the toString() method to generate its String representation, but it happened anyway. toString() is a method defined in the Object class that all other objects are subclasses of. This method is therefore known to exist for all objects due to inheritance, which you learn about next. For all objects, it is intended to return the String representation of itself for situations just as this. If you look at the API, documentation for this method, you will see that it is actually recommended that this method be overridden for every class.

Extending a Class

Another great benefit of object-oriented programming is that you can *extend* it to add more functionality to a class that already exists, instead of having to reinvent the wheel. When extending a class, you create a *subclass* that inherits some of the class's preexisting functionality. Earlier, you wrote the Automobile class. It's a fairly vague class that only generally defines what an automobile is. If you wanted to define a class that defines a more specific type of automobile such as a big truck, which you are going to do, you don't have to redefine the stuff that's already defined in Automobile. For instance, you don't have to redefine the variables that hold the color, name, and whether or not the engine is running, or operations such as starting the engine, driving it, and so on. Instead, you *subclass* the Automobile class. This concept is known as *inheritance*.

The extends keyword subclasses a class. When you subclass a class, the new class is called a (you guessed it) *subclass* and the original class is its *superclass*. A subclass inherits its superclass's members and methods. A subclass is created so that you can add more to it. Here is the syntax for extending a class, which is done when the class is declared.

```
public class MySubClass extends MyClass { ... }
```

The *BigTruck* Class

The BigTruck class is a subclass of the Automobile class. This means it *is* an Automobile. It inherits Automobile's variables and methods. Then it expands upon it, giving it operations that are specific to the BigTruck class, such as the capability to haul a trailer.

TRICK

If you want a quick view of public and protected member variables and methods, you can use the javap utility. By default (it has other options), javap lists the public and protected variables and methods. The syntax for this utility is:

javap ClassName

Here is another quick example that lists all of this chapter's project's variables and methods in a text file named t.txt:

javap BigTruck -private >t.txt

One drawback, though, is that it doesn't list any variables or methods that were inherited.

Here is the source listing for BigTruck.java:

```java
/*
 * BigTruck
 * Extends the Automobile class - is a subclass of Automobile
 */

public class BigTruck extends Automobile {

  // inherits all of Automobile's members & methods
  // and adds more
  protected boolean trailer;

  public BigTruck() {
    this(false, DEFAULT_COLOR, 0);
  }

  public BigTruck(boolean running, String color, int numMiles) {
    //calls the superclass constructor
    super(running, color, numMiles);
    trailer = false;
  }

  public void attachTrailer() {
    if (trailer) {
      System.out.println("There is already a trailer attached.");
    }
    else {
      trailer = true;
      System.out.println("Attached a trailer.");
    }
  }

  public void detachTrailer() {
    if (trailer) {
      trailer = false;
      System.out.println("Detached the trailer.");
    }
    else {
      System.out.println("There is no trailer attached.");
    }
  }

  public void haul() {
    if (trailer) {
      drive();
    }
    else {
      System.out.println("There is nothing to haul.");
    }
  }

  //overriding toString
  public String toString() {
```

```
        String str = super.toString();
        str += ", trailer = " + trailer;
        return str;
    }

}
```

The `BigTruck` class defines only one more member variable, `trailer`, which is a Boolean that specifies whether a trailer is attached. There are also some new methods to attach a trailer, detach a trailer, and haul a trailer if one is attached. Take a look at the constructor. Notice the `super` keyword? The `super` keyword specifies the superclass. In the line:

```
super(running, color, numMiles);
```

The superclass's (`Automobile`) constructor is called. You already wrote the code in the `Automobile` class's constructor, why not just call that constructor instead of rewriting code that does the same thing? You can also use `super` to call a superclass's method. You do this if you have overridden a method, but you specifically want to use the superclass's version of the method instead of the new one defined for the subclass. Another reason to do this is if in your subclass's method, you want to first call the superclass's method, and then add more stuff at the end in your subclass's override method. The syntax for calling a superclass method is:

```
super.methodName(arguments);
```

TRAP

If you do use a call to a superclass's constructor within a subclass's constructor, it must be done in the first statement or else you will get a compiler error. You must call a super class's constructor, or an overloaded constructor of this class if you are defining a brand spanking new constructor instead of overriding one in the subclass. This ensures that the subclass is also a valid instance of the superclass. You will get confusing compiler errors if you forget to do this. Java actually forces you to call the superclass's constructor. If you don't do it explicitly, the compiler will use the superclass's default no-argument constructor. You learned earlier that there are cases in which the default constructor does not exist. What then? In these cases, you must explicitly call the superclass's constructor or you will get a compiler error. The first line of any constructor (assuming the superclass does not have a default constructor) must either be a call to an overloaded constructor within the same class or a call to the superclass's constructor.

The `BigTruckTest` program gives your new `BigTruck` class a test drive (see Figure 5.10). Here is the source listing for `BigTruckTest.java`:

```
/*
 * BigTruckTest
 * Tests the BigTruck class
 */
```

```
public class BigTruckTest {

    public static void main(String args[]) {
        BigTruck truck = new BigTruck();
        System.out.println(truck);
        System.out.println("Starting...");
        truck.start();
        System.out.println("Driving...");
        truck.drive();
        System.out.println("Attaching Trailer...");
        truck.attachTrailer();
        System.out.println("Hauling...");
        truck.haul();
        System.out.println("Detaching trailer...");
        truck.detachTrailer();
        System.out.println("Shutting off...");
        truck.shutOff();
        System.out.println("Painting...");
        truck.setColor("black");
        System.out.println(truck);
    }

}
```

FIGURE 5.10

This is the output of the BigTruckTest application.

Overriding Methods

As you know, a subclass inherits its superclass's variables and members. It is possible, however, to take an inherited method and make it work differently for the subclass than it works for the superclass. You *override* a method by defining the same method signature in the subclass. Defining a method with the same name, but with a different number of arguments or argument types, just creates a new overloaded version of the superclass's method. You overrode an Automobile method in the BigTruck class. You overrode Automobile's toString() method. The toString() method in the Automobile class returns a String representing the name, whether or not it is running, the color, and the number of miles. The `toString()` method in the `BigTruck` class overrides this method to include whether or not a trailer is attached. First you used what you learned about the `super` keyword to call `Automobile`'s version of the method, and then you simply appended the `trailer` value.

Polymorphism

Polymorphism is another complicated word for a simple concept. It simply means that an instance of a subclass is also an instance of its superclass. A `BigTruck` instance is an `Automobile` too. All classes inherit from the `Object` class defined in the Java language, so every instance of `Automobile` and `BigTruck` is also an instance of `Object`. For example, if a method existed that accepted an `Automobile` object as a parameter:

```
public void doSomething(Automobile auto) { … }
```

You can pass in a `BigTruck` object, because it is an `Automobile`:

```
BigTruck truck = new BigTruck();
doSomething(truck);
```

Back to the *BlackJack* Game

You've learned a great deal about object-oriented programming in this chapter. Now you put this knowledge to good use by creating a text-based version of a blackjack game. In this section you subclass the `CardDeck` class, to create `RandomCardDeck`, a randomized deck of cards so the game isn't predictable. You also learn about the `java.util.Vector` class, which will help in creating the final game. Finally, you write the actual `BlackJack` application.

The *RandomCardDeck* Class

You've already written a class that represents a deck of cards, the `CardDeck` class. Now you just need to override it so that the `Cards` stored in the deck are randomized. To do this, you import the `java.util.Random` class. In the constructor, you call the superclass's constructor to build a regular `CardDeck`, and then you call the new `shuffle()` method to rearrange the `Cards` randomly. One other thing you need to do is override the `reset()` method so that when you reset the top card, you also shuffle the deck. Here is the source listing for `RandomCardDeck.java`:

```
/*
 * RandomCardDeck
 * Simulates a shuffled deck of cards
 */
```

```
import java.util.Random;

public class RandomCardDeck extends CardDeck {

  public RandomCardDeck () {
    super();
    shuffle();
  }

  public void shuffle() {
    Card[] shuffled = new Card[cards.length];
    Random rand = new Random();
    int cIndex;
    boolean placed;
    for (int c=0; c < cards.length; c++) {
      do {
        placed = false;
        cIndex = rand.nextInt(cards.length);
        if (shuffled[cIndex] == null) {
          shuffled[cIndex] = cards[c];
          placed = true;
        }
      } while (!placed);
    }
    cards = shuffled;
    top = 0;
  }

  public void reset() {
    super.reset();
    shuffle();
  }

}
```

The shuffle() method deserves some elaboration. A new Card array, shuffled, is
declared locally in this method. Its purpose is to be a temporary placeholder for
the deck of cards as it is being shuffled. It is initialized to the same size as the
cards array instance variable. This initializes the Card objects in the shuffled
array to null. The for loop loops on all the Cards in the existing cards array, one
at a time. Then a random index for the shuffled array is created. If a card has not
already been placed at this index, stored in cIndex (you can tell because the Card
object there is null), the card is placed there; if it is already occupied by another
Card, it continues to look for vacancies until it finds one.

So, the cards in the cards array are copied, one by one, randomly into the shuffled array, and then the shuffled array is assigned to the cards instance variable,
causing it to be shuffled, and then the top variable is reset to 0. The RandomCard-
DeckTest program tests to make sure that the RandomCardDeck class works the
way you expect it to. The output is shown in Figure 5.11. Here is the source code:

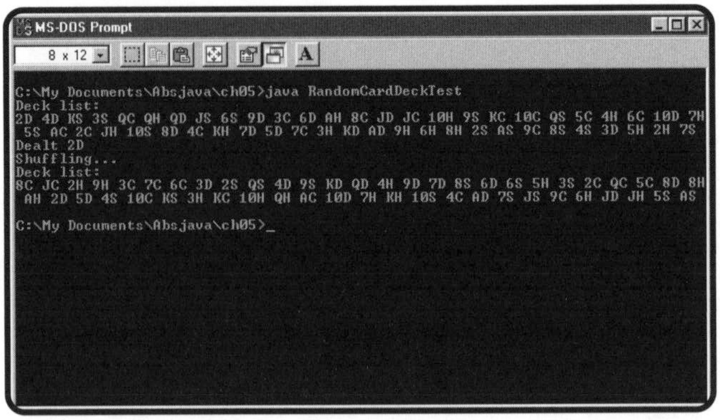

FIGURE 5.11

The RandomCardDeck class represents a random deck of playing cards.

```
/*
 * RandomCardDeckTest
 * Tests the RandomCardDeck class
 */

public class RandomCardDeckTest {

   public static void main(String args[]) {
      RandomCardDeck deck = new RandomCardDeck();
      System.out.println("Deck list:");
      deck.list();
      Card card = deck.deal();
      System.out.println("Dealt " + card);
      System.out.println("Shuffling...");
      deck.shuffle();
      System.out.println("Deck list:");
      deck.list();
   }

}
```

The *Vector* Class

The java.util package contains many useful classes, including the Random and Vector classes. The Vector class implements a growable array of objects. It acts similarly to an array except that the size automatically grows and shrinks as objects are added and removed. It is of interest here because you use the Vector class to represent the dealer's and the player's hand in the BlackJack game. Table 5.1 contains some useful Vector methods. Remember that because of polymorphism, any object can be passed to the methods that accept an Object instance.

The VectorVictor application demonstrates simple use of the Vector class. The source code for VectorVictor.java is as follows:

TABLE 5.1   VECTOR METHODS

Method	Description
void add(int *index*, Object *element*)	Inserts *element* at the specified *index*, shifting the remaining indices by adding 1.
boolean add(Object *element*)	Appends *element* to the end; returns true.
int capacity()	Returns the capacity (current maximum size).
void clear()	Removes all elements.
void copyInto(Object[] anArray)	Copies the Vector's elements into the given array.
Object elementAt(int *index*)	Returns the element at the given index.
Object remove(int *index*)	Removes and returns the object at the given index.
boolean remove(Object *element*)	Removes the first occurrence of *element*.
void trimToSize()	Sets the capacity of the Vector to its current size.

```
/*
 * VectorVictor
 * Demonstrates the Vector class
 */

import java.util.Vector;

public class VectorVictor {

  public static void main(String args[]) {
    //initialize a vector of capacity 5 and increment 5
    Vector v = new Vector(5, 5);
    System.out.println("size, capacity");
    System.out.println(v.size() + ", " + v.capacity());
    v.add(new String("Fuzzy"));
    System.out.println(v.size() + ", " + v.capacity());
    v.add(new String("Wuzzy"));
    System.out.println(v.size() + ", " + v.capacity());
    v.add(new String("was"));
    System.out.println(v.size() + ", " + v.capacity());
    v.add(new String("a"));
    System.out.println(v.size() + ", " + v.capacity());
    v.add(new String("bear"));
    System.out.println(v.size() + ", " + v.capacity());
    v.add(new String("Fuzzy"));
    System.out.println(v.size() + ", " + v.capacity());
    v.add(new String("Wuzzy"));
    System.out.println(v.size() + ", " + v.capacity());
```

```
      v.add(new String("had"));
      System.out.println(v.size() + ", " + v.capacity());
      v.add(new String("no"));
      System.out.println(v.size() + ", " + v.capacity());
      v.add(new String("hair"));
      System.out.println(v.size() + ", " + v.capacity());
      v.add(new String("Fuzzy"));
      System.out.println(v.size() + ", " + v.capacity());
      v.add(new String("Wuzzy"));
      System.out.println(v.size() + ", " + v.capacity());
      v.add(new String("wasn't"));
      System.out.println(v.size() + ", " + v.capacity());
      v.add(new String("fuzzy"));
      System.out.println(v.size() + ", " + v.capacity());
      v.add(new String("was"));
      System.out.println(v.size() + ", " + v.capacity());
      v.add(new String("he"));
      System.out.println(v.size() + ", " + v.capacity());
      v.trimToSize();
      System.out.println(v.size() + ", " + v.capacity());

      //copy into an array
      String[] str = new String[v.size()];
      v.copyInto(str);

      for (int s=0; s < str.length; s++) {
        System.out.print(str[s] + " ");
      }
   }
}
```

The constructor accepts two int arguments. The first argument is the initial capacity of the Vector and the second one is the capacity increment. The capacity increment is the amount by which the capacity increases any time adding an element to the Vector causes the size to be greater than its capacity. As you can see in the output shown in Figure 5.12, anytime the size of the Vector exceeds

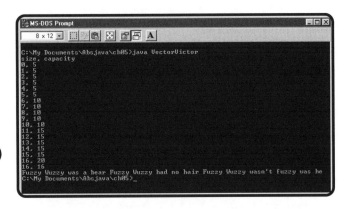

FIGURE 5.12

What's your
Vector, Victor?

the capacity, it grows by a factor of 5. This program also demonstrates copying the elements of the Vector into an array.

The *BlackJack* Program

Okay, here it is, the final project source code listing for BlackJack.java:

```java
/*
 * BlackJack
 * A simple BlackJack card game simulation
 */

import java.util.Vector;
import java.io.*;

public class BlackJack {

  protected RandomCardDeck deck;
  protected Vector dealerHand, playerHand;
  protected int dealerPoints, playerPoints;
  protected final static char HIT = 'H', STAND = 'S';

  public BlackJack() {
    Card card;
    dealerHand = new Vector();
    playerHand = new Vector();
    deck = new RandomCardDeck();
    for (int c=0; c < deck.getNumCards(); c++) {
      card = deck.getCard(c);
      if (card.isPictureCard()) {
        card.setValue(10);
      }
      else if (card.getFaceValue() == Card.ACE) {
        card.setValue(1);
      }
    }
  }

  public static void main(String args[]) {
    BufferedReader reader;
    char input;
    BlackJack bj = new BlackJack();
    reader = new BufferedReader(new InputStreamReader(System.in));
    do {
      bj.play();
      System.out.print("Play Again (Y/N)? ");
      try {
        input = Character.toUpperCase(reader.readLine().charAt(0));
      } catch (IOException ioe) { input = '?'; }
    } while (input == 'Y');
  }
```

```java
public void play() {
  int input;
  dealerHand.clear();
  playerHand.clear();
  if (deck.getNumCardsLeft() <= 15) {
    System.out.println("Shuffling deck...");
    deck.shuffle();
  }
  deal();
  output();

  if (playerBlackJack()) {
    System.out.println("Player has BlackJack!!!");
    ((Card)dealerHand.elementAt(0)).setVisible(true);
    output();
    if (dealerBlackJack()) {
      System.out.println("Dealer also has BlackJack.");
      System.out.println("Game is a PUSH.");
    }
    else {
      System.out.println("Player wins!");
    }
  }
  else if (dealerBlackJack()) {
    ((Card)dealerHand.elementAt(0)).setVisible(true);
    System.out.println("Dealer has BlackJack.");
    output();
    System.out.println("Player loses.");
  }
  else {
    // hit or stand loop.
    do {
      try {
        input = getUserInput();
      } catch (IOException ioe) { input = STAND; }
      if (input == HIT) {
        System.out.println("Dealt " + hitPlayer());
        output();
      }
      if (playerPoints > 21) {
        System.out.println("Player BUSTS!");
        ((Card)dealerHand.elementAt(0)).setVisible(true);
        output();
        System.out.println("Player loses.");
      }
    } while (input == HIT && playerPoints < 21);
    if (playerPoints <= 21) {
      System.out.println("Dealer's turn");
      ((Card)dealerHand.elementAt(0)).setVisible(true);
      output();
      while (dealerPoints <= 16) {
        System.out.println("Dealer gets " + hitDealer());
        output();
      }
```

```
        if (dealerPoints > 21) {
           System.out.println("Dealer BUSTS!");
           System.out.println("Player wins!");
        }
        else if (dealerBlackJack()) {
           System.out.println("Dealer has BlackJack.");
           System.out.println("Player loses.");
        }
        else if (dealerPoints == playerPoints) {
           System.out.println("The game is a PUSH.");
        }
        else if (dealerPoints > playerPoints) {
           System.out.println("Player loses.");
        }
        else {
           System.out.println("Player wins!");
        }
      }
    }
  }

  protected void deal() {
    Card card;
    playerHand.add(deck.deal());
    playerHand.add(deck.deal());
    card = deck.deal();
    card.setVisible(false);
    dealerHand.add(card);
    dealerHand.add(deck.deal());
    updatePoints();
  }

  protected void output() {
    String d = "Dealer's Hand: ";
    String p = "Your Hand     : ";
    for (int c=0; c < dealerHand.size(); c++) {
      d += (Card)dealerHand.elementAt(c) + " ";
    }
    for (int c=0; c < playerHand.size(); c++) {
      p += (Card)playerHand.elementAt(c) + " ";
    }
    if (d.indexOf('?') == -1) {
      d += " (" + dealerPoints +")";
    }
    p += " (" + playerPoints +")";
    System.out.println(d);
    System.out.println(p);
  }

  protected Card hitPlayer() {
    return hit(playerHand);
  }
```

```
protected Card hitDealer() {
  return hit(dealerHand);
}

protected char getUserInput() throws IOException {
  BufferedReader reader;
  char input;
  reader = new BufferedReader(new InputStreamReader(System.in));
  do {
    System.out.print("(H)it or (S)tand? ");
    input = Character.toUpperCase(reader.readLine().charAt(0));
  } while (input != HIT && input != STAND);
  return input;
}

protected boolean dealerBlackJack() {
  if (dealerHand.size() == 2) {
    if (((Card)dealerHand.elementAt(1)).getFaceValue() == Card.ACE
        || ((Card)dealerHand.elementAt(0)).getVisible()) {
      return dealerPoints == 21;
    }
  }
  return false;
}

protected boolean playerBlackJack() {
  if (playerHand.size() == 2) {
    return playerPoints == 21;
  }
  return false;
}

private Card hit(Vector hand) {
  Card card = deck.deal();
  hand.add(card);
  updatePoints();
  return card;
}

protected void updatePoints() {
  playerPoints = addUpPoints(playerHand);
  dealerPoints = addUpPoints(dealerHand);
}

private int addUpPoints(Vector hand) {
  int points = 0;
  int nAces = 0;
  Card[] cards = new Card[hand.size()];
  hand.copyInto(cards);
  for (int c=0; c < cards.length; c++) {
    points += cards[c].getValue();
    if (cards[c].getFaceValue() == Card.ACE) nAces++;
  }
```

```
    if (points <= 11 && nAces > 0) {
      points += 10;
    }
    return points;
  }

}
```

This class defines five instance variables. `deck` is a `RandomCardDeck` object that stores the deck of cards. `dealerHand` and `playerHand` are `Vector` objects that represent the dealer's cards and the player's cards, respectively. `dealerPoints` and `playerPoints` store the dealer's points and the player's points. There are also two class variable `char` constants, `HIT` and `STAND`. They are used as flags that are compared to user input in order to determine whether the user wants to hit or stand.

The constructor initializes the game for playing. The most notable thing in the game is where it calls the `isPictureCard()` method defined in the `Card` class. You do this so that you can set the value of all picture cards to 10. Also, it references the `Card.ACE` constant to find the Aces and set their initial values to 1.

The `main()` method creates a new `BlackJack` instance and calls the `play()` method in a `do-while` loop. It continues to call `play()` while the users enter Y to continue playing. Aside from the `main()` method, `play()` is the only other `public` method. In this implementation of the `BlackJack` game, it is not necessary to give everyone access to any other method. You allow instances to only call the `play()` method, which defines one hand of blackjack. If you decide to create a new version of the game, you can always subclass or redefine the `BlackJack` class itself.

The *play()* Method: *BlackJack* Driver

The `play()` method is the driver for the game. First it clears the dealer's and player's hands. Then it shuffles the deck if the number of remaining cards is running low (15 or fewer). It deals the cards by calling the `deal()` method, which basically deals the cards to the dealer (one face down and one face up) and the player (both cards visible). When it prints the cards, it calls the `output()` method, which builds a `String` representation of the hands. Note that when the `Vector`'s `elementAt()` method is called, the return value must be cast to a `Card` object in order to get its `String` representation:

```
p += (Card)playerHand.elementAt(c) + " ";
```

If after the cards are dealt, either the dealer or the player has blackjack, the hand is over; otherwise the player is prompted to hit or stand. The `getUserInput()` method prompts the users. It will accept only an H or an S and will continue to prompt the user until it gets one of those responses. This method throws an `IOException`, which is caught back in `play()`, where if it does occur, in order to end the hand gracefully, sets the user response to BlackJack.STAND, ending the player's turn. Once the player's turn is done, it moves on to the dealer. The dealer continues to hit until the dealer's hand is 17 or more, at which point a winner can be determined.

Other *BlackJack* Methods

There are some other methods in BlackJack that exist to make the implementation of the class easier. The hitPlayer() and hitDealer() are both protected methods. This allows any subclasses to call them. It is beneficial to have one method for hitting the player and another for hitting the dealer, so you can specify which hand will have a Card added to it without having to pass in a Vector representation of the hand. It is not a big deal, but would be possible to throw in any old Vector, giving the methods the capability to behave differently than they are intended to. Here, they should only be hitting the hands defined in this class. It is also true that hitting the dealer and player are similar operations, that's why there is a private hit() method that accepts a Vector argument and adds a Card to it. Being private, it is hidden from outside implementers and subclasses.

The dealerBlackJack() and playerBlackJack() methods return a Boolean value that indicates whether the dealer or player has blackjack. For the player's hand, this is straightforward. Does the player have two cards that add up to 21? If so then the player has blackjack. For the dealer, in this interpretation of the game, it is a bit different. The dealer can have two cards that add up to 21, but he has one card hidden. If the face-up card is an Ace, the dealer will show you right away if he has blackjack, but if he has blackjack, with the 10-card face up, he won't show you until its his turn. The guts of the method determine whether the card is hidden and handle these situations.

The updatePoints() method updates both the dealer's and the player's points by calling the private addUpPoints() method, which accepts a Vector argument, for both hands. The interesting things about this method are that first, it copies the Cards into a Card array from the Vector passed to it. Then it loops on this array, and adds up the points. An Ace can be either 1 or 11 points. This method calculates the points for Aces that bring the total points closest to 21 without going over.

Figure 5.13 shows the output of another session of the game, where the player plays multiple times.

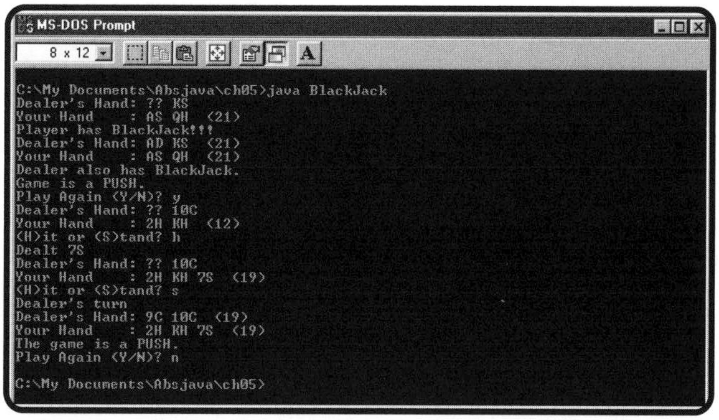

FIGURE 5.13

The player pushes a couple of games of BlackJack.

Summary

This chapter is arguably one of the most important chapters to understand. Java is an object-oriented programming language, and every Java program you write reflects this fact. In this chapter, you learned how to define a class. You learned about instance and class variables and methods. You also learned about the access modifiers public, protected, and private. You learned many other OOP concepts that you use in the rest of the book as well. In the next chapter, you move away from the text-based programs and learn about graphical user interface (GUI) programming.

CHALLENGES

1. Create a Holder class so that it maintains a list of objects, possibly represented by Strings, which you can add to or take from by using its methods. Hint: try overriding the Vector class.

2. Create a subclass of the Holder class. Use your imagination. Consider a Refrigerator class that holds food and keeps it cold, or a Wallet that holds money, perhaps. Try overriding methods defined in the Holder class. Try creating some overloaded methods as well.

3. Try adding more rules and functions to the BlackJack game. Create a subclass of BlackJack and for added fun, give the players some money and let them bet it on the game as a way of keeping score.

CHAPTER

Creating a GUI Using the Abstract Windowing Toolkit

This chapter breathes some new life into your Java programs. Up to this point, all your programs, aside from the simple applet in Chapter 1, have been command-prompt based. All input and output was completed through the command prompts using simple text. Java's *Abstract Windowing Toolkit* (*AWT*) package includes classes used to build a graphical interface for interacting with the users. A *Graphical User Interface* (*GUI*, pronounced "gooey") is the official term for this type of interface. In a GUI, graphics represent such components as text fields, buttons, menus, and so on, which the users interact with to pass information back and forth to the underlying program. In this chapter, you learn how to create a GUI using Java's AWT package, `java.awt`.

The Java AWT components covered in this chapter are:

- Frames
- Labels
- Buttons
- Text fields
- Text areas
- Check boxes
- Choices

- Lists
- Scroll bars
- Menus
- Canvases
- Panels
- Dialog boxes

The Project: *MadLib* Program

Are you familiar with the old pen and paper Mad-Lib games? Here is a description in case you're not. First, you are presented with requests for certain types of words such as nouns, verbs, adjectives, adverbs, and so on. Then you read a story that uses those words to form sentences that are usually pretty funny because they don't make much sense. They don't make much sense because the words are used out of context. Figure 6.1 shows a typical nonsensical example.

In this project, a dialog box opens first, prompting the users for some words using text fields, radio buttons, choices, a list, and a text area. Then once the users click the x to close the dialog box, another window opens and displays a story that uses the input given by the users. MadLib uses a GUI to interact with the users. Throughout the rest of this chapter, you learn all about the GUI components that make up the Java AWT. You can see the output for a typical session of the MadLib game in Figure 6.1.

The *java.awt* Package

Java's AWT package contains all the classes that are used for creating graphical user interfaces and for creating graphics and displaying images. It contains classes used for implementing GUI components such as labels, buttons, text fields, and so on. It also contains classes that are used for handling user-initiated

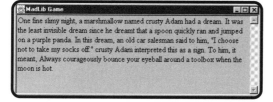

FIGURE 6.1

The users enter some words and the program generates a story in the MadLib game.

events; for example, when a user clicks a button or selects an item from a list. You can gain access to any of the java.awt package classes by importing them:

```
import java.awt.*;
```

This line imports (references, technically) any of the java.awt package classes used in your Java program, and no others. Basically, it just signifies where the classes can be found—in the java.awt package. Consult the API documentation for this package after you've learned the basics in this chapter for more detailed information.

Components

Components are the individual elements that collectively make up a graphical user interface. The Component class is the superclass for all the AWT components such as labels, buttons, text fields, and so on. Because all these components subclass the Component class, they all have a common set of methods. These methods are summarized in Table 6.1. Keep in mind throughout the rest of this chapter, as well in Chapters 7 and 8, that these methods are common for all java.awt components. They are used extensively throughout the rest of this book.

Java Programming for the Absolute Beginner

HINT

All the components defined in the java.awt package are called *heavyweight* components because they each have a native peer associated with them. This means that they are rendered using the underlying operating system's native API behind the scenes. Java is still platform-independent because the JRE makes references to the API associated with the operating system it is installed over without requiring any difference in Java source code or recompilation. You can create lightweight components that are not associated with a native peer by subclassing the Component class directly. Java also includes a package, called "Swing" (specifically, javax.swing) that defines lightweight components ready for you to use.

TABLE 6.1 SOME COMPONENT CLASS METHODS

Method	Description
getBackground()	Returns the background color for the Component.
getBounds()	Returns the bounds (x and y coordinates and width and height) of this Component as a Rectangle object.
getFont()	Returns the Font associated with the Component.
getForeground()	Returns a Color object that represents this Component's foreground color.
getHeight()	Returns an int that represents this Component's height in pixels.
getPreferredSize()	Returns a Dimension object that represents this object's optimal size.
getSize()	Returns a Dimension object that represents this object's current size.
getWidth()	Returns an int that represents this Component's width in pixels.
getX()	Returns an int that represents this Component's current position in pixels from the left side of the screen.
getY()	Returns an int that represents this Component's current position in pixels below the top of the screen.
boolean isEnabled()	Returns a boolean that indicates whether this Component is enabled.
boolean isFocusTraversable()	Returns a boolean that indicates whether this Component can be traversed using the Tab or Shift+Tab key operations.
boolean isLightWeight()	Returns whether this Component is lightweight. A Component is lightweight if it is not associated with a native peer.

TABLE 6.1   CONTINUED

Method	Description
paint(*Graphics*)	This method takes care of rendering the graphics that represent this Component's appearance.
repaint()	This method is called to repaint this Component's graphics after they are updated or moved.
setBackground(*Color*)	Sets this Component's background color to the given *Color* object.
setBounds(*Rectangle*)	Sets this Component's bounds (x and y coordinates and width and height) to the given *Rectangle* object's values.
setEnabled(*boolean*)	Sets whether this Component is enabled. Users can interact with it only if it's enabled.
setFont(*Font*)	Sets this Component's font to the specified *Font* object's values.
setLocation(*int*, *int*)	Sets this Component's location to the specified (*int, int*) coordinate.
setSize(*int*, *int*)	Sets this Component's size to the specified width and height.
setSize(*Dimension*)	Sets this Component's size to the specified *Dimension* object's width and height.
setVisible(*boolean*)	Shows this Component if the given parameter is true, or hides it if it is false.

Figure 6.2 shows the graphical representation of some of Java's AWT components, which are described here:

- Labels are used mainly for labeling other components or displaying a message for the user's benefit.
- The user interacts with Buttons to initiate some action.
- You use a TextField to accept some text input from the users.
- A Scrollbar defines a range of numerical values for the users to choose from.
- A Checkbox is either checked or unchecked and its associated label is used for describing what the state of the Checkbox signifies.
- You use the Canvas component mainly to display graphics in a confined area.

- The `Choice` component allows the users to choose one item out of a selection of items.

- The `List` component is similar to the `Choice` component, except it allows the users in some instances to choose more than one item from a list of items. It also allows the users to view multiple items at one time.

- The user interacts with the `TextArea` component to enter multiple lines of text, or you can use it to display longer messages to the users.

- The `Frame` component is also a `Container`, so it can hold other components. The `Frame` class is a top-level window including a border and a title bar. You work with these components as well as others not shown here throughout this chapter.

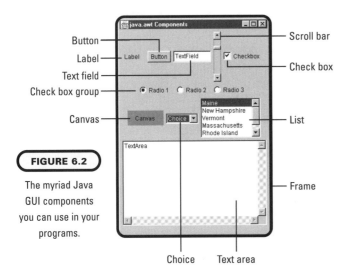

FIGURE 6.2

The myriad Java GUI components you can use in your programs.

IN THE REAL WORLD

In the real world GUIs are everywhere. You use them when interfacing with your operating system as well as when buying stuff on the Internet from e-commerce sites. An overlying GUI environment also makes it much easier to interface with a database via entries or queries. When GUIs are developed in Java, frequently developers will create their own packages and define their own unique look and feel. They will make reusable and extendable code that they can continue to build on. That is one of the benefits of an object-oriented GUI programming environment.

Events

Java's AWT events are defined within the java.awt.event package. Each component has associated events, themselves defined as Java classes, that users trigger by interacting with the components. You handle these events through interface classes known as *AWT event listener interfaces*. You explore this in more detail in Chapter 7, "Advanced GUI: Layout Managers and Event Handling," but you are exposed to it a bit in this chapter too. I had to at least explain how to handle a WindowEvent so that you don't have to write a bunch of GUI programs that won't exit when you try to close the window.

Basically, when the users interact with a GUI component, that component triggers an event. Any classes that "listen" to these events typically define a set of statements that handle the event. You make a class "listen" to these events by implementing an interface. An *interface* is an *abstract class* that predefines a set of methods. It is abstract because the methods themselves have no statements associated with them. The methods are simply predefined and must be overridden by a class that implements the interface.

Put differently, say there is an event that is triggered when the user attempts to close the window by clicking the little close button (an x) in the upper-right corner. There is an interface called WindowListener that declares a certain method to handle this, windowClosing(WindowEvent). If you want to create a class that listens to this event, you implement the WindowListener interface in your class. When you do this, you must define the windowClosing(WindowEvent) method within your class. Then when the user clicks the button, the method you defined in your class will be called to handle the event. Don't worry about it too much if you don't have a full grasp of this concept yet. You deal with event handling only a very little in this chapter and don't fully explore it until Chapter 7.

Graphics

The AWT also supports graphics programming. The Graphics class, defined in the java.awt package, has methods for drawing shapes, text, and images to the screen. It is responsible for rendering the actual graphics that make up all the AWT's GUI components. It draws the lines that make a button look raised when it is not clicked and pressed when it is clicked. You learn a bit about this aspect of Java's AWT in this chapter, and then learn even more advanced concepts in Chapter 7.

Using Frames

The Frame class is a GUI component that defines a top-level window. A Frame includes a border and a title bar. The Frame class extends the Window class, which is a top-level window without a border or title bar. The Window class subclasses the Container class, which is a component that can contain other components. Because Frame inherits from these other classes, it is itself a container able to hold other components. Table 6.2 summarizes some of the Frame class's methods. Remember also that Frame inherits from the Component class, so the methods shown in Table 6.1 are also present in the Frame class.

The *UselessFrame* Application

The UselessFrame class extends the Frame class and doesn't do much except set its size and display it. To write this application, first you must import the Frame class:

```
import java.awt.Frame;
```

Then you declare the UselessFrame class and indicate that it is a subclass of the Frame class:

```
public class UselessFrame extends Frame {
```

TABLE 6.2   SUMMARY OF FRAME METHODS

Method	Description
Frame()	Constructs a new Frame that is initially not visible.
Frame(*String*)	Constructs a new invisible Frame with the given *String* title.
Image getIconImage()	Returns this Frame's icon Image object.
MenuBar getMenuBar()	Returns this Frame's MenuBar.
String getTitle()	Returns this Frame's *String* title.
boolean isResizeable()	Returns a boolean that indicates whether this Frame can be resized by the users.
setIconImage(*Image*)	Sets the Frame's icon image to the given *Image* object.
setMenuBar(*MenuBar*)	Sets this Frame's menu bar to the given *MenuBar* object.
setResizeable(*boolean*)	Determines whether this Frame can be resized.
setTitle(*String*)	Sets this Frame's title to the given *String*.
setVisible(*boolean*)	Makes this Frame visible if the given parameter is true. If it is false, it makes the Frame invisible.

Frames are initially not visible and are automatically sized to their minimum size, which is quite small. So small, in fact, that you might not even notice them once they are displayed in the upper-left corner of your screen. The constructor takes care of creating a new UselessFrame with the title, Useless Frame, by calling its superclass's Frame(String) constructor. Then it sets the size to 300 pixels wide by 200 pixels high, by calling the setSize(300, 200) method defined in the Component class. Finally, the constructor shows the UselessFrame by calling setVisible(true). The main() method simply instantiates a new UselessFrame because the constructor takes care of the rest. The source code for Useless-Frame.java is listed here:

```
/*
 * UselessFrame
 * A Frame that does absolutely nothing aside from merely existing
 */

import java.awt.Frame;

public class UselessFrame extends Frame {

  public UselessFrame() {
    super("Useless Frame");
    setSize(300, 200);
    setVisible(true);
  }

  public static void main (String args[]) {
    UselessFrame uf = new UselessFrame();
  }

}
```

When you run this at the command prompt by typing **java UselessFrame**, a window will pop up with the title Useless Frame. You can see the window in Figure 6.3. I ran this from a Microsoft Windows 98 environment at a screen resolution of 800×600. Your window might look different if you ran it from a different operating system and/or screen resolution. The UselessFrame initially appears in the top-left corner of the computer screen, but I moved it by clicking the title bar and dragging it to a new location before I created the screen shot. When you run this you can go ahead and play around with it. Move it, minimize it, maximize it, deactivate it by clicking another window or on the desktop, reactivate it by clicking it, and so on. The one thing you can't do is close the window by clicking the x. That's because you haven't handled the window-closing event yet. You do this in the next section.

TRICK   When you create a window that won't close, or any Java program that hangs without any activity, try pressing Ctrl+C at the command prompt to stop the program from running if you are using a Windows environment. Another thing you can try is pressing Ctrl+Alt+Delete to end the task from the task manager. Be careful when using Ctrl+Alt+Del because after you press this combo once, pressing it again will cause your computer to reboot and you will lose any unsaved files.

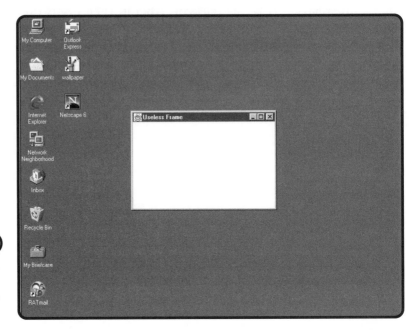

FIGURE 6.3

This is an example of a frame that does nothing other than display itself.

Learning about Containers

The Container class defines a Component that can contain other Components. The Container maintains a list of the Components it contains. You can add Components to it by calling its add(Component) method. Containers arrange their Components by using a layout manager. Layout managers are fully covered in Chapter 7, but in this chapter you do use the FlowLayout class, the simplest of the layout managers in this chapter to display multiple Components within a Frame.

Using the *WindowListener* Interface

The WindowListener interface handles WindowEvents. The UselessFrame window doesn't close when you click the close button because it does not implement the WindowListener interface. When you implement this abstract interface in your classes, you are required to define all the following methods:

```
public void windowClosing(WindowEvent)
public void windowActivated(WindowEvent)
public void windowClosed(WindowEvent)
public void windowIconified(WindowEvent)
```

```
public void windowDeiconified(WindowEvent)
public void windowDeactivated(WindowEvent)
public void windowOpened(WindowEvent)
```

These methods are defined in Chapter 7. In this chapter, you are only interested in the `windowClosing(WindowEvent)` method. This is what is called when the user clicks your window's close button to close it. They are all listed here because you have to define them in the `ComponentTestFrame` class because you want to be able to use the interface to actually close the window without having to manually intervene and halt your program.

The `ComponentTestFrame` class extends `Frame` and implements the `WindowListener` interface. How do you get it to do that? You just tell it the way it is:

```
public class ComponentTestFrame extends Frame implements WindowListener {
```

You use the `extends` word normally, followed by the superclass, `Frame`, and then you follow that with another keyword `implements` and the interface, `WindowListener`. As soon as you do this, you know that you have to define the methods shown previously. Take a look at the source code for `ComponentTestFrame.java` and then make sure you take the time to write it out and compile it. You need to use it throughout the rest of this chapter.

```
/*
 * ComponentTestFrame
 * A Simple Frame to use for testing components
 */

import java.awt.*;
import java.awt.event.*;

public class ComponentTestFrame extends Frame
                                 implements WindowListener {

  public ComponentTestFrame(String title) {
    super(title);
    setBackground(SystemColor.control);
    setSize(400, 300);
    setLocation(200, 150);
    setLayout(new FlowLayout());
    addWindowListener(this);
  }

  // the only WindowListener method I care about
  public void windowClosing(WindowEvent e) {
    dispose();
    System.exit(0);
  }

  // the rest of them that must be declared
  public void windowActivated(WindowEvent e) { }
  public void windowClosed(WindowEvent e) { }
```

```
public void windowIconified(WindowEvent e) { }
public void windowDeiconified(WindowEvent e) { }
public void windowDeactivated(WindowEvent e) { }
public void windowOpened(WindowEvent e) { }

}
```

The only method you care about here is the `windowClosing(WindowEvent)` method, so that's the only one you need to add statements to. You add two statements to the body of this method that take care of closing the window and exiting the program. `dispose()` releases the native resources owned by the `Frame` and those of its components as well (closes and disposes of the window's resources). The `System.exit(0)` statement terminates the program itself. The rest of the `WindowListener` methods are there only because you have to define them. In this case, you don't add any statements in the methods, so they don't actually do anything.

TRICK The `WindowListener` interface is defined within the `java.awt.event` package, so you need to import that package. It also defines the `WindowEvent` class. When you import a package using the asterisk character *, it indicates that only those classes that are referenced within the program should be imported. Actually, nothing is imported into the object code; remember that the `import` statement just indicates where to find the classes you're using.

This `ComponentTestFrame` component performs some other operations of interest as well. It sets its background color to `SystemColor.control`, which is the background color currently set for your operating system's control objects, such as windows, dialog boxes, buttons, and so on. This color is not the default color for `Frames`; however, so you need to set it explicitly if you want it to have that particular background color. It also sets its location to the (x, y) pixel coordinates (200, 150) and sets its layout to `FlowLayout`. Basically, this layout manager lays its `Components` out in a center-aligned row (by default) until there is no more room, and then wraps around to the next row and continues to do this until there are no more `Components` to align.

Using Components

In this section, you test the AWT `Components` by adding them to a `ComponentTestFrame` instance of the class you defined in the previous section. Because the layout is already set to `FlowLayout`, you create the `Components` and then add them to the `ComponentTestFrame`, using the `add(Component)` method. You learn about the different specifics of these `Components` by creating multiple instances of the same `Component` using different states. You then call different methods and compare their appearances and behaviors.

The *Label* Component

A Label contains read-only text that you display within a container. Like all other Components, you can change its background and foreground colors. You can also set the alignment of text within the Label's area. Table 6.3 shows some of the more common fields and methods of the Label class.

In the LabelTest program, you use the ComponentTestFrame to display four different Labels. You create the l1 object by using the Label(String) constructor, which builds a Label with the given String that is left aligned by default. The l2 label demonstrates that the font can be changed using the setFont(Font) method. You use the Label() constructor with no arguments to construct the l3 Label, and then set the text using the setText(String) method and also call setEnabled(false) to disable the Label. As you can see in Figure 6.4, the graphics for a disabled Label are grayed out. The l4 Label's foreground color is set to green and the background color is set to black. Its text is right-aligned because the constructor was called using Label.RIGHT.

Next, you create the ComponentTestFrame. Because that class itself does most of its own work, you only need to create a ComponentTestFrame object, frame, by passing a String title to its constructor. After you do that, you can add the Label components you created earlier by calling frame.add(Component) and passing the label as its Component parameter. Next, you call frame.setVisible(true) to show

TABLE 6.3 FIELDS AND METHODS OF THE LABEL COMPONENT

Field or Method	Description
static int CENTER	Indicates the Label should be center-aligned.
static int LEFT	Indicates the Label should be left-aligned.
static int RIGHT	Indicates the Label should be right-aligned.
Label()	Constructs a blank Label.
Label(*String*)	Constructs a Label with the given *String* text.
Label(*String, int*)	Constructs a Label with the given *String* text and *int* alignment.
int getAlignment()	Returns an int representation of this Label's alignment.
String getText()	Returns the String object that holds this Label's text.
setAlignment(*int*)	Sets the alignment of this object to the given *int*.
setText(*String*)	Sets the text of this Label to the given *String*.

the window and that's all you need to do. The window-closing event is already handled in the ComponentTestFrame class itself, so you don't have to worry about that here. Notice that if you resize the window, the Labels can be realigned. If you maximize the window, they will all form one row, but if you make the window narrow, the labels will all line up in one column. That fact further emphasizes how the FlowLayout layout manager works. Here is a listing of the source code:

```
/*
 * LabelTest
 * Tests the Label Component
 */

import java.awt.*;

public class LabelTest {

   public LabelTest() {
      //Make the Labels
      Label l1 = new Label("Label");
      Label l2 = new Label("I am a Label");
      l2.setFont(new Font("Timesroman", Font.BOLD, 18));
      Label l3 = new Label();
      l3.setText("I am disabled");
      l3.setEnabled(false);
      Label l4 = new Label("Colored, Right aligned", Label.RIGHT);
      l4.setForeground(Color.green);
      l4.setBackground(Color.black);

      //Make the Frame and add the labels to it
      ComponentTestFrame frame = new ComponentTestFrame("Label Test");
      frame.add(l1);
      frame.add(l2);
      frame.add(l3);
      frame.add(l4);
      frame.setVisible(true);
   }

   public static void main(String args[]) {
      LabelTest lt = new LabelTest();
   }
}
```

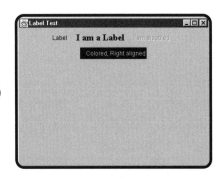

FIGURE 6.4

Four Labels are
displayed in the
Component-
TestFrame.

The `Font` and `Color` classes of the `java.awt` package are used here to change the font and color associated with the `Labels`. They are used throughout this chapter to emphasize the flexibility you have in changing the appearance of `Compo-nents`. The `Font` class defines a font face associated with a `Component` that is present on the system. In this chapter, you use the `Font(String, int, int)` constructor to build a `Font`. The first argument is the name of the `Font`, and the second argument is the style of the `Font`, which can be `Font.PLAIN`, `Font.BOLD`, `Font.ITALIC`, or `Font.BOLD + Font.ITALIC`. The third argument is the point size for the `Font`. In this chapter you also use `Color` constants to specify colors for your `Components`. Some of these constants are `Color.black`, `Color.blue`, `Color.cyan`, `Color.red`, and `Color.yellow`. The `Font` class and the `Color` class are revisited in Chapter 7 when you learn about graphics programming.

The *Button* Component

The `Button` class defines a labeled button. `Buttons` typically trigger some action when the user clicks them. There are two constructors. One accepts no arguments and just creates an empty `Button`. You can set its `label` later on using the `setLa-bel(String)` method. The other constructor accepts a `String` argument specified to be its `label`. Table 6.4 shows some of the other common `Button` methods.

In the `ButtonTest` program, you create four `Button` objects to get a feel for how to create and use the `Button` component. You construct b1 with the `Button(String)` constructor to set its label to "Button". You call the `Button()` constructor to instantiate the b2 `Button` object, creating an empty `Button`. Then you call two of its methods to set the label and change the font:

```
b2.setLabel("Press me!");
b2.setFont(new Font("Timesroman", Font.BOLD, 18));
```

TABLE 6.4   BUTTON METHODS

Method	Description
`Button()`	Constructs a `Button` with no text label.
`Button(String)`	Constructs a `Button` with the given *String* text label.
`addActionListener(ActionListener)`	Adds an *ActionListener* to this `Button`.
`String getLabel()`	Returns the `String` label of this `Button`.
`setLabel()`	Sets this `Button`'s label to the given `String`.
`removeActionListener(ActionListener)`	Removes the specified *ActionListener* from this `Button`.

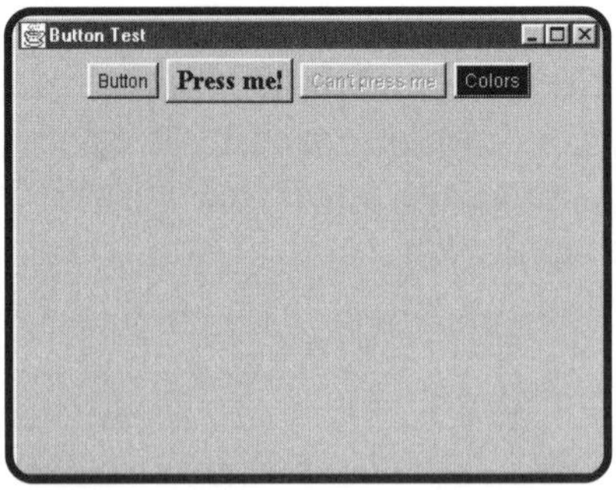

FIGURE 6.5

This is a test of the
Button
component.

When looking at Figure 6.5 from left to right, you can see that the font of the second Button is bigger, bold, and Times Roman. (The first Button is a standard one added for comparison.) You can also see that the third Button, b3 (called "Can't press me"), is not enabled. The label is grayed out and when you actually run this, you can see that you cannot click it. Disabling a Component has a visual and functional effect. Its appearance is altered and the users cannot interact with it. The fourth Button, b4 (called "Colors"), has a different appearance than the other buttons because you set its background color and foreground colors differently by calling its setBackground(Color) and setForeground(Color) methods. Here is a listing of ButtonTest.java.

```
/*
 * ButtonTest
 * Demonstrates the Button Component
 */

import java.awt.*;

public class ButtonTest {

  public ButtonTest() {
    //Make the Buttons
    Button b1 = new Button("Button");
    Button b2 = new Button();
    b2.setLabel("Press me!");
    b2.setFont(new Font("Timesroman", Font.BOLD, 18));
    Button b3 = new Button("Can't press me");
    b3.setEnabled(false);
    Button b4 = new Button("Colors");
    b4.setForeground(Color.green);
    b4.setBackground(Color.black);

    //Make the Frame and add the buttons to it
    ComponentTestFrame frame = new ComponentTestFrame("Button Test");
    frame.add(b1);
    frame.add(b2);
    frame.add(b3);
    frame.add(b4);
```

```
      frame.setVisible(true);
   }

   public static void main(String args[]) {
      ButtonTest bt = new ButtonTest();
   }

}
```

When you run the ButtonTest application, try traversing the buttons using Tab and Shift+Tab. You can see the appearance of the Button currently in focus is different and stands out as the one that has user input focus. A Component is said to have *focus* when it is immediately ready to accept user input. For instance, while traversing through the Buttons, press the spacebar. The Button that currently has focus will be clicked. Also take note that the disabled Button never receives user input focus.

The *TextField* Component

There are two text components in the AWT. They subclass the TextComponent superclass. Table 6.5 shows some of the TextComponent methods inherited by

TABLE 6.5 TEXTCOMPONENT METHODS

Method	Description
int getCaretPosition()	Returns the caret position of this TextComponent.
String getSelectedText()	Returns the selected (highlighted) text in this TextComponent.
int getSelectionStart()	Returns the position in this TextComponent where the selected text begins.
int getSelectionEnd()	Returns the position in this TextComponent where the selected text ends.
String getText()	Returns the String that represents the full text of this TextComponent.
select(*int*, *int*)	Causes the text between the first and the second argument positions to become selected.
setCaretPosition(*int*)	Sets the position of the caret (the blinking cursor where text is inserted).
setEditable(*boolean*)	Sets whether the users can edit the text within this TextComponent.
setSelectionStart(*int*)	Sets the beginning index of the selected text.
setSelectionEnd(*int*)	Sets the ending index of the selected text.
setText(*String*)	Sets this TextComponent's text to the given *String*.

both TextField and TextArea. The TextField class defines a text component that gives the users the capability to enter and edit a single line of text, whereas the TextArea class allows users to enter and edit multiple lines of text.

The TextField component has four constructors. These four constructors offer different options for instantiating a TextField object centering around two of its properties—its initial text and the number of columns wide it is. The number of columns is a somewhat vague concept. One column is an approximation of the average character width and is system dependent. The TextField will actually be able to fit varying numbers of characters (with proportional fonts) in its visible area. Table 6.6 shows this class's constructors as well as some of its other methods.

The TextFieldTest application uses a bunch of TextFields to demonstrate the versatility of the class. The source code for this application is listed here.

TABLE 6.6 TEXTFIELD METHODS

Method	Description
TextField()	Constructs a new TextField with no text and with the default number of columns.
TextField(int)	Constructs a new TextField with no text and the given number of columns.
TextField(String)	Constructs a new TextField with the specified String text.
TextField(String, int)	Constructs a new TextField with the specified String text and the given number of columns.
addActionListener(ActionListener)	Adds an ActionListener that will be listed for this TextField's ActionEvents.
boolean echoCharIsSet()	Returns a boolean value that indicates whether this TextField has an echo character set.
removeActionListener()	Removes the specified ActionListener from this TextField.
setColumns()	Sets this TextField's number of columns.
setEchoChar(char)	Sets the echo character for this TextField. An echo character is a character that is displayed in place of the actual characters that are typed. For example, a password field might use an asterisk as the echo character, so when a user types a password, the field will only display ********.
setText(String)	Sets this TextField's text.

```
/*
 * TextFieldTest
 * Demonstrates the TextField Component
 */

import java.awt.*;

public class TextFieldTest {

  public TextFieldTest() {
    //Make the TextFields
    TextField tf1 = new TextField();
    TextField tf2 = new TextField(25);
    tf2.setText("Type stuff here");
    tf2.setFont(new Font("Timesroman", Font.BOLD, 18));
    TextField tf3 = new TextField("I am disabled", 15);
    tf3.setEnabled(false);
    TextField tf4 = new TextField("Colors");
    tf4.setForeground(Color.green);
    tf4.setBackground(Color.black);
    TextField tf5 = new TextField("Not editable");
    tf5.setEditable(false);
    TextField tf6 = new TextField("I am selected text!!!");
    tf6.select(5, 13);
    TextField tf7 = new TextField("Caret Here -->><--");
    TextField tf8 = new TextField("username", 8);
    TextField tf9 = new TextField("password",8);
    tf9.setEchoChar('*');

    //Make the Frame and add the TextFields to it
    ComponentTestFrame frame = new ComponentTestFrame("TextField Test");
    frame.add(tf1);
    frame.add(tf2);
    frame.add(tf3);
    frame.add(tf4);
    frame.add(tf5);
    frame.add(tf6);
    frame.add(tf7);
    frame.add(tf8);
    frame.add(tf9);
    frame.setVisible(true);
    tf7.setCaretPosition(14);
  }

  public static void main(String args[]) {
    TextFieldTest tft = new TextFieldTest();
  }

}
```

Wondering what you do with the TextField objects in this application? Well, the t1 object is as simple as a TextField can get. The TextField() constructor is called and you don't call any other of its methods to alter its state. Figure 6.6

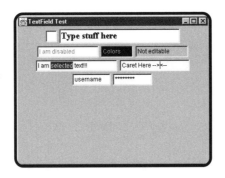

FIGURE 6.6

This shows different implementations of the TextField component.

shows that when a TextField is constructed this way, it appears as a tiny little TextField with no initial text. You can enter some text in it. You construct the tf2 object with 25 columns, and set its text after it is constructed by calling tf2.setText("Type stuff here"). You also change its font. You play around with tf4's colors, by setting its background to black and its foreground to green. You don't allow the user to edit the text in the tf5 TextField by calling tf5.setEditable(false). When a TextField is not editable, it is still traversable and you can copy its text to the Clipboard, but you cannot edit the text itself. You might want to create a TextField that is not editable if you want to use it to display information that might change, but the user should not be the one who's changing it. For example, if you wrote a clock program that displays the current time, which is updated every second, you could display it in a non-editable field. This program demonstrates how you can cause a TextField's text to be selected.

```
TextField tf6 = new TextField("I am selected text!!!");
tf6.select(5, 13);
```

This causes the word selected in tf6's text, "I am selected text!!!" to become selected because the letter s is at index 5, the first argument in the select(int, int) method and the second argument, 13, indicates the index after the d character. The length of any String that is selected by this method is equal to the second argument minus the first argument. After that, you create three more TextFields: tf7, tf8, and tf9. The interesting thing about tf7 is that you set the caret position. The caret is just the cursor that indicates the insertion location for when you are entering text. You set the caret position to 14, which puts it right between the arrows.

TRICK

For TextField tf9 of the TextFieldTest application, you call the setEchoChar(char) method. What this does is display the given character in place of all the characters in the TextField. You can use this to hide the actual value of the TextArea, which is useful when a user is entering a password and doesn't want anyone to see it on the screen.

The *TextArea* Component

The TextArea component is similar to the TextField component except that it allows editing of multiple lines of text. A TextField has a certain number of rows and columns that determines its size. It also can have scroll bars associated with it. Table 6.7 lists the fields and some methods of the TextArea class.

TABLE 6.7 TextArea Fields and Methods

Field or Method	Description
SCROLLBARS_NONE	Indicates that this TextArea should not use any scroll bars.
SCROLLBARS_VERTICAL_ONLY	Indicates that this TextArea should use only a vertical scroll bar.
SCROLLBARS_HORIZONTAL_ONLY	Indicates that this TextArea should use only a horizontal scroll bar.
SCROLLBARS_BOTH	Indicates that this TextArea should use both a horizontal and a vertical scroll bar.
TextArea()	Constructs a new, empty TextArea.
TextArea(*String*)	Constructs a new TextArea with the given *String* text.
TextArea(*int, int*)	Constructs a new TextArea with the given rows and columns.
TextArea(*String, int, int*)	Constructs a new TextArea with the given *String* text and the specified number of rows and columns.
TextArea(*String, int, int, int*)	Constructs a new TextArea with the given *String* text, the specified number of rows and columns as the second and third arguments and the *int* representation, such as SCROLLBARS_BOTH, of how the scroll bars are displayed.
append(*String*)	Appends the given *String* to the end of this TextArea's text.
int getColumns()	Returns the number of columns.
int getRows()	Returns the number of rows.
insert(*String, int*)	Inserts the given *String* at the specified text index.
replaceRange(*String, int, int*)	Replaces the currently existing text starting with the second argument beginning index and ending with the third argument ending index with the specified *String* argument.
setColumns(*int*)	Sets the number of columns.
setRows(*int*)	Sets the number of rows.

The `TextAreaTest` application is pretty straightforward. You create four `TextArea` objects and display them in the `ComponentTestFrame`. The first one on the left, `ta1`, is constructed with no text, 10 rows, and 20 columns. You can see in Figure 6.7 that the default for the scroll bars is `TextArea.SCROLLBARS_BOTH`, because both the horizontal and vertical scroll bars appear in this `TextArea`. The middle `TextArea`, `ta2`, changes its background and foreground colors and specifies its scroll bars as `TextArea.SCROLLBARS_NONE`. You can see that no scroll bars appear. The behavior of this `TextArea` is different as a result. In `ta1`, while you're typing, if your line becomes longer than the displayable width, the horizontal scroll bar will start to react to indicate this. You are allowed to continue typing on one single line. However, in `ta2`, if you attempt to type past the visible number of columns, the text will automatically be wrapped and no scrolling takes place.

One more thing to note is that when the text for `ta2` is initialized, a newline character \n is used. As you might expect, the `TextArea` correctly interprets it and the initial text becomes two lines long. As for the other two, `ta3` (on the right) is not editable, but it can gain focus and you can select its text, and `ta4` (on the bottom) is not enabled. It can't have focus, and the text is a bit grayed out to indicate this.

```
/*
 * TextAreaTest
 * Demonstrates the TextArea Component
 */

import java.awt.*;

public class TextAreaTest {

  public TextAreaTest() {
    //Make the TextAreas
    TextArea ta1 = new TextArea("", 10, 20);
    TextArea ta2 = new TextArea("TextArea\nText", 10, 10,
      TextArea.SCROLLBARS_NONE);
    ta2.setFont(new Font("Verdana", Font.ITALIC, 12));
    ta2.setForeground(Color.yellow);
    ta2.setBackground(Color.black);
    TextArea ta3 = new TextArea("This TextArea is not editable",
      10, 15, TextArea.SCROLLBARS_HORIZONTAL_ONLY);
    ta3.setEditable(false);
    TextArea ta4 = new TextArea("This TextArea is not enabled",
      4, 25, TextArea.SCROLLBARS_VERTICAL_ONLY);
    ta4.setEnabled(false);

    //Make the Frame and add the TextAreas to it
    ComponentTestFrame frame = new ComponentTestFrame("TextArea Test");
    frame.add(ta1);
    frame.add(ta2);
    frame.add(ta3);
    frame.add(ta4);
    frame.setVisible(true);
  }
```

```
public static void main(String args[]) {
  TextAreaTest tat = new TextAreaTest();
}
}
```

Here are four
TextArea
components.

The *Choice* Component

The Choice component allows the users to choose one item from a list of items. It is implemented as a drop-down menu. Initially, it is visibly about the size of a TextField, but when a user is selecting an item, a drop-down (also called pop-up) menu opens and the user selects the item from the list of items that appear within it. Once the user has selected an item, the Choice "shrinks" again; actually, the menu disappears, and the selected item will be the one visible item in the Choice. A Choice is used first by calling its only constructor, which accepts no arguments. Then you add items to it:

```
Choice myChoice = new Choice();
myChoice.add("Work");
myChoice.add("Play");
myChoice.add("Sleep");
```

This snippet of code constructs a Choice, called myChoice, and then adds three items to it, Work, Play, and Sleep. From a user standpoint, this is a choice between Work, Play, and Sleep. Note that you cannot pick more than one of these at a time—they are mutually exclusive. No contest, right—"Sleep". Table 6.8 lists some of Choice's more common methods.

The ChoiceTest application creates four Choice objects, c1, c2, c3, and c4. There is nothing out of the ordinary here except c3 shows that you can change its colors and c4 is not enabled. Figure 6.8 shows the output. Here is a listing of the ChoiceTest application source code, ChoiceTest.java.

```
/*
 * ChoiceTest
 * Demonstrates the Choice Component
 */
```

TABLE 6.8 CHOICE METHODS

Method	Description
Choice()	Constructs a new Choice object.
add(*String*)	Adds a new item to this Choice.
addItem(*String*)	Adds a new item to this Choice.
addItemListener(*ItemListener*)	Adds an ItemListener to this Choice.
String getItem(*int*)	Returns the item at the specified index.
int getItemCount()	Returns the number of items in this Choice.
int getSelectedIndex()	Returns the index of the currently selected item.
insert(*String*, *int*)	Inserts a *String* at the specified index.
remove(*int*)	Removes the item at the specified index.
remove(*String*)	Removes the first occurrence of the specified item.
removeAll()	Removes all the items from this Choice.
removeItemListener(*ItemListener*)	Removes the ItemListener from this Choice.
select(*int*)	Causes the item at the specified index to be selected.
select(*String*)	Causes the first occurrence of the specified item to be selected.

```
import java.awt.*;

public class ChoiceTest {

  public ChoiceTest() {
    //Make the Choices
    Choice c1 = new Choice();
    c1.add("Soup");
    c1.add("Salad");
    Choice c2 = new Choice();
    c2.add("Java");
    c2.add("C++");
    c2.add("HTML");
    c2.add("JavaScript");
    c2.add("COBOL");
    c2.add("FORTRAN");
    Choice c3 = new Choice();
    c3.add("One");
    c3.add("Two");
    c3.add("Three");
    c3.setForeground(Color.red);
    c3.setBackground(Color.black);
```

```
    c3.setFont(new Font("Courier", Font.PLAIN, 16));
    Choice c4 = new Choice();
    c4.add("Not Enabled");
    c4.add("Nope");
    c4.setEnabled(false);

    //Make the Frame and add the Choices to it
    ComponentTestFrame frame = new ComponentTestFrame("Choice Test");
    frame.add(c1);
    frame.add(c2);
    frame.add(c3);
    frame.add(c4);
    frame.setVisible(true);
  }

  public static void main(String args[]) {
    ChoiceTest ct = new ChoiceTest();
  }
}
```

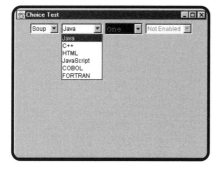

FIGURE 6.8

You use the Choice component to pick one item out of many.

The *List* Component

The List component is similar to the Choice component, except it shows multiple rows at a time and allows the users to scroll through the items. You typically use Lists over Choices when there are a significantly large number of items to choose from. Another difference is that you can set up a List component so that the users can select multiple items simultaneously. Similar to the Choice component, the List component is used by first constructing one, and then adding items to it:

```
List myList = new List(3, true);
myList.add("Milk");
myList.add("Eggs");
myList.add("Bread");
```

The myList component has three rows (specified in the call to the constructor) and three items to choose from. One is listed per row, so all three are visible. The second argument, true, indicates that multiple items can be selected simultaneously. The user can select from "Milk", "Eggs", and "Bread". All of them can be selected, or none of them. Also one or two can be selected as well. Table 6.9 shows some of the more important methods that belong to the List class.

Four List objects are created in the ListTest application. l1 (upper-left) is constructed using the no-parameter constructor and two items are added to it. All the items fit within its visible area, so the scroll bar is not displayed. Also the default multiple mode is false, so only one item can be selected at a time. The l2 (upper-right) object sets its multiple mode to true, so you can select more than one item at a time. The l3 (lower-left) object demonstrates that you can change its colors and fonts and also that when there are too many items for the List to display all at once, the scroll bar is used to scroll through them. The l4 (lower-right) object is not enabled, so you cannot select or deselect any of the items. Using the select(int) method, it selects the second item (because the index starts at zero), Nope. When you run this procedure, you will be unable to deselect it or select the other item. Here is the source code for ListTest.java. The execution of this program appears in Figure 6.9.

```
/*
 * ListTest
 * Demonstrates the List Component
 */

import java.awt.*;

public class ListTest {

    public ListTest() {
        //Make the Lists
        List l1 = new List();
        l1.add("Soup");
        l1.add("Salad");
        List l2 = new List(6, true);
        l2.add("Java");
        l2.add("C++");
        l2.add("HTML");
        l2.add("JavaScript");
        l2.add("COBOL");
        l2.add("FORTRAN");
        List l3 = new List(5, false);
        l3.add("One");
        l3.add("Two");
        l3.add("Three");
        l3.add("Four");
        l3.add("Five");
        l3.add("Six");
        l3.add("Seven");
        l3.add("Eight");
        l3.add("Nine");
        l3.add("Ten");
```

TABLE 6.9 LIST METHODS

Method	Description
List()	Constructs a new List object.
List(*int*)	Constructs a new List object with the specified number of visible rows.
List(*int*, *boolean*)	Constructs a new List object with the specified number of visible rows and a *boolean* that indicates whether this List allows multiple selections.
add(*String*)	Adds the specified item to this List.
add(*String*, *int*)	Adds the specified item to this List at the given index.
addActionListener(*ActionListener*)	Adds the given ActionListener to this List.
addItemListener(*ItemListener*)	Adds the given ItemListener to this List.
deselect(*int*)	Deselects the item at the given index.
String getItem(*int*)	Returns the String item at the given index.
String[] getItems()	Returns all the items as an array of Strings.
int getItemCount()	Returns the number of items in this List.
int getRows()	Returns the number of visible rows.
int getSelectedIndex()	Returns the index of the currently selected item. If either none or more than one item is selected, this method returns -1.
int[] getSelectedIndexes()	Returns an array of integers that represent all this List's selected item indices.
String getSelectedItem()	Returns the String item that is currently selected or null.
String[] getSelectedItems()	Returns all this List's selected items as an array of Strings.
boolean isMultipleMode()	Returns whether this List can have multiple selections.
remove(*int*)	Removes the item at the given index.
remove(*String*)	Removes the first occurrence of the given item.
removeAll()	Removes all the items from this List.
removeActionListener(*ActionListener*)	Removes the specified *ActionListener* from this List.
removeItemListener(*ItemListener*)	Removes the specified *ItemListener* from this List.
select(*int*)	Selects the specified item within this List.
setMultipleMode(*boolean*)	Sets whether this List can have multiple selections.

```
13.select(9);
13.setForeground(Color.red);
13.setBackground(Color.black);
13.setFont(new Font("Courier", Font.PLAIN, 16));
List 14 = new List();
14.add("Not Enabled");
14.add("Nope");
14.select(1);
14.setEnabled(false);

//Make the Frame and add the Lists to it
ComponentTestFrame frame = new ComponentTestFrame("List Test");
frame.add(l1);
frame.add(l2);
frame.add(l3);
frame.add(l4);
frame.setVisible(true);
}

public static void main(String args[]) {
    ListTest lt = new ListTest();
}

}
```

FIGURE 6.9

The List
component allows
the users to choose
only one, or more
than one, item,
depending on how
you set it up.

The *Checkbox* Component

Checkbox is a fairly simple component that defines one item that can be either checked or unchecked (true or false). It has a text label used to identify it. The Checkbox class has constructors that allow you to specify its label, its state (true or false), and the CheckboxGroup it belongs to. Table 6.10 shows some of the Checkbox class's methods.

The CheckboxTest application creates some Checkbox objects. Figure 6.10 shows the output. You can select or deselect any one of these objects except for the two disabled ones (Garlic and Sugar). Note that you can also select more than one of them simultaneously. Each time the user clicks a Checkbox, its state reverses from true to false, or from false to true.

TABLE 6.10   CHECKBOX METHODS

Method	Description
Checkbox()	Constructs a new Checkbox object.
Checkbox(*String*)	Constructs a new Checkbox object with the given *String* label.
Checkbox(*String, boolean*)	Constructs a new Checkbox with the given *String* label and the given state (true if it is initially checked, or false if it is not).
Checkbox(*String, boolean, CheckboxGroup*)	Constructs a new Checkbox with the given *String* label and the given state (true if it is initially checked, or false if it is not). It is specified as a member of the given *CheckboxGroup*.
Checkbox(*String, CheckboxGroup, boolean*)	Constructs a new Checkbox with the given *String* label and the given state (true if it is initially checked, or false if it is not). It is specified as a member of the given *CheckboxGroup*.
addItemListener(*ItemListener*)	Adds the given *ItemListener*.
CheckboxGroup getCheckboxGroup()	Returns this Checkbox's CheckboxGroup or null if it is not part of a CheckboxGroup.
String getLabel()	Returns the label associated with this Checkbox.
boolean getState()	Returns whether this Checkbox is checked.
removeItemListener(*ItemListener*)	Removes the specified *ItemListener*.
setCheckboxGroup(*CheckboxGroup*)	Sets this Checkbox's *CheckboxGroup*.
setLabel(*String*)	Sets this Checkbox's label.
setState(*boolean*)	Sets whether this Checkbox is checked.

```
/*
 * CheckboxTest
 * Demonstrates the Checkbox Component
 */

import java.awt.*;

public class CheckboxTest {

  public CheckboxTest() {
    //Make the Checkboxes
    Checkbox cb1 = new Checkbox("Peppers");
    Checkbox cb2 = new Checkbox("Onions");
```

```
            Checkbox cb3 = new Checkbox("Celery");
            Checkbox cb4 = new Checkbox("Garlic", true);
            cb4.setEnabled(false);
            Checkbox cb5 = new Checkbox("Tomatoes");
            Checkbox cb6 = new Checkbox("Salt", true);
            Checkbox cb7 = new Checkbox("Pepper", false);
            Checkbox cb8 = new Checkbox();
            cb8.setLabel("Sugar");
            cb8.setState(false);
            cb8.setEnabled(false);

            //Make the Frame and add the Checkboxes to it
            ComponentTestFrame frame = new ComponentTestFrame("Checkbox Test");
            frame.add(cb1);
            frame.add(cb2);
            frame.add(cb3);
            frame.add(cb4);
            frame.add(cb5);
            frame.add(cb6);
            frame.add(cb7);
            frame.add(cb8);
            frame.setVisible(true);
        }

    public static void main(String args[]) {
        CheckboxTest cbt = new CheckboxTest();
    }
}
```

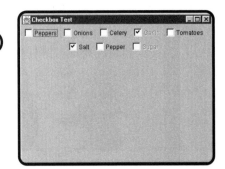

FIGURE 6.10

These Checkbox components are either checked or unchecked. More than one box can be checked at a time.

Using the *CheckboxGroup* Class

The CheckboxGroup class is used to group Checkbox objects together in such a way that only one of them can be selected at any given time. Simply specifying multiple Checkboxes as belonging to one CheckboxGroup does this:

```
CheckboxGroup group = new CheckboxGroup();
Checkbox cb1 = new Checkbox("One", true, group);
Checkbox cb2 = new Checkbox("Two", false, group);
Checkbox cb3 = new Checkbox("Three", false, group);
```

This code creates three Checkboxes that are all part of the same CheckboxGroup. Only one of them can be checked at any one time. cb1 is initially checked because of its second argument being true. Checking any of the other two will cause cb1 to become unchecked. The CheckboxGroup class defines methods used for setting and getting the selected Checkbox: Checkbox getSelectedCheckbox(), which returns the Checkbox in the group that is currently checked, and setSelected-Checkbox(Checkbox), which checks the given Checkbox.

 HINT   Checkboxes in a CheckboxGroup **are also sometimes called** *radio buttons*.

The CheckboxGroupTest application adds all its Checkboxes to the same Checkbox-Group. When you run it, notice that only one of them can be checked at any given time. The output is shown in Figure 6.11. Here is a listing of the source code:

```
/*
 * CheckboxGroupTest
 * Demonstrates the CheckboxGroup Class
 */

import java.awt.*;

public class CheckboxGroupTest {

  public CheckboxGroupTest() {
    //Make the CheckboxGroup
    CheckboxGroup cbg = new CheckboxGroup();
    Checkbox cb1 = new Checkbox("Red", false, cbg);
    Checkbox cb2 = new Checkbox("Green", false, cbg);
    Checkbox cb3 = new Checkbox("Blue", false, cbg);
    Checkbox cb4 = new Checkbox("Yellow", true, cbg);
    cb4.setEnabled(false);
    Checkbox cb5 = new Checkbox("Orange", false, cbg);
    Checkbox cb6 = new Checkbox("Purple", false, cbg);
    Checkbox cb7 = new Checkbox("Cyan", false, cbg);
    Checkbox cb8 = new Checkbox("Magenta", false, cbg);

    //Make the Frame and add the Checkboxes to it
    ComponentTestFrame frame = new ComponentTestFrame("CheckboxGroup Test");
    frame.add(cb1);
    frame.add(cb2);
    frame.add(cb3);
    frame.add(cb4);
    frame.add(cb5);
    frame.add(cb6);
    frame.add(cb7);
    frame.add(cb8);
    frame.setVisible(true);
  }
```

```
public static void main(String args[]) {
   CheckboxGroupTest cbgt = new CheckboxGroupTest();
}

}
```

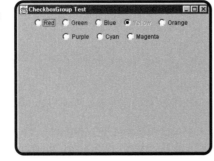

FIGURE 6.11

The
`CheckboxGroup`
class groups
`Checkbox`
components
together so that
only one can be
checked at a time.

The *Canvas* Component

A `Canvas` is a blank rectangular area primarily used for displaying graphics or for capturing user events. The `CanvasTest` application creates four `Canvas` objects and displays them in the frame. One important thing to note is that `CanvasTest` extends `Canvas`. It overrides its `paint(Graphics)` method, which is inherited from the `Component` class, so all other components have it too. It is responsible for rendering the component's graphics and drawing them on-screen. Although this is not covered in detail until the next chapter, I included a bit of it here because the `Canvas` component is not very useful without displaying some kind of graphical representation. Remember your first applet way back in Chapter 1? You used the `drawString(String, int, int)` method there too. This program simply creates the `Canvas`es, changes their colors, and displays them in the frame. Canvases are typically used in GUI interfaces to display an image, or some other graphic, such as a corporate logo, within a frame. The output is shown in Figure 6.12. Here is the source code:

```
/*
 * CanvasTest
 * Demonstrates the Canvas Component
 */

import java.awt.*;

public class CanvasTest extends Canvas {

   public static void main(String args[]) {
      //Make the Canvas
      CanvasTest c1 = new CanvasTest();
      c1.setSize(100, 100);
```

```
        CanvasTest c2 = new CanvasTest();
        c2.setSize(100, 100);
        c2.setBackground(Color.orange);
        c2.setForeground(Color.blue);

        CanvasTest c3 = new CanvasTest();
        c3.setSize(200, 50);
        c3.setBackground(Color.white);
        c3.setForeground(Color.lightGray);

        CanvasTest c4 = new CanvasTest();
        c4.setSize(80, 150);
        c4.setBackground(Color.darkGray);
        c4.setForeground(Color.white);

        //Make the Frame and add the Canvas
        ComponentTestFrame frame = new ComponentTestFrame("Canvas Test");
        frame.add(c1);
        frame.add(c2);
        frame.add(c3);
        frame.add(c4);
        frame.setVisible(true);
    }

    /* Override the paint() method to alter its graphics */
    public void paint(Graphics g) {
        g.setFont(new Font("Arial", Font.ITALIC + Font.BOLD, 16));
        g.drawString("Canvas", 15, 25);
    }

}
```

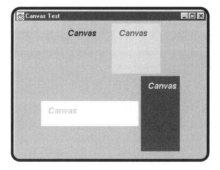

FIGURE 6.12

A Canvas is a component that can display graphics by overriding the paint() method.

The *Menu* Component

Every Frame object can be associated with a MenuBar. A Frame's MenuBar is usually at the top of the Frame, underneath the title bar. It contains a set of options, which themselves are Menus. A Menu appears when an option is selected from the MenuBar. Menus drop down from the MenuBar when they are selected and contain

MenuItems. A MenuItem is an option that exists within a Menu. Some of the more common MenuItem methods are summarized in Table 6.11. To use MenuItems, you must first create them, add them to Menus, then add the Menus to the MenuBar, and then finally associate the MenuBar with the Frame. Here's a quick example:

```
MenuItem myItem = new MenuItem("Some Option");
Menu myMenu = new Menu("Some Menu Title");
myMenu.add(myItem);
MenuBar myBar = new MenuBar();
myBar.add(myMenu);
frame.setMenuBar(myMenuBar);
```

This assumes that frame is a valid Frame object. Shortcut keys are also supported. You can assign a shortcut key to a MenuItem, so that instead of clicking the menu bar and selecting the menu and finally the MenuItem, you can use a keyboard shortcut. This is set either in the MenuItem(String, MenuShortcut) constructor or the setShortcut(MenuShortcut) method. The MenuShortcut class defines which key or key combo is the shortcut. You specify this combo using KeyEvent constants. The MenuTest application sets some shortcuts just to demonstrate how it's done.

TABLE 6.11 MENUITEM METHODS

Method	Description
MenuItem()	Constructs a new MenuItem object.
MenuItem(*String*)	Constructs a new MenuItem object with the given label.
MenuItem(*String*, *MenuShortcut*)	Constructs a new MenuItem object with the given label and MenuShortcut.
addActionListener(*ActionListener*)	Adds the specified ActionListener to this MenuItem.
String getLabel()	Returns this MenuItem's label.
MenuShortcut getShortcut()	Returns this MenuItem's MenuShortcut.
boolean isEnabled()	Returns whether this MenuItem is enabled.
removeActionListener(*ActionListener*)	Removes this MenuItem's ActionListener.
setEnabled(*boolean*)	Sets whether this MenuItem is enabled.
setLabel(*String*)	Sets this MenuItem object's label to the specified *String*.
setShortcut(*MenuShortcut*)	Sets this MenuItem's shortcut to the specified MenuShortcut.

The MenuTest application builds two Menus for the MenuBar and sets the MenuBar for the Frame. Here is the source:

```
/*
 * MenuTest
 * Demonstrates the MenuBar, Menu, and MenuItem classes
 */

import java.awt.*;
import java.awt.event.KeyEvent;

public class MenuTest {

  public MenuTest() {
    //create MenuBar object
    MenuBar menuBar = new MenuBar();

    //create a Menu object
    Menu fileMenu = new Menu("File");

    //create MenuItem objects
    MenuItem fm_new = new MenuItem("New");
    fm_new.setShortcut(new MenuShortcut(KeyEvent.VK_N));
    MenuItem fm_open = new MenuItem("Open");
    fm_open.setShortcut(new MenuShortcut(KeyEvent.VK_O));
    MenuItem fm_save = new MenuItem("Save");
    fm_save.setShortcut(new MenuShortcut(KeyEvent.VK_S));
    fm_save.setEnabled(false);
    MenuItem fm_saveAs = new MenuItem("Save As...");
    fm_saveAs.setShortcut(new MenuShortcut(KeyEvent.VK_A));
    fm_saveAs.setEnabled(false);
    MenuItem fm_exit = new MenuItem("Exit");

    //add the MenuItems to the Menu with a Separator
    fileMenu.add(fm_new);
    fileMenu.add(fm_open);
    fileMenu.add(fm_save);
    fileMenu.add(fm_saveAs);
    //separator
    fileMenu.addSeparator();
    fileMenu.add(fm_exit);

    //make another quick Menu
    Menu editMenu = new Menu("Edit");
    MenuItem em_options = new MenuItem("Options");
    editMenu.add(em_options);

    //add the Menus to the MenuBar
    menuBar.add(fileMenu);
    menuBar.add(editMenu);

    //create the Frame and add the MenuBar
    ComponentTestFrame frame = new ComponentTestFrame("Menu Test");
```

```
    frame.setMenuBar(menuBar);
    frame.setBackground(Color.white);
    frame.setVisible(true);
  }

  public static void main(String args[]) {
    MenuTest mt = new MenuTest();
  }

}
```

It demonstrates how creating a bunch of MenuItems and dumping them into the Menus then adding the Menus to the MenuBar does this. Here is an explanation for the more complicated parts. The fm_new MenuItem adds a shortcut:

```
fm_new.setShortcut(new MenuShortcut(KeyEvent.VK_N));
```

Basically, the KeyEvent.VK_N constant specifies the N key on your keyboard. You can see in the output in Figure 6.13 that this shortcut is indicated right next to the MenuItem's label. It is Ctrl+N, although it might vary for different operating systems. Menus can also have separator lines that are used to separate different groups of MenuItems (for cosmetic sake). You do this by calling the addSeparator() method in the Menu class. Here's an example from MenuTest.java.

```
fileMenu.addSeparator();
```

This line of code added a separator in the File menu, right in between the Save As... and Exit options. Some of the MenuItems were disabled. You can see the difference in their appearance.

TRICK Although it is not shown here, you can nest Menus. Menu is a subclass of MenuItem, so it is a MenuItem itself and can be added to other Menus. Try it out and see for yourself!

FIGURE 6.13

The Menu class allows users to select options from a Frame's MenuBar.

The *PopupMenu* Component

The PopupMenu component is a subclass of Menu that doesn't have to be attached to a MenuBar. It can pop up anywhere you specify it to by indicating a Component and an x and y position relative to that Component's coordinate space. You can attach a PopupMenu to a MenuBar or another Menu, but if you do, you can't show it at any old location that you choose because it is attached to something else. A PopupMenu is created similar to other Menus. It becomes visible by calling its show(Component, int, int) method. The specified Component's coordinate space is used as a reference and the top-left corner of the PopupMenu is set to the location specified by the second and third arguments (x, y). The PopupMenuTest application demonstrates these concepts. The output is shown in Figure 6.14. When you run it, the PopupMenu is initially shown, if you click anywhere at all, though, it will simply disappear. This example demonstrates the basics of creating a pop-up menu. In the real world, you would cause the pop-up menu to become visible based on some event, such as right-clicking the frame. Also, you should associate actions that are triggered when the user selects a menu item. Text editors might use a pop-up menu that offers the Clipboard options (cut, copy, paste). Here is a listing of the source code for the PopupMenuTest.java example.

```java
/*
 * PopupMenuTest
 * Demonstrates the PopupMenu Component
 */

import java.awt.*;

public class PopupMenuTest {

  public PopupMenuTest() {
    //create the PopupMenu
    PopupMenu popMenu = new PopupMenu("Clipboard");

    //create the MenuItems
    MenuItem pm_cut = new MenuItem("Cut");
    MenuItem pm_copy = new MenuItem("Copy");
    MenuItem pm_paste = new MenuItem("Paste");
    MenuItem pm_delete = new MenuItem("Delete");

    //add the MenuItems to the PopupMenu
    popMenu.add(pm_cut);
    popMenu.add(pm_copy);
    popMenu.add(pm_paste);
    popMenu.add(pm_delete);

    //create the Frame and make show the PopupMenu
    ComponentTestFrame frame = new ComponentTestFrame("PopupMenu Test");
    frame.add(popMenu);
    frame.setVisible(true);
    popMenu.show(frame, 50, 50);
  }
```

```
public static void main(String args[]) {
    PopupMenuTest pmt = new PopupMenuTest();
  }

}
```

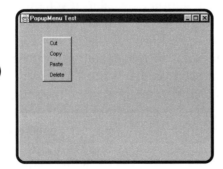

A PopupMenu is
similar to a Menu
except it's not
attached to a
MenuBar.

The *Panel* Component

The Panel class is a simple extension of Container. It can contain other components, including other Panels. To use a Panel, you can construct one, and then
add components to it like this:

```
Panel myPanel = new Panel();
myPanel.add(someComponent);
```

The PanelTest application is a simple example of this. It creates two Panel objects
and adds them to the Frame. Both Panels also have other components added to
them as well and they have different colors so they contrast with the Frame and
each other, making it easier to determine their bounds. Here is the source for
PanelTest.java. The output is shown in Figure 6.15.

```
/*
 * PanelTest
 * Demonstrates the Panel Component
 */

import java.awt.*;

public class PanelTest {

  public PanelTest() {
    //Create the Panels and add components to them
    Panel p1 = new Panel();
    p1.setBackground(Color.red);
    p1.add(new Label("URL:", Label.RIGHT));
    p1.add(new TextField(25));
    p1.add(new Button("Go"));
```

```
      Panel p2 = new Panel();
      p2.setBackground(Color.darkGray);
      p2.setForeground(Color.white);
      CheckboxGroup cbg = new CheckboxGroup();
      p2.add(new Label("Pick one:"));
      p2.add(new Checkbox("Lead Guitar", false, cbg));
      p2.add(new Checkbox("Bass Guitar", false, cbg));
      p2.add(new Checkbox("Drums", false, cbg));
      p2.add(new Button("OK"));
      p2.setSize(100, 500);

      ComponentTestFrame frame = new ComponentTestFrame("Panel Test");
      frame.add(p1);
      frame.add(p2);
      frame.setVisible(true);
   }

   public static void main(String args[]) {
      PanelTest pt = new PanelTest();
   }

}
```

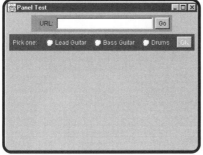

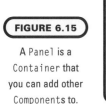

FIGURE 6.15

A Panel is a
Container that
you can add other
Components to.

The *Scrollbar* Component

The Scrollbar class allows a user in a GUI environment to select from a range of numerical values. It can have one of two orientations that are specified by the class constants Scrollbar.HORIZONTAL and Scrollbar.VERTICAL. A Scrollbar also has a minimum value, a maximum value, a visible amount, and a current value. Note that when you create a Scrollbar, its actual maximum value is the given maximum value minus the visible amount. The visible amount sets the size of the slider and its increment. Some of the Scrollbar fields and methods are described in Table 6.12.

The ScrollbarTest application creates two Scrollbars. One is oriented horizontally and the other is oriented vertically. This class is actually an extension of Scrollbar. The reason for this is so that you can override the Dimension

TABLE 6.12 SCROLLBAR **FIELDS AND METHODS**

Field or Method	Description
HORIZONTAL	Indicates that this Scrollbar should have horizontal orientation.
VERTICAL	Indicates that this Scrollbar should have vertical orientation.
Scrollbar()	Constructs a new Scrollbar object with vertical orientation.
Scrollbar(int)	Constructs a new Scrollbar object with the given orientation.
Scrollbar(int, int, int, int, int)	Constructs a Scrollbar with the given five int arguments. The first argument is the orientation, the second is its initial value, the third is its visible amount, the fourth is its minimum, and the fifth argument is the maximum value.
addAdjustmentListener(AdjustmentListener)	Adds the specified AdjustmentListener.
int getMaximum()	Returns the maximum value of this Scrollbar.
int getMinimum()	Returns the minimum value of this Scrollbar.
int getOrientation()	Returns this Scrollbar's orientation.
int getValue()	Returns this Scrollbar's current value.
int getVisibleAmount()	Returns this Scrollbar's visible amount.
removeAdjustmentListener(AdjustmentListener)	Removes the specified AdjustmentListener from this Scrollbar.
setMaximum(int)	Sets this Scrollbar's maximum value.
setMinimum(int)	Sets this Scrollbar's minimum value.
setOrientation(int)	Sets this Scrollbar's orientation.
setValue(int)	Sets this Scrollbar's value to the given int.
setVisibleAmount(int)	Sets this Scrollbar's visible amount.
setValues(int, int, int, int)	Respectively sets this Scrollbar's value, visible amount, minimum, and maximum values. (This method is preferred over setting them individually because it maintains consistency.)

getPreferredSize() method. Remember that you set the ComponentTestFrame's layout manager to FlowLayout()? Well, that actually resizes a component based on its preferred size, which is different for different components and different states of those components. Here, the override takes place because when the layout manager calls the method, getSize() is returned so the preferred size becomes whatever the current size is and the layout manager doesn't resize it. This method is inherited from Component. The source code for ScrollbarTest.java follows. You can see in the source code how the labels that represent the minimum and maximum values are built to be accurate. The output is shown in Figure 6.16.

```
/*
 * ScrollbarTest
 * Demonstrates the Scrollbar Component
 */

import java.awt.*;

public class ScrollbarTest extends Scrollbar {

  public ScrollbarTest(int orientation, int value, int visible,
                       int minimum, int maximum) {
    super(orientation, value, visible, minimum, maximum);
  }

  public Dimension getPreferredSize() {
    //Do this so FlowLayout won't resize the Scrollbar
    return getSize();
  }

  public static void main(String args[]) {
    //create the Scrollbars
    ScrollbarTest sbt1 = new ScrollbarTest(Scrollbar.HORIZONTAL,
      50, 20, 0, 100);
    sbt1.setSize(200, 15);
    ScrollbarTest sbt2 = new ScrollbarTest(Scrollbar.VERTICAL,
      0, 7, 0, 10);
    sbt2.setSize(50, 200);

    //add the Scrollbars to the Frame
    ComponentTestFrame ctf = new ComponentTestFrame("Scrollbar Test");
    ctf.add(new Label(String.valueOf(sbt1.getMinimum()), Label.RIGHT));
    ctf.add(sbt1);
    ctf.add(new Label(String.valueOf(sbt1.getMaximum()
                                     - sbt1.getVisibleAmount())));
    ctf.add(sbt2);
    ctf.setVisible(true);
  }

}
```

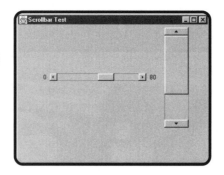

The *Dialog* Component

The Dialog object is a top-level window that has a title bar and a border. It is typically used to pop up and prompt the users for some input. A Dialog must have either a Frame or another Dialog as a parent and can be either modal or non-modal. A modal Dialog blocks input focus from other application windows when it's active. In order for you to change focus to another window in the application, the modal Dialog must be closed. When a Dialog is non-modal, it can traverse focus back and forth among other windows in the application. The Dialog constructors appear in Table 6.13.

TABLE 6.13 DIALOG CONSTRUCTORS

Constructor	Description
Dialog(*Dialog*)	Constructs a Dialog that has the specified *Dialog* as its owner.
Dialog(*Dialog*, *String*)	Constructs a Dialog that has the specified *Dialog* as its owner and the specified *String* title.
Dialog(*Dialog*, *String*, *boolean*)	Constructs a Dialog that has the specified *Dialog* as its owner, the specified *String* title, and a *boolean* that indicates whether this Dialog is modal.
Dialog(*Frame*)	Constructs a Dialog that has the specified *Frame* as its owner.
Dialog(*Frame*, *boolean*)	Constructs a Dialog that has the specified *Frame* as its owner and a *boolean* that indicates whether this Dialog is modal.
Dialog(*Frame*, *String*)	Constructs a Dialog that has the specified *Frame* as its owner and the specified *String* title.
Dialog(*Frame*, *String*, *boolean*)	Constructs a Dialog that has the specified *Frame* as its owner, the specified *String* title, and a *boolean* that indicates whether this Dialog is modal.

The `DialogTest` application basically creates two `Dialog` objects: one modal, the other non-modal. The `Label`s they have indicate which one is which. If you try to click the `Frame` or the non-modal `Dialog` while the modal `Dialog` is opened, you won't be able to gain focus there; however, if you close the modal `Dialog`, you can traverse focus between the two freely. Here is the source code for DialogTest.java:

```
/*
 * DialogTest
 * Tests the Dialog Component
 */

import java.awt.*;
import java.awt.event.*;

public class DialogTest implements WindowListener {

  public DialogTest() {
    //Make the Frame and add the Dialogs to it
    ComponentTestFrame frame = new ComponentTestFrame("Dialog Test");
    Dialog d1 = new Dialog(frame, "Non-modal Dialog", false);
    d1.add(new Label("This is a non-modal dialog box."));
    d1.addWindowListener(this);

    Dialog d2 = new Dialog(d1, "Modal Dialog", true);
    d2.add(new Label("This is a modal dialog box."));
    d2.addWindowListener(this);

    frame.setVisible(true);
    d1.pack();
    d1.setLocation(220, 170);
    d1.setVisible(true);
    d2.pack();
    d2.setLocation(250, 210);
    d2.setVisible(true);
  }

  public static void main(String args[]) {
    DialogTest dt = new DialogTest();
  }

  // the only WindowListener method I care about
  public void windowClosing(WindowEvent e) {
    ((Dialog)e.getSource()).setVisible(false);
  }

  // the rest of them that must be declared
  public void windowActivated(WindowEvent e) { }
  public void windowClosed(WindowEvent e) { }
  public void windowIconified(WindowEvent e) { }
  public void windowDeiconified(WindowEvent e) { }
  public void windowDeactivated(WindowEvent e) { }
  public void windowOpened(WindowEvent e) { }

}
```

The event handling is a bit funky, but you can ignore the specifics for now, until the next chapter. Simplified, the line

```
((Dialog)e.getSource()).setVisible(false);
```

just means whichever `Dialog` you clicked the close box for should close. You can see the dialog box generated with this code in Figure 6.17.

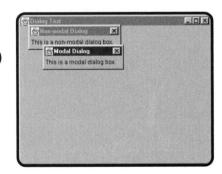

FIGURE 6.17

Modal `Dialog` windows must be closed before the `Frame` or `Dialog` it owns can gain user input focus.

Back to the *MadLib* Game Application

Okay, back to the `MadLib` game application! You use your newly acquired GUI programming skills to build this game. You are creating two program files for this application—`MadDialog.java` and `MadLib.java`. These programs work together to form the `MadLib` application.

Creating the *MadDialog* Component

The `MadDialog` component extends `Dialog`. It contains all the fields where user input is accepted. This component prompts the user for nouns, verbs, adjectives, adverbs, and so on. Here's how it works. First it declares its components. It has `Panels`, `TextFields`, `Labels`, `Checkboxes` and `CheckboxGroups`, a `Choice`, a `List`, and a `TextArea`. This component lines up its `Panels` in separate rows (by setting its width wider than the widest panel, but too thin for more than one `Panel` to fit in a single row). It puts like-types of input in these `Panels`, such as placing all noun prompts in one `Panel`, and so on. The users click the x to exit the `Dialog` when they are done entering all the input.

The `String[] getStringArray()` method is for the benefit of the `MadLib` class. It takes all the `Strings` associated with the user's input and adds them to a `Vector`, simply because it's easier that way, and then converts the `Vector` to a `String` array and returns it. Here is the source code:

```
/*
 * MadDialog
 * Used by MadLib to collect user input
 */

import java.awt.*;
import java.util.Vector;

public class MadDialog extends Dialog {
  private TextField a1, a2, a3, a4, av1, av2,
                    n1, n2, n3, v1, v2, v3,
                    body, occupation, animal, name;
  private CheckboxGroup mfg, mlg;
  private Checkbox male, female, most, least;
  private Choice color, time;
  private List prep;
  private TextArea text;

  public MadDialog(Frame owner) {
    super(owner, "Mad Dialog", true);
    setLayout(new FlowLayout());

    Panel nPanel = new Panel();
    nPanel.add(new Label("Nouns:"));
    n1 = new TextField(10);
    n2 = new TextField(10);
    n3 = new TextField(10);
    nPanel.add(n1); nPanel.add(n2); nPanel.add(n3);
    add(nPanel);

    Panel aPanel = new Panel();
    aPanel.add(new Label("Adjectives:"));
    a1 = new TextField(10);
    a2 = new TextField(10);
    a3 = new TextField(10);
    a4 = new TextField(10);
    aPanel.add(a1); aPanel.add(a2); aPanel.add(a3);
    aPanel.add(a4);
    add(aPanel);

    Panel vPanel = new Panel();
    vPanel.add(new Label("Verbs:"));
    v1 = new TextField(10);
    v2 = new TextField(10);
    v3 = new TextField(10);
    vPanel.add(v1);
    vPanel.add(new Label("Past Tense:"));
    vPanel.add(v2); vPanel.add(v3);
    add(vPanel);

    Panel avPanel = new Panel();
    avPanel.add(new Label("Adverbs:"));
    av1 = new TextField(10);
    av2 = new TextField(10);
```

```java
avPanel.add(av1); avPanel.add(av2);
add(avPanel);

Panel boPanel = new Panel();
boPanel.add(new Label("Bodypart:"));
body = new TextField(10);
boPanel.add(body);
boPanel.add(new Label("Occupation:"));
occupation = new TextField(10);
boPanel.add(occupation);
add(boPanel);

Panel naPanel = new Panel();
naPanel.add(new Label("Name:"));
name = new TextField(10);
naPanel.add(name);
naPanel.add(new Label("Animal:"));
animal = new TextField(10);
naPanel.add(animal);
add(naPanel);

Panel mfPanel = new Panel();
mfPanel.add(new Label("Male or Female:"));
mfg = new CheckboxGroup();
male = new Checkbox("male", true, mfg);
female = new Checkbox("female", false, mfg);
mfPanel.add(male);
mfPanel.add(female);
add(mfPanel);

Panel mlPanel = new Panel();
mlPanel.add(new Label("Most or Least:"));
mlg = new CheckboxGroup();
most = new Checkbox("most", true, mlg);
least = new Checkbox("least", false, mlg);
mlPanel.add(most);
mlPanel.add(least);
add(mlPanel);

Panel ctPanel = new Panel();
ctPanel.add(new Label("Choose a color: "));
color = new Choice();
color.add("red");
color.add("blue");
color.add("green");
color.add("orange");
color.add("yellow");
color.add("purple");
ctPanel.add(color);
ctPanel.add(new Label("Choose a timeframe:"));
time = new Choice();
time.add("Always");
time.add("Only sometimes");
time.add("Never");
```

```
    ctPanel.add(time);
    add(ctPanel);

    Panel ptPanel = new Panel();
    ptPanel.add(new Label("Prepositions:"));
    prep = new List(3, false);
    prep.add("under");
    prep.add("over");
    prep.add("inside of");
    prep.add("beside");
    prep.add("outside of");
    prep.add("around");
    prep.add("through");
    prep.select(0);
    ptPanel.add(prep);
    ptPanel.add(new Label("Text:"));
    text = new TextArea("Enter a sentence or two here", 3, 20,
                        TextArea.SCROLLBARS_NONE);
    ptPanel.add(text);
    add(ptPanel);

    setSize(480, 450);
  }

  public String[] getStringArray() {
    String[] s;
    Vector v = new Vector();
    v.add(a1.getText()); v.add(n1.getText());
    v.add(a2.getText()); v.add(name.getText());
    v.add(mlg.getSelectedCheckbox().getLabel());
    v.add(a3.getText());
    if (mfg.getSelectedCheckbox() == male)
      v.add("he");
    else v.add("she");
    v.add(n2.getText()); v.add(av1.getText());
    v.add(v2.getText()); v.add(v3.getText());
    v.add(color.getSelectedItem());
    v.add(animal.getText()); v.add(occupation.getText());
    v.add(text.getText()); v.add(a2.getText());
    v.add(name.getText());
    if (mfg.getSelectedCheckbox() == male)
      v.add("him");
    else v.add("her");
    v.add(time.getSelectedItem()); v.add(av2.getText());
    v.add(v1.getText()); v.add(body.getText());
    v.add(prep.getSelectedItem()); v.add(n3.getText());
    v.add(a4.getText());
    s = new String[v.size()];
    v.copyInto(s);
    return s;
  }

}
```

Telling the Story: Creating the *MadLib* Game Frame

The MadLib.java program uses a MadDialog object to retrieve user input. The MadLib class extends Frame. It listens for when the user closes the MadDialog dialog box and then builds the story and displays it in its un-editable TextArea. The MadDialog Frame itself will remain hidden until after the story is already built. Here's why. The MadDialog object is modal and it is shown first by calling dialog.setVisible(true). It will maintain focus until it is hidden again. When the user clicks the x on the MadDialog window, the buildStory() method is called before the dialog is actually closed. Once the story is done, the MadDialog will disappear and the MadLib will display the completed story.

The buildStory() method itself works by creating an array of Strings that represent segments of the story that break where words should be inserted. The String[] getStringArray() method defined in the MadDialog class returns the String array sorted in the order they should be inserted into the story. This makes the two arrays' indices correspond with each other, so they are processed in a for loop to build the story. Here is the source for MadLib.java.

```
/*
 * MadLib
 * A MadLib game
 */

import java.awt.*;
import java.awt.event.*;

public class MadLib extends Frame implements WindowListener {
  private TextArea display;
  private MadDialog dialog;

  public MadLib() {
    super("MadLib Game");
    display = new TextArea("", 7, 60,
      TextArea.SCROLLBARS_VERTICAL_ONLY);
    display.setFont(new Font("Timesroman", Font.PLAIN, 16));
    display.setEditable(false);
    add(display);
    addWindowListener(this);
    setLocation(100, 150);
    pack();

    dialog = new MadDialog(this);
    dialog.addWindowListener(this);
    dialog.setLocation(150, 100);
    dialog.setVisible(true);
    setVisible(true);
  }
```

```
public static void main(String args[]) {
  MadLib ml = new MadLib();
}

private void buildStory() {
  String story = "";
  String[] segs = {"One fine ", " night, a ", " named ",
    " ", " had a dream. It was the ", " ", " dream since ",
   " dreamt that a ", " ", " ", " and ", " on a ", " ",
   ". In this dream, an old ", " said to him, \"", "\" ", " ",
   " interpreted this as a sign. To ", ", ", it meant, ", " ", " ",
   " your ", " ", " a ", " when the moon is ", "." };

  String[] s = dialog.getStringArray();
  for (int i = 0; i < s.length; i++) {
    story += segs[i] + s[i];
  }
  story += segs[segs.length - 1];
  display.setText(story);
}

public void windowClosing(WindowEvent e) {
  if (e.getSource() == this) {
    dispose();
    System.exit(0);
  }
  else if (e.getSource() instanceof Dialog) {
    buildStory();
    ((Dialog)e.getSource()).setVisible(false);
  }
}

// the rest of them that must be declared
public void windowActivated(WindowEvent e) { }
public void windowClosed(WindowEvent e) { }
public void windowIconified(WindowEvent e) { }
public void windowDeiconified(WindowEvent e) { }
public void windowDeactivated(WindowEvent e) { }
public void windowOpened(WindowEvent e) { }

}
```

Summary

In this chapter, you learned all about GUI programming and Java's AWT. You learned about Containers and Components. You learned how to create a Frame and add components to it. You also learned how to close a Frame when the user clicks the close box. You learned about these specific components: Label, Button, TextField, TextArea, Choice, List, Checkbox, Canvas, Menu, PopupMenu, Panel,

Scrollbar, and Dialog. In the next chapter, you learn about layout managers, GUI event handling, and simple graphics programming.

CHALLENGES

1. Create a Frame that has many different Components in it similar to Figure 6.2. Hint: See ComponentTest.java on the CD.

2. Go back and try playing around with some of the methods that appeared in tables of this chapter, but never actually made it into any of the programs to see how their effects look.

Advanced GUI: Layout Managers and Event Handling

In the last chapter, you learned about GUI programming. You learned how to create components such as `Buttons`, `TextFields`, `Labels`, and the like. In this chapter, you learn how to use layout managers to have more control over the placement of your components. *Layout managers* are classes that define where and how to place components within a container. You will also learn about event handling. In a GUI, users interact with the components. *Event handling* describes the process of knowing when a user interacts with a component and then causing some action to occur based on the user's actions. By the end of this chapter, you will be able to use layout managers and event handling to create a more advanced version of the `MadLib` game, created in the previous chapter. This chapter covers the following AWT concepts:

• Use layout managers

• Handle GUI events

The Project: the *AdvancedMadLib* Application

This application has the same goal as the `MadLib` project from the previous chapter, which is to provide a graphical interface for the users to enter specific types of words and generate nonsensical output using those words within a story. However, it accomplishes it much differently. There are some more advanced features that make it more user-friendly. The term *user friendly* describes an interface that the user can easily understand and use to accomplish the desired task.

When the `AdvancedMadLib` application starts, a window entitled "Create your own Song" opens. In this chapter, you make this `MadLib` take the form of a song. The window has a label "Enter some nouns:" and then has some `TextField` prompts for the user to enter some nouns. There are also some `Buttons` on the bottom—Prev, Next, and Show/Refresh Story—and a `Choice` with the options Nouns, Verbs, and Other. These components on the bottom of the `Advanced-MadLib Frame` are used for navigating the input `Panels`. The entire application consists of three panels used for entering nouns, verbs, and other text, and also a `Frame` that displays the story based on the user's input. Figure 7.1 displays the Nouns panel and the completed story.

Here's how it works. The user first enters the nouns, and then clicks the Next button to get to the screen that allows the entry of the verbs. Once the verbs are entered, the user clicks Next again to get to the screen that allows entry of other text such as nicknames, adjectives, prepositions, and so on. Once all input is completed, the user clicks the Show/Refresh Story button to display the new #1 hit song.

The `AdvancedMadLib` application is actually more versatile than that. The users can click the Prev button to go back to a previous screen to enter some text they might have missed, or just want to edit. The `Choice` also allows users to go to any of the three screens instantly by selecting from Nouns, Verbs, or Other choices. The Show/Refresh Story button is also more versatile. The user initially clicks it to display the story in a second window, but the original input window stays open. The users can then make any edits to the `TextFields` and then click the button again to refresh the story to reflect the changes. Also, the users can close the window that contains the song (entitled "Your Song") and then reopen it by clicking the Show/Refresh Song button. All in all, it's a much better `MadLib` application interface.

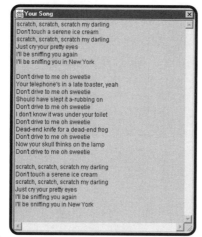

FIGURE 7.1

The `AdvancedMadLib` application creates a song by using the text entered by the users.

Using Layout Managers

In Chapter 6, "Creating a GUI Using the Abstract Windowing Toolkit," you used the `FlowLayout` layout manager to lay out your components. In this chapter, you learn more about the `FlowLayout` layout manager as well as some other layout managers. Layout managers are classes that implement the `LayoutManager` interface of the `java.awt` package and describe where and how your GUI application should put its components relative to the other components.

For example, if you created a frame and added six buttons to it, the layout manager would be responsible for knowing where, within that frame, to place those buttons and how to handle their placement when the frame is resized. When adding a great deal of components to your containers, it is essential to use layout managers to facilitate the programmatic description of the design of your GUI.

Using *FlowLayout*

The `FlowLayout` layout manager is the simplest of all the layout managers. It simply arranges the components you add to the container, in the order that you add them, from left to right, and wraps them onto a new line when it runs out of room. You can think of this as being similar to how your word processor wraps words within a paragraph. By default, each "line" of components is centered, but you can specify left, right, or center alignment. The FlowLayoutTest application shows you how to use the FlowLayout layout manager. Here is the source code:

```
/*
 * FlowLayoutTest
 * Demonstrates use of the FlowLayout layout manager.
 */

import java.awt.*;
import java.awt.event.*;

public class FlowLayoutTest extends Frame
                                    implements WindowListener {

   public FlowLayoutTest() {
      super("FlowLayout Test");
      addWindowListener(this);
      setLayout(new FlowLayout(FlowLayout.RIGHT, 20, 50));

      for (int b=1; b <= 15; b++) {
         add(new Button("Button " + b));
      }
      setSize(575, 300);
      setVisible(true);
   }

   public static void main(String args[]) {
      new FlowLayoutTest();
   }

   //WindowListener Interface
   public void windowClosing(WindowEvent e) {
      dispose();
      System.exit(0);
   }
   public void windowOpened(WindowEvent e) {}
   public void windowActivated(WindowEvent e) {}
   public void windowDeactivated(WindowEvent e) {}
   public void windowIconified(WindowEvent e) {}
   public void windowDeiconified(WindowEvent e) {}
   public void windowClosed(WindowEvent e) {}

}
```

As in all the layout manager examples in this chapter, the FlowLayoutTest application extends Frame and implements WindowListener, so it is a Frame. You can close it normally because the windowClosing(WindowEvent) method is implemented. If you are unsure how to create a Frame that implements the WindowListener interface, review Chapter 6, as this chapter builds on that information.

Okay, so here the `Frame` is created and its `setLayout(LayoutManager)` method, inherited from the `Container` class, is called. The argument to that method is `new FlowLayout(FlowLayout.RIGHT, 20, 50)`. This instantiates a new `FlowLayout` so that the "lines" of components are right aligned (because of the first static `int` argument `FlowLayout.RIGHT`). The second and third arguments are the horizontal and vertical gap arguments, respectively. They specify the horizontal and vertical pixel distance between components.

You can see the three `FlowLayout` constructor methods in Table 7.1. The alignment constants shown in Table 7.1 are pretty self-explanatory except for `FlowLayout.LEADING` and `FlowLayout.TRAILING`. `FlowLayout.LEADING` specifies that the components are justified from the leading edge of the container. What this means is that if the container is oriented left-to-right, the left side is the leading edge. If the container is oriented right-to-left, the leading edge is the right side. `FlowLayout.TRAILING` specifies that the components are justified from the trailing edge of the container, as you might have deduced.

TABLE 7.1   FLOWLAYOUT CONSTRUCTOR METHODS

Constructor	Description
FlowLayout()	Constructs a `FlowLayout` with a default center alignment and a five-pixel horizontal and vertical gap.
FlowLayout(*int*)	Constructs a `FlowLayout` with the specified alignment (can be one of the following: `FlowLayout.LEFT`, `FlowLayout.CENTER`, `FlowLayout.RIGHT`, `FlowLayout.LEADING`, or `FlowLayout.TRAILING`).
FlowLayout(*int, int, int*)	Constructs a `FlowLayout` with the specified alignment and horizontal and vertical component gaps.

In the `for` loop, 15 buttons are created and added to the `Frame`. The fact that the layout manager was set to `FlowLayout` beforehand lets the `Frame` know where to put them. You can see the output of the `FlowLayoutTest` application in Figure 7.2. When you run this application, resize the window so you can see how the `FlowLayout` layout manager repositions the buttons based on different window sizes.

Using *GridLayout*

The `GridLayout` class lays out its components in a grid of equally sized rectangular cells. You just need to specify the number of rows and columns and then add the components. The `GridLayout` layout manager adds the components from left

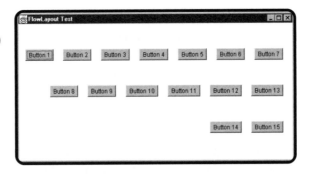

FIGURE 7.2

The
FlowLayoutTest
application lays out
15 buttons, right
aligned, using the
FlowLayout layout
manager.

to right in rows. When it reaches the end of a row, it creates a new row and adds columns in that row from left to right. Here is an example of a GridLayout that lays out 12 buttons in a grid of four rows by three columns. It also sets a horizontal gap of five and a vertical gap of 10 pixels in between components:

```
/*
 * GridLayoutTest
 * Demonstrates the GridLayout layout manager
 */

import java.awt.*;
import java.awt.event.*;

public class GridLayoutTest extends Frame
                                implements WindowListener {

   public GridLayoutTest() {
      super("GridLayout Test");
      addWindowListener(this);
      setLayout(new GridLayout(0, 3, 5, 10));

      for (int b=1; b <=12; b++) {
         add(new Button("Button " + b));
      }

      pack();
      setVisible(true);
   }

   public static void main(String args[]) {
      GridLayoutTest glt = new GridLayoutTest();
   }

   //WindowListener Interface
   public void windowClosing(WindowEvent e) {
      dispose();
      System.exit(0);
   }
   public void windowOpened(WindowEvent e) {}
   public void windowActivated(WindowEvent e) {}
```

```
public void windowDeactivated(WindowEvent e) {}
public void windowIconified(WindowEvent e) {}
public void windowDeiconified(WindowEvent e) {}
public void windowClosed(WindowEvent e) {}

}
```

Figure 7.3 shows how the GridLayout layout manager lays out the buttons created in the GridLayoutTest application and Table 7.1 summarizes the GridLayout class constructor methods.

TRICK

When you create a new GridLayout object, you can specify both the number of rows and the number of columns, but you can also just specify one or the other. For example, if you wanted to create a layout that had three columns and any number of rows, you can specify the number of columns to be three and the number of rows to be zero.

```
setLayout(new GridLayout(0, 3));
```

Java interprets this as meaning that there are strictly three columns, but there can be any number of rows. You cannot specify zero for both rows and columns at the same time.

FIGURE 7.3

The GridLayout manager has rows and columns of equal sized components.

TABLE 7.2 GRIDLAYOUT CONSTRUCTOR METHODS

Constructor	Description
GridLayout()	Constructs a GridLayout with a default of one row of components.
GridLayout(*int*, *int*)	Constructs a GridLayout with the given number of rows and columns.
GridLayout(*int*, *int*, *int*, *int*)	Constructs a GridLayout with the given number of rows and columns. The third and fourth arguments are the horizontal and vertical spacing in between components.

Using *BorderLayout*

The BorderLayout class divides a container into five areas based on its borders. The areas are designated by static constants in the BorderLayout class. The top border is designated BorderLayout.NORTH, the bottom is designated BorderLayout.SOUTH, and the right and left borders are BorderLayout.EAST, and BorderLayout.WEST, respectively. The center of the container is specified by BorderLayout.NORTH. This is the default layout manager for Frames, which is why you will see some code that assumes BorderLayout without explicitly specifying so. The BorderLayoutTest application lays out five buttons in each of BorderLayout's regions. Here is the source code:

```
/*
 * BorderLayoutTest
 * Demonstrates the BorderLayout layout manager
 */

import java.awt.*;
import java.awt.event.*;

public class BorderLayoutTest extends Frame
                              implements WindowListener {

  public BorderLayoutTest() {
    super("BorderLayout Test");
    addWindowListener(this);
    setLayout(new BorderLayout());

    add(new Button("Center"), BorderLayout.CENTER);
    add(new Button("North"), BorderLayout.NORTH);
    add(new Button("East"), BorderLayout.EAST);
    add(new Button("South"), BorderLayout.SOUTH);
    add(new Button("West"), BorderLayout.WEST);

    pack();
    setSize(400, 300);
    setVisible(true);
  }

  public static void main(String args[]) {
    BorderLayoutTest blt = new BorderLayoutTest();
  }

  //WindowListener Interface
  public void windowClosing(WindowEvent e) {
    dispose();
    System.exit(0);
  }
  public void windowOpened(WindowEvent e) {}
  public void windowActivated(WindowEvent e) {}
  public void windowDeactivated(WindowEvent e) {}
```

```
public void windowIconified(WindowEvent e) {}
public void windowDeiconified(WindowEvent e) {}
public void windowClosed(WindowEvent e) {}

}
```

Notice that when components are added, the `add(Component, int)` method is used. The `BorderLayout` constant specifying which region to add the component in is passed as the `int` argument. It is not necessary to add a component to all the regions. Figure 7.4 shows how the `BorderLayout` layout manager lays out a container's components and Table 7.3 summarizes the `BorderLayout` constructor methods.

 HINT When you resize a container that is using a `BorderLayout`, the center area takes precedence. The north, south, east, and west regions take up only their minimum space and the center region takes up the rest of the space.

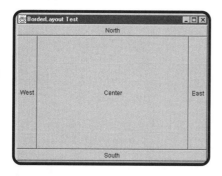

FIGURE 7.4

The `BorderLayout` manager has five main sections: center, north, south, east, and west.

TABLE 7.3 BORDERLAYOUT CONSTRUCTOR METHODS

Constructor	Description
`BorderLayout()`	Creates a `BorderLayout` object with no horizontal or vertical gaps.
`BorderLayout(int, int)`	Constructs a `BorderLayout` object with the given horizontal and vertical gaps in between components.

Using *GridBagLayout*

Get ready, the `GridBagLayout` manager is not as simple as the other layout managers. In fact, it's much more complicated, but also much more powerful. It's kind of like a loose grid and is less strict than the `GridLayout`'s grid that you stuff components into. I guess that's why they call it a grid bag? Unlike `GridLayout`, however, GridBagLayout does not force its components to be contained within equal sized cells. It also does not have a specified number of rows or columns. Instead, each GridBagLayout instance is associated with a set of rules, which are set for each of its components. These rules specify where the components need to be laid out. This set of rules is contained within the GridBagConstraints class. The GridBagConstraints class holds information, such as which coordinates to use with each component and what to do with the components when the container is resized. Table 7.4 lists some of the more important GridBagConstraints fields.

```
GridBagLayout gridbag = new GridBagLayout();
GridBagConstraints constraints = new GridBagConstraints();
setLayout(gridbag);
```

After that, you just specify values for the GridBagConstraints object and set the constraints to the component using GridBagLayout's setConstraints(Component, GridBagConstraints) method. Here is the source code for SimpleGridBag-Test.java, which illustrates an example of how to accomplish this:

```
/*
 * SimpleGridBagTest
 * Demonstrates a simple GridBagLayout
 */

import java.awt.*;
import java.awt.event.*;

public class SimpleGridBagTest extends Frame
                                implements WindowListener {

  public SimpleGridBagTest() {
    super("Simple GridBagLayout");
    Button b1, b2, b3, b4;

    //Create the GridBagLayout & GridBagConstraints objects
    GridBagLayout gridbag = new GridBagLayout();
    GridBagConstraints constraints = new GridBagConstraints();
    setLayout(gridbag);

    b1 = new Button("Button 1");
    //this makes the buttons fill their cells
    constraints.fill = GridBagConstraints.BOTH;
    //set the gridwidth to span multiple columns
    constraints.gridwidth = 2;
    //set the constraints for b1
    gridbag.setConstraints(b1, constraints);
    //add b1 to the frame
    add(b1);

    b2 = new Button("Button 2");
    //reset the gridwidth
    constraints.gridwidth = 1;
```

	TABLE 7.4 GRIDBAGCONSTRAINTS FIELDS

Field	Description
int anchor	This field specifies where to place a component within its cell if the cell area is larger than the component. Possible values are the static constants NORTH, NORTHEAST, EAST, SOUTHEAST, SOUTH, SOUTHWEST, WEST, NORTHWEST, and CENTER.
int fill	This field determines how to resize a component to fit its cell if the cell area is larger than the component. Possible values are the static constants HORIZONTAL, VERTICAL, BOTH, or NONE.
int gridheight	Specifies how many rows this cell spans.
int gridwidth	Specifies how many columns this cell spans.
int gridx	Specifies the x coordinate at the left side of this component, where the left-most cell has the value gridx=0.
int gridy	Specifies the y coordinate at the top of this component, where the top-most cell has the value gridy=0.
Insets insets	This value of type Insets specifies how much space to give around the outside of the component (*external padding*).
int ipadx	This value is the *internal horizontal padding*, or how much to add to the horizontal size of the component.
int ipady	This value is the *internal vertical padding*, or how much to add to the vertical size of the component.
int weightx	This specifies how much horizontal weight this component has when its container is resized. The greater the number, the larger it will be in comparison to other components when the container is enlarged.
int weighty	This is the same as weightx except that it specifies vertical weight.
static int RELATIVE	This value can be set to gridwidth or gridheight, in which case it signifies that this component is the next-to-last component in that row or column, respectively. It can also be set to gridx or gridy, in which case it signifies that this component should be placed right next to the previous component (just to the right for gridx and just underneath for gridy).
static int REMAINDER	This value can be set to gridwidth or gridheight to specify that it should be the last component in its row or column, respectively.

```
//change the gridheight to make it span multiple rows
constraints.gridheight = 2;
gridbag.setConstraints(b2, constraints);
add(b2);

b3 = new Button("Button 3");
//reset the gridheight
constraints.gridheight = 1;
```

```
    //make sure the button goes on the second row, first col
    constraints.gridy = 1;
    constraints.gridx = 0;
    gridbag.setConstraints(b3, constraints);
    add(b3);

    b4 = new Button("Button 4");
    //place this in the next column over
    constraints.gridx = GridBagConstraints.RELATIVE;
    gridbag.setConstraints(b4, constraints);
    add(b4);

    addWindowListener(this);
    pack();
    setVisible(true);
  }

  public static void main(String args[]) {
    new SimpleGridBagTest();
  }

  //WindowListener Interface
  public void windowClosing(WindowEvent e) {
    dispose();
    System.exit(0);
  }
  public void windowOpened(WindowEvent e) {}
  public void windowActivated(WindowEvent e) {}
  public void windowDeactivated(WindowEvent e) {}
  public void windowIconified(WindowEvent e) {}
  public void windowDeiconified(WindowEvent e) {}
  public void windowClosed(WindowEvent e) {}

}
```

In the SimpleGridBagTest application, a GridBagLayout object, gridbag, is created, along with its GridBagConstraints counterpart, constraints. Then, the application sets the constraints.fill field to the value GridBagConstraints. BOTH to signify that the components should be resized to fill their cells. I set the constraints.gridwidth field to 2 for Button b1. This makes it two cells wide or in other words, it spans two columns. After setting the values for b1, you have to explicitly set the constraints for b1:

```
gridbag.setConstraints(b1, constraints);
```

Then you add b1 to the Frame. Because b2 shouldn't span two rows, constraints.gridwidth is set back to 1 before setting the constraints for it. I set the constraints.gridheight to 2 to make it span two rows instead. For b3, you reset constraints.gridheight back to the default, which is 1. You also explicitly set its row to 1 and column to 0:

```
constraints.gridy = 1;
constraints.gridx = 0;
```

For b4, you set the `constraints.gridx` value to `GridBagConstraints.RELATIVE` so that it is placed directly to the right of b3. You can see how these constraints affect the buttons in Figure 7.5.

FIGURE 7.5

Four buttons are laid out using the `GridBagLayout` manager. The callouts show the row and column coordinates of the components.

(0, 0)　　　(1, 0)　　　(2, 0)

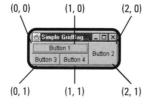

(0, 1)　　　(1, 1)　　　(2, 1)

Here is a more complicated example of how to use `GridBagLayout`:

```java
/*
 * GridBagLayoutTest
 * Demonstrates the GridBagLayout layout manager
 */

import java.awt.*;
import java.awt.event.*;

public class GridBagLayoutTest extends Frame
                                    implements WindowListener {

    public GridBagLayoutTest() {
        super("GridBagLayout Test");
        Button b1, b2, b3, b4, b5, b6, b7, b8;
        TextArea ta;
        addWindowListener(this);
        GridBagLayout gridbag = new GridBagLayout();
        GridBagConstraints constraints = new GridBagConstraints();

        setLayout(gridbag);
        b1 = new Button("Button 1");
        gridbag.setConstraints(b1, constraints);
        add(b1);

        b2 = new Button("Button 2");
        constraints.fill = GridBagConstraints.HORIZONTAL;
        gridbag.setConstraints(b2, constraints);
        add(b2);

        b3 = new Button("Button 3");
        constraints.fill = GridBagConstraints.NONE;
```

```
//end the row
constraints.gridwidth = GridBagConstraints.REMAINDER;
constraints.ipadx = 20;
constraints.ipady = 20;
gridbag.setConstraints(b3, constraints);
add(b3);

b4 = new Button("Button 4");
constraints.ipadx = 0;
constraints.ipady = 0;
constraints.gridwidth = 1;
//end this column
constraints.gridheight = GridBagConstraints.REMAINDER;
constraints.fill = GridBagConstraints.VERTICAL;
gridbag.setConstraints(b4, constraints);
add(b4);

ta = new TextArea("", 10, 30);
constraints.gridheight = 1;
constraints.weightx = 1;
constraints.weighty = 1;
constraints.fill = GridBagConstraints.BOTH;
constraints.insets = new Insets(5, 10, 15, 20);
gridbag.setConstraints(ta, constraints);
add(ta);

b5 = new Button("Button 5");
constraints.weightx = 0;
constraints.weighty = 0;
constraints.fill = GridBagConstraints.NONE;
constraints.anchor = GridBagConstraints.NORTHWEST;
constraints.insets = new Insets(0, 0, 0, 0);
gridbag.setConstraints(b5, constraints);
add(b5);

b6 = new Button("Button 6");
constraints.anchor = GridBagConstraints.SOUTHEAST;
constraints.gridwidth = GridBagConstraints.REMAINDER;
gridbag.setConstraints(b6, constraints);
add(b6);

b7 = new Button("Button 7");
constraints.fill = GridBagConstraints.BOTH;
//make this the second to last in this row
constraints.gridwidth = GridBagConstraints.RELATIVE;
gridbag.setConstraints(b7, constraints);
add(b7);

b8 = new Button("Button 8");
constraints.gridwidth = 1;
gridbag.setConstraints(b8, constraints);
add(b8);
```

```
    pack();
    setBackground(SystemColor.control);
    setVisible(true);
  }

  public static void main(String args[]) {
    new GridBagLayoutTest();
  }

  //WindowListener Interface
  public void windowClosing(WindowEvent e) {
    dispose();
    System.exit(0);
  }
  public void windowOpened(WindowEvent e) {}
  public void windowActivated(WindowEvent e) {}
  public void windowDeactivated(WindowEvent e) {}
  public void windowIconified(WindowEvent e) {}
  public void windowDeiconified(WindowEvent e) {}
  public void windowClosed(WindowEvent e) {}


}
```

The GridBagLayoutTest application lays out more components and uses more GridBagConstraints fields to lay them all out. There are eight Button objects—b1, b2, b3, b4, b5, b6, b7, and b8—and one TextArea object—ta. In this application, I add b1 without changing any of the constraints fields. For b2, I set the constraints.fill value to GridBagConstraints.HORIZONTAL to signify that it should completely fill its cell horizontally, even as the Frame is resized. For b3, I set constraints.fill to GridBagConstraints.NONE so that it doesn't completely fill its cell. I also set constraints.gridwidth to GridBagConstraints.REMAINDER to end the row that it's in. When I set constraints.ipadx = 20 and constraints.ipady = 20 for b3, I am telling gridbag to add 20 to its minimum width and height. For b4, I set these values back to 0, and the constraints.gridwidth back to 1. I also set constraints.gridheight to GridBagConstraints.REMAINDER so that it is the last component in its column and constraints.fill to GridBagConstraints.VERTICAL so that it will fill its cell vertically.

For the TextArea, ta, I set the constraints.weightx and constraints.weighty fields to 1 so that it will have precedence when the frame is resized. That's why, as you can see in Figure 7.6, the TextArea increases so much in size when the Frame is maximized. I also set its Insets so that it would have space in between it and the other components. For b5, I reset some of the constraints values and then set constraints.anchor to GridBagConstraints.NORTHWEST, so that it sticks (is anchored to) the top-left corner of its cell. I set this value to GridBagConstraints.SOUTHEAST for b6. I made b7 the second-to-last button in the row by setting constraints.gridwidth to GridBagConstraints.RELATIVE and then finally added the final component, b8. BINGO!

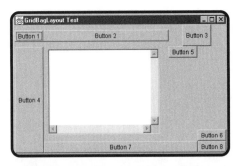

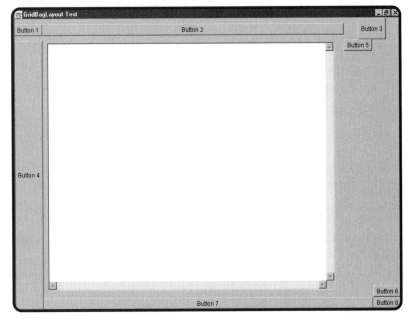

FIGURE 7.6

This is a more complex example of the `GridBagLayout` class.

TRICK

The `weightx` and `weighty` fields in the `GridBagConstraints` class can be confusing. Keep this in mind: The default value of these fields is zero. This value gives its components equal weight when the container is resized. One component typically takes precedence over the others, in which case you can set these values to 1 for that one component. If, however, your situation calls for a more complicated weight distribution among your components, you can try implementing it this way. Think of the weights of your components as adding up to 100 and each component's weight is a percentage of that. You can set a value to each of your components accordingly.

The `GridBagConstraints insets` field is an object of the `Insets` class. The `Insets` class is a simple way to specify insets, such as padding or margins. It has only one constructor, `Insets(int, int, int, int)`, which sets the top, left, bottom, and right insets, respectively. It also has four fields for these values, `top`, `left`, `bottom`, and `right`, oddly enough.

TRAP Be careful when working with only one `GridBagConstraints` object. It can get confusing to keep track of the constraints fields. One way to make this easier is to create a helper method that you pass a component to, along with some arguments that set `GridBagConstraints` fields for a new `GridBagConstraints` object, which is created each time the helper method is called. If your constraints get mixed up, you'll end up with an ugly GUI that's not very easily debugged.

Creating the *GUIFrame* Class

All the examples in the chapter up to this point have been using a new `Frame`. Now that you are going to be getting into some more complicated stuff, it's a good time to create a `Frame` subclass that encapsulates the functionality that you can use throughout the rest of the chapter. The `GUIFrame` class in this example has a few advanced features in it that you will come to understand more thoroughly as you continue reading this chapter. Here is a listing of `GUIFrame.java`:

```java
/*
 * GUIFrame
 * An extension of Frame that uses a WindowAdapter to
 * handle the WindowEvents and is centered.
 */

import java.awt.*;
import java.awt.event.*;

public class GUIFrame extends Frame {

  public GUIFrame(String title) {
    super(title);
    setBackground(SystemColor.control);

    addWindowListener(new WindowAdapter() {
      //only need to override the method needed
      public void windowClosing(WindowEvent e) {
        dispose();
        System.exit(0);
      }
    });
  }

  /* Centers the Frame when setVisible(true) is called */
  public void setVisible(boolean visible) {
    if (visible) {
      Dimension d = Toolkit.getDefaultToolkit().getScreenSize();
      setLocation((d.width - getWidth())/2,
                  (d.height - getHeight())/2);
    }
    super.setVisible(visible);
  }
}
```

First off, it extends Frame, so it is a Frame. It sets its background color to System-Color.control, which as you might remember from the previous chapter, is the color that your operating system uses for painting windows. Then it adds a WindowAdapter object as its WindowListener. Pay close attention to the syntax here. This is actually an inner-class declaration, which you'll learn about later on in this chapter.

Another cool thing it does is center itself, no matter what size it is when it becomes visible. I did this by overriding the setVisible(boolean) method. If the argument passed in is true, I get the screen size by calling Toolkit.getDefault-Toolkit().getScreenSize(), which returns a Dimension object representing the resolution of the computer screen, whether it is 640 by 480, 800 by 600, or whatever. The Toolkit class is the abstract subclass of all implementations of the AWT, the default of which is different depending on what operating system you are running. To center the GUIFrame on screen I needed to know the screen size and the size of the GUIFrame. The position of the GUIFrame is set with the setLocation(int, int) method, where the first int is the x location and the second int is the y location. The center location is half the difference of the screen width minus the GUIFrame width as the x position, and half the difference of the screen height minus the GUIFrame height as the y position. super.setVisible(visible) is called so that the corresponding method in the Frame class can take care of actually making the GUIFrame visible. Take a look at Figure 7.7 to see what the GUIFrame looks like. Here is a test of the GUIFrame class, GUIFrameTest:

```
/*
 * GUIFrameTest
 * Demonstrates the GUIFrame Class
 */

public class GUIFrameTest {

  public static void main(String args[]) {
    GUIFrame frame = new GUIFrame("GUIFrame Test");
    frame.setSize(400, 300);
    frame.setVisible(true);
  }

}
```

Using *CardLayout*

The CardLayout layout manager lays out its components as cards. You can think of each card as a card within a deck of playing cards. To make this analogy work, imagine that the cards are face up and only the top card is visible. You can take a card off the top of the deck and add it to the bottom to make the next card visible. Each card is actually a Java component. Only one of the components is visi-

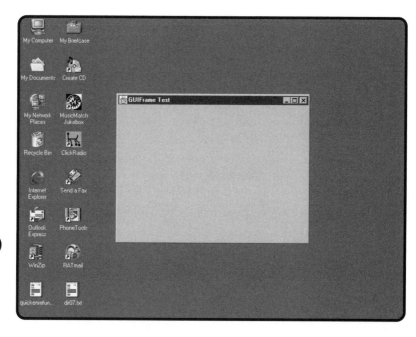

FIGURE 7.7

The GUIFrame class tested here is used throughout this chapter.

ble at a time. The first component added to the layout is visible when the container is initially visible. CardLayout has some methods that change which component is visible, as you can see in Table 7.5. When adding components to a CardLayout, you specify a string. That string is used as an identifier so that you can flip directly to that card when necessary. The name of the class is pretty self-explanatory. You can think of it as a deck of cards or a deck of components that

TABLE 7.5 CARDLAYOUT METHODS

Method	Description
CardLayout()	Constructs a CardLayout object with no horizontal or vertical gaps.
CardLayout(int, int)	Constructs a CardLayout object with the given horizontal and vertical gaps.
void first(Container)	Displays the first card of the given Container object.
void last(Container)	Displays the last card of the given Container object.
void next(Container)	Displays the next card of the given Container object.
void previous(Container)	Displays the previous card of the given Container object.
void show(String, Container)	Displays the card that was added to this Container using the specified String identifier.

can be traversed through, or dealt, one at a time. The `CardLayoutTest` application is an example:

```
/*
 * CardLayoutTest
 * Demonstrates the CardLayout layout manager
 */

import java.awt.*;
import java.awt.event.*;

public class CardLayoutTest extends GUIFrame
                            implements ActionListener {

  Panel cardPanel;
  Panel buttonPanel;
  Button nextButton;
  Button prevButton;
  Label l1, l2, l3;
  TextArea ta;
  CardLayout cardLayout;

  public CardLayoutTest() {
    super("CardLayout Test");
    cardLayout = new CardLayout();
    cardPanel = new Panel();
    cardPanel.setLayout(cardLayout);
    cardPanel.setBackground(Color.black);
    cardPanel.setForeground(Color.yellow);
    Font lFont = new Font("Verdana", Font.BOLD, 20);
    l1 = new Label("First", Label.LEFT);
    l1.setFont(lFont);
    l2 = new Label("Second", Label.CENTER);
    l2.setFont(lFont);
    ta = new TextArea("You can put any Components"
      + "\nthat you want, or even add a Container"
      + "\nthat itself contains multiple Components", 4, 35);
    ta.setForeground(Color.black);
    l3 = new Label("Last", Label.RIGHT);
    l3.setFont(lFont);
    cardPanel.add("C1", l1);
    cardPanel.add("C2", l2);
    cardPanel.add("C3", ta);
    cardPanel.add("C4", l3);
    add(cardPanel, BorderLayout.CENTER);

    buttonPanel = new Panel();
    prevButton = new Button("Previous");
    prevButton.addActionListener(this);
    buttonPanel.add(prevButton);
    nextButton = new Button("Next");
    nextButton.addActionListener(this);
    buttonPanel.add(nextButton);
    add(buttonPanel, BorderLayout.SOUTH);
```

```
    //pack sets the minimum size able to display the largest
    //Dimension Components
    pack();
    setVisible(true);
  }

  public static void main(String args[]) {
    CardLayoutTest clt = new CardLayoutTest();
  }

  public void actionPerformed(ActionEvent e) {
    if (e.getSource() == nextButton)
      cardLayout.next(cardPanel);
    else
      cardLayout.previous(cardPanel);
  }

}
```

CardLayoutTest extends GUIFrame, which itself has a BorderLayout by default, but contains a Panel, cardPanel, which has its layout set to cardLayout, a Card-Layout object. cardLayout lays out three labels: l1, l2, and l3, and a TextArea, ta, inside of cardPanel. The order that these are added is as follows:

```
    cardPanel.add("C1", l1);
    cardPanel.add("C2", l2);
    cardPanel.add("C3", ta);
    cardPanel.add("C4", l3);
```

Remember that the components are added along with a String identifier, which can call up any one of the cards to the front. After these four components are added to cardPanel, cardPanel is added to the GUIFrame at BorderLayout.CENTER. prevButton and nextButton are Button objects that I added to another Panel, buttonPanel, which in turn, I added to the GUIFrame at BorderLayout.SOUTH. Some event handling is required with these Buttons, covered in the next section. Basically prevButton causes cardLayout.previous(cardPanel) to be called and nextButton causes cardLayout.next(cardPanel) to be called when they are clicked. The output is shown in Figure 7.8.

FIGURE 7.8

The CardLayout manager displays its components one at a time.

Handling AWT Events

Up to this point, you've learned how to create components and lay them out within a container. However, you haven't had much use for these components yet. You were exposed to a bit of event handling already. This section concentrates on the `java.awt.event` package, which has classes that are used for handling events caused by user interaction with the AWT GUI interfaces you create. In this section, you'll learn about `WindowEvents`, `ActionEvents`, `FocusEvents`, `ItemEvents`, `AdjustmentEvents`, `TextEvents`, `MouseEvents`, and `KeyEvents`. The classes that you need to use to handle AWT events are in the `java.awt.event` package, so don't forget to import it into your applications. All the `Event` classes explored here directly extend the abstract `AWTEvent` class or the `ComponentEvent` class, which itself is a direct subclass of `AWTEvent`. `AWTEvent` is a subclass of the `EventObject` class. `KeyEvent` and `MouseEvent` extend `InputEvent`, which is a subclass of `ComponentEvent`.

You handle AWT events in Java (1.1 and higher) by implementing a *listener* interface that "listens" for events that can be triggered by components. A component that triggers events must *register* the listeners so that the listeners can "hear" the component's events. A component keeps a list of listeners that it informs when it triggers an event by calling one of its required methods. For example, you already know that to be a `WindowListener`, a class must implement all six of the `WindowListener` interfaces. When a `WindowEvent` occurs, the window will inform its listeners by calling one of those six methods, depending on which event has occurred. This will become more intuitive to you the more you do it, and because no GUI is useful without event handling, you will be using it every time you create one.

Handling *WindowEvents*

You've already implemented the `WindowListener` interface in the previous chapter and also in this chapter. Now you will learn about handling `WindowEvents` in more detail. To handle `WindowEvents`, you need to implement the `WindowListener` interface. When you implement the `WindowListener` interface or any other abstract interface, you need to implement its methods, which are listed in Table 7.6. These methods are called when corresponding actions have taken place. For `WindowListeners`, when a window is opened, closed, activated, deactivated, iconified (minimized), or deiconified (restored), the corresponding method is called to notify the interested "listener" class that the action has taken place.

The `WindowEventTest` application is a test of the `WindowListener` interface. It extends `GUIFrame` and implements `WindowListener`. The window opens and the events are handled simply by printing to standard output the event that has

TABLE 7.6 WINDOWLISTENER METHODS

Method	Description
void windowActivated(*WindowEvent*)	Called when a window becomes active (able to accept input events).
void windowClosed(*WindowEvent*)	Called when a window is closed (disposed).
void windowClosing(*WindowEvent*)	Called when a user attempts to close a window. You implement this method to conditionally close the window.
void windowDeactivated(*WindowEvent*)	Called when a window is deactivated (loses input focus).
void windowDeiconified(*WindowEvent*)	Called when a window is restored from a minimized state.
void windowIconified(*WindowEvent*)	Called when a window becomes minimized.
void windowOpened(*WindowEvent*)	Called when a window initially becomes visible.

taken place, so as you perform actions on the window that pops up, pay attention to the standard output so you can know when each method is called. Here is the source code for WindowEventTest.java:

```
/*
 * WindowEventTest
 * Tests WindowEvents
 */

import java.awt.*;
import java.awt.event.*;

public class WindowEventTest implements WindowListener {

  public WindowEventTest() {
    Frame frame = new Frame("WindowEvent Test");

    frame.add(new Label("See Command Prompt output for event log..."));
    frame.addWindowListener(this);
    frame.pack();
    frame.setVisible(true);
  }

  public static void main(String args[]) {
    WindowEventTest wet = new WindowEventTest();
  }

  //WindowListener Interface
  public void windowClosing(WindowEvent e) {
```

```
      System.out.println("windowClosing");
      ((Window)e.getSource()).dispose();
   }
   public void windowOpened(WindowEvent e) {
      System.out.println("windowOpened");
   }
   public void windowActivated(WindowEvent e) {
      System.out.println("windowActivated");
   }
   public void windowDeactivated(WindowEvent e) {
      System.out.println("windowDeactivated");
   }
   public void windowIconified(WindowEvent e) {
      System.out.println("windowIconified");
   }
   public void windowDeiconified(WindowEvent e) {
      System.out.println("windowDeiconified");
   }
   public void windowClosed(WindowEvent e) {
      System.out.println("windowClosed");
      System.exit(0);
   }

}
```

Most of the code here should be familiar. You've already used the methods of the `WindowListener` interface before, except that before now, you implemented them except for `windowClosing(WindowEvent)` as empty do-nothing methods. Previously, you had always called `System.exit(0)` in the `windowClosing(WindowEvent)` method. In this program, you wanted to see the `windowClosed(WindowEvent)` method triggered, so instead, you called:

```
((Window)e.getSource()).dispose();
```

As you learned in the previous chapter, the `dispose()` method releases all native resources used for the window and its subcomponents and closes the window. You can make the window displayable again, though, assuming `System.exit(0)` isn't called (which it is here) by calling `pack()` or `show()`. The `getSource()` method of the `WindowEvent` class, inherited from `EventObject`, is discussed in the next section. Basically, `e.getSource()` returns the object that initiated this WindowEvent, which in this case will always be the `WindowEventTest` object. In the `windowClosed(WindowEvent)` method, I called `System.exit(0)` to exit the Java VM after the window is closed. The `windowClosed(WindowEvent)` method is triggered when the `dispose()` method is called, closing the window.

The `WindowEventTest` class implements the `WindowListener` interface, so it becomes `WindowListener` itself, which is better than a window watcher, like the lady that lives across the street from me and calls the police if I forget about a holiday and bring my garbage out on the wrong day. Anyway, `WindowEventTest` is also a `Frame` because it extends `Frame`. It is the `Frame` and the `WindowListener` that listens to itself. It registers itself as a listener by calling the `addWindowListener(WindowListener)` method and passing itself as an argument by using the `this` keyword. Because of this, when a `WindowEvent` is triggered, it will call one of its own `WindowListener` methods so that it can handle its own events. This is not the only way to do it, though. It can register any `WindowListener`, or even multiple listeners, also by calling the `addWindowListener(WindowListener)` method for each of them.

You can see the output of this application in Figure 7.9. When I started the application, using the command:

```
java WindowEventTest
```

It ran the first two lines of output, `windowActivated` and `windowOpened`. After that, I minimized the window, running the next two lines, `windowIconified` and `windowDeactivated`. Then I restored the window (using Windows by clicking the icon on the taskbar), which triggered three events. These events—`windowActivated`, `windowDeiconified`, and `windowActivated`—generated the output, indicating that I activated the window by initially interacting with it on the taskbar. As the window was restored, the window triggered the `windowDeiconified(WindowEvent)` method; finally, the window was activated again.

When I closed the window by clicking the close button (the x), the `windowClosing` and `windowClosed` lines printed in the output.

Using Inner Adapter Classes

You're probably thinking, yeah, okay, Joe, what about that funky code in GUIFrame.java that closes the window? It doesn't implement WindowListener, nor does it define its methods, like you just told me I have to do, right? Well, actually it does, indirectly.

The WindowAdapter class implements the WindowListener interface and defines the methods as empty do-nothing methods. The sole purpose of the WindowAdapter class and other adapter classes, such as FocusAdapter, KeyAdapter, MouseAdapter, and MouseMotionAdapter, is to facilitate the implementation of their respective listener interfaces. Because they are classes that implement the listener's methods as do-nothing methods, you don't have to implement them all. You only need to implement the ones that you are interested in. In the GUIFrame class, you add the WindowListener as follows:

```
addWindowListener(new WindowAdapter() {
  //only need to override the method needed
  public void windowClosing(WindowEvent e) {
    dispose();
    System.exit(0);
  }
});
```

The code is even more confusing because the windowClosing(WindowEvent) method is overridden right within the call to the addWindowListener(WindowListener) method. The declaration of the WindowAdapter here is called an *anonymous inner class*. Here, I am creating a subclass of WindowAdapter and overriding its windowClosing(WindowEvent) method without actually giving that subclass a name and I am doing this within another class's definition. That's why it's called an anonymous inner class. Take a look at the files in the directory where you compiled GUIFrame.java. You will see a file named GUIFrame$1.class. This file holds the class definition of the anonymous `WindowAdapter` subclass. The syntax for creating an anonymous inner class is as follows:

```
OuterClass {
  new InnerClassName(constructor_arguments) {
    subclass_definition;
  }
}
```

Inner classes are Java classes that are defined within the curly braces of another class. An inner class has access to the outer classes' members and methods. For now, this is all you need to know about inner classes. You will revisit this topic in Chapter 11, "Custom Event Handling and File I/O."

Handling *ActionEvents*

`ActionEvents` are high-level events that are triggered by a component when it generates an event, such as a clicked `Button`. `ActionEvents` are listened to by implementing the `ActionListener` interface. This interface defines only one method `actionPerformed(ActionEvent)`. Take a look at `ButtonEventTest.java`, which implements the `ActionListener` interface:

```
/*
 * ButtonEventTest
 * Demonstrates using ActionListener to handle Button
 * events by counting the number of times a button is clicked.
 */

import java.awt.*;
import java.awt.event.*;

public class ButtonEventTest extends GUIFrame
                             implements ActionListener {

  Button button;
  int count;
  Label clicksLabel;

  public ButtonEventTest() {
    super("Button Event Test");
    button = new Button("Button");
    button.addActionListener(this);
    add(button, BorderLayout.CENTER);

    count = 0;
    clicksLabel = new Label();
    updateLabel();
    add(clicksLabel, BorderLayout.SOUTH);

    setSize(200, 200);
    setVisible(true);
  }
```

```
public static void main(String args[]) {
    new ButtonEventTest();
}

private void updateLabel() {
    String text = "Number of times clicked: ";
    clicksLabel.setText(text + String.valueOf(count));
}

public void actionPerformed(ActionEvent e) {
    count++;
    updateLabel();
}

}
```

The ButtonEventTest class has a Button, a Label, and an int, which are identified by the variable names button, clicksLabel, and count, respectively. Its action-Performed(ActionEvent) method is overridden to increment count, which is initialized to zero by the constructor and to update clicksLabel to display the current count value. This method is called each time that button is clicked, so in effect, this method just counts the number of times you click the button. As you can see in Figure 7.10, I clicked the button 27 times.

FIGURE 7.10

This application counts the number of times the button is clicked.

Note that the actionPerformed(ActionEvent) method is the only method. Because there is only one method, there is no corresponding ActionAdapter class. Table 7.7 lists some of ActionEvent's more common fields and methods.

Knowing the Source of an Event

If your event listener listens to multiple components, as it does the following example, you need to be able to determine which component triggered the event. No matter which component triggers the event, the same method is called. So if you have two buttons that your ActionListener is listening to, no matter which one is clicked, it will call the actionPerformed(ActionEvent) method. If the two buttons perform different actions, you need to determine the source of the ActionEvent and conditionally execute code based on which button triggered it. Here is a listing of ActionEventSourceTest.java:

TABLE 7.7 ACTIONEVENT FIELDS AND METHODS

Field or Method	Description
int ALT_MASK	Designates the Alt key modifier.
int CTRL_MASK	Designates the Ctrl key modifier.
int META_MASK	Designates the Meta key modifier.
int SHIFT_MASK	Designates the Shift key modifier.
int getModifiers()	Returns the modifier keys. Can be ALT_MASK, CTRL_MASK, META_MASK, SHIFT_MASK, or a combination (sum) of multiple key masks.
String getActionCommand()	Returns the *String* command associated with this ActionEvent.

```java
/*
 * ActionEventSourceTest
 * Demonstrates how to determine which Component triggered
 * the ActionEvent
 */

import java.awt.*;
import java.awt.event.*;

public class ActionEventSourceTest extends GUIFrame
                                    implements ActionListener {

Button button1, button2, button3;
int count1, count2, count3;
Label actionSource, click1, click2, click3;

  public ActionEventSourceTest() {
    super("ActionEvent Source Test");
    setLayout(new GridLayout(0, 2, 5, 10));
    actionSource = new Label("Action Source: <No Action>");
    add(actionSource);
    add(new Label("Click Counts"));

    button1 = new Button("Button 1");
    button1.addActionListener(this);
    add(button1);
    count1 = 0;
    click1 = new Label("0");
    add(click1);

    button2 = new Button("Button 2");
    button2.addActionListener(this);
```

```
//set the action command
button2.setActionCommand("Increment 2");
add(button2);
count2 = 0;
click2 = new Label("0");
add(click2);

button3 = new Button("Button 3");
//button3 has two action listeners
//this and an anonymous inner class
button3.addActionListener(this);
button3.addActionListener(new ActionListener() {
  public void actionPerformed(ActionEvent e) {
    click3.setText(String.valueOf(++count3));
  }
});
add(button3);
count3 = 0;
click3 = new Label("0");
add(click3);

pack();
setVisible(true);
}

public static void main(String args[]) {
  new ActionEventSourceTest();
}

public void actionPerformed(ActionEvent e) {
  actionSource.setText("Action Source: "
    + ((Button)e.getSource()).getLabel());
  //test by source
  if (e.getSource() == button1) {
    click1.setText(String.valueOf(++count1));
  }
  //test by action command
  else if (e.getActionCommand() == "Increment 2") {
    click2.setText(String.valueOf(++count2));
  }
}

}
```

This application is similar to the ButtonEventTest application, except that it separately counts three button clicks instead of just one. Each Button object has its associated int variable to count the number of clicks and Label to display the value. The stuff that is relevant to this section happens in the actionPerformed(ActionEvent) method.

In this method, you see the getSource() method again. This method is inherited from the EventObject class, so all classes that subclass EventObject have this method. It returns an `Object`, which is the source of the event. When you get the source of the `ActionEvent`, here using `e.getSource()`, an object of type `Object` is returned. An `Object` is not necessarily a `Button`, but a `Button` is an object. All objects in Java inherit from the `Object` class, but the `Object` class doesn't inherit from any other class. Because you know here that you can only expect a `Button`, you can cast the `Object` object to a `Button` object so you can call its methods that are defined in the `Button` class.

Here, because there are three `Button` objects, I decided to use three ways of handling a specific `Button`'s events. For `button1` and `button2`, this `ActionEventSourceTest` is the `ActionListener`. No matter which button is clicked, the `actionSource` label is updated with the button's label, obtained by the code:

```
((Button)e.getSource()).getLabel())
```

`button1` is tested as the source by testing the actual object reference:

```
if (e.getSource() == button1) {…}
```

Remember that the equality comparison operator ==, when applied to objects, tests whether both objects point to the same memory location (both are references to the exact same object... one object, two references). This condition is `true` if the user clicked `button1` to trigger the `ActionEvent`. `button2` is tested for by getting the action command associated with the `ActionEvent` by calling `e.getActionCommand()`. This only works because prior to this, I set the action command for the button:

```
button2.setActionCommand("Increment 2");
```

So by testing if the action command is `"Increment 2"`, I know that `button2` was clicked. `button3` is not listened to by this `ActionEventSource`. Instead, I used an anonymous inner class. If you choose to, you can create an anonymous inner class for each of the three buttons, so you never actually have to test for the source.

This `ActionListener` is set only to `button3`, so I don't have to call `e.getSource()`. I know right away that if the `actionPerformed(ActionEvent)` method here gets called, some chump clicked `button3`. You can see the results in Figure 7.11. I clicked Button 1, 19 times, Button 2, 21 times, and Button 3, 25 times (I didn't have anything better to do, or maybe I enjoy spending my free time clicking buttons).

FIGURE 7.11

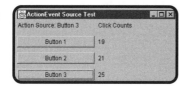

Finding the source of the action allows you to determine which button is clicked.

More *ActionEvent* Handling

Not only Button objects trigger ActionEvents. MenuItem, TextField, and List objects can also generate ActionEvents. ActionListenerTest is an example that displays the component that triggered the event. In this application, a MenuItem, a TextField, a Button, and a List are added to the GUIFrame. The "Who done it" TextField tells you which component triggered the event and is added to the GUIFrame, in its own Panel, at BorderLayout.NORTH. The "Action Command" TextField is at BorderLayout.SOUTH, and displays the action command that's associated with the component's ActionEvent. If you don't explicitly set the action command for the button, the button's label will be the action command. The action command for a TextField is the text it contains. The action command for a List is the text of the item. To get a TextField to trigger an ActionEvent, press the Enter key while it has your input focus. To get List to trigger an Action-Event, double-click one of the items it contains. Figure 7.12 shows the output.

```
/*
 * ActionListenerTest
 * Uses the ActionListener interface to listen to components.
 */

import java.awt.*;
import java.awt.event.*;

public class ActionListenerTest extends GUIFrame
                                  implements ActionListener {

    Panel controlPanel, whoDoneItPanel, commandPanel;
    MenuBar menuBar;
    Menu menu;
    MenuItem menuItem;
    Button button;
    List list;
    Label whoDoneItLabel, commandLabel;
    TextField whoDoneItTextField, commandTextField, textField;

    public ActionListenerTest() {
        super("ActionListener Test");
        controlPanel = new Panel();

        menuBar = new MenuBar();
        menu = new Menu("A Menu");
        menuItem = new MenuItem("A MenuItem",
                                new MenuShortcut(KeyEvent.VK_M));
        menuItem.addActionListener(this);
        menu.add(menuItem);
        menuBar.add(menu);
        setMenuBar(menuBar);
```

```
      controlPanel.add(new Label("A TextField:", Label.RIGHT));
      textField = new TextField(15);
      textField.addActionListener(this);
      controlPanel.add(textField);
      button = new Button("A Button");
      button.setActionCommand("My Action Command");
      button.addActionListener(this);
      controlPanel.add(button);
      controlPanel.add(new Label("A List:", Label.RIGHT));
      list = new List(5, false);
      list.add("Breakfast");
      list.add("Brunch");
      list.add("Lunch");
      list.add("Snack");
      list.add("Dinner");
      list.add("Dessert");
      list.addActionListener(this);
      controlPanel.add(list);

      add(controlPanel, BorderLayout.CENTER);

      whoDoneItPanel = new Panel();
      whoDoneItPanel.setBackground(Color.pink);
      whoDoneItLabel = new Label("Who done it:", Label.RIGHT);
      whoDoneItPanel.add(whoDoneItLabel);
      whoDoneItTextField = new TextField(15);
      whoDoneItTextField.setEditable(false);
      whoDoneItPanel.add(whoDoneItTextField);

      add(whoDoneItPanel, BorderLayout.NORTH);

      commandPanel = new Panel();
      commandPanel.setBackground(Color.pink);
      commandLabel = new Label("Action Command:", Label.RIGHT);
      commandPanel.add(commandLabel);
      commandTextField = new TextField(15);
      commandTextField.setEditable(false);
      commandPanel.add(commandTextField);

      add(commandPanel, BorderLayout.SOUTH);

      pack();
      setVisible(true);
   }

   public static void main(String args[]) {
      new ActionListenerTest();
   }

   public void actionPerformed(ActionEvent e) {
      if (e.getSource() == menuItem) {
         whoDoneItTextField.setText("A MenuItem");
      }
```

```
    else if (e.getSource() == textField) {
      whoDoneItTextField.setText("A TextField");
    }
    else if (e.getSource() == button) {
      whoDoneItTextField.setText("A Button");
    }
    else if (e.getSource() == list) {
      whoDoneItTextField.setText("A List");
    }

    commandTextField.setText(e.getActionCommand());
  }

}
```

FIGURE 7.12

This application tests actions caused by `MenuItems`, `TextFields`, `Buttons`, and `Lists`.

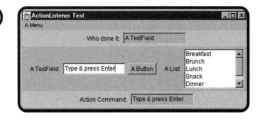

Handling Focus Events

The idea of a component having *focus* is that it is the component that is immediately awaiting user input. If you traverse through a GUI, a component's graphics will likely change to let you know that it has focus. For example, in Windows, a dotted rectangular shape appears around a `Button`'s label when it has focus and pressing the spacebar will cause the button to be pressed. Active `TextFields` have a blinking cursor. The `FocusTest` application tests the handling of `FocusEvents` by changing the color of the currently focused component to green. Here is the source code:

```
/*
 * FocusTest
 * Demonstrates listening to focus events
 */

import java.awt.*;
import java.awt.event.*;

public class FocusTest extends GUIFrame
                       implements FocusListener {

  Label label;
  Button button;
```

```
TextField textField;
Checkbox checkBox;

public FocusTest() {
  super("FocusListener Test");
  setLayout(new GridLayout(4, 0, 0, 10));
  label = new Label("Who has focus? No one does.");
  add(label);

  textField = new TextField("Track 1", 15);
  textField.addFocusListener(this);
  add(textField);

  button = new Button("Play Track");
  button.addFocusListener(this);
  add(button);

  checkBox = new Checkbox("Repeat", true);
  checkBox.addFocusListener(this);
  add(checkBox);
  add(button);

  pack();
  setVisible(true);
}

public static void main(String args[]) {
  new FocusTest();
}

public void focusGained(FocusEvent e) {
  ((Component)e.getSource()).setForeground(Color.green);
  if (e.getSource() == textField) {
    label.setText("Who has focus? The TextField.");
  }
  else if (e.getSource() == button) {
    label.setText("Who has focus? The Button.");
  }
  else if (e.getSource() == checkBox) {
    label.setText("Who has focus? The Checkbox.");
  }
}

public void focusLost(FocusEvent e) {
  ((Component)e.getSource()).setForeground(Color.black);
  label.setText("Who has focus? No one does.");
}

}
```

The addFocusListener(FocusListener) method is inherited from the Component class, so all components that are traversable can trigger FocusEvents. This application updates the "Who has focus?" method with the component that gains focus as well as changes the color of the component's foreground. The color change is hard to see in the screen shot because it's not in color, but you can see the label. Try running this on your own to see it for yourself. You can see this in action in Figure 7.13.

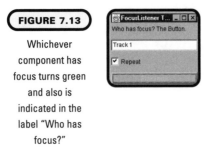

FIGURE 7.13

Whichever component has focus turns green and also is indicated in the label "Who has focus?"

There are two `FocusListener` methods. `focusGained(FocusEvent)`, which is called when a component gains keyboard focus, and `focusLost(FocusEvent)`, which is called when a component loses keyboard focus. There is also a `FocusAdapter` class that you can use to implement just one of these methods if you choose to.

Handling *ItemEvents*

`ItemEvents` are triggered by components that allow for a selection of items, such as `Checkbox`, `Choice`, and `List`. The `ItemListener` interface listens for these events. It contains only one method, `itemStateChanged(ItemEvent)`. It is called when an item is either selected or deselected. The `ItemTest` application tests the `ItemListener` interface. Here is the source code for `ItemTest.java`:

```
/*
 * ItemTest
 * Demonstrates the ItemListener interface
 */

import java.awt.*;
import java.awt.event.*;

public class ItemTest extends GUIFrame
                          implements ItemListener {
  Checkbox checkBox;
  Choice choice;
  List list;
  Label eventLabel;

  public ItemTest() {
    super("ItemListener Test");
    Panel itemPanel = new Panel();
    itemPanel.setLayout(new GridLayout(0, 4, 10, 0));
    checkBox = new Checkbox("Bass Boost", true);
```

```java
    checkBox.addItemListener(this);
    itemPanel.add(checkBox);

    itemPanel.add(new Label("Volume:", Label.RIGHT));
    choice = new Choice();
    for (int i=1; i <= 10; i++) {
      choice.add(String.valueOf(i));
    }
    choice.addItemListener(this);
    itemPanel.add(choice);

    list = new List(5, true);
    list.add("Coal Chamber");
    list.add("Disturbed");
    list.add("Godsmack");
    list.add("Kittie");
    list.add("Korn");
    list.addItemListener(this);
    itemPanel.add(list);
    add(itemPanel, BorderLayout.CENTER);

    eventLabel = new Label("Event:");
    add(eventLabel, BorderLayout.SOUTH);

    pack();
    setVisible(true);
  }

  public static void main(String args[]) {
    new ItemTest();
  }

  public void itemStateChanged(ItemEvent e) {
    String event = "Event: ";
    String selDesel = " ";
    if (e.getStateChange() == ItemEvent.SELECTED) {
      selDesel += "selected from ";
    }
    else if (e.getStateChange() == ItemEvent.DESELECTED) {
      selDesel += "deselected from ";
    }

    if (e.getSource() == checkBox) {
      event += e.getItem() + selDesel + "Checkbox";
    }
    else if (e.getSource() == choice) {
      event += e.getItem() + selDesel + "Choice";
    }
    else {
      event += list.getItem(((Integer)e.getItem()).intValue()) + selDesel + "List";
  }

      eventLabel.setText(event);
  }
}
```

The output for this application is shown in Figure 7.14. Within the `itemState-Changed(ItemEvent)` method, two string objects are built based on which event occurred. The `getStateChange()` method determines whether the item was selected or deselected by comparing the returned value to `ItemEvent.SELECTED` or `ItemEvent.DESELECTED`. The program then obtains the value of the item depending on what type of component it is. The `getItem()` method in the `ItemEvent` class returns an `Object` object that represents the item that triggered the event. For the `Checkbox` and the `Choice`, this works out great because the object returned is a string that can be added to the `"Event:"` string. For the `List`, however, I had to use the code:

```
list.getItem(((Integer)e.getItem()).intValue())
```

FIGURE 7.14

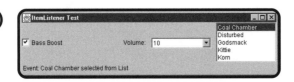

ItemEvents are
triggered by
Checkboxes,
Choices, and
Lists.

because `e.getItem()` returns the `Integer` index of the `List` item that was either selected or deselected. I had to explicitly cast it to an `Integer` object and call its `intValue()` method, which returns an `int` type value of the `Integer` object. Then I had to take that `int` value and pass it into `list.getItem(int)` so that I could get the `String` value of the `List` item. Table 7.8 lists some of the more common `ItemEvent` fields and methods.

TABLE 7.8 ITEMEVENT FIELDS AND METHODS

Field or Method	Description
int DESELECTED	Signifies that the ItemEvent occurred because an item was deselected.
int SELECTED	Signifies that the ItemEvent occurred because an item was selected.
int getStateChange()	Returns a value, either ItemEvent.DESELECTED or ItemEvent.SELECTED depending on what type of state change is associated with this ItemEvent.
Object getItem()	Returns an Object that represents the item whose state changed.

Handling *AdjustmentEvents*

The AdjustmentListener interface listens for AdjustmentEvents, which are triggered by objects that are adjustable, such as the Scrollbar component. AdjustmentListener has only one method, adjustmentValueChanged(AdjustmentEvent), which is invoked when the value of an adjustable object is changed, as you can probably guess from the name of the method. The AdjustmentTest application tests this:

```
/*
 * AdjustmentTest
 * Demonstrates the AdjustmentListener Interface on a scroll bar
 */

import java.awt.*;
import java.awt.event.*;

public class AdjustmentTest extends GUIFrame
                            implements AdjustmentListener {
  Scrollbar bar;
  Label minimum, maximum, current;

  public AdjustmentTest() {
    super("AdjustmentListener Test");
    GridBagLayout gridbag = new GridBagLayout();
    GridBagConstraints constraints = new GridBagConstraints();
    int min = 0, max = 100, curr = 50;

    setLayout(gridbag);
    minimum = new Label(String.valueOf(min), Label.RIGHT);
    gridbag.setConstraints(minimum, constraints);
    add(minimum);

    bar = new Scrollbar(Scrollbar.HORIZONTAL, curr, 1, min, max + 1);
    constraints.ipadx = 200;
    gridbag.setConstraints(bar, constraints);
    bar.addAdjustmentListener(this);
    add(bar);

    maximum = new Label(String.valueOf(max));
    constraints.gridwidth = GridBagConstraints.REMAINDER;
    constraints.ipadx = 0;
    gridbag.setConstraints(maximum, constraints);
    add(maximum);

    current = new Label(String.valueOf(curr), Label.CENTER);
    gridbag.setConstraints(current, constraints);
    add(current);

    setSize(300, 150);
    setVisible(true);
  }
```

```
public static void main(String args[]) {
  new AdjustmentTest();
}

public void adjustmentValueChanged(AdjustmentEvent e) {
  current.setText(String.valueOf(e.getValue()));
}

}
```

This application is fairly straightforward. It creates a `Scrollbar` and some `Labels` that represent the `Scrollbar`'s minimum, maximum, and current values. The `adjustmentValueChanged(AdjustmentEvent)` method updates the current value of the `Scrollbar` by calling `e.getValue()`. You can see the output in Figure 7.15. Table 7.9 shows some useful fields and methods of the `AdjustmentEvent` class.

FIGURE 7.15

You use the
Adjustment-
Listener interface
to determine when
a Scrollbar value
is being changed.

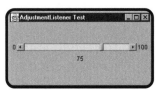

TABLE 7.9 ADJUSTMENTEVENT FIELDS AND METHODS

Field or Method	Description
int BLOCK_DECREMENT	Block decrement adjustment type.
int BLOCK_INCREMENT	Block increment adjustment type.
int TRACK	Absolute tracking adjustment type.
int UNIT_DECREMENT	Unit decrement adjustment type.
int UNIT_INCREMENT	Unit increment adjustment type.
int getAdjustmentType()	Returns the *int* representation of the adjustment type.
int getValue()	Returns the *int* current value of the adjustable object.

Handling *TextEvents*

TextEvents are generated by high-level objects such as text components. The `TextComponent` class has the `addTextListener(TextListener)` method, and both `TextField` and `TextArea` are subclasses of `TextComponent`. The `TextListener` interface has only one method, `textValueChanged(TextEvent)`. This method is invoked any time the value of the text is changed, such as when text is added or deleted. The TextTest application implements the TextListener interface to copy what you are typing into a TextField. Here is the source code for TextTest.java:

```java
/*
 * TextTest
 * Demonstrates the TextListener interface
 */

import java.awt.*;
import java.awt.event.*;

public class TextTest extends GUIFrame
                      implements TextListener {
  TextField text;
  TextField copyCat;

  public TextTest() {
    super("TextListener Test");
    GridBagLayout gridbag = new GridBagLayout();
    GridBagConstraints constraints = new GridBagConstraints();

    setLayout(gridbag);
    constraints.gridwidth = GridBagConstraints.REMAINDER;

    text = new TextField(25);
    gridbag.setConstraints(text, constraints);
    text.addTextListener(this);
    add(text);

    copyCat = new TextField(25);
    copyCat.setEnabled(false);
    gridbag.setConstraints(copyCat, constraints);
    add(copyCat);

    setSize(300, 150);
    setVisible(true);
  }

  public static void main(String args[]) {
    new TextTest();
  }

  public void textValueChanged(TextEvent e) {
    copyCat.setText(text.getText());
  }
}
```

This application simply creates two TextField objects, text and copyCat. text is the TextField that the user will be typing into. copyCat is a disabled TextField that will mimic the value of text each time its text value changes. You can see the TextListenerTest application in Figure 7.16.

FIGURE 7.16

This application copies your text as you write it and displays it below.

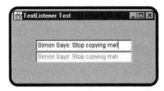

Handling *MouseEvents*

Your computer's mouse triggers MouseEvents. There are two types of mouse events. There are mouse motion events that are triggered by moving your mouse and regular mouse events that are triggered by clicking your mouse buttons or by moving your mouse into or out of a listener's area. These two types of events have two listener classes: MouseListener, which listens for mouse button triggered events and entry and exit events, and MouseMotionListener, which listens for the motion (change in pointer location) of your mouse and also dragging (mouse moved while button is down) events.

TRICK

MouseInputListener of the javax.swing.event package, which is not covered in this book, is a subinterface of both MouseListener and MouseMotionListener, so you can implement MouseInputListener and add it using addMouseListener(MouseListener) or addMouseMotionListener(MouseMotionListener), or both, to listen to any of these types of MouseEvents.

The MouseTest application implements both MouseListener and MouseMotionListener interfaces to capture MouseEvents. Here is the source code for MouseTest.java:

```
/*
 * MouseTest
 * Demonstrates the MouseListener and MouseMotionListener interfaces
 */

import java.awt.*;
import java.awt.event.*;

public class MouseTest extends GUIFrame
                        implements MouseListener, MouseMotionListener {

  Canvas canvas;
  Label location, event;

  public MouseTest() {
    super("Mouse Event Test");
    canvas = new Canvas();
    canvas.setBackground(Color.white);
    canvas.setSize(450, 450);
```

```
    canvas.addMouseListener(this);
    canvas.addMouseMotionListener(this);
    add(canvas, BorderLayout.CENTER);

    Panel infoPanel = new Panel();
    infoPanel.setLayout(new GridLayout(0, 2, 10, 0));
    location = new Label("Location:");
    infoPanel.add(location);
    event = new Label("Event:");
    infoPanel.add(event);
    add(infoPanel, BorderLayout.SOUTH);

    pack();
    setVisible(true);
  }

  public static void main(String args[]) {
    new MouseTest();
  }


  //The five MouseListener methods...

  public void mouseClicked(MouseEvent me) {
    String text = "Event: Clicked Button ";
    switch(me.getModifiers()) {
      case (InputEvent.BUTTON1_MASK):
        text += "1";
        break;
      case (InputEvent.BUTTON2_MASK):
        text += "2";
        break;
      case (InputEvent.BUTTON3_MASK):
        text += "3";
        break;
      default:
        text += "?";
    }
    text += " (" + me.getClickCount() + "x)";
    event.setText(text);
  }

  public void mouseEntered(MouseEvent me) {
    event.setText("Event: Entered");
  }

  public void mouseExited(MouseEvent me) {
    event.setText("Event: Exited");
  }

  public void mousePressed(MouseEvent me) {
    event.setText("Event: Pressed");
  }
```

```
public void mouseReleased(MouseEvent me) {
  event.setText("Event: Released");
}

//The two MouseMotionListener methods...

public void mouseMoved(MouseEvent me) {
  Point p = me.getPoint();
  location.setText("Location: (" + p.x + ", " + p.y + ")");
}

public void mouseDragged(MouseEvent me) {
  Point p = me.getPoint();
  event.setText("Event: Dragged");
  location.setText("Location: (" + p.x + ", " + p.y + ")");
}

}
```

The `MouseTest` object adds itself as a `MouseListener` and a `MouseMotionListener` to the `Canvas`, `canvas`. It overrides the listener methods to display on-screen the current location of the mouse cursor as well as the current event. `MouseEvent` methods are summarized in Table 7.10, and `MouseListener` and `MouseMotionListener` methods are summarized in Table 7.11. I overrode the `MouseListener` methods as follows: The `mouseClicked(MouseEvent)` method updates the `event` Label as to which button was clicked by testing the value returned by `getModifiers()` against the static variables `InputEvent.BUTTON1_MASK`, `InputEvent.BUTTON2_MASK`, and `InputEvent.BUTTON3_MASK`. This method also counts the clicks for the events. A double-click, for example, will show up as (2x). This number is obtained by getting the `getClickCount()` method of the `MouseEvent` class, which returns an `int` value of the number of times the mouse button was successively clicked. The `mouseEntered(MouseEvent)`, `mouseExited(MouseEvent)`, `mousePressed(MouseEvent)`, and `mouseReleased(MouseEvent)` methods just update the `event` Label, indicating which event occurred.

TABLE 7.10 MOUSEEVENT METHODS

Method	Description
int getClickCount()	Returns the number of successive mouse clicks.
Point getPoint()	Returns a Point that represents the cursor location relative to the source component.
int getX()	Returns the horizontal portion of the location point.
int getY()	Returns the vertical portion of the location point.

TABLE 7.11   MOUSELISTENER AND MOUSEMOTIONLISTENER METHODS

Method	Listener	Description
void mouseClicked(*MouseEvent*)	MouseListener	Invoked when a mouse clicks (is pressed, and then released) on a component.
void mouseEntered(*MouseEvent*)	MouseListener	Invoked when the mouse cursor enters the source component's area.
void mouseExited(*MouseEvent*)	MouseListener	Invoked when the mouse cursor exits the source component's area.
void mousePressed(*MouseEvent*)	MouseListener	Invoked when the mouse button is pressed down.
void mouseReleased(*MouseEvent*)	MouseListener	Invoked when the mouse button is released.
void mouseMoved(*MouseEvent*)	MouseMotionListener	Invoked when the mouse moves while within a component's area.
void mouseDragged(*MouseEvent*)	MouseMotionListener	Invoked when the mouse moves while the mouse button is down while within a component's area.

I updated the MouseMotionListener method mouseMoved(MouseEvent) to update the current location of the mouse cursor, and the mouseDragged(MouseEvent) method to update the current event to indicate the mouse is being dragged and also to update the current location of the mouse cursor. Figure 7.17 shows the output where I double-clicked mouse button 1 at location (277, 151). The location returned by getLocation() is a Point object. The Point class maintains two public variables x and y, which represent a point. There are some methods associated with the class, but basically, for your purposes, it's just that simple.

Handling *KeyEvents*

KeyEvents are triggered by keyboard actions performed by the users. The KeyListener interface defines three methods, shown in Table 7.12. The addKeyListener(KeyListener) method is defined in the Component class, so all components can process KeyEvents. The KeyEvent class has an insane number of static integers that represent each of the possible keys of different types of keyboards. There are

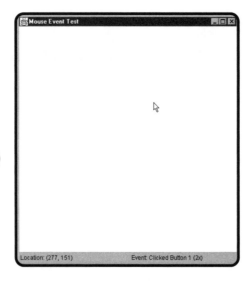

FIGURE 7.17

Listening to
MouseEvents
allows you to know
what the user is
doing with the
mouse.

TABLE 7.12 KEYLISTENER METHODS

Method	Description
void keyPressed(*KeyEvent*)	Invoked when a key is pressed down.
void keyReleased(*KeyEvent*)	Invoked when a key is released.
void keyTyped(*KeyEvent*)	Invoked when a key is typed.

too many to list here. Refer to the JDK 1.3 documentation of the KeyEvent class for a full list. Basically, these constants start with the letters VK (which stand for virtual key codes) followed by an underscore and a string representation of the key. For instance, the keyboard keys are represented by the constants KeyEvent.VK_A through KeyEvent.VK_Z, and the arrow keys are KeyEvent.VK_UP, KeyEvent.VK_DOWN, KeyEvent.VK_LEFT, and KeyEvent.VK_RIGHT. The more important KeyEvent methods are listed in Table 7.13.

The keyTyped(KeyEvent) method is only invoked by keys that generate valid characters, such as alpha characters and numerical characters. Even the Esc key generates a valid character. Experiment with the KeyTest application and see which keys do and do not update the "Last Typed:" field. Another thing to note is that holding a key down can sometimes generate multiple key typed events without ever generating a key release event if a keyboard is enabled with auto-repeat.

TABLE 7.13   KeyEvent Methods

Method	Description
char getKeyChar()	Returns the character associated with the key.
int getKeyCode()	Returns an integer representation of the key.
String getKeyModifiersText(*int*)	Returns a *String* representation of the modifier keys such as Ctrl based on the given integer representation of the modifiers.
String getKeyText(*int*)	Returns a *String* representation of a key based on the given key code.

The KeyTest application tests the handling of KeyEvents. Basically, it adds a KeyListener, which is itself, to a TextArea, textArea, and updates three labels with either pressed, released, or typed events. It gets the text representation of the key by first calling the getKeyCode() method of the KeyEvent class and passing it into the getKeyText(int) method. In the keyPressed(KeyEvent) method, the lastPressed variable is displayed when the keyTyped(KeyEvent) method is called. This is done in the keyPressed(KeyEvent) method instead of in the keyTyped(KeyEvent) method because key typed events always return VK_UNDEFINED when getKeyCode() is called. Here is the source listing of KeyTest.java. Sample output is shown in Figure 7.18.

```
/*
 * KeyTest
 * Demonstrates handling key events
 */

import java.awt.*;
import java.awt.event.*;

public class KeyTest extends GUIFrame
                     implements KeyListener {
  TextArea textArea;
  Label pressed, released, typed;
  String lastPressedText;

  public KeyTest() {
    super("KeyListener Test");
    textArea = new TextArea(10, 30);
    textArea.addKeyListener(this);
    add(textArea, BorderLayout.CENTER);

    Panel infoPanel = new Panel();
    infoPanel.setLayout(new GridLayout(3, 0, 0, 10));
    pressed = new Label("Last Pressed: <none>");
```

```
    infoPanel.add(pressed);
    released = new Label("Last Released: <none>");
    infoPanel.add(released);
    typed = new Label("Last Typed: <none>");
    infoPanel.add(typed);
    add(infoPanel, BorderLayout.SOUTH);

    pack();
    setVisible(true);
  }

  public static void main(String args[]) {
    new KeyTest();
  }

  public void keyPressed(KeyEvent e) {
    lastPressedText = e.getKeyModifiersText(e.getModifiers())
      + " " + KeyEvent.getKeyText(e.getKeyCode());
    pressed.setText("Last Pressed: "
                    + KeyEvent.getKeyText(e.getKeyCode()));
  }

  public void keyReleased(KeyEvent e) {
    released.setText("Last Released: "
                     + KeyEvent.getKeyText(e.getKeyCode()));
  }

  public void keyTyped(KeyEvent e) {
    typed.setText("Last Typed: " + lastPressedText);
  }
}
```

FIGURE 7.18

Implementing the
KeyListener
interface lets you
know when the
users are using the
keyboard.

Getting Back to the *AdvancedMadLib* Application

The AdvancedMadLib application uses much of what you have learned in this chapter. It uses layout managers to lay out its components, including a CardLayout. It also uses event handling to cause events for buttons that are pressed, or selections made from a Choice menu. Let's get ready to rumble!

Creating the *MadInputPanel* Class

The `MadInputPanel` class is responsible for all user text input. It has three `Panels`, which are laid out by the `CardLayout` layout manager. Each `Panel` gets its own type of input. One is for obtaining nouns, one is for obtaining verbs, and the last one is for obtaining all other types of words. Each card has its own array of `TextFields`: `nFields` for nouns, `vFields` for verbs, and `oFields` for other fields. Each card lays out its components using a `GridBagLayout` manager. This process is facilitated by the private method `addComponent(Panel, Component)`; it is basically there to reduce the number of lines in the source code and keep it from getting too confusing. It sets the `GridBagConstraints` to the passed in component and then adds the component to the passed in `Panel`. It also has two public methods that traverse through the cards, called `previous()` and `next()`. Another method, `show(String)`, shows a specific card based on its `String` name—Nouns, Verbs, or Other.

Similar to the `MadDialog` class from the previous chapter, the `MadInputPanel` class has a `String[] getStringArray()` method that returns the values of its `TextFields` in the order that they should be inserted into the story. It also implements it in a similar way. It creates a `Vector`, copies it into an array of `Strings`, and returns it to the caller. The source listing for `MadInputPanel.java` is as follows:

```
/*
 * MadInputPanel
 * The AdvancedMadLib game's input panel.
 * All input is accepted here
 */

import java.awt.*;
import java.awt.event.*;
import java.util.Vector;

public class MadInputPanel extends Panel {
    protected GridBagLayout gridbag;
    protected GridBagConstraints constraints;
    protected CardLayout cards;
    protected Panel nouns, verbs, others;
    protected TextField[] nFields, vFields, oFields;

    public MadInputPanel() {
        super();
        gridbag = new GridBagLayout();
        constraints = new GridBagConstraints();
        constraints.anchor = GridBagConstraints.WEST;
        cards = new CardLayout();
        setLayout(cards);
```

```java
//Nouns
nouns = new Panel();
nouns.setLayout(gridbag);
addComponent(nouns, new Label("Enter some nouns:"));
nFields = new TextField[8];
//put all noun fields in the second column
constraints.gridx = 1;
constraints.gridy = GridBagConstraints.RELATIVE;
for (int n=0; n < nFields.length; n++) {
  nFields[n] = new TextField(20);
  addComponent(nouns, nFields[n]);
}
add("Nouns", nouns);

//Verbs
verbs = new Panel();
verbs.setLayout(gridbag);
constraints.gridx = constraints.gridy = 0;
addComponent(verbs, new Label("Enter some verbs:"));
vFields = new TextField[8];
//put all verb Fields in the second column
constraints.gridx = 1;
constraints.gridy = GridBagConstraints.RELATIVE;
for (int v=0; v < vFields.length; v++) {
  vFields[v] = new TextField(20);
  addComponent(verbs, vFields[v]);
}
//add other field descriptions.
constraints.gridx = 2;
constraints.gridy = 4;
addComponent(verbs, new Label("(ends with \"ing\")"));
constraints.gridy = GridBagConstraints.RELATIVE;
addComponent(verbs, new Label("(ends with \"ing\")"));
addComponent(verbs, new Label("(past tense)"));
addComponent(verbs, new Label("(present tense)"));
add("Verbs", verbs);

//Other Fields
others = new Panel();
others.setLayout(gridbag);
constraints.gridx = GridBagConstraints.RELATIVE;
constraints.gridy = GridBagConstraints.RELATIVE;
addComponent(others, new Label("Enter affectionate nicknames:"));
oFields = new TextField[7];
//create Other text fields, but don't lay them out yet
for (int o=0; o < oFields.length; o++) {
  oFields[o] = new TextField(20);
}
addComponent(others, oFields[0]);
constraints.gridwidth = GridBagConstraints.REMAINDER;
addComponent(others, oFields[1]);
constraints.gridwidth = 1;
```

```java
    addComponent(others, new Label("Enter adjectives:"));
    addComponent(others, oFields[2]);
    constraints.gridwidth = GridBagConstraints.REMAINDER;
    addComponent(others, oFields[3]);
    constraints.gridwidth = 1;
    addComponent(others, new Label("Enter a preposition:"));
    constraints.gridwidth = GridBagConstraints.REMAINDER;
    addComponent(others, oFields[4]);
    constraints.gridwidth = 1;
    addComponent(others, new Label("Enter a body part:"));
    constraints.gridwidth = GridBagConstraints.REMAINDER;
    addComponent(others, oFields[5]);
    constraints.gridwidth = 1;
    addComponent(others, new Label("Enter a location:"));
    addComponent(others, oFields[6]);
    add("Other", others);
  }

  private void addComponent(Panel p, Component c) {
    gridbag.setConstraints(c, constraints);
    p.add(c);
  }

  public void previous() {
    cards.previous(this);
  }

  public void next() {
    cards.next(this);
  }

  public void show(String panel) {
    cards.show(this, panel);
  }

  public String[] getStringArray() {
    String[] s;
    Vector v = new Vector();
    v.add(vFields[0].getText()); v.add(vFields[0].getText());
    v.add(vFields[0].getText()); v.add(oFields[0].getText());
    v.add(vFields[1].getText()); v.add(oFields[2].getText());
    v.add(nFields[0].getText());
    v.add(vFields[0].getText()); v.add(vFields[0].getText());
    v.add(vFields[0].getText()); v.add(oFields[0].getText());
    v.add(vFields[2].getText()); v.add(oFields[5].getText());
    v.add(vFields[4].getText());
    v.add(vFields[4].getText()); v.add(oFields[6].getText());
    v.add(vFields[3].getText()); v.add(oFields[1].getText());
    v.add(nFields[1].getText()); v.add(oFields[3].getText());
    v.add(nFields[2].getText());
    v.add(vFields[3].getText()); v.add(oFields[1].getText());
    v.add(vFields[6].getText()); v.add(vFields[5].getText());
    v.add(vFields[3].getText()); v.add(oFields[1].getText());
```

```
        v.add(oFields[4].getText()); v.add(nFields[3].getText());
        v.add(vFields[3].getText()); v.add(oFields[1].getText());
        v.add(nFields[4].getText()); v.add(nFields[5].getText());
        v.add(vFields[3].getText()); v.add(oFields[1].getText());
        v.add(nFields[6].getText()); v.add(vFields[7].getText());
        v.add(nFields[7].getText());
        v.add(vFields[3].getText()); v.add(oFields[1].getText());
        v.add(vFields[0].getText()); v.add(vFields[0].getText());
        v.add(vFields[0].getText()); v.add(oFields[0].getText());
        v.add(vFields[1].getText()); v.add(oFields[2].getText());
        v.add(nFields[0].getText());
        v.add(vFields[0].getText()); v.add(vFields[0].getText());
        v.add(vFields[0].getText()); v.add(oFields[0].getText());
        v.add(vFields[2].getText()); v.add(oFields[5].getText());
        v.add(vFields[4].getText());
        v.add(vFields[4].getText()); v.add(oFields[6].getText());

        s = new String[v.size()];
        v.copyInto(s);
        return s;
    }
}
```

Creating the *AdvancedMadLib* Application

The AdvancedMadLib application is the heart of this game. It extends GUIFrame
and uses the default layout manager, BorderLayout. It creates a MadInputPanel
object, inputPanel, and adds it at BorderLayout.CENTER. It also creates a Panel,
navPanel, which it adds the prev, next, and showStory buttons to. It also adds a
Choice called inputChoice. To the prev Button, an ActionListener is added so
that when it is clicked, the previous card of inputPanel is displayed. Oppositely,
to the next Button, an ActionListener is added so that when it is clicked the
next card is shown by calling its next() method. The inputChoice menu is set up
with items that represent the names of inputPanel's cards. An ItemListener is
added to it so that when an Item is chosen, the corresponding card is shown by
calling:

```
inputPanel.show((String)e.getItem());
```

The showStory button calls up the Dialog, storyDialog. Before calling up the
storyDialog window, the private createStory() method builds the story using
an array of String segments that represent the segments of the story. It merges
these segments with the segments returned by the getStringArray() method of
the MadInputPanel class. Once the story is displayed, you can change the values
of the text and redisplay the story as many times as you want. Here is the source
listing for AdvancedMadLib.java:

```
/*
 * AdvancedMadLib
 * A MadLib Application that demonstrates layout managers and events
 */

import java.awt.*;
import java.awt.event.*;

public class AdvancedMadLib extends GUIFrame {
  Panel navPanel;
  MadInputPanel inputPanel;
  Button prev, next, showStory;
  Choice inputChoice;
  Dialog storyDialog;
  TextArea story;

  public AdvancedMadLib() {
    super("Create your own Song");

    //Card Panel (contains other panels in a CardLayout)
    inputPanel = new MadInputPanel();
    add(inputPanel, BorderLayout.CENTER);

    //Navigation Panel
    navPanel = new Panel();
    navPanel.setLayout(new GridLayout(0, 4, 10, 0));
    prev = new Button("<- Prev");
    prev.addActionListener(new ActionListener() {
      public void actionPerformed(ActionEvent e) {
        inputPanel.previous();
      }
    });
    navPanel.add(prev);
    inputChoice = new Choice();
    inputChoice.add("Nouns");
    inputChoice.add("Verbs");
    inputChoice.add("Other");
    inputChoice.addItemListener(new ItemListener() {
      public void itemStateChanged(ItemEvent e) {
        inputPanel.show((String)e.getItem());
      }
    });
    navPanel.add(inputChoice);
    next = new Button("Next ->");
    next.addActionListener(new ActionListener() {
      public void actionPerformed(ActionEvent e) {
        inputPanel.next();
      }
    });
    navPanel.add(next);
    showStory = new Button("Show/Refresh Story");
```

```
    showStory.addActionListener(new ActionListener() {
      public void actionPerformed(ActionEvent e) {
        createStory();
        storyDialog.setVisible(true);
      }
    });
    navPanel.add(showStory);

    add(navPanel, BorderLayout.SOUTH);
    storyDialog = new Dialog(this, "Your Song");
    storyDialog.addWindowListener(new WindowAdapter() {
      public void windowClosing(WindowEvent e) {
        storyDialog.setVisible(false);
      }
    });
    story = new TextArea("", 27, 50);
    story.setEditable(false);
    storyDialog.add(story);
    storyDialog.pack();

    pack();
    setVisible(true);
  }

  public static void main(String args[]) {
    new AdvancedMadLib();
  }

  private void createStory() {
    String song = "";
    String[] segs = {", ", ", ", " my ", "\nDon't ", " a ", " ",
      "\n", ", ", ", ", ", ", " my ", "\nJust ", " your pretty ",
      "\nI'll be ", " you again \nI'll be ", " you in ",
      "\n\nDon't ", " to me oh ",
      "\nYour ", "'s in a ", " ",
      ", yeah \nDon't ", " to me oh ",
      "\nShould have ", " it a-",
      " on\nDon't ", " to me oh ",
      "\nI don't know it was ", " your ",
      "\nDon't ", " to me oh ",
      "\nDead-end ", " for a dead-end ",
      "\nDon't ", " to me oh ",
      "\nNow your ", " ", " on the ",
      "\nDon't ", " to me oh ",
      "\n\n", ", ", ", ", " my ", "\nDon't ", " a ", " ",
      "\n", ", ", ", ", ", ", " my ", "\nJust ", " your pretty ",
      "\nI'll be ", " you again \nI'll be ", " you in "};

    String[] s = inputPanel.getStringArray();
    for (int i = 0; i < segs.length; i++) {
      song += s[i] + segs[i];
    }
```

```
        song += s[s.length - 1];

        story.setText(song);
    }

}
```

Summary

In this chapter, you learned all about layout managers, including `FlowLayout`, `GridLayout`, `BorderLayout`, `GridBagLayout`, and `CardLayout`. You also learned how to handle GUI events using the `java.awt.event` package. You can now handle `ActionEvents`, `WindowEvents`, `FocusEvents`, `ItemEvents`, `AdjustmentEvents`, `TextEvents`, `MouseEvents`, and `KeyEvents`. In the next chapter, you learn all about applets.

CHALLENGES

1. **Create a Frame that does not close normally by using the `windowClosing(WindowEvent)` method, but instead, closes when you click a Button labeled `Close`.**

2. **Create an application that has multiple Buttons with different labels for each of them. When any one of those Buttons is clicked, a `TextField` is updated with the text of that one Button. Also include a `TextArea` that appends the text displayed in the `TextField` to its text by listening for `TextEvents`. The end result will be that the `TextArea` will contain an audit trail of all of the button clicks, in the order they were clicked. The `TextField` displays the most recently clicked button. Lay out these components as you desire, but use a `GridBagLayout` manager.**

3. **Create a numerical keypad that uses Buttons to update an uneditable `TextField` by appending the clicked number to the end of its current number. Use a `BorderLayout` for the `Frame`. At `BorderLayout.NORTH`, place the `TextField`. In the center, create a panel that uses a `GridLayout` to lay out Buttons 1 through 9 in a three by three grid. At `BorderLayout.SOUTH`, create another `Panel` that has the zero key and also a "clear" key that deletes the current number in the `TextField`.**

CHAPTER

8

Writing Applets

With the Internet as widely used as it is today, one of the more exciting features of Java is its use as a tool for Internet development. You can embed Java right into a Web document by writing an applet and adding some HTML to include that applet. In this chapter, you learn all about applets—how to create them, how to write the HTML to make use of them, and all about security restrictions and other differences between applets and applications. This chapter covers the following topics:

- Understand applet basics

- Learn the difference between applets and applications

- Use the `Applet` class

- Include an applet in an HTML Web page

- Write programs that can run as either an applet or an application

- Display images and play sounds

The Project: *QuizShow* Applet

The QuizShow applet asks a series of true or false questions. The user selects either true or false and then clicks the "That's my final answer!" button for the next question. The label at the top indicates whether the previous answer was correct. After the user answers the final question, the QuizShow applet shows the final score. The applet is driven by parameters set within the HTML. None of the questions are hard coded in the applet itself. The questions are specified within the HTML parameters, which enable you to ask any number of questions by modifying the HTML file and without having to rewrite or recompile the applet code. Figure 8.1 shows the project for this chapter.

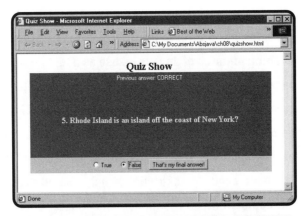

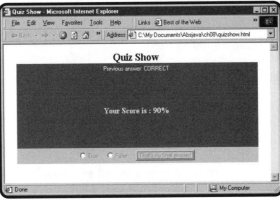

FIGURE 8.1

The QuizShow applet asks true or false questions and shows you your score.

Understanding Applets

An *applet* is a small program that runs embedded within another application. Popular browsers such as Microsoft Internet Explorer and Netscape Navigator support Java applets. This means that the browsers themselves are interpreting the Java byte code as part of a Web document, not the Java VM that is installed on your system that runs applications. There are often differences in how the browsers interpret the Java to the extent that you will notice a significant difference in how the applets run. Sometimes an applet will run fine in one browser, but not in another. If you experience any difficulty running these applets in your browser, make sure you have the latest version of the Java interpreter, or Virtual Machine (VM), installed. In this chapter, I tested all my applets using the SDK's appletviewer utility (part of the development kit included on the CD) as well as using Microsoft Internet Explorer 5 with the latest Microsoft VM installed.

If you are having trouble with Internet Explorer, from the Tools menu, select Windows Update, where you will be taken to the Windows Update Web site, and look for the Microsoft Virtual Machine update if one is available. If you are using any other browser, visit your browser vendor's Web site to get more information about the particular browser you are using and its Java support. If all else fails, use the appletviewer utility; it should work just fine.

 To use the appletviewer utility in Windows, Solaris, and Linux, at your command prompt type `appletviewer` *myhtmlfile.html*, where *myhtmlfile.html* is the HTML file that has the `<applet>` tags that reference your applet. The appletviewer will show only the applet itself and none of the surrounding HTML.

Knowing the Difference between Applets and Applications

So far in this book, you've dealt almost exclusively with applications. The only exposure you had to an applet was a brief example back in Chapter 1, "Getting Started." Applications are stand-alone programs because they run on their own and are not interpreted by any program other than your computer's Java Interpreter. Applets are found on the Internet and are run by your browser, so they force security restrictions on applets. You wouldn't want to surf to the wrong Web site and have your hard drive erased, would you? There are other differences between Java applets and applications, but the main difference is that applets are restricted from reading or writing files on your client (your computer, to the Internet), whereas applications can do whatever they want to do.

How Do Applets Work?

To create an applet, you have to subclass the `Applet` class. The `Applet` class is found in the `java.applet` package, which is quite small—just the `Applet` class and a few interfaces. Applets have a method called `init()`. Typically, operations that you perform in a constructor are done in this `init()` method for applets. After you've written and compiled your applet, you need to include in an HTML document so that your browser can interpret it and include the `<applet>` tag so that your browser can find the applet and run it. You therefore have your class that extends `Applet`, the HTML file, and your browser. That's all you need to run a simple applet. This is all just briefly described here so you will be able to understand the early examples in this chapter. These topics are covered in more detail later in this chapter, so don't worry about it too much just yet.

Hello Again!

In Chapter 1, you wrote the `HelloWeb` applet. It only displayed a string, `"Hello, Web!"`. That applet works by overriding the `paint(Graphics)` method, which you'll learn about in the next chapter. The `HelloAgainApplet` works differently. To understand how it works, first off, you need to understand that the `Applet` class extends `java.awt.Panel`. That's right, an `Applet` is a `Panel` that is displayable by your browser. That means that you can add other AWT components to it right away, as long as you remember to import the `java.awt` package. The `HelloAgainApplet` applet says `"Hello Again!"` by adding a `Label`. Here is the source code for `HelloAgainApplet.java`:

```
/*
 * HelloAgainApplet
 * This is another version of the HelloWeb applet
 * that uses a Label to say Hello.
 */

import java.applet.Applet;
import java.awt.Label;

public class HelloAgainApplet extends Applet {

  public void init() {
    add(new Label("Hello Again!", Label.CENTER));
  }

}
```

You can see that this program imports the `java.applet.Applet` class. This is necessary so that `HelloAgainApplet` can subclass the `Applet` class. `java.awt.Label` is also imported so that it can add a label. The only other thing that this applet does is override the `init()`. It is inside of this method where the label is added.

Here is the `helloagain.html` file listing. Using HTML to include an applet is described in greater detail in the next section. For now, just type the following into a text editor and save it as `helloagain.html`. The output is shown in Figure 8.2.

HINT   The file name isn't all that important when naming an HTML document that contains an applet. Unlike a Java source file, the name of the HTML document does not have to match the class name. You can name it whatever you want.

```
<html>
<head>
  <title>Hello Again Applet</title>
</head>

<body>
<h1 align=center>Hello Again Applet</h1>
<center>

<applet code="HelloAgainApplet.class" width=200 height=100>
</applet>

</center>
</body>
</html>
```

FIGURE 8.2

The `HelloAgain-Applet` says hello using a `Label`.

As in all the HTML source files, you use a text editor to enter the HTML, and then save it with the file extension `.html` or `.htm`. Then you can double-click the resulting icon to have your default browser open it up. Again, you can also run it by using the appletviewer utility. Make sure you pass the HTML file as the argument to the appletviewer, not the. java or the `.class` file.

The *Applet* Class

In order for a Java program to be an applet and have the capability to run within a Web browser, it must subclass the Applet class. It provides the interface that browsers need to embed Java code. It is important to know what the methods of the Applet class do in order to use them properly. Table 8.1 lists some important Applet methods.

TABLE 8.1   APPLET METHODS

Method	Description
destroy()	Called by the browser to indicate that the applet is being unloaded from memory and that it should perform any clean up now.
String getAppletInfo()	Returns a String object that represents information about this applet. It is meant to be overridden by subclasses to provide information such as author, version, and so on.
AudioClip getAudioClip(URL)	Returns the AudioClip object at the specified URL.
AudioClip getAudioClip(URL, String)	Returns the AudioClip object at the specified base URL, having the specified name.
URL getCodeBase()	Returns the URL object that represents this applet's base URL.
URL getDocumentBase()	Returns the absolute (complete, not relative) URL object that represents the directory that contains this applet.
Image getImage(URL)	Returns the Image at the given URL.
Image getImage(URL, String)	Returns the Image at the given URL, with the specified name.
String getParameter(String)	Returns the String value of the parameter having the given name or null, if the parameter isn't set.
String[][] getParameterInfo()	Returns a String[][] that represents the parameter information of this applet. This method is intended to be overridden by subclasses of Applet.
void init()	Called by the browser to indicate that the applet has been loaded.
void start()	Called by the browser to indicate that the applet should begin execution.
void stop()	Called by the browser to indicate that the applet should stop execution.

Including an Applet in a Web Page

You need to know a little bit of HTML here to get your applets to run in a Web page. In this section, I'll go over the bare bones of HTML—just the stuff you need to get your applets up and running. First I'll talk about basic HTML tags, and then the `<applet>` tag and after that I'll explain how to pass parameters to applets using the `<param>` tag.

HTML stands for Hypertext Markup Language and is used to develop Web documents. HTML tags are formatting instructions that surround text, giving the text certain attributes that affect the way your browser displays it. Tags are specified within angle brackets (`<` and `>`) and typically there is a start and an end tag with some text in between. Here is an example:

```
<tag>Here Is some text that the tag affects</tag>
```

where *tag* is the name of the tag. An open tag goes at the beginning of the text you are formatting. A closing tag is placed at the end of the text. The label within the tag is preceded with a forward slash (/). An example of opening and closing tags is `<b>bold text</b>`. The bold tags (`<b>` and `</b>`) surround text to make it appear bold when displayed within your browser. An opening tag can also specify certain *attributes*, or parameters that tweak the tag's effect. The attributes are listed, separated by spaces and typically their values are placed within quotation marks, but sometimes they are omitted:

```
<tag attribute1="value1" attribute2="value2">Formatted text</tag>
```

An ending tag is also the name of the tag within angle brackets, but the name is prefaced with a forward-slash (/) to indicate that it is an ending tag. Some tags do not require ending tags. Table 8.2 lists the tags that I use in this book and

TABLE 8.2 RELEVANT HTML TAGS

Tag	Purpose
`<HTML></HTML>`	These are top-level tags that indicate this is an HTML file.
`<HEAD></HEAD>`	Surrounds information about the HTML document, such as the title.
`<TITLE></TITLE>`	Specifies the title that appears in the title bar of the browser window.
`<BODY></BODY>`	Surrounds the main body of the HTML document.
`<H1></H1>`	Specifies header text that is used as titles for sections of the document.
`<CENTER></CENTER>`	Centers the text that it surrounds.
`<APPLET></APPLET>`	Embeds an applet in the document.

what they do. HTML is much more robust than what this book explains, but that's why there are entire series of books dedicated to HTML and Web development, so not every attribute of every tag is covered here, just the ones you'll see in the HMTL files you are going to create.

The *<applet>* HTML Tag

The ⟨applet⟩ tag embeds a Java applet within a browser window. It specifies the .class file of the applet as well as the width, height, and other attributes. When a Java-enabled browser encounters a set of ⟨applet⟩⟨/applet⟩ tags, it invokes the applet at the location where the tags appear. It does not display any text that it finds within the opening and closing tags, but browsers that do not understand Java will, so you can write the applet tag in the helloagain.html file like this:

```
<applet code="HelloAgainApplet.class" width=200 height=100>
Your browser does not support Java. Time for an upgrade, methinks!
</applet>
```

If you then opened the document with a browser that either does not support Java or has Java disabled, instead of seeing the applet, you would see the text "Your browser does not support Java. Time for an upgrade, methinks!". The ⟨applet⟩ tag has a set of attributes. Here are some of them:

CODE	Specifies the .class file that defines the applet.
WIDTH	Specifies the width within the browser window reserved for the applet.
HEIGHT	Specifies the height within the browser window reserved for the applet.
CODEBASE	Specifies the URL of the applet. Required if the applet resides in a different directory.
MAYSCRIPT	Its presence (has no value assigned to it) indicates that the applet can access JavaScript functionality within the page.
NAME	Specifies the name of the applet that identifies it from other applets on the same document.

Passing Parameters to Applets

Applets can accept run-time parameters just like applications can. You specify applet parameters within ⟨param⟩ tags. These tags belong within the opening and closing ⟨applet⟩ tags of the applet they are intended for. When specifying a parameter for an applet, you need to specify the parameter name and the parameter value using the corresponding ⟨param⟩ tag attributes:

```
<param name="fontcolor" value="blue">
```

The names of the attributes, as well as their actual implementations, are up to you to define within the applet source code. The applet retrieves this parameter information by using the getParameter(String) method of the Applet class. The String that is passed to this method is the name of the parameter. The String value that it returns is the value that is set for that parameter. For example, the previous parameter is retrieved with the following code within the applet source file:

```
String myColor = getParameter("fontcolor");
```

Note that the getParameter(String) method always returns a String. This means that if the value you need to use in your actual applet is not a String, you need to parse the returned String value to whatever type you need or use conditional logic based on the parameter's value to get the result you need. For example, check out this code, which would come after the previous parameter retrieval:

```
if (myColor == "blue") myColorObject = Color.blue;
```

The SayWhatApplet applet demonstrates how to use parameters and how different parameter settings cause differences in how your applet runs. Here is the SayWhatApplet.java source code:

```
/*
 * SayWhatApplet
 * Says whatever the "say" parameter tells it to say
 */

import java.applet.Applet;
import java.awt.Label;

  public class SayWhatApplet extends Applet {

  public void init() {
    String sayThis;
    sayThis = getParameter("say");
    if (sayThis == null) {
      sayThis = "...";
    }
    add(new Label(sayThis));
  }

  public String[][] getParameterInfo() {
    return new String[][] {
      { "say", "String", "Message to display" }
    };
  }

  public String getAppletInfo() {
    return "Author: Joseph P Russell";
  }
}
```

TRAP

After the SayWhatApplet applet retrieves the say parameter, it checks if it is null. This is how it can tell whether the HTML document that contains this applet has specified the value for this parameter. This is important, because if you don't test for null, your applet might crash with a NullPointerException. It is good practice to test for null parameter values in your applet code and handle those situations accordingly. In the case of the SayWhatApplet, the text "…" is displayed instead if no say parameter is specified.

Although not required, I overrode the getParameterInfo() and getAppletInfo() methods to return information that might be useful. It is up to the application that embeds this applet to display this information. For example, to see these values that I set here, you can run the appletviewer tool on the HTML files listed next and select Info from the Applet menu. There are also some other useful menu options such as Reload, Restart, and Tag, that you can play around with.

The getParameterInfo() method returns a two dimensional String array. It is an array of arrays. Each subarray should be a set of three Strings that specify the parameter name, the parameter type, and a description of the parameter.

TRICK

Overriding the getParameterInfo() method anytime your applet accepts parameters is good practice. It allows you as well as others to make use of your parameters without having to refer to the source code and explains settable features of your applet that would otherwise remain unknown to others. From the getAppletInfo() method, you can return any information about the applet that you want to share with others. You can show off by including your name as the author of the applet, specify your company's name, applet version number, and so on. That's what these methods are there for, so why not take advantage of them?

Here is an HTML file that does not pass any parameters to the SayWhatApplet applet, saywhat1.html:

```
<html>
<head>
<title>Say What Applet 1 - No Parameter Set</title>
</head>
<body>
<h1 align=center>Say What Applet 1 - No Parameter Set</title>
<center>

<applet code="SayWhatApplet.class" width=300 height=100>
</applet>

</center>
</body>
</html>
```

You can see the SayWhatApplet running in Figure 8.3.

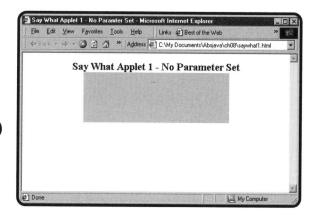

FIGURE 8.3

No parameters were passed into the applet, so all you get is "…".

Here is a listing for `saywhat2.html`, which passes a `String`, `"Adrenaline starts to flow!"`, to the `say` argument of the `SayWhatApplet` applet:

```
<html>
<head>
<title>Say What Applet 2</title>
</head>
<body>
<h1 align=center>Say What Applet 2</h1>
<center>

<applet code="SayWhatApplet.class" width=300 height=100>
<param name="say" value="Adrenaline starts to flow!">
</applet>

</center>
<body>
</html>
```

You can see how `SayWhatApplet` interprets the parameter in Figure 8.4.

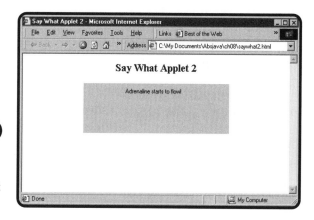

FIGURE 8.4

The `SayWhatApplet` says what you tell it to say.

Here is one more example to show that the SayWhatApplet will run differently each time its parameter is different. Here is a listing of saywhat3.html, which tells the SayWhatApplet to say "You're thrashing all around!"

```
<html>
<head>
<title>Say What Applet 3</title>
</head>
<body>
<h1 align=center>Say What Applet 3</h1>
<center>

<applet code="SayWhatApplet.class" width=300 height=100>
<param name="say" value="You're thrashing all around!">
</applet>

</center>
<body>
</html>
```

Now that the parameter has changed yet again; take a look at Figure 8.5 for the result.

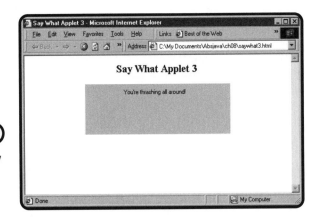

FIGURE 8.5

Private Gump, why did you say that? Because you told me to, Sergeant?

Using Frames with Applets

You can call up Frames from within Java applets. They look just like normal Frames except there is a warning on the bottom to let the users know that this is not an application, but an applet and might not be trustworthy. There are security restrictions that prevent applets from messing with your hard drive, so there is nothing to worry about, but it is possible to trust an applet and give it access to your computer. That's why the warning is there, just as a friendly reminder not to take candy from strangers. You can use Frames pretty much just like you do in applications. FrameTestApplet calls up a Frame. Here is the source listing for FrameTestApplet.java:

```
/*
 * FrameTestApplet
 * Shows how to call up a Frame from an Applet
 */

import java.awt.*;
import java.applet.Applet;
import java.awt.event.*;

public class FrameTestApplet extends Applet
                                implements ActionListener {
  Button button;
  Frame frame;
  Label label;

  public void init() {
    button = new Button("Show 'da Frame");
    button.addActionListener(this);
    add(button);
    frame = new Frame("An Applet Frame: I'm Framous!");
    frame.setBackground(SystemColor.control);
    label = new Label("15 Minutes of Frame", Label.CENTER);
    frame.add(label, BorderLayout.CENTER);
    frame.addWindowListener(new WindowAdapter() {
      public void windowClosing(WindowEvent we) {
        frame.setVisible(false);
      }
    });
    frame.setSize(300, 200);
  }

  public void actionPerformed(ActionEvent e) {
    frame.setVisible(true);
  }

}
```

Basically, the applet adds a Button, called button, to itself. It implements Action-Listener and overrides the actionPerformed(ActionEvent) method to make the Frame named frame visible. In the init() method, button is instantiated, and the ActionListener, this, is added to it and it is added to the Applet panel. Then frame is created and a WindowListener is added to it using methods that you are already familiar with from Chapters 6, "Creating a GUI Using the Abstract Windowing Toolkit," and 7, "Advanced GUI: Layout Managers and Event Handling." The Label is added to the frame just to demonstrate that frame works like the other Frame objects you've used up to this point.

Here is the frametest.html source listing:

```
<html>
<head>
  <title>Frame Test Applet</title>
```

```
</head>
<body>
<h1 align="center">Frame Test Applet</h1>

<center>
<applet code="FrameTestApplet.class" width=125 height=50>
</applet>
</center>

</body>
</html>
```

Take a look at Figure 8.6 to see how this looks when run from Internet Explorer.

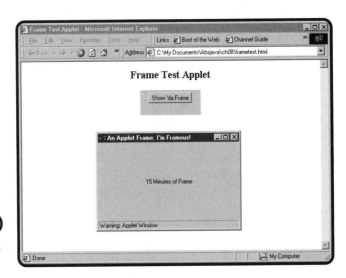

FIGURE 8.6

This applet calls up an applet window.

Security Restrictions

There are other security features in place that keep someone from destroying your computer files or corrupting your operating system with viruses while surfing the net. An applet cannot load libraries or define native methods. This basically means that your system's specific APIs are inaccessible. An applet can only use its own methods or the methods provided by the application's Java applet API. An applet also cannot read or write files on your computer. There are ways around this that are not covered in this book, but basically an applet cannot read or write files on your computer unless you give it permission to. An applet can't start any applications that reside on your computer, nor can it read any of your system properties.

Learning Applet Methods: *init()*, *start()*, *stop()*, and *destroy()*

When a Web browser runs an applet, it calls its init(), start(), stop(), and destroy() methods in a particular order at specific times of the applet's life cycle. The init() method is called once the browser has loaded the applet and you typically perform operations that normally are performed in a constructor in an application here. The start() method is called when the applet should begin execution and the stop() method is called when the applet should stop. Finally destroy() is called when the applet is unloaded from system resources; you override this method to perform any clean-up actions that you need to perform when the applet dies. The AppletInit applet overrides these methods to print a text message to standard output to let you know exactly when these methods are called. Here is the source code for AppletInit.java:

```
/*
 * AppletInit
 * Tests which methods are called during initialization
 */

import java.applet.Applet;

public class AppletInit extends Applet {

  public void init() {
    System.out.println("init()");
  }

  public void start() {
    System.out.println("start()");
  }

  public void stop() {
    System.out.println("stop()");
  }

  public void destroy() {
    System.out.println("destroy()");
  }

}
```

Here is the appletinit.html file source code listing:

```
<html>
<head>
  <title>Applet Test</title>
</head>
<body>
<h1 align="center">Applet Test</h1>
<center>
```

```
<applet code="AppletInit.class" width=100 height=100>
</applet>

</center>
</body>
</html>
```

You can see the MS-DOS output from AppletInit, which is running in appletviewer, in Figure 8.7, and you can see Internet Explorer's Java Console in Figure 8.8.

The standard output print stream can be different for each application that runs your applet. For instance, the appletviewer tool prints its output to your system's standard output (the same one as your applications) and Internet Explorer prints to the Java Console. To view the Java Console, select the Java Console option from the View menu. If you can't find it or it is disabled, select Internet Options from the Tools menu. Then click the Advanced tab and check the Java Console Enabled option, which will require that you restart your computer. If that option is not available, you need to install the Microsoft VM (again, this is done by selecting Windows Update from the Tools menu). Netscape also has a Java Console, which is found on the Options menu.

FIGURE 8.7

I started AppletInit with the appletviewer and then closed the appletviewer window. You can see the order these methods were called.

FIGURE 8.8

From Internet Explorer, I started the applet. Then, I reloaded and visited another page and you can see the resulting order of method calls here.

Printing Status Messages

The `AppletInit` applet prints messages to the standard output stream, but there is another way to display status messages. You can do this by using the `showStatus(String)` method provided by the `Applet` class. The string that is passed to this method is displayed, typically, somewhere in your browser's frame or at the bottom of the appletviewer window if you are running your applets by using the appletviewer tool. Here is the source code for `StatusBarApplet.java`, an applet that displays a message when your mouse enters it and displays a different message when your mouse cursor exits it by using the `MouseListener` interface:

```
/*
 * StatusBarApplet
 * Demonstrates how to print text in the status bar
 */

import java.applet.Applet;
import java.awt.event.*;

public class StatusBarApplet extends Applet {

  public void init() {
    addMouseListener(new MouseAdapter() {
      public void mouseEntered(MouseEvent e) {
        showStatus("Stop touching me...");
      }

      public void mouseExited(MouseEvent e) {
        showStatus("Thanks!");
      }
    });
  }

}
```

Here is the source code for `statusbar.html`; the output is shown in Figure 8.9.

```
<html>
<head>
  <title>Status Bar Applet</title>
</head>

<body>
<h1 align=center>Status Bar Applet</h1>
<center>

<applet code="StatusBarApplet.class" width=100 height=100>
</applet>

</body>
</html>
```

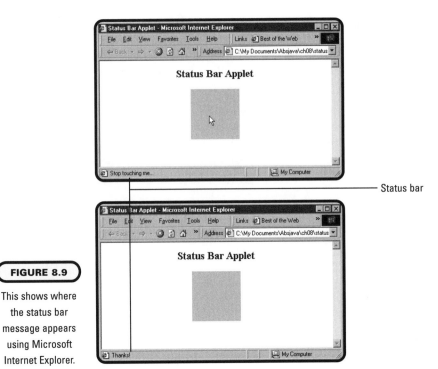

Status bar

FIGURE 8.9

This shows where the status bar message appears using Microsoft Internet Explorer.

Writing Java Programs that Can Run as Applets or Applications

It is possible to write a Java program that can run as an application or an applet. This is kind of cool, don't you think? Basically, this is done by extending `Applet`, which as you know, is required if you want to be able to run your program as a Java applet. You also need to create a `main()` method, which as you know, is required in order for your program to run as an application. The distinction between an applet and application lies in the way the program is started. If you go into your command prompt window and type the following:

```
java MyProgram
```

the program will run as an applet. The `init()` method will be ignored unless you directly make a call to it, so you only need to define things that your application will do within the `main()` method. On the other hand, if you have the following applet tag:

```
<applet code="MyProgram.class" width=100 height=100></applet>
```

it will be interpreted by your browser. The `main()` method will be ignored. Instead the `init()`, `start()`, `stop()`, and `destroy()` methods are called, so that is where you put your applet-specific code. The next section takes the project from Chapter 7, the MadLib game, and rewrites it so that you can run it as either an application or an applet.

TRICK Because the `Applet` class extends `java.awt.Panel`, and the operations performed in the `init()` method are like those typically done in a constructor, you can write a program that runs as an application and an applet without duplicating your code too much. You can do this by calling the `init()` method from the `main()` method to build up the applet as a `Panel`, and then add the `Panel` to a `Frame`.

Rewriting *MadInputPanel*

The `MadInputPanel` class would optimally not need to be written. The only reason it needed to be rewritten is because of the differences between the Java VM installed on my hard drive (SDK 1.3) and the version I have installed in my browser, 5.0.0.3802. The problem here was the `Vector` class. Internet Explorer, with the version of Microsoft VM that I have installed just a few days ago, does not recognize the `add(Object)` method of the `Vector` class, which was introduced in JDK 1.2. It also does not understand the `remove(Object)` or `get(int)` methods. These methods were added because the `Vector` class was retrofitted to implement the `List` interface. The original versions of these methods, `addElement(Object)`, `removeElement(Object)`, and `elementAt(int)`, are used to circumvent the fact that Internet Explorer does not support the newer methods as of the writing of this book. The appletviewer utility, however, does support the new `List` interface methods. Here is the new listing for `MadInputPanel.java`:

```
/*
 * MadInputPanel
 * The AdvancedMadLib game's input panel.
 * All input is accepted here
 */

import java.awt.*;
import java.awt.event.*;
import java.util.Vector;

public class MadInputPanel extends Panel {
  protected GridBagLayout gridbag;
  protected GridBagConstraints constraints;
  protected CardLayout cards;
  protected Panel nouns, verbs, others;
  protected TextField[] nFields, vFields, oFields;

  public MadInputPanel() {
    super();
    gridbag = new GridBagLayout();
    constraints = new GridBagConstraints();
```

```
constraints.anchor = GridBagConstraints.WEST;
cards = new CardLayout();
setLayout(cards);

//Nouns
nouns = new Panel();
nouns.setLayout(gridbag);
addComponent(nouns, new Label("Enter some nouns:"));
nFields = new TextField[8];
//put all noun fields in the second column
constraints.gridx = 1;
constraints.gridy = GridBagConstraints.RELATIVE;
for (int n=0; n < nFields.length; n++) {
  nFields[n] = new TextField(20);
  addComponent(nouns, nFields[n]);
}
add("Nouns", nouns);

//Verbs
verbs = new Panel();
verbs.setLayout(gridbag);
constraints.gridx = constraints.gridy = 0;
addComponent(verbs, new Label("Enter some verbs:"));
vFields = new TextField[8];
//put all verb Fields in the second column
constraints.gridx = 1;
constraints.gridy = GridBagConstraints.RELATIVE;
for (int v=0; v < vFields.length; v++) {
  vFields[v] = new TextField(20);
  addComponent(verbs, vFields[v]);
}
//add other field descriptions.
constraints.gridx = 2;
constraints.gridy = 4;
addComponent(verbs, new Label("(ends with \"ing\")"));
constraints.gridy = GridBagConstraints.RELATIVE;
addComponent(verbs, new Label("(ends with \"ing\")"));
addComponent(verbs, new Label("(past tense)"));
addComponent(verbs, new Label("(present tense)"));
add("Verbs", verbs);

//Other Fields
others = new Panel();
others.setLayout(gridbag);
constraints.gridx = GridBagConstraints.RELATIVE;
constraints.gridy = GridBagConstraints.RELATIVE;
addComponent(others, new Label("Enter affectionate nicknames:"));
oFields = new TextField[7];
//create Other text fields, but don't lay them out yet
for (int o=0; o < oFields.length; o++) {
  oFields[o] = new TextField(20);
}
addComponent(others, oFields[0]);
constraints.gridwidth = GridBagConstraints.REMAINDER;
```

```
    addComponent(others, oFields[1]);
    constraints.gridwidth = 1;
    addComponent(others, new Label("Enter adjectives:"));
    addComponent(others, oFields[2]);
    constraints.gridwidth = GridBagConstraints.REMAINDER;
    addComponent(others, oFields[3]);
    constraints.gridwidth = 1;
    addComponent(others, new Label("Enter a preposition:"));
    constraints.gridwidth = GridBagConstraints.REMAINDER;
    addComponent(others, oFields[4]);
    constraints.gridwidth = 1;
    addComponent(others, new Label("Enter a body part:"));
    constraints.gridwidth = GridBagConstraints.REMAINDER;
    addComponent(others, oFields[5]);
    constraints.gridwidth = 1;
    addComponent(others, new Label("Enter a location:"));
    addComponent(others, oFields[6]);
    add("Other", others);
}

private void addComponent(Panel p, Component c) {
    gridbag.setConstraints(c, constraints);
    p.add(c);
}

public void previous() {
    cards.previous(this);
}

public void next() {
    cards.next(this);
}

public void show(String panel) {
    cards.show(this, panel);
}

public String[] getStringArray() {
    String[] s;
    Vector v = new Vector();
    v.addElement(vFields[0].getText()); v.addElement(vFields[0].getText());
    v.addElement(vFields[0].getText()); v.addElement(oFields[0].getText());
    v.addElement(vFields[1].getText()); v.addElement(oFields[2].getText());
    v.addElement(nFields[0].getText()); v.addElement(vFields[0].getText());
    v.addElement(vFields[0].getText()); v.addElement(vFields[0].getText());
    v.addElement(oFields[0].getText()); v.addElement(vFields[2].getText());
    v.addElement(oFields[5].getText()); v.addElement(vFields[4].getText());
    v.addElement(vFields[4].getText()); v.addElement(oFields[6].getText());
    v.addElement(vFields[3].getText()); v.addElement(oFields[1].getText());
    v.addElement(nFields[1].getText()); v.addElement(oFields[3].getText());
    v.addElement(nFields[2].getText()); v.addElement(vFields[3].getText());
    v.addElement(oFields[1].getText()); v.addElement(vFields[6].getText());
    v.addElement(vFields[5].getText()); v.addElement(vFields[3].getText());
    v.addElement(oFields[1].getText()); v.addElement(oFields[4].getText());
```

```
        v.addElement(nFields[3].getText()); v.addElement(vFields[3].getText());
        v.addElement(oFields[1].getText()); v.addElement(nFields[4].getText());
        v.addElement(nFields[5].getText()); v.addElement(vFields[3].getText());
        v.addElement(oFields[1].getText()); v.addElement(nFields[6].getText());
        v.addElement(vFields[7].getText()); v.addElement(nFields[7].getText());
        v.addElement(vFields[3].getText()); v.addElement(oFields[1].getText());
        v.addElement(vFields[0].getText()); v.addElement(vFields[0].getText());
        v.addElement(vFields[0].getText()); v.addElement(oFields[0].getText());
        v.addElement(vFields[1].getText()); v.addElement(oFields[2].getText());
        v.addElement(nFields[0].getText()); v.addElement(vFields[0].getText());
        v.addElement(vFields[0].getText()); v.addElement(vFields[0].getText());
        v.addElement(oFields[0].getText()); v.addElement(vFields[2].getText());
        v.addElement(oFields[5].getText()); v.addElement(vFields[4].getText());
        v.addElement(vFields[4].getText()); v.addElement(oFields[6].getText());

        s = new String[v.size()];
        v.copyInto(s);
        return s;
    }
}
```

When you are writing an applet, it is best to refrain from using the newest Java features, because browser support for the newest releases always comes later than the release dates of the Java API. Another potential problem is that even when new versions are released, most users do not keep their Java VMs up to date. To reach the widest possible audience, try to use features and classes of Java that are well established. Be careful, however, about deprecation. A class, field, or method is deprecated when the standard version of Java encourages you not to use it (usually because a better method has been developed or because the future releases will not support this aging method). The newest version of Java might support it, but when you compile your code, you will get a warning. Future releases of Java will probably omit the deprecated features altogether.

Rewriting the *MadLib* Game

This section describes the changes that I made to the AdvancedMadLib.java source code, which I renamed to MadLibApplet.java to differentiate it from the original. The first visible change is the fact that I imported the java.applet.Applet package and extended Applet instead of GUIFrame. Instead of extending GUIFrame, I included a GUIFrame member, frame, which I use when this is run as an application or to its own dialog box when it runs as an applet. I moved the code that used to reside in the AdvancedMadLib constructor to the init() method. I also added the instantiation of the frame object to the init() method. The reason for using the GUIFrame even when this is run as an applet is because, when you create a Dialog object, you have to pass either a Frame or another Dialog to be its owner. You can see that when I construct the storyDia-log object, I pass in frame instead of this because the Applet class does not extend either Frame or Dialog. Okay, so far, that's all you need to do to run this as an applet.

To be able to run this as an application also, I added a main() method. The main() method creates a new MadLibApplet object, mla, calls its init() method to build up its GUI, and then adds the Applet to the frame object by calling showIn-Frame(). showInFrame()adds this MadLibApplet to frame, packs it, and makes it visible. There, once the HTML is written, this game can be run as both an applet and an application. Here is the source code for MadLibApplet.java:

```
/*
 * MadLibApplet
 * A Rewrite of the AdvancedMadLib Application from Chapter 7
 * so that it can be run as an Applet or an Application.
 */

import java.applet.Applet;
import java.awt.*;
import java.awt.event.*;

public class MadLibApplet extends Applet {
  GUIFrame frame;
  Panel navPanel;
  MadInputPanel inputPanel;
  Button prev, next, showStory;
  Choice inputChoice;
  Dialog storyDialog;
  TextArea story;

  public void init() {
    setLayout(new BorderLayout());
    frame = new GUIFrame("Create your own Song");
    //Card Panel (contains other panels in a CardLayout)
    inputPanel = new MadInputPanel();
    add(inputPanel, BorderLayout.CENTER);

    //Navigation Panel
    navPanel = new Panel();
    navPanel.setLayout(new GridLayout(0, 4, 10, 0));
    prev = new Button("<- Prev");
    prev.addActionListener(new ActionListener() {
      public void actionPerformed(ActionEvent e) {
        inputPanel.previous();
      }
    });
    navPanel.add(prev);
    inputChoice = new Choice();
    inputChoice.add("Nouns");
    inputChoice.add("Verbs");
```

```
      inputChoice.add("Other");
      inputChoice.addItemListener(new ItemListener() {
        public void itemStateChanged(ItemEvent e) {
          inputPanel.show((String)e.getItem());
        }
      });
      navPanel.add(inputChoice);
      next = new Button("Next ->");
      next.addActionListener(new ActionListener() {
        public void actionPerformed(ActionEvent e) {
          inputPanel.next();
        }
      });
      navPanel.add(next);
      showStory = new Button("Show/Refresh Story");
      showStory.addActionListener(new ActionListener() {
        public void actionPerformed(ActionEvent e) {
          createStory();
          storyDialog.setVisible(true);
        }
      });
      navPanel.add(showStory);

      add(navPanel, BorderLayout.SOUTH);
      storyDialog = new Dialog(frame, "Your Song");
      storyDialog.addWindowListener(new WindowAdapter() {
        public void windowClosing(WindowEvent e) {
          storyDialog.setVisible(false);
        }
      });
      story = new TextArea("", 27, 50);
      story.setEditable(false);
      storyDialog.add(story);
      storyDialog.pack();
    }

    public void showInFrame() {
      frame.add(this);
      frame.pack();
      frame.setVisible(true);
    }

    public static void main(String args[]) {
      MadLibApplet mla = new MadLibApplet();
      mla.init();
      mla.showInFrame();
    }

    private void createStory() {
      String song = "";
      String[] segs = {", ", ", ", " my ", "\nDon't ", " a ", " ",
        "\n", ", ", ", ", ", ", " my ", "\nJust ", " your pretty ",
```

```
          "\nI'll be ", " you again \nI'll be ", " you in ",
          "\n\nDon't ", " to me oh ",
          "\nYour ", "'s in a ", " ",
          ", yeah \nDon't ", " to me oh ",
          "\nShould have ", " it a-",
          " on\nDon't ", " to me oh ",
          "\nI don't know it was ", " your ",
          "\nDon't ", " to me oh ",
          "\nDead-end ", " for a dead-end ",
          "\nDon't ", " to me oh ",
          "\nNow your ", " ", " on the ",
          "\nDon't ", " to me oh ",
          "\n\n", ", ", ", ", " my ", "\nDon't ", " a ", " ",
          "\n", ", ", ", ", " my ", "\nJust ", " your pretty ",
          "\nI'll be ", " you again \nI'll be ", " you in "};

      String[] s = inputPanel.getStringArray();
      for (int i = 0; i < segs.length; i++) {
        song += s[i] + segs[i];
      }
      song += s[s.length - 1];

      story.setText(song);
    }

}
```

Here is the HTML file to include the MadLibApplet applet:

```
<html>
<head>
  <title>Mad Lib</title>
</head>
<body>
<h1>Mad Lib</h1>

<applet code="MadLibApplet.class" width=550 height=250></applet>

</body>
</html>
```

The MadLibApplet is shown in Figure 8.10 running as an applet. You can also run it as an application by typing java MadLibApplet at your command prompt. It will look and run exactly as it did in Chapter 7.

Using Sounds and Images

The Applet class has built-in support for playing sounds and loading and displaying images. In this section, you learn how to do both of these things from applets. First, I'll go over playing audio files, and then get into displaying images.

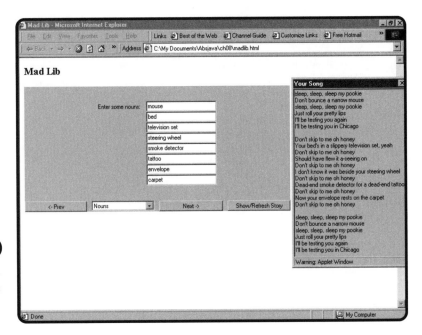

FIGURE 8.10

The MadLibApplet
program can run as
an applet or an
application.

Playing Sound Files

Playing sound files from applets is actually very easy. You can use getAudio-
Clip(URL) or getAudioClip(URL, String) to load an audio clip as an AudioClip
instance. AudioClip is actually an interface in the java.applet package. It has
three methods:

void play()	Plays an audio clip from beginning to end.
void loop()	Continuously plays this audio clip in a loop from beginning to end.
void stop()	Stops playing the audio clip.

The URL object specifies the location of the audio clip. As you would imagine, it's
just a class in the java.net package that encapsulates a Uniform Resource Loca-
tor. It isn't covered in this book, so for more information, consult the Java API
documentation, which you can find at the URL **http://java.sun.com/j2se/1.3/docs/
api/index.html**. Instead of getting into URLs, I use the getCodeBase() method
from the Applet class, which returns the URL where the applet class file exists.
That's all you need to know about the URL class in this book.

The SoundTestApplet applet loads a sound file and gives you the option of playing, looping, and stopping the audio clip, by adding those corresponding methods to three buttons ActionListener, this. Any time you click one of those
buttons, the method associated with that button is called. You can therefore see

first hand how the buttons work. I load the sound into the `AudioClip` member, `sound`, as follows:

```
sound = getAudioClip(getCodeBase(), "stooges.au");
```

The second argument is the file name. `stooges.au` is a Sun audio file. I chose this format because Internet Explorer does not support other audio files to be loaded in this way. Appletviewer didn't have a problem playing other types of sound files. Sound file types supported by Java include AU, AIFF, MIDI, and WAV. Keep in mind, that when you're using sounds and images, the applet takes time to load these. Users with slow Internet connections can get frustrated waiting for your applet to start running. Here is the source code listing for `SoundTestApplet.java`:

```java
/*
 * SoundTestApplet
 * Tests playing a sound file from an applet
 */

import java.applet.*;
import java.awt.*;
import java.awt.event.*;

public class SoundTestApplet extends Applet
                             implements ActionListener {
  AudioClip sound;
  Button playButton, stopButton, loopButton;

  public void init() {
    playButton = new Button("Play");
    playButton.addActionListener(this);
    add(playButton);

    loopButton = new Button("Loop");
    loopButton.addActionListener(this);
    add(loopButton);

    stopButton = new Button("Stop");
    stopButton.addActionListener(this);
    add(stopButton);

    sound = getAudioClip(getCodeBase(), "stooges.au");
  }

  public void actionPerformed(ActionEvent e) {
    if (e.getSource() == playButton) {
      sound.play();
    }
    else if (e.getSource() == loopButton) {
      sound.loop();
    }
    else if (e.getSource() == stopButton) {
      sound.stop();
    }
  }
}
```

Here is the HTML:

```html
<html>
<head>
  <title>Sound Test Applet</title>
</head>
<h1 align=center>Sound Test Applet</h1>
<body>
<center>

<applet code="SoundTestApplet.class" width=200 height=100>
</applet>

</center>
</body>
</html>
```

Figure 8.11 shows what the GUI interface of the SoundTestApplet looks like.

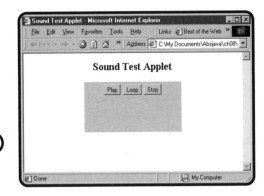

This applet can play sound files.

Loading and Displaying Images

An applet can also load and display images. You will learn all about images in Chapter 9, "The Graphics Class: Drawing Shapes, Images, and Text," but images are displayed slightly differently in applets so I'll just show you how to load an image here and in Chapter 9, you can learn more about images as well as other graphics programming. You can get an Image object by calling the getImage(URL) or getImage(URL, String) methods, which are similar to the getAudioClip() methods.

```java
/*
 * ImageApplet
 * Demonstrates displaying an image in an applet and using
 * MediaTracker to wait for the images to load
 */

import java.applet.Applet;
import java.awt.*;
```

```
public class ImageApplet extends Applet {
  Image img;

  public void init() {
    showStatus("Loading Image...");
    MediaTracker mt = new MediaTracker(this);
    img = getImage(getCodeBase(), "misty2.jpg");
    mt.addImage(img, 0);
    //An InterruptedException might occur
    try {
      mt.waitForID(0);
    } catch (InterruptedException ie) {}
    showStatus("Image Loaded.");
  }

  public void paint(Graphics g) {
    g.drawImage(img,
                (getSize().width - img.getWidth(this)) / 2,
                (getSize().height - img.getHeight(this)) / 2,
                this);
  }

}
```

This example also demonstrates how to wait for an image to load. This is done through the use of the MediaTracker class found in the java.awt package. Here, I use the MediaTracker class to wait for the misty2.jpg image to load. I created a new MediaTracker object, mt, by passing this to the constructor. The one and only constructor accepts a Component argument, which specifies the component on which the image will eventually be drawn (the component that owns the Image object).

I then added the image to mt by calling the addImage(Image, int) method. The Image object passed as the first argument is the one that you want to track and the int argument is the ID number. After I added the Image to the MediaTracker, I called mt.waitForID(0), which is a method that waits for the image specified by the int argument (the ID that is passed to addImage(int)). There is also a method for waiting for all images that were added to the MediaTracker object to load, waitForAll(). Currently, MediaTracker does not support waiting for other file types such as audio files, but that can be added in future releases.

This is a listing of the imagetest.html source code:

```
<html>
<head>
  <title>Image Applet</title>
</head>
<body>
<h1 align=center>Image Applet</h1>
```

```
<center>
<applet code="ImageApplet.class" width=350 height=250>
</applet>
</center>

</body>
</html>
```

Figure 8.12 shows ImageApplet displaying an image.

FIGURE 8.12

This applet displays
an image.

Back to the *QuizShowApplet* Applet

All right, now you know a lot about how to create and run applets. In this section, you use this information to build the QuizShowApplet applet. In this applet that you saw at the beginning of this chapter, the users are prompted with a series of true or false questions and get a score at the end based on how many they answered correctly. This applet is actually parameter-driven. It is versatile in that it accepts parameters that build the whole thing up. You can change the parameters at any time to change the questions that are asked, the answers to those questions, and also the number of questions that the QuizShowApplet asks. These are the parameters:

nQuestions   The number of questions asked by the QuizShowApplet.

Q*n*   Each question is specified in its own parameter. Q stands for "Question" and the *n* represents the question number, which must start with 1 and be incremented to the number of questions specified in nQuestions without skipping any numbers.

key   A string of Ts and Fs that indicate the answers to the questions in order. The length of this string must be equal to the number of questions.

Here is the source code for `QuizShowApplet.java`:

```java
/*
 * QuizShowApplet
 * Asks a series of True and False Questions that
 * are passed in as parameters and grades the results
 *
 * See the getParameterInfo() method for parameter info
 */

import java.applet.Applet;
import java.awt.*;
import java.awt.event.*;

public class QuizShowApplet extends Applet
                            implements ActionListener {
  String[] questions;
  char[] answers;
  int score, nCorrect, currQ;
  Label questionLabel, rightWrong;
  Checkbox t, f;
  CheckboxGroup groupTorF;
  Button okButton;

  public void init() {
    boolean paramsOK = false;
    try {
      paramsOK = readParams();
    } catch (Exception e) { System.out.println(e); }
    if (paramsOK) {
      setLayout(new BorderLayout());
      setBackground(Color.blue);
      nCorrect = currQ = 0;
      questionLabel = new Label("1. " + questions[0], Label.CENTER);
      questionLabel.setFont(new Font("TimesRoman",
                                     Font.BOLD, 16));
      questionLabel.setForeground(Color.yellow);
      add(questionLabel, BorderLayout.CENTER);
      Panel controlPanel = new Panel();
      controlPanel.setBackground(SystemColor.control);
      groupTorF = new CheckboxGroup();
      t = new Checkbox("True", false, groupTorF);
      controlPanel.add(t);
      f = new Checkbox("False", false, groupTorF);
      controlPanel.add(f);
      okButton = new Button("That's my final answer!");
      okButton.addActionListener(this);
      controlPanel.add(okButton);
      add(controlPanel, BorderLayout.SOUTH);
      rightWrong = new Label("", Label.CENTER);
      rightWrong.setForeground(Color.white);
      add(rightWrong, BorderLayout.NORTH);
    }
```

```java
    else {
      add(new Label("Parameters not properly set"));
    }
  }

  protected boolean readParams() throws Exception {
    questions = new String[Integer.parseInt(getParameter("nQuestions"))];
    answers = getParameter("key").toCharArray();

    if (questions.length != answers.length) return false;

    for (int i=0; i < questions.length; i++) {
      questions[i] = getParameter("Q" + (i + 1));
      if (questions[i] == null
          || answers[i] != 'T' && answers[i] != 'F') return false;
    }
    return true;
  }


  /*
   * Parameters:
   * nQuestions - number of questions
   * Qn - A question: Qstands for question and n is the question #
   *       the question number starts at zero and has at least
   *       nQuestion number of questions e.g. Q1, Q2, Q3, etc.
   * key - a series of T's and F's - The answer key. The length
   *        of the string must be >= nQuestions
   */
  public String[][] getParameterInfo() {
    return new String[][] {
      {"nQuestions", "int", "Number of questions"},
      {"Qn", "String", "A Question (n=question#)"},
      {"key", "String of T's & F's in order, CAPS", "Answer Key"}
    };
  }

  public void actionPerformed(ActionEvent e) {
    Checkbox selected = groupTorF.getSelectedCheckbox();
    if (selected == null) return;
    if (selected == t && answers[currQ] == 'T'
        || selected == f && answers[currQ] == 'F') {
      nCorrect++;
      rightWrong.setText("Previous answer: CORRECT");
    }
    else {
      rightWrong.setText("Previous answer: INCORRECT");
    }
    groupTorF.setSelectedCheckbox(null);
    if (currQ == questions.length - 1) {
      //very last question
      t.setEnabled(false);
      f.setEnabled(false);
      okButton.setEnabled(false);
```

```
    questionLabel.setText("Your Score is : "
       + Math.round( ((double)nCorrect) / questions.length * 100)
       + "%");
    }
    else {
      currQ++;
      questionLabel.setText((currQ + 1) + ". " + questions[currQ]);
    }
  }
}
```

questions is the array that holds the questions that this applet will ask. answers is an array of characters that represents the answers to these questions. The subscript of the questions array corresponds to the subscript of the answers array so that the answer to questions[2], for example, has the correct answer stored in answers[2]. The int, called score, calculates the score at the end of the game, nCorrect counts the number of correct answers, and currQ indicates the index of the current question. There are two Label objects: questionLabel, which displays the current question, and rightWrong, which tells the users whether the previously answered question was correct. The Checkbox objects, t and f, select true or false as the answer to the question and okButton actually submits the currently selected answer.

The init() method declares a boolean variable, paramsOK, which indicates whether the parameters are loaded properly. It is initialized to false. Then the readParams() method is called which returns true if the parameters are loaded, or false if they are not. It might also cause an exception if the parameters are specified using Strings that cannot be parsed correctly. This Exception will be caught, so the program doesn't crash. At this point the paramsOK variable will still be false, and as you can see, if this is false later in the init() method, a message indicating that the parameters are not set correctly is displayed.

The readParams() method works by first reading the nQuestions parameter. It parses the value to an int and initializes the questions array size with that value. Then it reads the key parameter. If the length of the answer key is not equal to the length of the number of questions, there must be a problem, so the program returns false to indicate that the parameters didn't load correctly. After nQuestions and key are read in, the program loops on the questions array and reads the Qn parameters. Note here that the n specified will be one higher than the index of the questions array that stores that question. If no such corresponding Qn exists or if the answer in the key that corresponds to this question is not T or F (caps matters here), the program also returns false. If all is okay, it returns true.

If the parameters are loaded correctly, the rest of the init() method creates the GUI, which is self-explanatory, and adds itself as the ActionListener for the okButton. The program checks to see whether the answer given by the user is correct by comparing it to the answers array. It will update the rightWrong Label and move on to the next question. It also increments nCorrect if the answer is correct. If no answer is selected when the button is clicked, nothing happens. If it is the last question, the button and check box answers are disabled and the score is calculated as the percentage of the number of correct answers. The game ends. To play again, the users must click the Reload button on their browser's toolbar.

Here is the HTML source code listing. Pay close attention to the <param> tags:

```
<html>
<head>
<title>Quiz Show</title>
</head>
<body>
<h1 align=center>Quiz Show</title>
<center>

<applet code="QuizShowApplet.class" width=500 height=200>
  <param name="nQuestions" value=10>
  <param name="Q1" value="This is the first question?">
  <param name="Q2" value="Jason Newstead is Metallica's bass player?">
  <param name="Q3" value="Dracula translates to 'Son of the Dragon'?">
  <param name="Q4" value="Don Vito Corleone was born Vito Andolini?">
  <param name="Q5" value="Rhode Island is an island off the coast of New York?">
  <param name="Q6" value="Two bits is 25 five cents?">
  <param name="Q7" value="In Monopoly, Pennsylvania Ave costs $300?">
  <param name="Q8" value="In Poker, a four of a kind beats a straight flush?">
  <param name="Q9" value="A tomato is a vegetable?">
  <param name="Q10" value="Bruce Leroy is the master?">
  <param name="key" value="TFTTFTFFFT">
</applet>

</center>
</body>
</html>
```

IN THE REAL WORLD

In the real world, you probably would not make it so easy for someone to see the answers to your quiz. Anyone that can read a text file can probably crack the T and F string code and figure out the answers before taking the quiz. This would be better implemented either as some code that only you understand and can interpret in your applet's class file or better yet, stored in a file on the server that is inaccessible to the users. Java Server programming is a huge subject in its own right and is not covered in this book, but is another great way to use Java.

Summary

In this chapter, you learned all about how to create and run applets. You learned how to run them in a browser, as well as by using the appletviewer. You learned a bit of HTML and learned how to pass parameters to applets. You also learned how browsers interpret Java. You now know that an applet that runs fine in one browser or the appletviewer, might not run at all in another browser, because it all depends upon the application the applet is embedded in. You learned about applet security restrictions. You also learned how to load and play sound files and display images. In the next chapter, you learn about Java graphics programming in detail.

CHALLENGES

1. Rewrite the `quizshow.html` file's parameters to create a different quiz.

2. Add some sounds to the `QuizShow` applet so that a loud buzzer goes off when you answer incorrectly and a bell or some other pleasant sound is played when the answer is correct.

3. Try rewriting some of the other applications from Chapters 6 and 7, or some of your own applications, so that you can run them as applets or as applications.

CHAPTER

9

The Graphics Class: Drawing Shapes, Images, and Text

Although you have already learned a great deal about the `java.awt` package, there is still more to learn. This chapter focuses on the `Graphics` class and how the `paint(Graphics)` method in the `Component` class works. In this chapter, you will learn how to draw shapes. You will also learn how to use the `Font` and `FontMetrics` classes to obtain graphical information about your fonts. You also learn about the `Color` class in more detail.

The main points covered in this chapter are:

- Use the `Graphics` class

- Render lines

- Render rectangles

- Render ovals

- Render arcs

- Render polygons

- **Render text**

- **Use the** `FontMetrics` **class**

- **Display images**

- **Understand the** `Color` **class**

The Project: Memory Game

The project for this chapter is the Memory application. In this game, a window opens up with 16 cells. Initially they are all covered with question marks. There are eight pairs of identical pictures hidden under the question marks. The goal here is to find all the matches with as few mismatches as possible. You interact with the cells by clicking them. First you click one and its contents are revealed and surrounded by a red border. Next you try to find its counterpart. If the next cell you click is not a match, both of the borders will remain red. The cells will remain visible until you click another cell, in which case the mismatch will be hidden again. You try to remember where the cells were, so when you find another cell that is a match for one of them, you will know where to find it again. When you do find a match, the borders around the cells turn green to signify a match. The green border will stick around until you click another cell. The number of mismatches are counted and displayed below the cells, next to the Reset button. The lower that number, the better you did. Also, the Reset button comes in handy when you want to play another round.

You will program this game by the end of this chapter. Figure 9.1 shows a typical game. You can see that I made my first match after having only one mismatch. You also see the whole board solved with only five mismatches.

The *Graphics* Class

The `Graphics` class contains methods that allow a component to draw onto itself. The `Graphics` object is passed into an object's `paint(Graphics)` method. To take control of a component's graphics rendering, you only need to override the `paint(Graphics)` method. The `Graphics` object that is passed into the `paint(Graphics)` method stores the component's graphics. This class has methods for drawing shapes such as lines, rectangles, and ovals, as well as for rendering text and images.

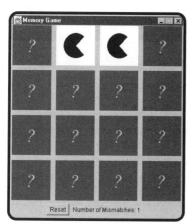 

FIGURE 9.1

The Memory game
in action. I only
missed five. See if
you can do better!

Drawing Lines

Drawing a line onto a component is as simple as overriding its `paint(Graphics)`
method and calling the `drawLine(int x1, int y1, int x2, int y2)` method of
the `Graphics` class. This method draws a line from the point (x1, y1) to the point
(x2, y2) relative to the component's coordinate system (the top-left corner of the
component is point (0, 0)). The `LineTest` application draws three lines. Here is the
source code for `LineTest.java`:

```
/*
 * LineTest
 * Demonstrates drawing lines
 */

import java.awt.*;

public class LineTest extends Canvas {

  public LineTest() {
    super();
    setSize(300, 200);
    setBackground(Color.white);
  }

  public static void main(String args[]) {
    LineTest lt = new LineTest();
    GUIFrame frame = new GUIFrame("Line Test");
    frame.add(lt);
    frame.pack();
    frame.setVisible(true);
  }

  public void paint(Graphics g) {
    g.drawLine(10, 10, 50, 100);
    g.setColor(Color.blue);
```

```
    g.drawLine(60, 110, 275, 50);
    g.setColor(Color.red);
    g.drawLine(50, 50, 300, 200);
  }

}
```

LineTest is a subclass of Canvas. In the constructor, the size is set to 300 by 200 and the background color is set to white. The paint(Graphics) class is overridden so that when it is painted on-screen, its graphics will show three lines of three different colors. The first line is drawn from the point (10, 10) to the point (50, 100):

```
g.drawLine(10, 10, 50, 100);
```

Notice that I used the Graphics object that was passed into the paint(Graphics) method to render the line. The initial color associated with the Graphics object is the component's foreground color, and this is the color that the first line will be drawn in. Before I draw the second line, I set the color to blue by calling the setColor(Color) method of the Graphics class:

```
g.setColor(Color.blue);
```

Any graphical operations beyond this point will be done in the color blue unless it is changed again. The Graphics object, g, renders the second line from the point (60, 110) to the point (275, 50). Then the color is set to red and the third line is drawn between the points (50, 50) and (300, 200). Because the red line is drawn after the blue one, the red line is drawn over the blue line where they intersect.

The main() method creates a new LineTest instance and adds it to a GUIFrame, a class that you created back in Chapter 7, "Advanced GUI: Layout Managers and Event Handling." If you don't remember, it's a frame that handles its own WindowEvents and centers itself on-screen when it becomes visible. You can see the output of the LineTest application in Figure 9.2.

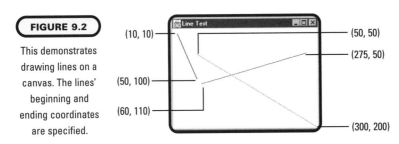

FIGURE 9.2

This demonstrates drawing lines on a canvas. The lines' beginning and ending coordinates are specified.

Drawing Rectangles

The `Graphics` class has four different methods for rendering rectangles, as follows:

- The `drawRect(int x, int y, int width, int height)` method draws the outline of a rectangle using the top-left corner at point (x, y) and having the specified width and height.

- The `fillRect(int x, y, int width, int height)` method fills a rectangle at the given position with the given width and height.

- The `drawRoundRect(int x, int y, int width, int height, int arcWidth, int arcHeight)` method draws the outline of a rectangle with rounded corners. The rounded rectangle's bounding area's top-left corner is at the point (x, y) and its width and height are `width` and `height`, respectively. The other two arguments are the rounded corner's horizontal and vertical diameters. If you picture an oval in the corner of the rectangle it is easier to understand. Take the top-left corner for instance. Picture an oval pushed into that corner such that the top of the oval is touching the top of the rectangle and the left side of the oval is touching the left side of the rectangle. Using the oval's edge as the rectangle's corner instead of the rectangle's actual corner rounds the rectangle.

- The fourth method is `fillRoundRect(int x, int y, int width, int height, int arcWidth, int arcHeight)`, which works the same as the previous method except the rectangle is filled with the `Graphics` object's current color. Figure 9.3 shows a graphical representation of this.

 HINT The `drawRect(int x, int y, int width, int height)` method draws the outline of a rectangle. The actual width of a drawn rectangle is x + `width` and the actual height is y + `height`. This differs from the `fillRect(int x, int y, int width, int height)`. The actual width for a filled rectangle is x + `width` - 1 and the actual height is y + `height` - 1. If you were to draw a rectangle and then fill a rectangle of the same size over it in a different color, you would still see the right and bottom edges of the drawn rectangle because it is one pixel wider and taller. For example:

```
g.setColor(Color.black);
g.drawRect(10, 10, 100, 100);
g.setColor(Color.green);
g.fillRect(10, 10, 100, 100);
```

Using this code in the paint(Graphics) method, you would see a green rectangle with a black right and bottom edge. This same idea holds true for all draw and fill methods of the Graphics class. Try it out and see for yourself.

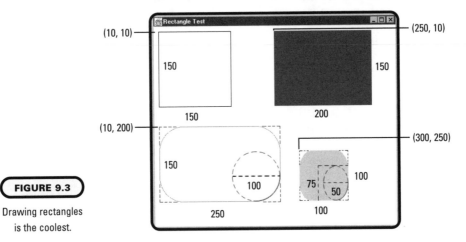

FIGURE 9.3

Drawing rectangles is the coolest.

Here is the source code for RectTest.java, an application that illustrates these methods:

```
/*
 * RectTest
 * Demonstrates drawing Rectangles
 */

import java.awt.*;

public class RectTest extends Canvas {

    public RectTest() {
        super();
        setSize(300, 200);
        setBackground(Color.white);
    }

    public static void main(String args[]) {
        RectTest rt = new RectTest();
        GUIFrame frame = new GUIFrame("Rectangle Test");
        frame.add(rt);
```

```
      frame.pack();
      frame.setVisible(true);
   }

   public void paint(Graphics g) {
      g.drawRect(10, 10, 150, 150);
      g.setColor(Color.blue);
      g.fillRect(250, 10, 200, 150);
      g.setColor(Color.red);
      g.drawRoundRect(10, 200, 250, 150, 100, 100);
      g.setColor(Color.green);
      g.fillRoundRect(300, 250, 100, 100, 50, 75);
   }

}
```

This application renders four rectangles, as shown in Figure 9.3. The first one (upper-left) is drawn at point (10, 10) and is 150 wide by 150 high. The second rectangle (upper-right) is filled with the color blue at position (250, 10) with dimensions 200 by 150. The next rectangle (lower-left) is rounded, drawn at position (10, 200), with a width of 250 and a height of 150. An arc of a circular diameter of 100 rounds the corners. The fourth and final rectangle (lower-right) is a round rectangle filled at position (300, 250), with a dimension of 100 by 100 and rounded at the corners by an arc with a horizontal diameter of 50 and a vertical diameter of 75.

Drawing 3D Rectangles

3D rectangles have the appearance of either being raised above or sunk below the surface by using highlighting colors. The colors that are used for highlighting are dependent upon the current color. The method for drawing a 3D rectangle is `draw3DRect(int x, int y, int width, int height, boolean raised)` for drawing a rectangle at the given (x, y) position with the given `width` by `height` dimensions and a `boolean` value that is `true` if the 3D rectangle should be raised, or `false` if it should be sunken. The method for filling a 3D rectangle is `fill3DRect(int x, int y, int width, int height, boolean raised)`. The `Rect3DTest` application illustrates these methods:

```
/*
 * Rect3DTest
 * Draws 3D Rectangles
 */
import java.awt.*;

public class Rect3DTest extends Canvas {

   public Rect3DTest() {
      super();
```

```
    setSize(300, 200);
    setBackground(SystemColor.control);
}

public static void main(String args[]) {
    Rect3DTest rt3d = new Rect3DTest();
    GUIFrame frame = new GUIFrame("3D Rectangle Test");
    frame.add(rt3d);
    frame.pack();
    frame.setVisible(true);
}

public void paint(Graphics g) {
    g.setColor(Color.gray);
    g.draw3DRect(5, 5, 140, 90, true);
    g.draw3DRect(150, 5, 140, 90, false);
    g.fill3DRect(5, 100, 140, 90, true);
    g.fill3DRect(150, 100, 140, 90, false);

}

}
```

Let the rendering begin! First the color is set to gray. The first rectangle is drawn at location (5, 5) and the width and height are 140 by 90, which is the same width and height for all four of these 3D rectangles. The fifth argument is true, so the first rectangle should appear raised. In Figure 9.4, the first 3D rectangle appears in the upper-left portion of the frame. The second 3D rectangle is on the upper-right and the fifth argument is false, so it should appear sunken. The next two 3D rectangles are filled underneath the drawn rectangles. The one on the left is raised, whereas the one on the right is not.

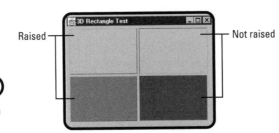

Raised ——   —— Not raised

FIGURE 9.4

3D Rectangles can
be raised or not.

HINT

Notice that the drawn 3D rectangle appears raised when the lighter color is on the top and left side and the darker color is on the bottom and the right side. The opposite is true to make the 3D rectangle appear sunken. In fact if you look at Figure 9.4 upside down, the raised rectangle will appear sunk and the sunken rectangle will appear raised.

Drawing Ovals

Drawing ovals is similar to drawing rectangles. In fact the arguments to the methods that render the ovals specify the rectangular bounds of the oval. There are two methods for rendering ovals. The drawOval(int x, int y, int width, int height) method draws the outline of an oval that fits in the rectangle specified by the arguments. The position is at (x, y) and the width and height are given as the third and fourth arguments. The fillOval(int x, int y, int width, int height) method fills the oval with the current color. The OvalTest application uses these methods to render two ovals. Here is the source code for OvalTest.java:

```
/*
 * OvalTest
 * Demonstrates drawing Ovals
 */

import java.awt.*;

public class OvalTest extends Canvas {

  public OvalTest() {
    super();
    setSize(300, 200);
    setBackground(Color.white);
  }

  public static void main(String args[]) {
    OvalTest ot = new OvalTest();
    GUIFrame frame = new GUIFrame("Oval Test");
    frame.add(ot);
    frame.pack();
    frame.setVisible(true);
  }

  public void paint(Graphics g) {
    g.fillOval(10, 10, 100, 100);
    g.setColor(Color.blue);
    g.drawOval(110, 110, 150, 50);
  }

}
```

The first oval is filled at position (10, 10) and has a width and a height of 100. The second oval is drawn at (110, 110). Unlike the first oval, this second oval is not an exact circle. Its width is 150 and its height is 50. You can see these ovals rendered in Figure 9.5.

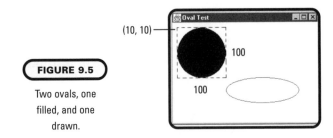

FIGURE 9.5

Two ovals, one filled, and one drawn.

Drawing Arcs

Rendering arcs is similar to rendering ovals except there are two more arguments in its methods. Arcs are also known as semicircles. The drawArc(int x, int y, int width, int height, int startAngle, int arcAngle) method draws an arc at the given position and having the given dimensions. The fifth argument specifies the starting angle, which is where on the oval specified by the first four arguments to start drawing the arc. If you think of the oval as the face of a clock, 0 degrees is at three o'clock, 90 degrees is at twelve o'clock, 180 degrees is at nine o'clock, 270 degrees is at six o'clock, and so it goes for all the angles in between these right angles. The sixth argument is the arc angle; it is the arc length along the oval. 360 degrees makes a whole circle, 180 degrees makes half a circle, and so on, from the starting point. The direction in which the arc is drawn is dependent on the sign of the sixth argument. A positive value indicates a counter-clockwise direction, whereas a negative value indicates a clockwise direction.

The fillArc(int x, int y, int width, int height, int startAngle, int arcAngle) method takes the same arguments but it fills the arc instead of drawing the outline. The shape of a filled arc is like that of a piece of pie. "mmmm-mmm pie," as Homer would say. If that doesn't draw a clear enough picture for you think of it as the minute hand of a clock (that can go both ways). The tip of the minute hand moves along the arc outline and the whole thing leaves a trail as it moves. The ArcTest application uses these methods to render a couple of arcs.

```
/*
 * ArcTest
 * Demonstrates drawing Arcs
 */

import java.awt.*;

public class ArcTest extends Canvas {

  public ArcTest() {
    super();
    setSize(300, 200);
```

```
    setBackground(Color.white);
  }

  public static void main(String args[]) {
    ArcTest at = new ArcTest();
    GUIFrame frame = new GUIFrame("Arc Test");
    frame.add(at);
    frame.pack();
    frame.setVisible(true);
  }

  public void paint(Graphics g) {
    g.drawArc(10, 10, 100, 100, 0, 270);
    g.setColor(Color.green);
    g.fillArc(150, 150, 50, 50, 90, -270);
  }

}
```

The first arc, shown in the upper-left corner of Figure 9.6, is drawn along at position (10, 10). The width and height are both 100. These bounds define the oval that the arc is drawn along. The starting angle is 0, so the arc will start at 3:00. The sixth argument is 270, so the arc will be drawn 270 degrees along the oval in a counter-clockwise direction. The second arc (in the lower-right corner of the figure) is drawn at (150, 150). Its width and height are both 50. The starting angle is 90, so the arc will start at 12:00. The arcAngle is −270, so it will be filled 270 degrees along the oval in a clockwise direction. The third arc, the Arc of the Covenant, has yet to be found.

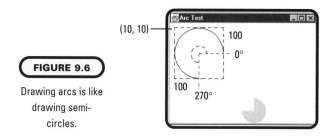

FIGURE 9.6

Drawing arcs is like drawing semi-circles.

Drawing Polygons

Polygons are multisided, enclosed shapes that are rendered by connecting a series of points together with lines. There are four methods for rendering polygons, described here:

- The drawPolygon(int[] xPoints, int[] yPoints, int nPoints) method draws the outline of a polygon defined by an array of x-coordinate points, xPoints, and an array of y-coordinate points, yPoints that correspond to

the x-coordinate points by the same array index. The third argument specifies the number of points of the polygon.

- The drawPolygon(Polygon) method draws the outline of a polygon based
on the Polygon object passed to it.
- The other two methods are the draw methods' corresponding fill methods
and fill the polygonal shapes with the current color.

The PolyTest application renders a few polygons. Here is the source code:

```
/*
 * PolyTest
 * Demonstrates drawing Polygons
 * and also the translate() method in the Graphics class
 */

import java.awt.*;

public class PolyTest extends Canvas {

    public PolyTest() {
        super();
        setSize(300, 200);
        setBackground(Color.white);
    }

    public static void main(String args[]) {
        PolyTest pt = new PolyTest();
        GUIFrame frame = new GUIFrame("Polygon Test");
        frame.add(pt);
        frame.pack();
        frame.setVisible(true);
    }

    public void paint(Graphics g) {
        Polygon p = new Polygon();
        p.addPoint(150, 10);
        p.addPoint(150, 75);
        p.addPoint(290, 75);
        g.drawPolygon(p);
        int[] xs = {50, 75, 10, 90, 25};
        int[] ys = {10, 90, 40, 40, 90};
        g.fillPolygon(xs, ys, 5);
        g.translate(150, 100);
        g.drawPolygon(xs, ys, 5);
    }

}
```

The first polygon is rendered by passing a Polygon object to the
drawPolygon(Polygon) method. The Polygon class itself is not that important in

this particular book, so I'll just go over how I used it here. I created a new Poly-gon object, p, by using the no-argument constructor. Then I added points by call-ing the addPoint(int x, int y) method. The points I added are the ones that were used to draw the triangle shown in Figure 9.7.

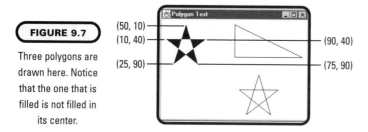

FIGURE 9.7

Three polygons are drawn here. Notice that the one that is filled is not filled in its center.

The second polygon is star shaped and the lines cross each other. It is filled using the even-odd, or alternating fill, rule. That's why the center of the star remains unfilled. Think of it sort of like a checkerboard. When lines of a polygon cross and the polygon is filled, only every other enclosed area is filled.

The third polygon is drawn using the same arrays as the second polygon, but the translate(int x, int y) method is called beforehand. This method changes the origin, which is (0, 0) by default to the specified position. The third polygon is drawn relative to the new origin, (150, 100) instead of (0, 0), so all the points of the second polygon shift over by 150 to the right, and 100 down to draw the third polygon.

TRAP
Be careful when rendering polygons. The third argument, which specifies the number of points of the polygon, can cause an ArrayIndexOutOfBounds excep-tion if the arrays passed as the first and second arguments don't have the capac-ity to hold that number of integers.

TRICK
Did you notice that when the polygons were rendered in the PolyTest applica-tion, the first point does not have to be repeated to close the polygon? This hap-pens automatically. The last point is automatically connected to the first point to close the polygon. There is a way to draw a polygon that remains unclosed. This is referred to as a *poly line*. The one method that allows you to do this is the drawPolyline(int[] xPoints, int[] yPoints, int nPoints) method. As you can see it takes the same arguments as one of the drawPolygon() methods, but when you use drawPolyline() method, the polygon is not closed. Note that a poly line cannot be filled because it is not closed. That's why there is no such thing as a fillPolyline() method.

Drawing Strings

The drawString(String str, int x, int y) method draws the given String object at the given (x, y) location. The given location indicates the position of the baseline of the left-most character in the string. The string is drawn using the Graphics object's current font and color. The StringTest application draws some strings onto a Canvas. Here is the source code for StringTest.java:

```
/*
 * StringTest
 * Demonstrates drawing Strings
 */

import java.awt.*;

public class StringTest extends Canvas {

  public StringTest() {
    super();
    setSize(300, 200);
    setBackground(Color.white);
  }

  public static void main(String args[]) {
    StringTest st = new StringTest();
    GUIFrame frame = new GUIFrame("String Test");
    frame.add(st);
    frame.pack();
    frame.setVisible(true);
  }

  public void paint(Graphics g) {
    g.drawString("Metallica...", 10, 10);
    g.setColor(Color.lightGray);
    g.setFont(new Font("Timesroman", Font.ITALIC, 48));
    g.drawString("New Bassist?", 25, 150);
    g.setColor(Color.black);
    g.setFont(new Font("Courier", Font.BOLD, 20));
    g.drawString("James", 20, 40);
    g.drawString("Lars", 30, 60);
    g.drawString("Dave", 40, 80);
    g.drawString("Kirk", 60, 100);
    g.drawString("Ron", 80, 120);
    g.drawString("Cliff", 100, 140);
    g.drawString("Jason", 120, 160);
  }

}
```

The StringTest application sets two different fonts by calling the Graphics class' setFont(Font) method. You'll learn more about fonts in the next section. This application draws a bunch of strings onto the Canvas. You can see the output in Figure 9.8.

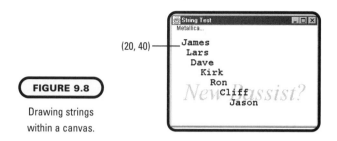

(20, 40)

FIGURE 9.8

Drawing strings within a canvas.

Fonts and *FontMetrics*

A font, as you probably know, is a collection of graphical representations of characters. You are probably very familiar with fonts such as Times New Roman or Arial. A graphics object has a font associated to it, implemented as a Font object. The Font class of the java.awt package represents fonts as you know them. The FontMetrics class has information about fonts that is useful to Graphics objects, such as the width and height of a string rendered with the current font.

The *Font* Class

The Font class encapsulates fields and methods that define fonts. The Font constructor method used in this book is the Font(String name, int style, int size) constructor. The first argument is the name of the font. The second argument is the style. Styles are represented by static integers in the font classes Font.PLAIN, Font.BOLD, and Font.ITALIC. The style can also be the combination (sum) Font.BOLD + Font.ITALIC. The third argument is the font point size. Here are a couple of examples:

```
Font f1 = new Font("Timesroman", Font.PLAIN, 24);
Font f2 = new Font("Helvetica", Font.BOLD + Font.ITALIC, 12);
```

Table 9.1 lists some important fields and methods of the Font class.

It is possible to get all of a system's available fonts. Here's how. First, you need to get the GraphicsEnvironment object that represents the system's local graphics environment. The GraphicsEnvironment class is part of the java.awt package. The local graphics environment describes graphics devices and fonts that are available to the Java VM. The way to get the local graphics environment is to call the static method GraphicsEnvironment.getLocalGraphicsEnvironment(). Once you have the local GraphicsEnvironment object, you can call its getAllFonts() method, which returns an array of Font objects of point size 1. You can also call getAvailableFontFamilyNames() to return a String array containing the font family names of all the available fonts. Here's a brief example:

```
GraphicsEnvironment ge =
  GraphicsEnvironment.getLocalGraphicsEnvironment();
String[] fontList = ge.getAvailableFontFamilyNames();
```

TABLE 9.1   FONT FIELDS AND METHODS

Field or Method	Description
static int BOLD	Represents a bold style.
static int ITALIC	Represents an italic style.
static int PLAIN	Represents a plain style (not bold or italic).
Font deriveFont(int style)	Derives a new Font object based on this Font, but with the given style.
String getFamily()	Returns the family name of this Font object.
String getFontName()	Returns this Font object's font face name.
int getSize()	Returns the point size of this Font.
int getStyle()	Returns the int representation of this Font's style.
boolean isBold()	Returns a *boolean* value that indicates whether this Font is bold.
boolean isItalic()	Returns a *boolean* value that indicates whether this Font is italic.
boolean isPlain()	Returns a *boolean* value that indicates whether ot this Font is plain.

After this snippet of code has executed, the fontList array will contain an array of available font family names.

The *FontMetrics* Class

The FontMetrics class encapsulates information that is used to render a font. The FontMetrics object that represents properties of the Graphics object's current Font is obtained by calling the getFontMetrics() method of the Graphics class. You can also get the FontMetrics object associated with any Font by calling the getFontMetrics(Font) method. The FontMetrics object will be based on the Font passed to this method. Table 9.2 lists some useful FontMetrics methods.

As you know, you draw strings by specifying a point location for the baseline of the left-most character. Parts of the characters of the strings can rise above or drop below the baseline certain distances. You use FontMetrics objects to measure these distances as well as other metrics of the font. A font's *ascent* is the distance that most characters rise above the baseline. A font's *descent* is the distance that most characters drop below the baseline. Some characters will exceed these values. A font's *leading* is the space reserved for interline spacing (the space in between lines of text). This value is part of the calculation of a font's height. The

TABLE 9.2   FontMetrics Methods

Method	Description
int getAscent()	Returns the *ascent,* which is the distance above the baseline of the font.
int getDescent()	Returns the *descent,* which is the distance that the font drops below the baseline.
int getFont()	Returns the Font object associated with this FontMetrics object.
int getHeight()	Returns the font height for one line of text.
int getLeading()	Returns the leading of the font. The *leading* is the distance between two lines of text.
int getMaxAdvance()	Returns the maximum advance width of any character of this font. The *advance* is the distance from the leftmost point to the rightmost point on the baseline.
int getMaxAscent()	Returns the maximum ascent of the font.
int getMaxDescent()	Returns the maximum descent of the font.
int stringWidth(*String*)	Returns the width of the given String rendered in the font.

height is calculated by adding a font's leading to the ascent and descent. The FontMetricsTest application illustrates the FontMetrics class. Here is a listing of the source code:

```
/*
 * FontMetricsTest
 * Demonstrates the FontMetrics Class
 */

import java.awt.*;
import java.awt.event.*;

public class FontMetricsTest extends Canvas
                             implements ItemListener {
  protected String string, font;

  public FontMetricsTest(String s, String f) {
    super();
    string = s;
    font = f;
    setSize(500, 250);
    setBackground(Color.white);
  }

  public static void main(String args[]) {
    FontMetricsTest fmt;
```

```java
    if (args.length == 1) {
      fmt = new FontMetricsTest(args[0], "Timesroman");
    }
    else if (args.length == 2) {
      fmt = new FontMetricsTest(args[0], args[1]);
    }
    else {
      fmt = new FontMetricsTest("Giggle", "Timesroman");
    }
    Panel fontPanel = new Panel();
    Choice fontChoice = new Choice();
    //get all available Fonts
    GraphicsEnvironment ge =
      GraphicsEnvironment.getLocalGraphicsEnvironment();
    String[] fontList = ge.getAvailableFontFamilyNames();
    for (int i=0; i < fontList.length; i++) {
      fontChoice.add(fontList[i]);
    }
    fontChoice.addItemListener(fmt);
    fontPanel.add(fontChoice);
    GUIFrame frame = new GUIFrame("FontMetrics Test");
    frame.add(fmt, BorderLayout.CENTER);
    frame.add(fontPanel, BorderLayout.SOUTH);
    frame.pack();
    frame.setVisible(true);
  }

  public void paint(Graphics g) {
    g.setFont(new Font(font, Font.PLAIN, 72));
    FontMetrics fm = g.getFontMetrics();
    int base = 150,
        start = 50,
        width = fm.stringWidth(string),
        height = fm.getHeight(),
        ascent = fm.getAscent(),
        descent = fm.getDescent(),
        leading = fm.getLeading();
    //draw a light gray box that represents the String's bounds
    g.setColor(Color.lightGray);
    g.fillRect(start, base + descent - height, width, height);
    g.setColor(Color.black);
    g.drawString(string, start, base);
    //draw the baseline
    g.drawLine(0, base, getSize().width, base);
    //draw lines to show the width of the string
    g.drawLine(start, 0, start, getSize().height);
    g.drawLine(start + width, 0, start + width, getSize().height);
    g.drawLine(start, descent + base + 10, start + width,
                descent + base + 10);
    //draw a line for the ascent
    g.drawLine(0, base - ascent, getSize().width, base - ascent);
    //draw a line for the descent
    g.drawLine(0, base + descent, getSize().width, base + descent);
    //draw the leading line
```

```
        g.drawLine(0, base - ascent - leading, getSize().width,
                base - ascent - leading);
        //draw the height line
        g.drawLine(start - 10, base + descent, start - 10,
                base + descent - height);
    }
    public void itemStateChanged(ItemEvent e) {
        font = ((Choice)e.getItemSelectable()).getSelectedItem();
        repaint();
    }
}
```

The FontMetrics class extends Canvas. The main() method optionally accepts one or two command-line arguments. The first argument is the string that will be displayed and the second argument is the name of the font that will be used initially to display the string. The default string is "Giggle", and the default font is "Timesroman". Also in the main() method, I get all the system's font family names in the same way that you learned in the previous section. I set up each of the fonts in a Choice menu, fontChoice. I added an ItemListener (this FontMetricsTest object, which implements that interface) to fontChoice. Therefore, when users select a font, the program sets the Font object, font to the selected font, and then calls repaint(), which results in a call to paint(Graphics).

 HINT If you need to invoke the paint(Graphics) method when you need to update your component's appearance on-screen, such as in the FontMetricsTest application, the preferred way is to call the repaint() method. This method ultimately results in a call to the paint(Graphics) method. Here is how this works. The repaint() method makes a call to the update(Graphics) method. The update(Graphics) method clears the component by painting it with the background color. Then it sets the Graphics object's color to the foreground color and passes it to the paint(Graphics) method. You never have to call the paint(Graphics) method directly unless you are sure that you don't need the graphics cleared before painting.

The paint(Graphics) method is overridden to draw lines based on the FontMetrics values. It sets the font style to Font.PLAIN, and the point size to 72. The local variables used here are fm, the FontMetrics object gotten by calling g.getFontMetrics(), base, which is the baseline and is set to 150. start is the left side of the painted string's coordinates and is passed to drawString(string, start, base). width is the actual width of the string and height is the font height. ascent is the font's ascent value and descent is the font's descent value. Finally, leading is the font's leading value. These variables get their values by calling the appropriate FontMetrics methods. After these variables are set, their values graphically represent the FontMetrics of the font. The bounds of the string are painted as a light gray rectangle:

```
g.setColor(Color.lightGray);
g.fillRect(start, base + descent - height, width, height);
```

The location of this rectangle must be relative to the string, so the x coordinate is set to the same as the x coordinate of the string and the y coordinate is set to `base + descent - height`.

Here's why: the bottom of the string is `base + descent` because `base` is the y coordinate of the string's baseline and the `descent` variable describes the amount by which characters can drop below the baseline. `height` is subtracted from this because you need to get the y coordinate of the top-left corner of the rectangle and `height`, as you remember is `leading + ascent + descent`. The width and height of the rectangle are `width` and `height`. This rectangle is drawn first and the string and lines that represent the fonts' metrics properties are drawn over it. After this rectangle is drawn, I set the color to black, draw the string, and start drawing lines.

The baseline is drawn the entire width of the canvas:

```
g.drawLine(0, base, getSize().width, base);
```

The lines that are drawn to show the width of the string are:

```
    g.drawLine(start, 0, start, getSize().height);
    g.drawLine(start + width, 0, start + width, getSize().height);
    g.drawLine(start, descent + base + 10, start + width,
            descent + base + 10);
```

The first two lines are drawn vertically on either side of the string and span the entire height of the canvas. The x coordinate of the left-side line is `start` and the x coordinate for the right side line is `start + width`. The third line is drawn horizontally, 10 pixels below the descent line and the length of the line is `width`, the width of the string.

The line that is drawn to represent the ascending value of the font is drawn horizontally across the canvas. The y coordinate is calculated as `base - ascent`, which shows the ascent by being `ascent` higher than the baseline of the string (the distance between the baseline and the ascent line is equal to the ascent of the font).

```
g.drawLine(0, base - ascent, getSize().width, base - ascent);
```

The descent line follows the same logic as ascent. This line spans the width of the canvas at the descent of the string and the leading line at the leading of the string:

```
g.drawLine(0, base + descent, getSize().width, base + descent);
g.drawLine(0, base - ascent - leading, getSize().width,
            base - ascent - leading);
```

Finally, the `Graphics` object draws the height line, a vertical line drawn to the left of the string whose height is equal to the string's height.

```
g.drawLine(start - 10, base + descent, start - 10,
          base + descent - height);
```

Figure 9.9 shows what this application looks like while it's running.

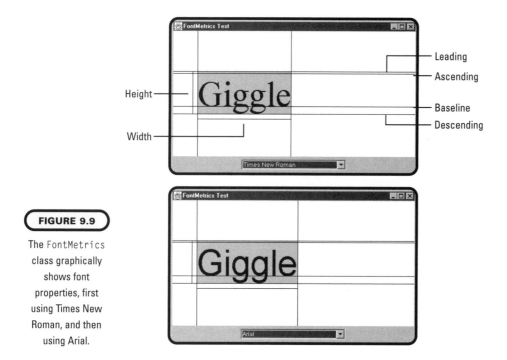

FIGURE 9.9

The `FontMetrics` class graphically shows font properties, first using Times New Roman, and then using Arial.

Drawing Images

You can actually draw images directly inside of your components using the `draw-Image()` methods. You've seen this a bit in the previous chapter when you learned how to display images inside of your applets. Loading images without the use of an applet works a bit differently. Here is how you load an application's image:

```
Image img = Toolkit.getDefaultToolkit().getImage(Image_filename);
```

Okay, it's probably a bit more complicated than you were expecting, so I'll explain. Here goes. You learned about the system's default toolkit in Chapter 7. To recap, it is your system's specific implementation of the AWT. You need that object to get the image using its `getImage(String)` method. The file name of the image you want to load is passed in as the `String` argument. Currently, Java supports the JPEG, GIF, and PNG file formats. The `ImageTest` application draws two images onto itself. Here is the source code. You can see the result in Figure 9.10.

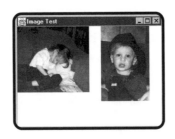

FIGURE 9.10

Displaying two images within a canvas using the `Graphics` class.

```
/*
 * ImageTest
 * Demonstrates drawing Images.
 */

import java.awt.*;

public class ImageTest extends Canvas {

   public ImageTest() {
      super();
      setSize(300, 200);
      setBackground(Color.white);
   }

   public static void main(String args[]) {
      ImageTest it = new ImageTest();
      GUIFrame frame = new GUIFrame("Image Test");
      frame.add(it);
      frame.pack();
      frame.setVisible(true);
   }

   public void paint(Graphics g) {
      Image img1 = Toolkit.getDefaultToolkit().getImage("britired.jpg");
      Image img2 = Toolkit.getDefaultToolkit().getImage("ty_hat.jpg");
      g.drawImage(img1, 0, 0, this);
      g.drawImage(img2, 175, 0, this);
   }

}
```

The arguments that are passed to the `drawImage()` method are an `Image` object, and then the x and y coordinates of the upper-left corner of the image. The fourth argument is an `ImageObserver`. `ImageObserver` is an interface that the `Component` class implements. It allows `Component` objects to receive image information. Any component can be passed as an image observer. Here, `this` is passed in because `ImageTest` extends `Canvas`, which extends `Component` and therefore is a `Component` and an `ImageObserver`. The `Image` class represents graphical images. Table 9.3 shows some of the more common methods of the `Image` class.

TABLE 9.3 IMAGE METHODS

Method	Description
Graphics getGraphics()	Returns a Graphics object that represents the graphics of this image.
int getHeight(*ImageObserver*)	Returns the image's height or −1 if it is not known.
int getWidth(*ImageObserver*)	Returns the image's width or −1 if it is not known.

An Image object's width and height are not known until the image has been loaded, so until then, the getHeight() and getWidth() methods return −1. The ImageTest2 method uses these methods to size the window and display the image. Because the size is not known until the image is loaded, yet you need the frame to be the correct size based on the image's size, there needs to be a way to wait for the images to load before setting the size of the frame (which packs the canvas in). This application does that. Here is a listing of the source code for ImageTest2.java:

```
/*
 * ImageTest2
 * Demonstrates how to wait for an image to load, how to
 * size the Frame initially based on the image size, and
 * how to resize the image when the Frame is resized.
 *
 * May pass args: [none] (default image and size are used)
 *              : [image] (displays image, original size
 *              : [image, width, height] (resizes image)
 */

import java.awt.*;

public class ImageTest2 extends Canvas {
  Image img;
  Dimension size;

  public ImageTest2(String imgName) {
    this(imgName, null);
  }

  public ImageTest2(String imgName, Dimension size) {
    //MediaTracker waits for the image to load for sizing
    MediaTracker mt =  new MediaTracker(this);
    img = Toolkit.getDefaultToolkit().getImage(imgName);
    mt.addImage(img, 0);
    //An InterruptedException might occur
    try {
      mt.waitForID(0);
```

```
      } catch (InterruptedException ie) {}
      if (size != null) setSize(size);
      else setSize(img.getWidth(this), img.getHeight(this));
    }


    public static void main(String args[]) {
      ImageTest2 it2;
      try {
        if (args.length == 1) {
          it2 = new ImageTest2(args[0]);
        }
        else if (args.length == 3) {
          it2 = new ImageTest2(args[0],
                        new Dimension(Integer.parseInt(args[1]),
                                      Integer.parseInt(args[2])));
        }
        else {
          it2 = new ImageTest2("bri_bass.jpg");
        }
      } catch (Exception e) {
        System.out.println("Args: [image] OR [image, width, height]");
        return;
      }
      GUIFrame frame = new GUIFrame("Image Test 2");
      frame.add(it2);
      frame.pack();
      frame.setVisible(true);
    }

    public void paint(Graphics g) {
      g.drawImage(img, 0, 0, getSize().width, getSize().height, this);
    }

}
```

When you run the ImageTest2 application, it can accept no arguments, one argument, or three arguments. The first argument is the name of the image you want to display and the second and third arguments are the width and height. If there are no arguments, the bri_bass.jpg image will be used and the size of the canvas will be the size of the image. If one argument is passed, the image specified will be displayed at its current size. If three arguments are passed, the image specified will be displayed with the specified width and height. I put the argument parsing in a try…catch so that if the arguments aren't in the right format, a message is issued to standard output indicating what the arguments are.

This application uses the MediaTracker class you learned about in the previous chapter to wait for the images to load. After the images are loaded, the size can be set by calling:

```
setSize(img.getWidth(this), img.getHeight(this));
```

This works only when no size command-line arguments were passed in. If size arguments are passed, those dimensions are used instead. The paint(Graphics) method is very simple. It just draws the image to fill the whole size of the canvas. If the users resize the canvas, the image will be resized right along with it. You can see the output in Figure 9.11.

FIGURE 9.11

The ImageTest2 application opens up just the right size to display its image.

Using the *Color* Class

You've used colors throughout this book starting with Chapter 6 "Creating a GUI Using the Abstract Windowing Toolkit." Every component has a background color and a foreground color and you've already used the setColor(Color) method of the Graphics class. Here you learn about the Color class in more detail. The Color class provides some predefined static Color objects, some of which you have already seen. They are black, blue, cyan, darkGray, gray, green, lightGray, magenta, orange, pink, red, white, and yellow. Yellow moons, green clovers, blue diamonds...where was I? Remember that because these are static variables, they should be prefixed by the Color class name, such as Color.blue. Table 9.4 shows some useful Color methods.

The ColorTest application creates a Canvas, palette, which it sets the background color of based on the arguments passed in. It accepts three integer arguments that range from 0-255. It makes sure that these values range between 0 and 255, like this:

```
r = r >= MIN && r <= MAX ? r : MIN;
g = g >= MIN && g <= MAX ? g : MIN;
b = r >= MIN && b <= MAX ? b : MIN;
```

If you don't remember how the conditional operator works, refer back to Chapter 3, "The Fortune Teller: Random Numbers, Conditionals, and Arrays." This application also makes use of two Buttons: bright, and dark. Once the initial color is set, clicking these buttons will invoke either brighter() or darker(), depending

TABLE 9.4	COLOR METHODS

Method	Description
Color(int r, int g, int b)	Constructs a Color object with the given red, green, and blue values that range from 0-255.
Color(int r, int g, int b, int a)	Constructs a Color object with the given red, green, blue, and alpha values, which range from 0-255.
Color brighter()	Returns a brighter version of this Color.
Color darker()	Returns a darker version of this Color.
int getAlpha()	Returns the alpha value of this Color.
int getBlue()	Returns the blue value of this Color.
int getGreen()	Returns the green value of this Color.
int getRed()	Returns the red value of this Color.

on which button you press. The canvas will change color accordingly. Here is the source code for ColorTest.java; the result can be seen in Figure 9.12.

```
/*
 * ColorTest
 * Demonstrates the Color class
 */

import java.awt.*;
import java.awt.event.*;

public class ColorTest extends GUIFrame {
  Canvas palette;
  Button bright, dark;
  public final static int MIN = 0,
                          MAX = 255;

  public ColorTest(int r, int g, int b) {
    super("Color Test");
    r = r >= MIN && r <= MAX ? r : MIN;
    g = g >= MIN && g <= MAX ? g : MIN;
    b = r >= MIN && b <= MAX ? b : MIN;
    palette = new Canvas();
    palette.setBackground(new Color(r, g, b));
    palette.setSize(200, 150);
    add(palette, BorderLayout.CENTER);

    Panel controlPanel = new Panel();
    controlPanel.setLayout(new GridLayout(1, 0));
    bright = new Button("Brighter");
```

```
      bright.addActionListener(new ActionListener() {
        public void actionPerformed(ActionEvent e) {
          Color c = palette.getBackground().brighter();
          palette.setBackground(c);
        }
      });
      controlPanel.add(bright);
      dark = new Button("Darker");
      dark.addActionListener(new ActionListener() {
        public void actionPerformed(ActionEvent e) {
          Color c = palette.getBackground().darker();
          palette.setBackground(c);
        }
      });
      controlPanel.add(dark);
      add(controlPanel, BorderLayout.SOUTH);

      pack();
      setVisible(true);
    }

    public static void main(String args[]) {
      if (args.length != 3) {
        new ColorTest(0, 0, 0);
      }
      else {
        new ColorTest(Integer.parseInt(args[0]),
                      Integer.parseInt(args[1]),
                      Integer.parseInt(args[2]));
      }
    }
  }
```

FIGURE 9.12

The ColorTest
application
demonstrates the
brighter() and
darker()
methods.

 HINT   Calling darker() on a Color object and reassigning its value a certain number
of times and then subsequently calling brighter() the same number of times
will not necessarily result in the original color. For instance, initially setting the
color to Color.yellow and then calling this:

```
color = color.darker()
```

15 or so times, and then attempting to reverse it by calling:

```
color = color.brighter()
```

the same number of times ends up with color being white. **Calling** darker() **that many times gives you black, and subsequent calls to** brighter() **will give you grays, from darker to brighter, until you get white. There is no trace of yellow. If you need to keep track of the original color, use multiple** Color **objects—one to hold the original color and another to hold the changed colors so you can always get back to the original.**

Color Values

The different values that make up colors are red, green, blue, and alpha values. The values must range from 0 to 255. The lower the number is, the less of that color used to make up the resulting color. Red, green, and blue are concepts that you already know. Having a 0 red value means that there is no red in the color. If red, green, and blue are all 0, this results in the color being black. If they are all 255, the color will be white. The alpha value, on the other hand, indicates its transparency or opacity, where 0 means the color is completely transparent and 255 indicates that the color is completely opaque. Values in between indicate different levels of translucency. The ColorSliders application demonstrates this concept. It is made up of three classes:

- ColorCanvas is the definition of the canvas used to paint the color.
- ColorChanger is a panel with sliders that allow for the adjustment of the color values.
- ColorSliders is the actual Frame of the application.

Here is the source code for the ColorCanvas application. As you can see, all it does is set its background color to white and override the paint(Graphics) method. In paint(Graphics), it just draws a black oval and then sets the color to the foreground color and paints the whole canvas with it over the oval. This is done so that you can see the level of transparency when you run the example.

```
/*
 * ColorCanvas
 * Displays its foreground color over a black oval
 * so that the color's alpha value can be noticed more
 * easily
 */

import java.awt.*;

public class ColorCanvas extends Canvas {

  public ColorCanvas() {
    setBackground(Color.white);
  }
```

```
  public void paint(Graphics g) {
    g.setColor(Color.black);
    g.fillOval(0, 0, getSize().width, getSize().height);
    g.setColor(getForeground());
    g.fillRect(0, 0, getSize().width, getSize().height);
  }

}
```

The ColorChanger class is a panel with four scroll bars that represent red, green, blue, and alpha values. Its constructor takes five arguments. The first argument is the component whose foreground color the sliders will be adjusting and the four other arguments are the initial red, green, blue, and alpha values. As you can see, it just lays out its sliders and labels that indicate the current values. When any of the sliders are adjusted, the values are updated, the component's foreground color is updated, and the component is repainted.

```
/*
 * ColorChanger
 * A Panel with scroll bars that represent red, green, blue,
 * and alpha values that change the foreground color of the
 * given Component
 */

import java.awt.*;
import java.awt.event.*;

public class ColorChanger extends Panel
                          implements AdjustmentListener {
  protected Scrollbar red, green, blue, alpha;
  protected Label redLabel, greenLabel, blueLabel, alphaLabel;
  protected int redVal, greenVal, blueVal, alphaVal;
  protected Color color;
  protected Component component;
  public final static int MIN = 0,
                          MAX = 255;

  public ColorChanger(Component c, int r, int g, int b, int a) {
    super();
    redVal = r >= MIN && r <= MAX ? r : MIN;
    greenVal = g >= MIN && g <= MAX ? g : MIN;
    blueVal = b >= MIN && b <= MAX ? b : MIN;
    alphaVal = a >= MIN && a <= MAX ? a : MIN;
    color = new Color(redVal, greenVal, blueVal, alphaVal);
    component = c;
    component.setForeground(color);

    GridBagLayout gridbag = new GridBagLayout();
    GridBagConstraints constraints = new GridBagConstraints();
    setLayout(gridbag);

    red = new Scrollbar(Scrollbar.HORIZONTAL, redVal, 1,
                        MIN, MAX + 1);
```

```java
        red.addAdjustmentListener(this);
        constraints.ipadx = 200;
        gridbag.setConstraints(red, constraints);
        add(red);
        redLabel = new Label("Red: " + redVal);
        constraints.gridwidth = GridBagConstraints.REMAINDER;
        gridbag.setConstraints(redLabel, constraints);
        add(redLabel);
        constraints.gridwidth = 1;

        green = new Scrollbar(Scrollbar.HORIZONTAL, greenVal, 1,
                              MIN, MAX + 1);
        green.addAdjustmentListener(this);
        gridbag.setConstraints(green, constraints);
        add(green);
        greenLabel = new Label("Green: " + greenVal);
        constraints.gridwidth = GridBagConstraints.REMAINDER;
        gridbag.setConstraints(greenLabel, constraints);
        add(greenLabel);
        constraints.gridwidth = 1;

        blue = new Scrollbar(Scrollbar.HORIZONTAL, blueVal, 1,
                             MIN, MAX + 1);
        blue.addAdjustmentListener(this);
        gridbag.setConstraints(blue, constraints);
        add(blue);
        blueLabel = new Label("Blue: " + blueVal);
        constraints.gridwidth = GridBagConstraints.REMAINDER;
        gridbag.setConstraints(blueLabel, constraints);
        add(blueLabel);
        constraints.gridwidth = 1;

        alpha = new Scrollbar(Scrollbar.HORIZONTAL, alphaVal, 1,
                              MIN, MAX + 1);
        alpha.addAdjustmentListener(this);
        gridbag.setConstraints(alpha, constraints);
        add(alpha);
        alphaLabel = new Label("Alpha: " + alphaVal);
        constraints.gridwidth = GridBagConstraints.REMAINDER;
        gridbag.setConstraints(alphaLabel, constraints);
        add(alphaLabel);
    }

    public void adjustmentValueChanged(AdjustmentEvent e) {
        redVal = red.getValue();
        greenVal = green.getValue();
        blueVal = blue.getValue();
        alphaVal = alpha.getValue();

        redLabel.setText("Red: " + redVal);
        greenLabel.setText("Green: " + greenVal);
        blueLabel.setText("Blue: " + blueVal);
        alphaLabel.setText("Alpha: " + alphaVal);
```

```
        color = new Color(redVal, greenVal, blueVal, alphaVal);
        component.setForeground(color);
        component.repaint();
    }

}
```

The `ColorSliders` application puts it all together. It lays out the `ColorCanvas` and the `ColorChanger` components and lets them do their work. As you can see, it passes the `ColorCanvas` object, `palette`, to the `ColorChanger` class as the component that is updated by the sliders. This application also optionally takes four arguments to initialize the color with red, green, blue, and alpha values. No care is taken to look for `NumberFormatException` occurrences. The default color when no arguments are passed is black, completely opaque. Try running this application for yourself to get a better idea of how the color values affect the color they make up. A sample run can be seen in Figure 9.13.

```
/*
 * ColorSliders
 * Tests a color's red, green, blue, and alpha values
 * through the use of ColorCanvas and ColorChanger
 */

import java.awt.*;

public class ColorSliders extends GUIFrame {
  ColorCanvas palette;
  ColorChanger sliders;

  public ColorSliders(int r, int g, int b, int a) {
    super("Color Values Test");
    palette = new ColorCanvas();
    sliders = new ColorChanger(palette, r, g, b, a);
    palette.setSize(150, 150);

    add(palette, BorderLayout.CENTER);
    add(sliders, BorderLayout.EAST);

    pack();
    setVisible(true);
  }

  public static void main(String args[]) {
    if (args.length != 4) {
      new ColorSliders(0, 0, 0, 255);
    }
    else {
      new ColorSliders(Integer.parseInt(args[0]),
                       Integer.parseInt(args[1]),
                       Integer.parseInt(args[2]),
                       Integer.parseInt(args[3]));
    }
  }
}
```

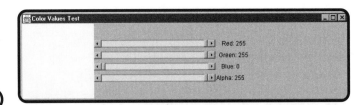

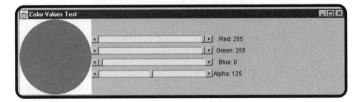

FIGURE 9.13

The `ColorSliders` application demonstrates a color's red, green, blue, and alpha values.

HINT

Ugh! What's that ugly flickering all about? When you run the `ColorSliders` application, you might notice some flickering while you are adjusting the color value sliders. This occurs because of the way the component's graphics are updated each time they are repainted. This flickering problem is solved in Chapter 10, "Animation, Sounds, and Threads."

Getting Back to the Memory Game

Now you know just about everything you need to know to program the Memory game. It is made up of two classes, the `MemoryCell` class that describes one picture cell of the game, and the `Memory` class, which uses multiple cells to create the game board and contains the `main()` method that drives the game.

Creating the *MemoryCell* Class

The `MemoryCell` class defines a single cell in the Memory game. It is a `Canvas` that is able to paint any of the shapes, the string, or the image, that makes up its symbol. Remember that in the memory game, the goal is to match like symbols with a minimum number of mismatches. This class has nine static integer constants that represent which symbol the `Memory` cell is able to display. They are `NONE` for no symbol (blank), `RECTANGLE`, `OVAL`, `ARC`, `TRIANGLE`, `SQUIGGLE`, `LINES`, `JAVA`, which is the graphical string `"Java"`, and `IMAGE`, a GIF image (lucy.gif).

This class also has `protected` variables that it uses to keep track of its states. They are:

`int symbol`	The symbol that this `MemoryCell` has. It can be one of the nine constants.
`static Image image`	This stores the image that is used for cells with the `IMAGE` symbol.

boolean matched	This indicates whether this cell has been matched with another cell.
boolean hidden	This indicates whether this MemoryCell's symbol is hidden.
boolean focused	This indicates whether the user is focusing on this cell (by clicking it).

Because these are protected variables, this class provides get and set methods that can be called to modify them from other classes that don't have direct access to these variables. Some of the set methods also call repaint() because the graphical representation of the cell is dependant on the value, such as the hidden variable. If the cell is hidden, a question mark appears, if it is not hidden, its symbol appears instead. Another useful method is the matches(MemoryCell) method. This method returns true if the symbol of the MemoryCell passed in matches the symbol of this MemoryCell object, otherwise it returns false. Here is the source code for MemoryCell.java:

```
/*
 * MemoryCell
 * Defines one cell of the Memory game
 */

import java.awt.*;

public class MemoryCell extends Canvas {

  //symbol shape constants
  public final static int NONE = -1,
                          RECTANGLE = 0,
                          OVAL = 1,
                          ARC = 2,
                          TRIANGLE = 3,
                          SQUIGGLE = 4,
                          LINES = 5,
                          JAVA = 6,
                          IMAGE = 7;
  protected int symbol;
  protected static Image image;
  protected boolean matched;
  protected boolean hidden;
  protected boolean focused;

  public MemoryCell(int shape) {
    super();
    setSymbol(shape);
    matched = false;
    hidden = true;
    focused = false;
    setBackground(Color.white);
    image = Toolkit.getDefaultToolkit().getImage("lucy.gif");
```

```java
    setSize(80, 80);
  }

  public void setSymbol(int shape) {
    if (shape >= -1 && shape <= 7) symbol = shape;
    else symbol = NONE;
  }

  public int getSymbol() {
    return symbol;
  }

  public boolean matches(MemoryCell otherMemoryCell) {
    return symbol == otherMemoryCell.symbol;
  }

  public void setMatched(boolean m) {
    matched = m;
    repaint();
  }

  public boolean getMatched() {
    return matched;
  }

  public void setHidden(boolean h) {
    hidden = h;
    repaint();
  }

  public boolean getHidden() {
    return hidden;
  }

  public void setFocused(boolean f) {
    focused = f;
    repaint();
  }

  public boolean getFocused() {
    return focused;
  }

  public void paint(Graphics g) {
    if (hidden) {
      g.setColor(Color.darkGray);
      g.fillRect(0, 0, getSize().width, getSize().height);
      g.setColor(Color.lightGray);
      g.setFont(new Font("Timesroman", Font.ITALIC, 36));
      Point p = centerStringPoint("?", g.getFontMetrics());
      g.drawString("?", p.x, p.y);
    }
```

```
    else switch (symbol) {
      case RECTANGLE:
        g.fillRect(15, 15, 50, 50);
        break;
      case OVAL:
        g.fillOval(15, 15, 50, 50);
        break;
      case ARC:
        g.fillArc(15, 15, 50, 50, 45, 270);
        break;
      case TRIANGLE:
        g.fillPolygon(new int[] {40, 15, 65},
                      new int[] {15, 65, 65}, 3);
        break;
      case SQUIGGLE:
        g.drawPolyline(new int[] {15, 25, 35, 45, 55, 65},
                       new int[] {15, 65, 15, 65, 15, 65}, 6);
        break;
      case LINES:
        g.drawLine(15, 15, 65, 15);
        g.drawLine(15, 25, 65, 25);
        g.drawLine(15, 35, 65, 35);
        g.drawLine(15, 45, 65, 45);
        g.drawLine(15, 55, 65, 55);
        g.drawLine(15, 65, 65, 65);
        break;
      case JAVA:
        g.setFont(new Font("Timesroman", Font.BOLD, 24));
        Point p = centerStringPoint("Java", g.getFontMetrics());
        g.drawString("Java", p.x, p.y);
        break;
      case IMAGE:
        g.drawImage(image, 15, 15, 50, 50, this);
        break;
      default:
        super.paint(g);
    }
    if (focused) {
      if (matched) g.setColor(Color.green);
      else g.setColor(Color.red);
      g.drawRect(0, 0, getSize().width - 1, getSize().height - 1);
    }
  }

  private Point centerStringPoint(String s, FontMetrics fm) {
    Point cp = new Point();
    int w = fm.stringWidth(s);
    int h = fm.getHeight() - fm.getLeading();
    cp.x = (getSize().width - w) / 2;
    cp.y = (getSize().height + h) / 2 - fm.getDescent();
    return cp;
  }
}
```

The paint(Graphics) method is basically the heart of this class, because its main purpose is to graphically represent itself based on its members. If this MemoryCell is hidden, it sets the background to dark gray and draws a light gray question mark in the center. If it's not hidden, the symbol variable is used as the condition of a switch statement.

Depending on what the symbol is, it will draw a shape, a string, or an image in the cell. Also, to make it easier for the users to distinguish the cells they are currently working with, a red border appears around the cell when the cell is active but doesn't have a match yet. If the cell has been matched, its border appears green.

It's important to understand how the strings are centered in the MemoryCells when they are drawn. The program invokes the private centerStringPoint (String, FontMetrics) method. This method returns the Point at which the given String should be drawn in the cell, based on the FontMetrics object passed in, so that the string will be centered both horizontally and vertically. Here's how that works.

The width and height of the String are determined through calls to the getWidth(String) and getHeight() methods of the FontMetrics class. The local variable w holds the width and h holds the height. Note that the leading value is subtracted from the height. This allows for better vertical aligning of most fonts. The x position is determined by finding the center of the canvas first (get-Size().width / 2). The paint() method can't draw the image here because the left side of the picture will be centered. If half the width of the image is subtracted from the x position, the center of the image will be aligned with the horizontal center of the canvas, as follows:

```
cp.x = (getSize().width / 2) - (w / 2);
```

And by using simple algebra:

```
cp.x = (getSize().width - 2) / 2;
```

The y position is obtained similarly except, instead of *subtracting* half of the height of the image, you add the height in order to move the image down instead of up. I also subtracted the descent from the y position. In many cases, a font's ascent is very large in comparison to its descent and can make the string appear to be too low. Subtracting the descent seemed to work pretty well at making the strings appear more centered for most fonts. (Note that there are more advanced ways to center strings graphically, but they are not covered in this book.)

Creating the *Memory* Class

The Memory class maintains an array, called cells, of sixteen MemoryCell objects that it lays out in a four-by-four grid. first and second are also MemoryCell object pointers. Because the goal is to match two cells, the users interact with two cells at a time. They click a cell and at that time first will point to that cell. The users then click another cell and second will point to that second cell. The program does this so that it can compare the two pointers and also determine how many cells the users are currently working with. If first and second are both null, the users aren't currently interacting with any cells, so when they click a cell, that cell becomes the first cell.

You can see how this reasoning works in the logic in the mousePressed (MouseEvent) method of the inner MouseAdapter class, ml. It makes sure that the first and second cells are not the same (first != second) and that only hidden cells can be in play. It also determines whether the first and second cells are matches. If they are not matches, nMisMatches, the variable that counts the number of mismatches, is incremented. The randomize() method randomizes the board, but makes sure that there are eight pairs of different symbols. The reset button calls the randomize() method.

```
/*
 * Memory
 * Defines a Memory game
 */

import java.awt.*;
import java.awt.event.*;
import java.util.Random;

public class Memory extends GUIFrame {
  protected MemoryCell[] cells;
  //first and second are the two cells trying to be matched
  protected MemoryCell first, second;
  protected Panel cellPanel, controlPanel;
  protected Label mismatches;
  protected Button reset;
  protected int nMismatched;

  public Memory() {
    super("Memory Game");
    MouseListener ml = new MouseAdapter() {
      public void mousePressed(MouseEvent e) {
        MemoryCell clickedCell = (MemoryCell)e.getSource();
        if (second != null) {
          first.setFocused(false);
          second.setFocused(false);
          if (!first.matches(second)) {
            first.setHidden(true);
            second.setHidden(true);
            nMismatched++;
            mismatches.setText("Number of Mismatches: "
                               + nMismatched);
          }
          first = second = null;
        }
```

```
        if (clickedCell.getHidden()) {
            clickedCell.setFocused(true);
            clickedCell.setHidden(false);
          if (first == null) {
            first = clickedCell;
          }
          else {
            second = clickedCell;
            if (first.matches(second)) {
              first.setMatched(true);
              second.setMatched(true);
            }
          }
        }
      }
    }
  };
  first = second = null;
  cellPanel = new Panel();
  cellPanel.setLayout(new GridLayout(4, 0, 10, 10));
  cells = new MemoryCell[16];
  for (int c=0; c < cells.length; c++) {
    cells[c] = new MemoryCell(MemoryCell.NONE);
    cells[c].addMouseListener(ml);
    cellPanel.add(cells[c]);
  }
  add(cellPanel, BorderLayout.CENTER);

  controlPanel = new Panel();
  controlPanel.setLayout(new FlowLayout());
  reset = new Button("Reset");
  reset.addActionListener(new ActionListener() {
    public void actionPerformed(ActionEvent e) {
      randomize();
    }
  });
  controlPanel.add(reset);
  mismatches = new Label("Number of Mismatches: 0");
  controlPanel.add(mismatches);
  add(controlPanel, BorderLayout.SOUTH);

  randomize();
  pack();
  setResizable(false);
  setVisible(true);
}

protected void randomize() {
  //for all possible symbol pairs
  int[] symbols = new int[cells.length];
  int pos;
  Random rand = new Random();
  //reinitialize all cells
  for (int c=0; c < cells.length; c++) {
    cells[c].setMatched(false);
```

```
      cells[c].setHidden(true);
      cells[c].setFocused(false);
      cells[c].setSymbol(MemoryCell.NONE);
      symbols[c] = c % 8;
    }
    for (int s=0; s < symbols.length; s++) {
      do {
        pos = rand.nextInt(cells.length);
      } while (cells[pos].getSymbol() != MemoryCell.NONE);
      cells[pos].setSymbol(symbols[s]);
    }
    //reset first and second & mismatches
    first = second = null;
    if (isVisible()) repaint();
    nMismatched = 0;
    mismatches.setText("Number of Mismatches: 0");
  }

  public static void main(String args[]) {
    new Memory();
  }
}
}
```

Summary

In this chapter, you learned all about AWT graphics programming. You learned how to draw shapes such as lines, rectangles, ovals, and polygons, as well as how to draw strings and images. You learned about the Font class and how to use the FontMetrics class to get useful information when positioning fonts in a graphical context. In the next chapter, you learn about animations, sounds, and thread programming.

CHALLENGES

1. **Create an application that allows you to draw lines by clicking the initial point and dragging the mouse to the second point. The application should be repainted so that you can see the line changing size and position as you are dragging the mouse. When the mouse button is released, the line is drawn.**

2. **Write an application that displays an image. The size of the frame should be just the right size to display the image. Over the image, draw a string that is centered both horizontally and vertically.**

3. **Create a Canvas that paints a gradient that's dark on one side and slowly gets lighter as it moves to the other side.**

CHAPTER 10

Animation, Sounds, and Threads

In this chapter, you learn all about how to use threads in Java. You will create multithreaded applications that perform animation. You will learn how to protect your code from multiple threads that run concurrently on the same objects. You also learn how to play sounds from applications. The final project of this chapter includes these tasks to build the ShootingRange **game:**

- **Create multithreaded applications**

- **Create thread-safe code**

- **Perform animation**

- **Play sounds from an application**

The Project: *ShootingRange* Game

The ShootingRange game animates aliens flying across the screen. Don't worry, no real aliens were harmed during the creation of this game. They're only fake aliens. This is just a shooting range. The goal here is very simple. Even my kids can play this game! They're only 4 and 1. You just press the spacebar to fire at the alien. The black square thingy at the bottom of the screen is supposed to be a gun of some sort. The bullet, which appears as a red sphere, shoots up toward the top of the screen. You have to try to time it so that your bullet hits the alien as it's flying by. You lose points if you miss a shot, even if you hit all the aliens; you also lose points if you fail to hit one of the aliens. The game shows you your score as a percentage. If you hit all the aliens, using only one shot per alien, you can get 100%. You can press the spacebar again to start up a new game. Figure 10.1 shows you what the game looks like.

Threading

Threads are independently executing "jobs." Multiple threads appear to be running concurrently, and you can think of them that way, as if two processors are running them simultaneously, although that's not *exactly* how it works. The processor—most machines have only one—switches between the threads to make them appear to be running at the same time. Here's a conceptual example. Say you call a method that lists some integers and you call another method that prints the letters of the alphabet. Without using a second thread, your code first prints the integers, and then proceeds to print the letters. It works like an

---

IN THE REAL WORLD

In the real world, threading is used for many reasons. One of the most common uses is to dispatch events to event handlers. Take a graphical user interface (GUI), for example. When you implement the ActionListener interface, you direct some action to occur when a button is clicked. It can be one line of code, or it can be a big huge program that takes forever to complete. If you didn't use multithreading, your program would just hang there until the task defined by the actionPerformed(ActionEvent) method completed. By using multithreading, that event can go do whatever it needs to and not hold everything else up.

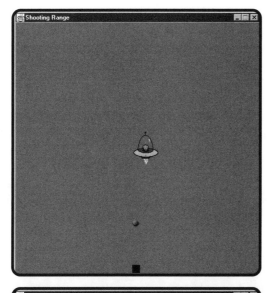

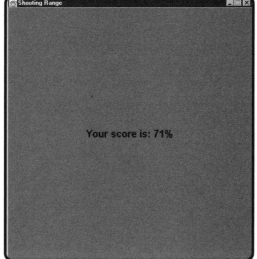

FIGURE 10.1

I missed on
purpose!

ordered step-by-step process, which it is. If you ran the two methods in two separate threads, you would have output like:

```
1 2 A 3 B 4 C D 5 …
```

There is no guarantee what order the output will print in because there is no guarantee which thread will get control and when. Java has support for threading in the Thread class, the Object class, and in the virtual machine.

Extending the *Thread* Class

One way to create a thread is to subclass the Thread class and override its run()
method. When you create a thread, its run() method drives the thread. Once you
have a Thread object, you invoke its start() method to make it run in its own
thread. Don't invoke run() directly.

TRAP Make sure that if you want to make a Thread instance to actually run its own
thread, you don't directly call the run() method. If you do that, the current
Thread will run the run() method. Calling start() is the way to go. Calling
start() doesn't immediately fire off the thread. Instead it registers the thread
with the virtual machine as eligible for running. At some point in the future, the
thread scheduler will allow your thread to run.

The Thread class is part of the java.lang package, so you don't have to import
anything to access it. The ThreadTest application is a simple example of how
to create and run a thread. It subclasses Thread and overrides the run() method
to print the numbers 1 through 10. The main() method just creates a new
ThreadTest instance and invokes the start() method so that the thread will
eventually run. Here is the source code for this program:

```
/*
 * ThreadTest
 * Demonstrates how to create a thread by extending the Thread class
 */

public class ThreadTest extends Thread {

  //override the run method
  public void run() {
    for (int i=1; i <=10; i++) {
      System.out.println(i);
    }
  }

  public static void main(String args[]) {
    ThreadTest test = new ThreadTest();
    //start the thread
    test.start();
  }

}
```

Figure 10.2 shows the output. Table 10.1 shows some members and methods of
the Thread class.

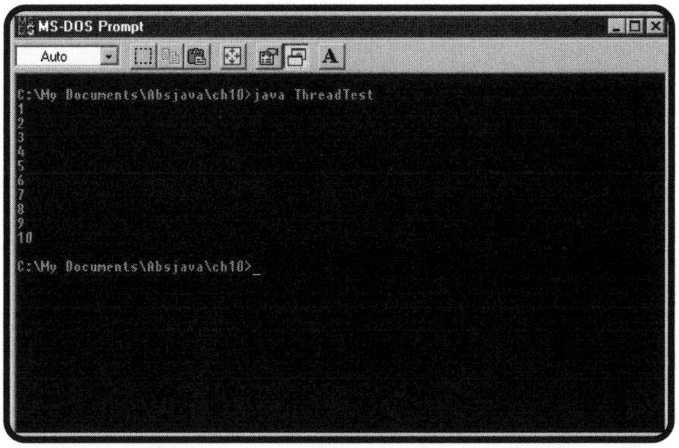

FIGURE 10.2

The ThreadTest program creates a new thread, which counts to 10.

TABLE 10.1 THE THREAD CLASS FIELDS AND METHODS

Member or Method	Description
MAX_PRIORITY	The maximum priority for a thread. The Thread scheduler might consider this priority when deciding which thread to dispatch.
MIN_PRIORITY	The minimum priority for a thread.
NORM_PRIORITY	The default priority for a thread.
Thread()	Constructs a new thread.
Thread(*Runnable*)	Constructs a new thread that runs the given *Runnable*.
Thread currentThread()	Static method that returns a reference to the currently running thread.
boolean isAlive()	Returns true if the thread has been started and has not yet died.
void interrupt()	Interrupts this thread (wakes it up if it is sleeping).
void join()	Waits for this thread to die.
void run()	The driver of the thread.
void sleep(*long*)	Makes this thread sleep (stop executing) for the specified number of milliseconds.
void stop()	*Deprecated*, unsafe method that stops threads (avoid calling this).

Implementing the *Runnable* Interface

There is another way to create a thread. Instead of extending the Thread class, you can implement the Runnable interface. The Runnable interface requires that you override one method. You guessed it: the run() method. To run a Runnable object in a thread, you pass it to the Thread(Runnable) constructor. When you invoke start() on the thread, it results in a call to the Runnable's run() method.

 The Thread class, itself, implements the Runnable interface. That's why when you extend Thread, you implement the run() method.

The RunnableTest application is an example of how to implement the Runnable interface to create a thread. Its run() method is exactly the same as the Thread-Test class's run() method. It just counts to 10. To get this thread started, you need to create a new Thread object (called t) in the main() method This Runnable object is passed into its constructor and then its start() method is invoked. Here is a listing of the source code:

```
/*
 * RunnableTest
 * Demonstrates how to implement the Runnable interface
 */

public class RunnableTest implements Runnable {

  //must implement the run method
  public void run() {
    for (int i=1; i <= 10; i++) {
      System.out.println(i);
    }
  }

  public static void main(String args[]) {
    RunnableTest test = new RunnableTest();
    //Construct a thread with this Runnable
    Thread t = new Thread(test);
    //start the thread
    t.start();
  }
}
```

You can see the output of the RunnableTest application in Figure 10.3.

 What's the difference between extending Thread and implementing Runnable? Why would you choose one over the other? Generally, it is better to implement the Runnable interface. One good reason for this is that if you are defining a subclass of another class, such as GUIFrame, you can't also subclass the Thread class. Inheritance can come from only one direct superclass. To get around this problem, you can extend GUIFrame and implement the Runnable interface too.

FIGURE 10.3

The output of the
RunnableTest
application is
exactly the same as
the ThreadTest
application.

Problems Associated with Multithreading

When two threads are running concurrently, there is no guarantee which thread
will be running at any given time. The MultiThreadTest application demonstrates this. It has two threads: the original program's execution thread and a second thread, an instance of MultiThreadTest, that the original thread starts. One
of the threads lists letters in order and the other lists numbers. The output of
this program is not exactly predictable and multiple runs can produce different
output. Here is the source code:

```
/*
 * MultiThreadTest
 * Demonstrates the unpredictability of multithreading
 */

public class MultiThreadTest extends Thread {

  public void run() {
    for (char a='A'; a <= 'J'; a++) {
      System.out.println(a);
    }
  }

  public static void main(String args[]) {
    MultiThreadTest t = new MultiThreadTest();
    //fire off the thread
    t.start();
    //continue on simultaneously
    for (int i=1; i <= 10; i++) {
      System.out.println(i);
    }
  }

}
```

You can see the output of the MultiThreadTest application in Figure 10.4.

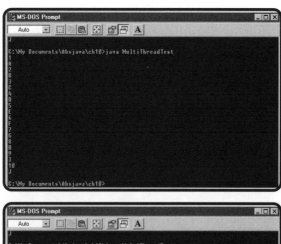

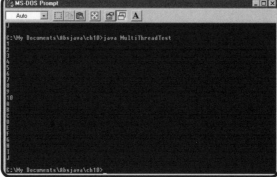

FIGURE 10.4

The `MultiThreadTest` application ran twice with totally different output.

This is just a simple example, but I'm sure you can imagine what kinds of disasters can result if you expect code to be executed in a particular order and you have multiple threads doing different things simultaneously. Your data can become corrupted!

Writing Thread-Safe Code

Java provides ways to write *thread-safe code,* that is, code that can have multiple threads executing it simultaneously, and not become unstable because of corruption of some kind. You can use the `synchronized` keyword as a modifier for methods. This keyword makes sure that only one thread can be executing the method at a time. It works by locking `this`, the object that owns the code. Only one thread at a time can own a lock for an object. Entering a `synchronized` method ensures that while a thread is inside it, it has an exclusive lock on `this`. Any other thread that needs to get into this method has to wait until the lock is released. When a thread passes out of synchronized code, the lock is automatically released.

```
public synchronized void mySafeMethod() { … }
```

To enter mySafeMethod(), the thread must gain a lock to the instance of the class that defines the method. When it gets into mySafeMethod(), it automatically gains the lock to this and when it passes out of the method, the lock is released, allowing other threads to enter mySafeMethod(). You can use the synchronized keyword also to lock blocks of code. You can lock on any object:

```
synchronized (myObject) {
    ...
}
```

myObject must not be locked by another thread to enter the block of code defined in the curly braces. Any thread that gets into the curly braces gains a lock to myObject. This second method of synchronization is much less commonly used because it can be dangerous to lock any object other than the one that owns the code.

HINT volatile is another keyword that has use in multithreaded environments. Only variables can be volatile. This keyword is not used very often. It indicates to the compiler that the variable might be modified out of synch and that multiple threads should be careful when working with it.

Using *wait(), notify(),* and *notifyAll()*

The wait(), notify(), and notifyAll() methods allow for threads to be paused and then restarted. These methods are defined in the Object class. They must be called from within synchronized code. When a thread enters the wait() method, it releases the object lock and pauses execution until another thread invokes the notify() or notifyAll() method. notify() wakes up one thread waiting on this object and notifyAll() notifies all the threads waiting on this object. The wait() method can throw an InterruptedException. A thread can be interrupted while it is waiting or asleep if you invoke the interrupt() method of the Thread class.

```
public synchronized void getValue() {
  if (valueNotSetYet) {
    try { wait();
    } catch (InterruptedException e) { }
  }
  x = value;
}
public synchronized void setValue() {
  value = y;
  valueNotSetYet = false;
  notify();
}
```

In the previous snippet of code, one thread is responsible for getting a value that is set by a different thread. Because you can't predict exactly when the value will be set, you need to determine whether the value has been set before you try to get it (assume valueNotSetYet is a boolean variable that indicates whether the value has been set). If the value hasn't been set, you wait for it. Calling wait() releases the lock and allows the second thread to synchronize on this and set the value valueNotSetYet to false, and then call notify() to allow the first thread to retrieve the value it so desperately needs to get.

Putting a Thread to Sleep

You can pause a thread for a set number of milliseconds by calling the static Thread.sleep(long) method. You will see the importance this feature has for animation when you get to that point to pause between each frame of animation. The long parameter specifies the number of milliseconds the thread sleeps (1000 milliseconds is one second). A sleeping thread can be interrupted, so calling Thread.sleep(long) requires that you handle InterruptedExceptions. Here is an example of an application that calls Thread.sleep(long). It alternatively prints "Tic" and "Toc" to standard output, pausing one second in between each print. Here is the source code for SleepTest.java:

```
/*
 * SleepTest
 * Demonstrates how to make a Thread sleep
 */

public class SleepTest extends Thread {

  public void run() {
    for (int i=0; i < 10; i++) {
      if (i % 2 == 0) System.out.println("Tic");
      else System.out.println("Toc");
      try {
        Thread.sleep(1000);
      } catch (InterruptedException e) {}
    }
  }

  public static void main(String args[]) {
    SleepTest t = new SleepTest();
    t.start();
  }

}
```

Figure 10.5 shows the output.

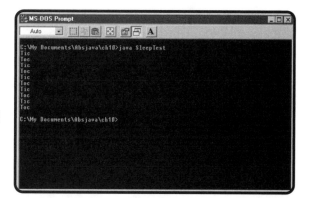

Performing Animation

Animation is basically done by showing a series of pictures that differ slightly
from each other in a way that makes the image appear to be moving. If the pictures change fast enough, the animation looks smooth. In this section, I'll take
you through the process of using threads to animate sprites.

The *Sprite* Class

A *sprite*, in its simplest definition, is any graphical image that moves, especially
when in relation to computer games. A sprite is typically made up of a series of
images that are used to animate a motion. It also has an (x, y) position and a
direction and speed of its movement. The Sprite class I defined for this chapter
is a simple class that encapsulates these concepts. It has an array of images,
images[], a Point location, location, and another Point, called deltaPoint,
which indicates the direction and speed of the sprite.

The way this works is the location point is ignored by deltaPoint. deltaPoint
indicates the distance the sprite will move in both the x direction and the y direction from where it currently is, wherever that might be, every time the sprite is
updated. There is another member, currentImgIndex, which keeps track of the
images[] Image element (the actual image) that is set as the current image to be
displayed. The Sprite class has its get and set methods for modifying the protected members. The constructor accepts the array of images, the starting location, and also the deltaPoint Point object.

The update() method sets the current image to the next image (if it gets past the
last image, it loops back to the first one), and then it moves the current location
based on the value of deltaPoint by calling the translate(int, int) method.
This method belongs to the Point class and moves the Point object's location
based on the change in x and the change in y that you pass in as its parameters.

The Sprite class doesn't perform any animation on its own. It relies on other classes to call its update() method, which creates the illusion of motion. Here is the source listing for Sprite.java:

```
/*
 * Sprite
 * Encapsulates images for animation.
 */

import java.awt.*;

public class Sprite {
  protected Image[] images;
  protected Point location;
  //indicates the change in (x, y)
  protected Point deltaPoint;
  protected int currentImgIndex;

  public Sprite(Image[] imgs, Point loc, Point delta) {
    images = imgs;
    currentImgIndex = 0;
    location = new Point(loc.x, loc.y);
    deltaPoint = new Point(delta.x, delta.y);
  }

  public Image getCurrentImage() {
    return images[currentImgIndex];
  }

  public void setLocation(Point loc) {
    location = new Point(loc.x, loc.y);
  }

  public Point getLocation() {
    return new Point(location.x, location.y);
  }

  public void setDeltaPoint(Point dest) {
    deltaPoint = new Point(dest.x, dest.y);
  }

  public Point getDeltaPoint() {
    return new Point(deltaPoint.x, deltaPoint.y);
  }

  public void update() {
    currentImgIndex = (currentImgIndex + 1) % images.length;
    location.translate(deltaPoint.x, deltaPoint.y);
  }

}
```

Testing the *Sprite* Class

The SpriteTest class tests the Sprite class by giving it some images, specifying its location, and delta point, and repeatedly calling its update() method from within a thread. Figure 10.6 shows the three images that make up the animation.

FIGURE 10.6

It's BoitMan! These images are animated by the SpriteTest class.

Here is the source code for SpriteTest.java:

```java
/*
 * SpriteTest
 * Tests the Sprite class
 */

import java.awt.*;

public class SpriteTest extends GUIFrame implements Runnable {
  Sprite sprite;

  public SpriteTest(Image[] images, Point loc, Point dest) {
    super("Sprite Animation Test");
    MediaTracker mt = new MediaTracker(this);
    for (int i=0; i < images.length; i++) {
      mt.addImage(images[i], i);
    }
    try {
      mt.waitForAll();
    } catch (InterruptedException e) {}

    sprite = new Sprite(images, loc, dest);
  }

  public static void main(String args[]) {
    Image[] imgs = { Toolkit.getDefaultToolkit().getImage("b1.gif"),
                     Toolkit.getDefaultToolkit().getImage("b2.gif"),
                     Toolkit.getDefaultToolkit().getImage("b3.gif") };

    SpriteTest spriteTest = new SpriteTest(imgs, new Point(0, 0),
                                               new Point(3, 3));
    spriteTest.setSize(300, 300);
    spriteTest.setVisible(true);

    Thread runner = new Thread(spriteTest);
    runner.start();
  }
```

```
//assumes animation moves to the right, down, or both
public void run() {
   while (sprite.getLocation().x < getSize().width
         && sprite.getLocation().y < getSize().height) {
     repaint();
     sprite.update();
     try {
       Thread.sleep(50);
     } catch (InterruptedException e) {}
   }
}

public void paint(Graphics g) {
  g.drawImage(sprite.getCurrentImage(), sprite.getLocation().x,
              sprite.getLocation().y, this);
}

}
```

It is a GUIFrame that constructs a Sprite object by passing in an array of images consisting of b1.gif, b2.gif, and b3.gif. The second argument to the constructor is new Point(0, 0) so the sprite starts in the top-left corner of the GUIFrame. The third argument is new Point(3, 3), so every time the sprite is updated by calling its update() method, it will move three generic units (often pixels) to the right and three down.

SpriteTest implements the Runnable interface and overrides run() to move the sprite until it is no longer in the visible GUIFrame area. It calls repaint() to display the image, and then calls sprite.update() to update the sprite to its next frame, sleeps for 50 milliseconds, and then repeats this dance. The paint(Graphics) method paints sprite's image at its current location, which it gets by calling sprite.getLocation().x and sprite.getLocation().y. Figure 10.7 hints at what this looks like; however, you have to run it for yourself to actually see the animation.

FIGURE 10.7

Go BoitMan, Go!

Double Buffering

Did you notice that ugly flickering while BoitMan was running across the screen? This is because the drawing is taking place directly onto the screen. To eliminate the flickering, you need to paint the image to an off-screen buffer first, and then copy the entire off-screen image to the screen. This technique is called *double buffering*. Here's how it works.

Calling a component's repaint() method results in a call to the update(Graphics) method, which clears the component's graphics with the background color. You actually see this happening on-screen, which is the main cause of the flickering. Then the update(Graphics) method sets the color to the foreground color and invokes paint(Graphics). You see the background color for a split second, and then you see the image again. This is where the flickering comes from.

To prevent the flickering, override update(Graphics) so that it doesn't clear the background. It just calls paint(Graphics) directly. Then from paint(), create an image buffer, which is an invisible image. You create the off-screen image buffer by invoking the createImage(int, int) method that is defined in the Component class. The arguments are its width and its height. Then draw on to the buffered image and then copy the whole thing to the screen. The SpriteNoFlickerTest application performs double-buffering:

```java
/*
 * SpriteTest
 * Tests the Sprite class
 */

import java.awt.*;

public class SpriteNoFlickerTest extends GUIFrame implements Runnable {
  Sprite sprite;
  Image offImg;

  public SpriteNoFlickerTest(Image[] images, Point loc, Point dest) {
    super("Sprite Animation Test (No Flicker)");
    MediaTracker mt = new MediaTracker(this);
    for (int i=0; i < images.length; i++) {
      mt.addImage(images[i], i);
    }
    try {
      mt.waitForAll();
    } catch (InterruptedException e) {}

    sprite = new Sprite(images, loc, dest);
  }

  public static void main(String args[]) {
    Image[] imgs = { Toolkit.getDefaultToolkit().getImage("b1.gif"),
                     Toolkit.getDefaultToolkit().getImage("b2.gif"),
                     Toolkit.getDefaultToolkit().getImage("b3.gif") };
```

```
      SpriteNoFlickerTest test = new SpriteNoFlickerTest(imgs,
                                   new Point(0, 0), new Point(3, 3));
      test.setSize(300, 300);
      test.setVisible(true);

      Thread runner = new Thread(test);
      runner.start();
   }

   //assumes animation moves to the right, down, or both
   public void run() {
      while (sprite.getLocation().x < getSize().width
             && sprite.getLocation().y < getSize().height) {
        repaint();
        sprite.update();
        try {
          Thread.sleep(50);
        } catch (InterruptedException e) {}
      }
   }

   //override update()
   public void update(Graphics g) {
      paint(g);
   }

   //on-screen image buffer
   public void paint(Graphics g) {
      offImg = createImage(getSize().width, getSize().height);
      Graphics offg = offImg.getGraphics();
      paintOffScreen(offg);
      g.drawImage(offImg, 0, 0, null);
   }

   //off-screen image buffer
   public void paintOffScreen(Graphics g) {
      // clear the off-screen image
      g.setColor(getBackground());
      g.fillRect(0, 0, getSize().width, getSize().height);
      g.drawImage(sprite.getCurrentImage(), sprite.getLocation().x,
                  sprite.getLocation().y, this);
      g.setColor(getForeground());
   }
}
```

This application is the same as the SpriteTest application except for the following differences. It declares an Image object, offImg, which will hold the reference to the off-screen image buffer. It overrides the update(Graphics) method, which you learned is required for double buffering. It just calls paint(Graphics). It creates the off-screen image buffer by calling the following:

```
offImg = createImage(getSize().width, getSize().height);
```

The paintOffScreen(Graphics) method is new. It basically does the work that was originally done in the SpriteTest's paint(Graphics) method. The paint(Graphics) method passes the offImg's graphics by invoking offImg.get-Graphics(). After offImge is all set, paint(Graphics) draws that image just like it draws any other image. The result of this effort? No annoying flickering!

Playing Sound from Applications

You already learned how to play sounds in Java, but that was specific to applets. In this section, you learn how to play sounds from applications, which is actually not all that different from playing sounds from applets. In fact, you can do it by invoking a static method provided in the Applet class, Applet.newAudio-Clip(URL). You pass in a URL object that tells where the audio file is and, presto, you got yourself an AudioClip instance! The SoundApplication application demonstrates how to do this:

```
/*
 * SoundApplication
 * Demonstrates how to play sounds from an application
 */

import java.awt.*;
import java.awt.event.*;
import java.applet.*;
import java.net.*;

public class SoundApplication extends GUIFrame
                                   implements ActionListener {

  AudioClip taught;

  public SoundApplication() {
    super("Sound Application");
    //call Applet's static method to load AudioClip
    try {
      taught = Applet.newAudioClip(new URL("file:taught.au"));
    } catch (MalformedURLException e) {}
    Button play = new Button("Play");
    play.addActionListener(this);
    add(play, BorderLayout.CENTER);
    setSize(200, 200);
    setVisible(true);
  }

  public static void main(String args[]) {
    new SoundApplication();
  }

  public void actionPerformed(ActionEvent e) {
    taught.play();
  }
}
```

The SoundApplication class imports the java.applet package so it can access the Applet class and the AudioClip class, which are both part of that package. It imports the java.net package for the URL class and the MalformedURLException class. Calling Applet.getAudioClip(URL) can cause a MalformedURLException if the given URL is not valid. Notice that when this method is called, the new URL object is created with a string representation of the URL. It begins with the word "file:" and is followed by the file name, which in this case is taught.au. After you have the AudioClip reference, you are ready to play it by invoking its play() method. Here I set it up so that when you click the Play button, it will play the audio file. Figure 10.8 shows the output, but you have to run it for yourself to hear the audio. You should hear Darth Vader giving Luke Skywalker a compliment.

FIGURE 10.8

Thanks, dad!

Back to the *ShootingRange* Game

Okay, now you know everything you need to know to build the ShootingRange game. Figure 10.9 shows the images of the aliens and the bullet that will be animated.

FIGURE 10.9

These images are
used by the
ShootingRange
game.

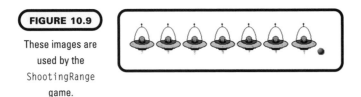

Here is the source code listing for ShootingRange.java:

```
/*
 * ShootingRange
 * Animates sprites for the user to try to shoot
 */

import java.awt.*;
import java.awt.event.*;
import java.applet.*;
import java.net.*;
```

```java
public class ShootingRange extends Canvas implements Runnable {
  protected AudioClip shoot, fly;
  protected Sprite bullet, target;
  protected Point bulletStartPt;
  //array of point pairs: starting points & delta points
  protected Point[] targetStartDeltaSet;
  public final static int LEFT = 0, RIGHT = 1;
  //keeps track of whether or not the sprites are on-screen
  protected boolean bulletOnScreen, targetOnScreen;
  protected boolean gameOver;
  protected Image offImg;
  protected int shots, hits;
  protected Thread runner;

  public ShootingRange() {
    try {
      shoot = Applet.newAudioClip(new URL("file:shoot.au"));
      fly = Applet.newAudioClip(new URL("file:fly.au"));
    } catch (MalformedURLException e) {}
    MediaTracker mt = new MediaTracker(this);
    Image[] bImg = { Toolkit.getDefaultToolkit().getImage("bullet.gif") };
    mt.addImage(bImg[0], 0);
    Image[] tImgs = { Toolkit.getDefaultToolkit().getImage("s1.gif"),
                      Toolkit.getDefaultToolkit().getImage("s2.gif"),
                      Toolkit.getDefaultToolkit().getImage("s3.gif"),
                      Toolkit.getDefaultToolkit().getImage("s4.gif"),
                      Toolkit.getDefaultToolkit().getImage("s5.gif"),
                      Toolkit.getDefaultToolkit().getImage("s6.gif"),
                      Toolkit.getDefaultToolkit().getImage("s7.gif") };
    for (int i=0; i < tImgs.length; i++) {
      mt.addImage(tImgs[i], i + 1);
    }
    try {
      mt.waitForAll();
    } catch (InterruptedException e) {}
    setSize(500, 500);
    bulletStartPt = new Point(
      (getSize().width - bImg[0].getWidth(this)) / 2,
      getSize().height - bImg[0].getHeight(this));
    bullet = new Sprite(bImg, new Point(0, 0), new Point(0, -30));
    //just initialize the target Sprite
    target = new Sprite(tImgs, new Point(0, 0), new Point(0, 0));
    targetStartDeltaSet = new Point[] {
      getTargetStart(LEFT, 100), new Point(5, 0),
      getTargetStart(RIGHT, 100), new Point(-5, 0),
      getTargetStart(LEFT, 200), new Point(6, 0),
      getTargetStart(RIGHT, 200), new Point(-6, 0),
      getTargetStart(LEFT, 300), new Point(7, 0),
      getTargetStart(RIGHT, 300), new Point(-7, 0),
      getTargetStart(LEFT, 400), new Point(5, 0),
      getTargetStart(RIGHT, 400), new Point(-6, 0),
      getTargetStart(LEFT, 400), new Point(7, 2),
      getTargetStart(RIGHT, 400), new Point(-10, 5) };
```

```java
    addKeyListener(new KeyAdapter() {
      public void keyPressed(KeyEvent e) {
        if (e.getKeyCode() == KeyEvent.VK_SPACE
            && !(bulletOnScreen || gameOver)) {
          bullet.setLocation(bulletStartPt);
          shots++;
          bulletOnScreen = true;
          shoot.play();
        }
        //reset if game over
        else if (gameOver) {
          playGame();
        }
      }
    });
    setFont(new Font("Arial", Font.BOLD, 20));
}

public static void main(String args[]) {
  GUIFrame frame = new GUIFrame("Shooting Range");
  ShootingRange range = new ShootingRange();
  range.setBackground(new Color(125, 100, 200));
  frame.add(range, BorderLayout.CENTER);
  frame.pack();
  frame.setResizable(false);
  frame.setVisible(true);
  //request keyboard focus for the shooting range
  range.requestFocus();
  range.playGame();
}

public void playGame() {
  if (runner == null || !runner.isAlive()) {
    runner = new Thread(this);
    runner.start();
  }
}

/* returns the starting point based on the parameters
 * side is LEFT or RIGHT, distance is distance from gun */
private Point getTargetStart(int side, int distance) {
  Point p = new Point(getWidth(), getHeight());
  if (side == LEFT)
    p.x = 0 - target.getCurrentImage().getWidth(this);
  p.y -= target.getCurrentImage().getHeight(this);
  p.y -= bullet.getCurrentImage().getHeight(this);
  p.y -= distance;
  return p;
}

public void run() {
  gameOver = false;
  hits = shots = 0;
```

```
    for (int i=0; i < targetStartDeltaSet.length - 1; i += 2) {
      target.setLocation(targetStartDeltaSet[i]);
      target.setDeltaPoint(targetStartDeltaSet[i + 1]);
      targetOnScreen = true;
      fly.play();
      repaint();
      while (targetOnScreen) {
        target.update();
        if (bulletOnScreen) bullet.update();
        try {
          Thread.sleep(50);
        } catch (InterruptedException e) {}
        repaint();
        checkSprites();
      }
    }
    targetOnScreen = bulletOnScreen = false;
    gameOver = true;
    repaint();
  }

  // checks sprites for collision or for going off-screen
  protected void checkSprites() {
    Rectangle r, bounds;
    bounds = new Rectangle(0, 0, getSize().width, getSize().height);
    if (collision()) {
      bulletOnScreen = false;
      targetOnScreen = false;
      hits++;
      return;
    }
    //don't fire bullet automatically
    if (bulletOnScreen) {
      r = new Rectangle(bullet.getLocation().x, bullet.getLocation().y,
                        bullet.getCurrentImage().getWidth(this),
                        bullet.getCurrentImage().getHeight(this));
      bulletOnScreen = r.intersects(bounds);
    }
    r = new Rectangle(target.getLocation().x, target.getLocation().y,
                      target.getCurrentImage().getWidth(this),
                      target.getCurrentImage().getHeight(this));
    targetOnScreen = r.intersects(bounds);
  }

  protected boolean collision() {
    Rectangle r1, r2;
    if (!(bulletOnScreen && targetOnScreen)) return false;
    //bullet bounds
    r1 = new Rectangle(bullet.getLocation().x, bullet.getLocation().y,
                       bullet.getCurrentImage().getWidth(this),
                       bullet.getCurrentImage().getHeight(this));
```

```java
    //target bounds
    r2 = new Rectangle(target.getLocation().x, target.getLocation().y,
                       target.getCurrentImage().getWidth(this),
                       target.getCurrentImage().getHeight(this));
    return r1.intersects(r2);
  }

  //for keyboard focus
  public boolean isFocusTraversable() {
    return true;
  }

  //override update()
  public void update(Graphics g) {
    paint(g);
  }

  //on-screen image buffer
  public void paint(Graphics g) {
    offImg = createImage(getSize().width, getSize().height);
    Graphics offg = offImg.getGraphics();
    paintOffScreen(offg);
    g.drawImage(offImg, 0, 0, null);
  }

  //off-screen image buffer
  public void paintOffScreen(Graphics g) {
    double score;
    // clear the off-screen image
    g.setColor(getBackground());
    g.fillRect(0, 0, getSize().width, getSize().height);
    if (!gameOver) {
      if (targetOnScreen) {
        g.drawImage(target.getCurrentImage(), target.getLocation().x,
                    target.getLocation().y, this);
      }
      if (bulletOnScreen) {
        g.drawImage(bullet.getCurrentImage(), bullet.getLocation().x,
                    bullet.getLocation().y, this);
      }
      g.setColor(getForeground());
      g.fillRect(bulletStartPt.x, bulletStartPt.y,
                 bullet.getCurrentImage().getWidth(this),
                 bullet.getCurrentImage().getHeight(this));
    }
    else {
      score = (double)hits / (targetStartDeltaSet.length / 2);
      score += (double)hits / shots;
      score = Math.rint(score * 50);
      String s = "Your score is: " + (int)score + "%";
      FontMetrics fm = g.getFontMetrics();
      int w = fm.stringWidth(s);
```

```
        int h = fm.getHeight();
        g.setColor(getForeground());
        g.drawString(s, (getSize().width - w) / 2,
          (getSize().height + h) / 2 - fm.getDescent());
      }
   }

}
```

The game uses two AudioClip objects, shoot and fly. shoot plays when you fire the gun and fly plays when each alien enters the screen. The ShootingRange game defines two Sprite objects, bullet and target. As you'd imagine, bullet is the Sprite for animating the bullet and target is the Sprite that animates the alien. bulletStartPt is a Point; it specifies where the bullet starts, which is where it is fired (the bottom middle of the screen).

The targetStartDeltaSet[] Point array needs explanation. It is one array that holds the starting points of the aliens as well as their delta points. Even numbered indices indicate the starting points and odd numbered indices indicate the delta points that come directly after their corresponding starting points. The LEFT and RIGHT constants just make it easier later to set up which side the aliens are coming from.

The bulletOnScreen and targetOnScreen boolean variables indicate whether the bullet and target Sprite object images currently appear on-screen. The gameOver member indicates whether the game is over. This information is used later to determine when it's time to display the score. The offImg is the off-screen image buffer used for double buffering; shots and hits count the number of times the gun is fired and the number of aliens that are hit, respectively. Thread runner runs this Runnable object.

The constructor loads the sounds and the images, sets up the targetStart-DeltaSet array, and calculates the bullet's starting point by finding the bottom center of this Canvas. The constructor also adds a KeyAdapter for listening to the spacebar. To fire the gun, the player presses the spacebar. It won't let you fire more than one bullet at a time and also won't let you fire a bullet if the game is over. Instead, if the game is over, pressing the spacebar (or any other key) will reset the game, so you can play again.

The playGame() method determines whether the runner thread is null or is not alive. In either case, it starts a new thread. The getTargetStart(int, int) method determines the starting point of the target sprite based on its parameters. The first parameter indicates which side the alien will come in from, either LEFT or RIGHT. Therefore, the x location of the variable is set based on placing the sprite just outside of the canvas on the side it will be introduced from. The y position is built off of the second argument, which specifies the distance between the sprite and the bullet.

The run() method loops on targetStartDeltaSet[]. The total number of aliens is half the length of this array. The run() method reuses the same sprite for all the aliens and just updates the point location for each new target. The run() method increments the index, i, by two because the points are stored in sets of starting points and delta points. Then it puts the target sprite on-screen and plays the fly AudioClip. While the target remains on-screen, the run() method updates the target and repaints. It also updates the bullet if there is one on the screen.

The checkSprites() method called from the run() method checks for a collision between the bullet and the target. It also checks for those sprites moving out of the play area. The way it checks for collisions and for being out of the play area is by getting a Rectangle object that represents the Sprite's bounds and also the Canvas's bounds. If a Sprite object appears on-screen, its bounds will intersect with the Canvas's bound. If a Sprite object collides with another Sprite object, their bounds will intersect with each other. There is a nifty method in the Rectangle class that is built just for doing this, intersects(Rectangle). Rectangles intersect each other if they share any pixels.

Summary

In this chapter you learned about using threads in general and then how to apply them to create animation effects. You also learned some safe multithreading techniques. You learned how to play sounds from applications, too. In the next chapter, you learn about custom event handling and inner classes and how to build a larger-scale game using those techniques.

CHALLENGES

1. **Create your own animation using the Sprite class and your own set of images.**

2. **Add a sound to the ShootingRange program that plays when the aliens are hit with bullets.**

Custom Event Handling and File I/O

In this chapter, you focus on building a puzzle game using custom event handling techniques. In developing this game, you will also use a great deal of what you've learned in previous chapters. The project in this chapter, and also the project in Chapter 12, "Creating Your Own Components and Packages," is much bigger than in the previous chapters. The goal is to reiterate much of what you have learned throughout the book, learn some new, more advanced stuff, and put it all together in a larger scale project. The Block Game programs use GUI components, threads, graphics, animation, and inner classes. You also learn to read and write files to save your high scores. You will use the following concepts to build a really fun game:

- Multithreading

- Animation

- Collision detection

- File I/O

- Inner classes

- Custom interfaces and event handling

The Project: The Block Game

The Block Game is similar in concept to the well-known Tetris game, owned by the Tetris Company, and originally developed by Alexey Pajitnov. The Block Game project in this book is for learning purposes only and can't truly compare to the actual Tetris game.

When you run the game, a window pops up with a black play area on the left side and some scoring information on the right side. The Play/Reset button also appears on the right; you click it to start a new game. When you click the button, blocks start falling from the top of the black play area, one at a time. There are seven shapes of blocks, each consisting of four squares. As the blocks fall, you can move them left and right and also rotate them clockwise and counter-clockwise using the key commands shown in Table 11.1. The goal is to complete rows of squares. When squares completely fill horizontal rows of the play area, those rows flash, and then disappear. Any blocks that are above the cleared rows fall down to fill up the vacated space. The game is over when no more blocks can fall into the play area because the existing blocks are in the way. Figure 11.1 shows how the game looks.

Building the *Block* Class

The blocks that fall into the play area of the Block Game application are what you directly have control of when you play. The blocks themselves consist of a specific orientation of squares that form one of seven shapes. You can flip the blocks around and the blocks can land on other blocks, so the blocks need to have some

TABLE 11.1 BLOCK GAME CONTROLS

Key Command	Action
Left arrow	Moves block to the left.
Right arrow	Moves block to the right.
Down arrow	Makes block drop down faster.
Up arrow or X	Rotates block clockwise one quarter turn.
Ctrl or Z	Rotates block counter-clockwise one quarter turn.

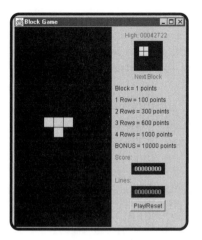

FIGURE 11.1

The Block Game
in action!

Chapter 11   Custom Event Handling and File I/O

representation of their orientation and area. In this section, I show you how to represent the blocks using the Java language.

Representing the Block's Area and Shape

Because a block is basically made up of a collection of four squares, it made sense to represent a block as a grid. The grid cells either contain a square or they don't. I used a two-dimensional boolean array, called matrix[][], for this:

```
protected boolean[][] matrix;
```

matrix has a certain number of rows and columns and each cell is either true (when it contains a square), or false, when it doesn't. The resulting block's shape is defined by the cells that are true. I also implemented the class in such a way that the number of rows and the number of columns of the block's area must be equal. You'll see in a bit that this makes the block easier to flip. The number of rows and columns is the block's size, which is stored in the size variable. The size must be at least one square's worth, so I added the MIN_SIZE constant to enforce that rule:

```
protected int size;
public final static int MIN_SIZE = 1;
```

Being that you know the block is ultimately going to be represented graphically, you can associate a color to the block:

```
protected Color color;
```

HINT The matrix[][] array of the Block class uses the column number as the first index and the row number as the secondary index (such as matrix[col][row]), which might seem unintuitive at first because most people think of tables in terms of rows of columns, not columns of rows. Don't forget that these blocks are going to be represented graphically using the (x, y) coordinate system. Because x is the horizontal axis, as x changes and you move horizontally, you change columns. Therefore, x is used as the column number and y, the vertical axis, is used as the row number. This facilitates painting the blocks later.

When creating a new Block object, you need to specify its size, the positions of its squares, and its color. Here is the constructor method:

```java
public Block(int size, Point[] squares, Color color) {
   this.size = size >= MIN_SIZE ? size : MIN_SIZE;
   this.color = color;
   matrix = new boolean[this.size][this.size];
   //add the block's squares to the matrix.
   for (int p=0; p < squares.length; p++) {
     if (squares[p].x < this.size && squares[p].y < this.size) {
       matrix[squares[p].x][squares[p].y] = true;
     }
   }
}
```

The first argument, size, is of course, the block's size. The second argument is an array of points that specifies the x and y coordinates within the block's area—where its squares are. This makes it much easier to work with other classes that don't need to know the details of how the Block object is implemented behind the scenes. To set up the corresponding boolean[][] array, I just looped through the points and set the values of the matrix variable of the specified point indices to true. If one of the points was (0, 1), the assignment matrix[0][1] = true would take place, putting a square in the first column, second row.

Including Useful *Block* Methods

The Block class includes methods that you can call to rotate the blocks 90 degrees clockwise or counter-clockwise. They are named rotateClockwise() and rotateCounterClockwise(), respectively. They don't use a lot of code, but they can still be confusing, so I'll explain how they work here. Here is the code for rotateClockwise():

```java
public void rotateClockwise() {
   //last is last (highest) index which is size - 1
   int last = size - 1;
   boolean[][] mRotateBuf = new boolean[size][size];
   for (int c=0; c < size; c++) {
     for (int r=0; r < size; r++) {
       mRotateBuf[c][r] = matrix[r][last - c];
     }
   }
   matrix = mRotateBuf;
}
```

I included the last variable just for the sake of readability (it makes the code a bit easier to follow). It is the index for the last row or column (because the number of rows is the same as the number of columns). mRotateBuf is a new two-dimensional Boolean array. This method uses it to build the matrix for the rotated block. When you turn a grid on its side, the rows become columns and the columns become rows. That's why the assignment mRotateBuf[c][r] = matrix[r][last - c] has the row and column number indices swapped. The easiest way to understand how this works conceptually is to physically draw out the grid and label each cell with its (row, col) coordinates, and then take that drawing and turn it 90 degrees clockwise. Then, using another sheet of paper, draw out the grid again and label the row and column coordinates that correspond to the original rotated grid. Then turn the original drawing back the way it was and compare the two grids. This is already done in Figure 11.2.

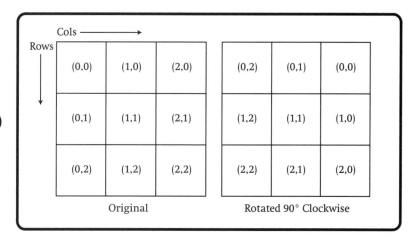

FIGURE 11.2

This shows the original grid on the left and the effect of rotating it 90 degrees clockwise on the right side.

Notice that in the second grid in Figure 11.2, the column indices decrease as you move to the right. That is why last - c is used as the second matrix index instead of just using c. The rotateCounterClockwise() works exactly the same way except, because the rotating is happening in the opposite direction, the assignment is as follows:

```
mRotateBuf[c][r] = matrix[last - r][c];
```

There are some other methods included. Here is a brief description of what they do:

int getSize()	Returns the size of the block's matrix.
Color getColor()	Returns the block's color.
boolean squareAt(int, int)	Returns true if there is a square at the given (col, row) location.

boolean squareAt(*Point*)	Returns true if there is a square at the given point's (x, y) matrix coordinate.
String toString()	Returns a string representation of the block.

Here is the complete source code listing for Block.java:

```
/*
 * Block
 * Defines a collection of squares within a square grid area
 * that can be rotated and have a certain color.
 */

import java.awt.Point;
import java.awt.Color;

public class Block {
  protected int size;
  public final static int MIN_SIZE = 1;
  protected boolean[][] matrix;
  protected Color color;


  /* Constructs a Block object having size x size grid
   * containing squares within the grid specified by
   * squares[] and has the given color. */
  public Block(int size, Point[] squares, Color color) {
    this.size = size >= MIN_SIZE ? size : MIN_SIZE;
    this.color = color;
    matrix = new boolean[this.size][this.size];
    //add the block's squares to the matrix.
    for (int p=0; p < squares.length; p++) {
      if (squares[p].x < this.size && squares[p].y < this.size) {
        matrix[squares[p].x][squares[p].y] = true;
      }
    }
  }

  //This works because size must be square
  public int getSize() {
    return size;
  }

  public Color getColor() {
    return color;
  }

  public boolean squareAt(int c, int r) {
    return squareAt(new Point(c, r));
  }
```

```java
public boolean squareAt(Point p) {
  if (p.x < size && p.y < size)
    return matrix[p.x][p.y];
  else return false;
}


/* Rotates the entire grid clockwise */
public void rotateClockwise() {
  //last is last (highest) index which is size - 1
  int last = size - 1;
  boolean[][] mRotateBuf = new boolean[size][size];
  for (int c=0; c < size; c++) {
    for (int r=0; r < size; r++) {
      mRotateBuf[c][r] = matrix[r][last - c];
    }
  }
  matrix = mRotateBuf;
}


/* Rotates the entire grid counter-clockwise */
public void rotateCounterClockwise() {
  //last is last (highest) index which is size - 1
  int last = size - 1;
  boolean[][] mRotateBuf = new boolean[size][size];
  for (int c=0; c < size; c++) {
    for (int r=0; r < size; r++) {
      mRotateBuf[c][r] = matrix[last - r][c];
    }
  }
  matrix = mRotateBuf;
}


public String toString() {
  String str = "Color: " + color.toString();
  str += "; Size: " + size;
  str += "; State ('*' = true, '-' = false):" ;
  String[] lines = new String[size];
  for (int c=0; c < size; c++) {
    for (int r=0; r < size; r++) {
      if (c == 0) lines[r] = "\n[";
      lines[r] += matrix[c][r] ? "*" : "-";
      if (c == (size - 1)) lines[r] += "]";
    }
  }

  for (int l=0; l < lines.length; l++) {
    str += lines[l];
  }
  return str;
}

}
```

What do you say you test the `Block` class? The `BlockTest` application creates a `Block` object, `block`, and accepts simple user input for testing the block rotation methods. Because this test is text-based, the string representation displays the orientation and the color isn't used. Entering C will rotate the block clockwise and entering X will rotate the block counter-clockwise. Typing nothing and pressing the Enter key will end the application. Here is the source code for `BlockTest.java`:

```
/*
 * BlockTest
 * Tests out the Block class
 */

import java.awt.*;
import java.io.*;

public class BlockTest {
  public static void main(String args[]) {
    String command;
    BufferedReader reader = new BufferedReader(new
                                  InputStreamReader(System.in));
    Point[] pnts = {new Point(0, 0), new Point(1, 0), new Point(2, 0),
                      new Point(1, 1), new Point(1, 2)};
    Block block = new Block(3, pnts, Color.blue);
    System.out.println(block);
    try {
      do {
        System.out.print("(C) Clockwise or (X) Counter-clockwise? ");
        command = reader.readLine();

        if (command.length() > 0) {
          if (command.toUpperCase().charAt(0) == 'C')
            block.rotateClockwise();
          else if (command.toUpperCase().charAt(0) == 'X')
            block.rotateCounterClockwise();
          System.out.println(block);
        }
      } while (command.length() > 0);
    } catch (IOException ioe) {}
  }
}
```

You can see in Figure 11.3 that asterisks represent the block's squares and dashes represent cells that don't contain squares.

Creating the *BlockGrid* Class

Now that you have the `Block` class, you need a way to represent it graphically so that you can show it on the screen instead of looking at it in standard output format (which isn't any fun). The `BlockGrid` class extends `Canvas` and represents the

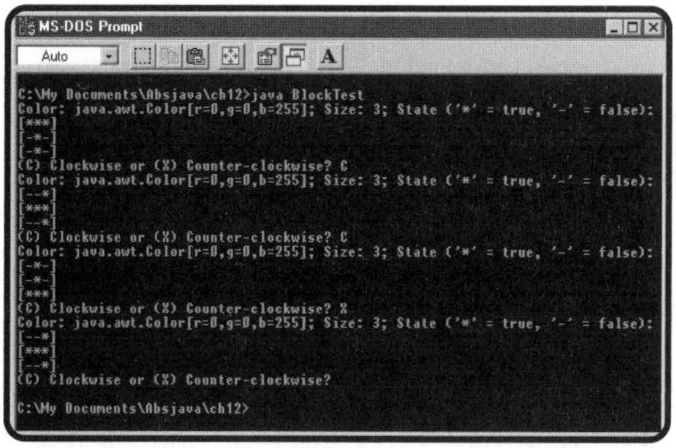

FIGURE 11.3

The rotation of the blocks seems to be working just fine, don't you think?

area that will contain the blocks. It draws the blocks in its area, so you can actually see them looking like blocks on your computer screen.

Representing the Block's Area

You already know that a canvas's area is a rectangular shape whose coordinate system starts at (0, 0) in the top-left corner and has the dimensions defined by the canvas's width and height. How do you put a block in there? Well, as you've seen, the Block class represents blocks in a grid. Each cell in the grid either contains a square, or it doesn't. The BlockGrid class works pretty much the same way. The BlockGrid class divides its area into a grid of cells, using a two-dimensional array named matrix[][]. The difference is that each cell of the Block class's grid is either true, meaning there is a square there, or false, meaning there is not. Because the BlockGrid class needs to actually paint the blocks, matrix[][] is a two-dimensional array of Color objects instead of boolean values. Each cell either contains a Color object or it doesn't (in which case, it contains null). Any cell that contains a block's square represents that fact by holding a Color object that represents that Block's color.

The BlockGrid class makes use of the following members:

int MIN_ROWS	The minimum number of rows.
int MIN_COLS	The minimum number of columns.
Color matrix[][]	Two-dimensional array of colors that represents the BlockGrid's area.
int cellsize	The square size (both width and height) of each cell in the BlockGrid.
Block block	The Block object that this BlockGrid contains (can only hold one at a time).

Point blockPos	The Point where the block is relative to the BlockGrid's cells' coordinate system.
Image offImg	Off-screen buffer used for double buffering.

The matrix[][] array is indexed by the columns and rows of the BlockGrid. Just as in the Block class, the first index is the column number and the second one is the row number, starting at 0. The variable cellsize holds the size for each cell. The total size of the BlockGrid is cellsize times the number of columns for the width by cellsize, times the number of rows for the height. The BlockGrid can hold only one Block object at a time, which is stored in block. blockPos is the (x, y) position of the Block relative to the BlockGrid's matrix system. It specifies the cell's coordinate (column, row) where the Block area's top-left corner is.

Remember how the Block class has its own matrix of columns and rows? Well, think of placing that whole grid inside of the bigger BlockGrid's grid. The block-Pos variable specifies which BlockGrid cell is the Block's (0, 0) cell.

BlockGrid Methods

The BlockGrid class includes some methods for getting and setting BlockGrid member values, for adding and removing the block's graphics, and for clearing the whole grid. Table 11.2 lists the methods along with some brief descriptions of what they do.

OK, now I'll explain the not-so-obvious methods. The setBlock(Block) method doesn't actually add the block's squares to the matrix. Instead, it just associates the given Block object to this BlockGrid. To add or remove the block's squares to the matrix, you need to call addBlock() or removeBlock(), respectively. Here's the addBlock() method:

```
public void addBlock() {
  if (block != null) {
    for (int c=0; c < block.getSize(); c++) {
      for (int r=0; r < block.getSize(); r++) {
        if (matrixContains(c + blockPos.x, r + blockPos.y)
          && block.squareAt(c, r))
          matrix[c + blockPos.x][r + blockPos.y] = block.getColor();
      }
    }
  }
}
```

If the block is not null, which is the case when there is no Block object associated with this BlockGrid, it adds the squares to its grid based on the block's color and position. It loops on the cells in the Block object's area and if the BlockGrid's matrix contains that cell, relative to the block's position, and the block has a

TABLE 11.2 THE BLOCKGRID METHODS

Method	Action
BlockGrid(*int*, *int*, *int*)	Constructs a BlockGrid with the given rows, columns, and cellsize, respectively.
int getRows()	Returns the number of rows.
int getCols()	Returns the number of columns.
void setBlock(*Block*)	Sets the Block object that this BlockGrid contains.
Block getBlock()	Returns the Block object held by this BlockGrid.
Point getBlockPos()	Returns the block's position within the BlockGrid's matrix.
void addBlock()	Adds the block's square's colors to the matrix for painting.
void removeBlock()	Removes the block's squares colors so they will not be painted.
void clear()	Removes the colors from the matrix and sets the block to null.
boolean BlockOutOfBounds()	Indicates whether the block is at least partially out of the BlockGrid's area. The top bound is not considered. Only the left, right, and bottom bounds count.
boolean BlockOutOfArea()	Indicates whether the block is at least partially out of the BlockGrid's area. All bounds are considered.
boolean matrixContains(*Point*)	Indicates whether the given point (column, row) is contained by this BlockGrid's matrix.
Dimension getPreferredSize()	Returns the size of this BlockGrid based on its cell size, number of columns, and number of rows. Overriding this method lets layout managers know what size is preferred if they attempt to resize this BlockGrid.

square in that cell, it adds the block's color at that position within the Block-Grid's matrix. To understand how blockPos comes into play here, consider the first cell of the block (0, 0). This is the top-left corner of the block's area. The block won't necessarily be positioned in the top-left corner of the BlockGrid, however, so that's why you need the blockPos variable. If the block's top-left corner was in the third column, second row down, blockPos would be (2, 1), so if there was a square in this cell, you don't paint it at (0, 0). Instead it gets painted at (0 + 2, 0 + 1), which is (2, 1). The block cell (1, 0) translates to (3, 1), and so on. The removeBlock() method works similarly except for the fact that it removes the colors of the block's squares instead of adding them.

HINT

The BlockGrid class doesn't force the colors of the current block to be removed if another block is added (remember, a BlockGrid can hold only one block at a time). If this happens, the colors of the original square remain where they are (however, you will lose the reference to the Block object), and the new block's squares are added. I designed the BlockGrid class this way so that many blocks can appear in the grid without needing a bunch of useless Block object references lying around wasting memory. You will see how this is used later. The Block object reference only needs to be around for as long as you need to continue manipulating the block's position. Once the block has "landed," the reference is no longer needed, so you just keep the squares around and get a new block to manipulate

The blockOutOfBounds() method returns true if any of the block's squares are out of the BlockGrid's area or if there is already another block's square there. This method is protected because it is very important when you call it. You should call it only when the block's squares are not added to the BlockGrid's color matrix yet (call it before addBlock(), not after) or it will always return true. What follows is the if statement that checks whether a block is out of bounds.

```
if (matrixContains(c + blockPos.x, r + blockPos.y)
    && block.squareAt(c, r)
    && matrix[c + blockPos.x][r + blockPos.y] != null)
  return true;
```

Because this is taken out of context here I need to tell you that r and c represent the row and column within the Block object's matrix (not the BlockGrid's). What this is checking for in plain English is if the BlockGrid contains this cell, given the block's position and the block has a square there (that isn't added to the BlockGrid yet) and there is already some other block's leftover square there, this block is out of bounds because you don't want to "overwrite" the old blocks with this one. This becomes more useful when you need to make new blocks land on top of the old ones (collision detection). Another instance where a block is out of bounds is when the block is too far left or right, or past the bottom row. You're probably wondering why I don't care about the upper bound. I don't care if the block is above the top of the BlockGrid's area because the Block Game application drops blocks down, starting above the BlockGrid's area. There is never an instance where a block needs to be past any of the other bounds. This is the code where it checks for this:

```
else if (!matrixContains(c + blockPos.x, r + blockPos.y)
        && block.squareAt(c, r))
    if (c + blockPos.x < 0 || c + blockPos.x >= getCols()
      || r + blockPos.y >= getRows())
      return true;
```

If the BlockGrid doesn't contain this cell, (!matrixContains(c + blockPos.x, r +blockPos.y)), and the block does have a square there, it might be out of bounds.

If it is too far left (c + blockPos.x < 0), too far right (c + blockPos.x >= get-Cols()), or too far down, (r + blockPos.y >= getRows()), return true because the block is out of bounds.

The blockOutOfArea() method is a public method. It doesn't matter when you call it. It is similar to blockOutOfBounds() except it checks all bounds, including the top. Basically, if a block has a square that is not in the BlockGrid's matrix, the block is out of area. This is useful in knowing when to end the game. If the block "lands" and is still out of area (specifically, over the top), the game is over and no more blocks should fall.

Painting the Picture

Okay, so you know about the members and methods that describe how the matrix should look (the number of rows and columns), where the block's squares are within the matrix, and what color they are. Most of the information you need to paint the squares of the matrix is stored in the matrix[][] array. Each color is stored in a matrix element by column and row. Basically, to draw the state of this BlockGrid, loop through the matrix's rows and columns and if a color exists at this particular matrix[*column*][*row*] index, fill a rectangle at that location the size of the cell, using that color and then draw an outline around it. That's it. The BlockGrid uses double buffering, which you learned about in the previous chapter, "Animation, Sounds, and Threads," so the update(Graphics) method is overridden, and the off-screen image buffer is painted using the OffImg Image object in the paintOffScreen(Graphics) method. After it clears the background, it loops on the matrix to paint its squares. Here is the code for that loop:

```
for (int c=0; c < matrix.length; c++) {
  for (int r=0; r < matrix[c].length; r++) {
    if (matrix[c][r] != null) {
      g.setColor(matrix[c][r]);
      g.fillRect(c * cellsize, r * cellsize, cellsize, cellsize);
      g.setColor(Color.black);
      g.drawRect(c * cellsize, r * cellsize, cellsize, cellsize);
    }
  }
}
```

Okay, now that you looked at the pieces of the BlockGrid class separately, here is the full source code listing:

```
/*
 * BlockGrid
 * Defines a Grid of colored squares that is able to
 * contain and paint a Block object.
 */
```

```java
import java.awt.*;

public class BlockGrid extends Canvas {
  public final static int MIN_ROWS = 1;
  public final static int MIN_COLS = 1;
  protected Color[][] matrix;
  protected int cellsize;
  protected Block block;
  //x, y coords of the top-left square of the block matrix
  protected Point blockPos;
  private Image offImg;

  /* Constructs a grid with the given columns, rows and
   * square size of the cells */
  public BlockGrid(int cols, int rows, int cellsize) {
    super();
    rows = rows >= MIN_ROWS ? rows : MIN_ROWS;
    cols = cols >= MIN_ROWS ? cols : MIN_COLS;
    matrix = new Color[cols][rows];
    this.cellsize = cellsize;
    block = null;
    blockPos = new Point(0, 0);
    setSize(cellsize * cols, cellsize * rows);
  }

  public int getRows() {
    return matrix[0].length;
  }

  public int getCols() {
    return matrix.length;
  }

  public void setBlock(Block b) {
    block = b;
  }

  public Block getBlock() {
    return block;
  }

  public void setBlockPos(Point bp) {
    blockPos = bp;
  }

  public Point getBlockPos() {
    return new Point(blockPos.x, blockPos.y);
  }

  /* adds the colors of the block to the matrix at blockPos
   * for painting */
  public void addBlock() {
    if (block != null) {
```

```
      for (int c=0; c < block.getSize(); c++) {
        for (int r=0; r < block.getSize(); r++) {
          if (matrixContains(c + blockPos.x, r + blockPos.y)
              && block.squareAt(c, r))
            matrix[c + blockPos.x][r + blockPos.y] = block.getColor();
        }
      }
    }
  }

  /* removes the colors of the block from the matrix
   * so the block is not painted at blockPos */
  public void removeBlock() {
    if (block != null) {
      for (int c=0; c < block.getSize(); c++) {
        for (int r=0; r < block.getSize(); r++) {
          if (matrixContains(c + blockPos.x, r + blockPos.y)
              && block.squareAt(c, r))
            matrix[c + blockPos.x][r + blockPos.y] = null;
        }
      }
    }
  }

  /* removes all of the colors from the matrix and nulls the block */
  public synchronized void clear() {
    block = null;
    for (int c=0; c < matrix.length; c++) {
      for (int r=0; r < matrix[c].length; r++) {
        matrix[c][r] = null;
      }
    }
  }

  /* A block is out of bounds if a square is out of the
   * playarea's matrix or in a cell already containing a square.
   * Note: over the top is not considered out of bounds */
  protected boolean blockOutOfBounds() {
    for (int c=0; c < block.getSize(); c++) {
      for (int r=0; r < block.getSize(); r++) {
        if (matrixContains(c + blockPos.x, r + blockPos.y)
            && block.squareAt(c, r)
            && matrix[c + blockPos.x][r + blockPos.y] != null)
          return true;
        else if (!matrixContains(c + blockPos.x, r + blockPos.y)
              && block.squareAt(c, r))
          if (c + blockPos.x < 0 || c + blockPos.x >= getCols()
              || r + blockPos.y >= getRows())
            return true;
      }
    }
    return false;
  }
```

```java
/* A block is out of area if a block square is out of the
 * playarea's matrix */
public boolean blockOutOfArea() {
  for (int c=0; c < block.getSize(); c++) {
    for (int r=0; r < block.getSize(); r++) {
      if (!matrixContains(c + blockPos.x, r + blockPos.y)
          && block.squareAt(c, r))
        return true;
    }
  }
  return false;
}

protected boolean matrixContains(int c, int r) {
  return matrixContains(new Point(c, r));
}

protected boolean matrixContains(Point p) {
  return p.x >= 0 && p.x < matrix.length
    && p.y >= 0 && p.y < matrix[0].length;
}

public Dimension getPreferredSize() {
  return new Dimension (matrix.length * cellsize,
                          matrix[0].length * cellsize);
}

public void update(Graphics g) {
  paint(g);
}

/* This is the on-screen image buffer */
public void paint(Graphics g) {
  Dimension d = getSize();
  offImg = createImage(d.width, d.height);
  Graphics offg = offImg.getGraphics();
  paintOffScreen(offg);
  g.drawImage(offImg, 0, 0, null);
}


/* This is the off-screen image buffer */
private void paintOffScreen(Graphics g) {
  Dimension d = getSize();
  // clear the image
  g.setColor(getBackground());
  g.fillRect(0, 0, d.width, d.height);
  g.setColor(getForeground());
  for (int c=0; c < matrix.length; c++) {
    for (int r=0; r < matrix[c].length; r++) {
      if (matrix[c][r] != null) {
        g.setColor(matrix[c][r]);
        g.fillRect(c * cellsize, r * cellsize, cellsize, cellsize);
```

```
            g.setColor(Color.black);
            g.drawRect(c * cellsize, r * cellsize, cellsize, cellsize);
        }
      }
    }
  }

}
```

Phew! Okay, so you did all the work to build this class up, you can now put it to the test and make sure your efforts weren't fruitless. The BlockGridTest application, listed next, extends the now familiar GUIFrame class. It uses a BlockGrid object to display a Block object and also gives a button that rotates the block clockwise. Here's how it creates the block:

```
Point[] p = { new Point(1, 0), new Point(0, 1),
              new Point(1, 1) };
block = new Block(3, p, Color.white);
```

The block's area is three by three cells and has squares at points (1, 0), (0, 1), and (1, 1). The color is set to Color.white. Next, it constructs the BlockGrid object, grid.

```
grid = new BlockGrid(5, 5, 30);
```

This makes grid a five-by-five BlockGrid of cells. Each cell has size 30 by 30. Next, it sets block as grid's block, sets the position to (1, 1), and then adds the block's squares:

```
grid.setBlock(block);
grid.setBlockPos(new Point(1, 1));
grid.addBlock();
```

The rotate button causes the block to rotate clockwise. Here's how this is done:

```
grid.removeBlock();
block.rotateClockwise();
grid.addBlock();
grid.repaint();
```

First, you have to remove the block's squares, and then call block's rotateClockwise() method, which rotates the block, and then add the block's squares back to the grid. Finally, you need to explicitly repaint the BlockGrid because removing and adding blocks doesn't do it automatically. It lets you play around with moving the blocks around first and when you decide where you want the block to be, you call repaint(). Here is the source code listing for BlockGridTest.java:

```
/*
 * BlockGridTest
 * Tests out the BlockGrid Class
 */
```

```java
import java.awt.*;
import java.awt.event.*;

public class BlockGridTest extends GUIFrame {
  Block block;
  BlockGrid grid;

  public BlockGridTest() {
    super("BlockGrid Test");
    Point[] p = { new Point(1, 0), new Point(0, 1),
                  new Point(1, 1) };
    block = new Block(3, p, Color.white);
    grid = new BlockGrid(5, 5, 30);
    grid.setBlock(block);
    grid.setBlockPos(new Point(1, 1));
    grid.addBlock();
    add(grid, BorderLayout.CENTER);

    Button rotate = new Button("Rotate");
    rotate.addActionListener(new ActionListener() {
      public void actionPerformed(ActionEvent e) {
        grid.removeBlock();
        block.rotateClockwise();
        grid.addBlock();
        grid.repaint();
      }
    });
    add(rotate, BorderLayout.SOUTH);

    pack();
    setVisible(true);
  }

  public static void main(String args[]) {
    new BlockGridTest();
  }

}
```

You can see a picture of this in action in Figure 11.4.

FIGURE 11.4

This shows the block as it initially appears (left), and then again after it rotates clockwise one time (right).

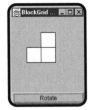

Building the *PlayArea* Event Model

The PlayArea class and its associated event classes—PlayAreaEvent and PlayArea-Listener—are the meat and potatoes of this chapter. The PlayArea class encapsulates the area of the Block Game application where the blocks fall and are manipulated by the users. Before you get into the actual PlayArea class, it's good to build the event classes. You've used events before, predefined ones in the java.awt.event package. Here you'll actually create your own event model.

Building Your Own Event Model

You're going to build the PlayArea event model to work similarly to the way the AWT event model works. To do this, you need to create an event class to define the types of events you need to fire, an event listener interface for listening for these events, and a mechanism for firing the events and adding and removing event listeners.

A simple way to create an event class is to subclass the java.util.EventObject class. It has a protected source field that stores the source of the event—that is, who triggered the event. It also has a constructor EventObject(Object), which accepts an object as a source argument and also has a getSource() method that returns the source of the event. The AWT's ActionEvent class is an example of an event class.

To create a listener that listens to your events, you need to define an abstract interface. You'll learn more about abstract classes in Chapter 12, "Creating Your Own Components and Packages," but briefly, abstract classes are shells of classes that need to be subclassed. You can never have an instance of an abstract class. Abstract interfaces need to be implemented to be of any use. To create an interface, you need to use the interface keyword. Then you need to declare methods. No method in an interface definition can have a body. The implementing class must provide the bodies by overriding these methods. Here is an example interface definition:

```
public abstract interface Loveable {
  public void love();
}
```

HINT

All interfaces are implicitly abstract and the abstract keyword is redundant and is not required. The Java Language Specification actually refers to using this keyword in interface declarations as obsolete and suggests that it should not be used when creating new interfaces. A good reason for not using the abstract keyword for interface declarations is that, in a way, it suggests that there can be interfaces that are not abstract. I chose to use the abstract keyword anyway

throughout this chapter as a reminder to you that the interfaces are abstract. Feel free to omit them when you are writing your own interfaces and keep in mind that all interfaces are abstract, whether you specify that explicitly or not.

See how useless this is on its own? There is no body for the love() method. The declaration of this method is simply followed by a semicolon. It is only useful in guaranteeing that any implementing classes have a love() method defined. To implement this interface, use the implements keyword, which you should be familiar with by now:

```
public class JavaProgrammer Implements Loveable {
...
//must Implement this method
  public void love() {

    ...
  }
  ...
}
```

Any class that implements the Loveable interface is referred to as a Loveable and must implement the love() method, even as a do-nothing method, or you will get a compiler error. To create an event listener interface, you typically create methods that are descriptive of some kind of event and accept the actual event as an argument. As an example, assume BabyEvent is an event that babies can fire. A possible listener interface would look like:

```
public abstract interface BabyListener {
  public void babyWokeUp(BabyEvent e);
  public void babyPooped(BabyEvent e);
  public void babyCried(BabyEvent e);
}
```

A possible implementing class would look like:

```
public class Dad Implements BabyListener {
  public void babyWokeUp(BabyEvent e) { //take baby out of crib }
  public void babyPooped(BabyEvent e) { //change baby's diaper }
  public void babyCried(BabyEvent e) { //pacify baby }
}
```

You also need to have a class that fires these events. Keeping with the previous examples, a BabyEvent might be fired by an object of the Baby class. This class would keep track of a list of other objects that register as listeners. These classes would implement BabyListener. The Baby class would also provide the methods used for registering BabyListeners, which could be named addBabyListener (*BabyListener*) and removeBabyListener(*BabyListener*). When the Baby object fires a BabyEvent, hopefully not babyPooped(*BabyEvent*), it loops through its listeners and invokes their respective methods.

Now you're ready to put this knowledge to good use. In the next couple of sections that follow, you will create the PlayAreaEvent model.

The *PlayAreaEvent* Class

The PlayAreaEvent class encapsulates the events that can be fired from the PlayArea class. It has two protected members, int numRows and boolean ooa. num-Rows specifies how many rows were completed as a result of this PlayAreaEvent. Remember, rows that are completed flash and disappear. You get this value from a PlayAreaEvent object by invoking its getRows() method. You will see later that this is used to keep score. The ooa member indicates whether the PlayAreaEvent was fired while the PlayArea's block was out of its area. You use this later to end the game when appropriate. Here is the listing for PlayAreaEvent.java:

```java
public class PlayAreaEvent extends java.util.EventObject {
  protected int numRows;
  protected boolean ooa;

  public PlayAreaEvent(Object source) {
    this(source, 0, false);
  }

  public PlayAreaEvent(Object source, int nRows) {
    this(source, nRows, false);
  }

  public PlayAreaEvent(Object source, int nRows, boolean out) {
    super(source);
    numRows = nRows;
    ooa = out;
  }

  public int getRows() { return numRows; }
  public boolean isOutOfArea() { return ooa; }
}
```

The *PlayAreaListener* Interface

This class is very simple. PlayAreas, as they are defined in this chapter, can fire only one event, blockLanded(PlayAreaEvent), so the definition for this interface is really tiny. Any class that implements this interface is required to implement the blockLanded(PlayAreaEvent) class. Here is the listing for PlayAreaListener.java:

```java
public abstract interface PlayAreaListener {
  public abstract void blockLanded(PlayAreaEvent pae);
}
```

Registering *PlayAreaListeners*

The registering of PlayAreaListeners takes place in the PlayArea class. You won't see the entire source listing for PlayArea.java until a bit later, but I feel it is most relevant to discuss how it registers listeners here, and how it fires events in the next section, "Firing PlayAreaEvents." Registering the listeners is not that complicated. Basically, PlayArea uses a Vector to maintain a dynamic list of PlayAreaListeners:

```
protected Vector listeners;
```

The PlayArea class also provides two methods for updating this Vector object, addPlayAreaListener(PlayAreaListener) and removePlayAreaListener(PlayAreaListener). addPlayAreaListener(PlayAreaListener) adds the passed PlayAreaListener, any class that implements the PlayAreaListener interface, to listeners and removePlayAreaListener(PlayAreaListener) removes the specified PlayAreaListener. Here is what they look like:

```
public void addPlayAreaListener(PlayAreaListener pal) {
   listeners.addElement(pal);
}

public void removePlayAreaListener(PlayAreaListener pal) {
   listeners.removeElement(pal);
}
```

You can see that they work just by calling the Vector class's methods. That's all it takes. Now you have a list of nosy classes that you need to notify when you fire PlayAreaEvents.

Firing *PlayAreaEvents*

You fire PlayAreaEvents from the PlayArea class by creating an instance of the PlayAreaEvent class and then calling the registered PlayAreaListeners' blockLanded(BlockEvent) methods. The PlayArea class has a private method for doing this:

```
private void fireBlockLanded(PlayAreaEvent pae) {
   for (int 1 = 0; 1 < listeners.size(); 1++) {
      ((PlayAreaListener)listeners.elementAt(1)).blockLanded(pae);
   }
}
```

fireBlockLanded(PlayAreaEvent) loops on the elements in the listeners Vector and calls their blockLanded(PlayAreaEvent) methods, passing in the given pae reference. As you can see, the PlayAreaEvent object must be created prior to calling fireBlockLanded(PlayAreaEvent). It does this by counting the number of rows completed and checking whether the block is out of area and passing those values along with this as the source of the event (meaning this PlayArea object was the source of the event) and passing these values to the PlayAreaEvent constructor method. I'll talk more about the details of creating and firing PlayAreaEvents, such as firing them in their own threads, in the next section, "Creating the PlayArea Class."

Creating the *PlayArea* Class

The PlayArea class is the most significant part of this project. It extends the BlockGrid class, which provides the graphical representation and already defines the methods for adding, removing, flipping, and painting blocks. The PlayArea class adds the capability to accept user input (as keyboard commands). It also implements the Runnable interface and animates the block. It animates falling blocks as time goes by and also repaints the blocks as users interact with them, flipping them around and such. It also handles the clearing of rows as they are completed and fires events, informing PlayAreaListeners, of them.

Inner Classes

The PlayArea class defines inner classes. Now is a good a time as any to start talking about inner classes because I'm close to the end of the book. An *inner class* is a class that is defined within another class, that is, within the curly braces of some other class, which is called the *outer class*. Inner classes are also sometimes called *nested classes*. Consider the following simple example:

```
public class Outer {
  private int x;
  Inner inner;

  public Outer() {
    inner = new Inner();
    inner.innerMethod();
  }

  public class Inner {
    private int y;
    public Inner() {
      x = 1;
      y = 2;
    }
    public void innerMethod() {
      System.out.println("x = " + x + ", y = " + y);
    }
  }

  public static void main(String args[]) {
    new Outer();
  }
}
```

This code would appear in a file named `Outer.java` because it is a definition of the class named `Outer`. Inside of the curly braces of the `Outer` class definition is where I defined the inner class, `Inner`. The `Inner` class definition looks like any other class definition. The main differences are the fact that it is defined within another class, `Outer`, and has access to the `Outer` class's members and methods, including private ones. The `y` variable is declared to be private and yet, the `Inner` class has access to it. See the `inner` variable declared as a member of `Outer`? That's an `Inner` object. In the previous example, the `Inner` object is created by using the code `new Inner()`. The `Inner` class is directly accessible, as if it were a member itself, from the `Outer` class, but it is also accessible from other classes because it is declared to be public. To access the `Inner` class from a static method or from another class that has access to it, you do it as follows:

```
Outer.Inner inner = new Outer().new Inner();
```

The `inner` class is referenced by `Outer.Inner` and a new instance of it is created by invoking the `Inner()` constructor as if it were an instance method. I wouldn't blame you for scratching your head looking at this code. I did a shortcut. I could have done it this way too:

```
Outer outer = new Outer();
Outer.Inner inner = outer.new Inner();
```

I created an instance of `Outer`, called `outer`, and then on a second line, I created an instance of `Inner` through `outer`. Before, I just did it all on one line.

You saw me reference the `Inner` class using the syntax `Outer.Inner`, but that's not the actual class name. If you take the time to write out this program and compile it, you will see two new class files generated by the compiler: `Outer.class` and `Outer$Inner.class`. The dollar sign ($) separates outer classes from inner classes, so the actual name of the `Inner` class is `Outer$Inner`.

Inner classes can also be created from within methods of an enclosing class and you don't even have to give them a name. You've done this before when you created listeners for your AWT components. Does this look familiar?

```
addWindowListener(new WindowAdapter() {
  public void windowClosing(WindowEvent e) {
    dispose();
    System.exit(0);
  }
});
```

The previous code was taken from `GUIFrame.java`. It creates an anonymous inner class that implements the `WindowListener` interface (by subclassing `WindowAdapter`, which implements `WindowListener`). Anonymous inner classes are defined when you construct the object, right after the `new` keyword. Anonymous inner classes have no name, but Java does create a .class file for them. It uses the enclosing class's name, and then a dollar sign followed by a number. An example of this is GUIFrame$1.class. That is in fact the name of the class file that Java creates for the anonymous WindowAdapter. What you might not know is that you can even create an anonymous inner class for any other class. Here is an example:

```
Canvas canvas = new Canvas() {
  //define an anonymous subclass of Canvas, such as overriding paint()
  public void paint(Graphics g) {
    g.fillRect(0, 0, 10, 10);
  }
};
```

In the preceding example, an anonymous inner class, which is a subclass of Canvas, is created. The paint(Graphics) method is overridden and it fills a rectangle. This eliminates the need to define a completely separate class, just to subclass Canvas to do something as simple as filling a rectangle.

Accepting User Input for Block Movements

The PlayArea class accepts user input in the form of KeyEvents. Before you get into the KeyListener implementation, take a look at the PlayArea members and methods that are available to facilitate block movements. First off, there are the static integer constants that represent possible block movements. Their names are self-explanatory; they are BLOCK_DOWN, BLOCK_UP, BLOCK_LEFT, BLOCK_RIGHT, BLOCK_CLOCKWISE, and BLOCK_COUNTERCLOCKWISE. The motions that are the opposite of each other are stored with opposite values (negatives of each other). For example, BLOCK_LEFT is −2 and BLOCK_RIGHT is 2. So, BLOCK_LEFT is the same as −BLOCK_RIGHT. This just makes it easier to reverse a movement.

You reverse a movement when attempting one movement causes the block to move out of bounds. Performing 0 minus the number constant that represents whatever the original move was, reverses that movement, which caused the block to go out of bounds. For example, (0 - BLOCK_DOWN == BLOCK_UP), (0 - BLOCK_LEFT == BLOCK_RIGHT), and so on. The moveBlock(int) method accepts these constants as its arguments and uses the aid of a private helper method, performMove(int), to actually move the block. Here's how they work:

```
/* Returns true if successful. If block movement causes block
 * to be out of bounds, movement is not performed, returning false;
 */
protected synchronized boolean moveBlock(int movement) {
  boolean moved = true;
  if (block == null) return false;
  removeBlock();
  performMove(movement);
```

```
        if (blockOutOfBounds()) {
          performMove(-movement);
          if (movement == BLOCK_DOWN) {
            addBlock();
            blockOut = blockOutOfArea();
            block = null;
            return false;
          }
          moved = false;
        }
        addBlock();
        return moved;
      }

      private void performMove(int movement) {
        switch (movement) {
          case BLOCK_DOWN: blockPos.translate(0, 1); break;
          case BLOCK_UP: blockPos.translate(0, -1); break;
          case BLOCK_LEFT: blockPos.translate(-1, 0); break;
          case BLOCK_RIGHT: blockPos.translate(1, 0); break;
          case BLOCK_CLOCKWISE: block.rotateClockwise(); break;
          case BLOCK_COUNTERCLOCKWISE: block.rotateCounterClockwise(); break;
        }
      }
    }
```

The moveBlock(int) method is synchronized so that you can be sure that there is at most only one thread in this method moving the block around at any given time. It returns a boolean value that indicates whether the originally intended movement was performed successfully. The way it determines this is it removes the block's square's colors from the matrix, and then calls the performMove(int) method to actually move the block by either translating its position point for up, down, left, and right movements, or by calling the block's rotate methods for rotation movements.

Note that nothing is repainted at this point, nor are there any colors added to the matrix; only the squares of the block are rearranged. Next, it checks if the movement causes the block to go out of bounds. If it does, it recalls the perform-Move(int) method, only passing in the negative of the original movement this time to reverse the movement. Don't forget that the BlockGrid class considers *out of bounds* to be when a block's square moves into an area where there is already a square. When the blocks are either to the left or to the right of the moving block, it simply doesn't allow the block to be moved in the occupied direction, but when a block falls down out of bounds that means it landed on something, either another block's square or the bottom of the play area.

When a block lands in this way there's no more need for the reference to the Block object, so you add the block by calling addBlock(), and then set the Block to null. Remember that this doesn't remove the colors from the matrix, but instead, it just allows you to use another `Block` object reference in the `block` member. On the other hand, if the movement is a success, there's no need to reverse it or set the block to `null`. Instead, it just adds the colors to the matrix and returns `true`.

To accept user input, the `PlayArea` class uses a `KeyAdapter`, which incidentally is defined as an anonymous inner class. The `KeyAdapter` listens for key presses. Specifically, it listens for the key presses that correspond to the keyboard commands listed in Table 11.1. For example, it listens for `KeyEvent.VK_LEFT` and attempts to move the block left. If it is successfully moves the block (`moveBlock(int)` returns `true`), it will repaint the `PlayArea` so that you can see the block move:

```
if (ke.getKeyCode() == KeyEvent.VK_LEFT) {
  if (moveBlock(BLOCK_LEFT)) repaint();
}
```

It does this for all the keyboard commands it's interested in. The only one that works a bit differently is handling the down arrow (`KeyEvent.VK_DOWN`). There is already a thread that moves the block down, which I'll get to next; it pauses once every second. Pressing down is supposed to make the block drop faster, so it causes the sleep interval, which is stored in `currentDropPeriod`, to be faster. `fastDropPeriod` is assigned the value 50 in the `PlayArea` constructor method. The normal drop period, stored in `dropPeriod`, is 1000.

Another thing I checked for was automatic key repeating (holding a key might automatically cause it to quickly repeat). That's fine for the other movements, especially right and left, but not okay for pressing down because there is an interrupt that tells the block not to wait any more and just fall. Automatic repeating would cause the block to fall as fast as possible, which is too fast! I just set up a `boolean` variable `pressingDown` that gets set to `true` the first time it detects a `KeyEvent.VK_DOWN`, and doesn't get set back to `false` until the down arrow key is released. Here is the code for handling the down arrow key press:

```
else if (!pressingDown && ke.getKeyCode() == KeyEvent.VK_DOWN) {
  pressingDown = true;
  currentDropPeriod = fastDropPeriod;
  blockDrop.interrupt(); //causes immediate effect
}
```

The code that handles the release of the down arrow sets `currentDropPeriod` back to `dropPeriod` and sets `pressingDown` to `false`.

As you know, `Canvas`es normally display graphics and don't accept user input. `PlayArea` extends `BlockGrid`, which extends `Canvas`, so `PlayArea` is a `Canvas`. In order to let the `PlayArea` gain user focus, I overrode the `isFocusTraversable()` method to return `true`. It indicates whether the `Canvas` should normally gain focus using `Tab` or `Shift+Tab` focus traversal. If it returns `false`, it can still get focus by calling `requestFocus()`, but any component that you want the user to be able to focus on should return `true` here to make it easier.

Making Blocks Fall

The `PlayArea` class implements the `Runnable` interface. It overrides the `run()` method to animate the block falling down. It uses a `Thread` object, called `block-Drop`, to run the `PlayArea` block dropping animation. Here is the code for the `run()` method:

```
public void run() {
  stopRequest = false;
  try {
    Thread.sleep (dropPeriod);
  } catch (InterruptedException ie) {}
  while (block != null && !stopRequest) {
    if (moveBlock(BLOCK_DOWN)) repaint();
    if (block != null) {
      try {
        Thread.sleep(currentDropPeriod);
      } catch (InterruptedException ie) {}
    }
  }
  if (!stopRequest) handleBlockLanded();
}
```

`stopRequest` is a `boolean` variable that is `true` if the thread is told to stop running because you shouldn't call the deprecated `stop()` method. The first `Thread.sleep(long)` call exists so that no matter what, the block will pause at the top of the `PlayArea` at least the amount of time specified by `dropPeriod`, which is the normal pause between each successive down movement. The `while` loop continues while `block` is not `null` (or it doesn't have anything to move) and while there is no request to stop running. It attempts to move the block down and repaints if it does, and then checks if `block` is `null` again (because `moveBlock(int)` sets `block` to `null` when the block lands), and then it sleeps and repeats.

After the `while` loop, the `run()` method checks whether it stopped because of a `stop` request. If it didn't, it assumes that it stopped because the block landed on something and calls `handleBlockLanded()` as a result.

TRICK

The `PlayArea` class implements the `Runnable` interface. Its `run()` method moves the block down. However, the `block` must be provided by a different class by calling the `introduceBlock(Block)` method. Doing this triggers a `Thread`, `blockDrop` to start running the `PlayArea`, which moves one block as far down as it can go, and then stops. No outside class needs to run the `PlayArea` in a different thread because `PlayArea` takes care of it itself. In the real world, you

probably don't want to do it this way. If you needed to hide the thread from the outside world, you are better off creating a protected or private inner class that extends Thread so that classes that don't need to start the thread can't run the thread by creating a new Thread object using an instance of PlayArea.

The handleBlockLanded() method checks if any rows were completed and calls rowClear(int[]) if there were any. Here's how this works. It declares a boolean array, rows[], which is the same size as the number of rows. true indicates rows, that, by their index, are completed and need to be cleared. Initially, they are all explicitly set to true and a variable, nComplete, which counts the number of rows that are completed, is set to the number of rows. Then it loops on the columns and rows, checking whether there is one square in every column of the rows (these rows are complete). Any time it finds a cell that doesn't contain a square, it sets that row's rows[] array to false and decrements nComplete. It won't check that row again. The loop will also stop as soon as it knows for sure there aren't any completed rows (nComplete is zero):

```
for (int c=0; c < getCols() && nComplete >= 0; c++) {
  for (int r=0; r < getRows(); r++) {
    if (matrix[c][r] == null && rows[r]) {
      rows[r] = false;
      nComplete--;
    }
  }
}
```

After this loop, the rows[] array is true at the index of every row that is complete and needs to be cleared. It rearranges this information so that an array, rowsTo-Clear[], which is the size of the number of rows that are complete is created and the elements of the array are set to the row indices of the matrix array that actually need to be cleared. Using the subscript Rindex++ sets the current value of the index to Rindex before incrementing it, so it is initially zero:

```
int Rindex = 0;
int[] rowsToClear = new int[nComplete];
for (int r=0; r < getRows(); r++) {
  if (rows[r]) rowsToClear[Rindex++] = r;
}
```

Next it calls the rowClear(int[]) method, passing in rowsToClear[] as the parameter. rowClear(int[]) animates all the rows that need to be cleared with flashing colors. The flashing colors are set up in the flashColors[] array. It does this by looping on this array and on all the cells in the rows that need to be cleared, and then setting the color of the squares to the different colors and repainting after each color is set. The last color of the flashColors[] array is null, so that makes the squares disappear.

Now there is the matter of making the blocks piled up on top of the rows fall down to fill up the newly vacated space. This isn't as straight-forward as you might think. You have to consider the possibility that when multiple rows are cleared simultaneously, they might not necessarily be successive rows (for example, row 10 and row 12 need to be cleared, but not row 11).

You also have to handle the fact that as you're moving rows down, new rows are being formed at the top because there aren't any rows above the play area to fall down. Here is the complicated loop that handles this:

```
for (int c=0; c < getCols(); c++) {
    nRows = 1;
    for (int r = rows[rows.length - 1]; r >= 0; r--) {
        while (nRows < rows.length
                && r - nRows == rows[rows.length - nRows - 1]) {
            nRows++;
        }
        if (r >= nRows) matrix[c][r] = matrix[c][r - nRows];
        else matrix[c][r] = null;
    }
}
repaint();
}
```

It loops on all the columns of the PlayArea matrix and sets the nRows variable to 1. nRows counts the number of rows that have been cleared. It loops on the rows, starting at the bottom-most row that was cleared, indicated by the last element of the rows array, rows[rows.length - 1] and works its way up to the top of the PlayArea. nRows starts at 1 for each column because it already accounts for the bottom-most row that was cleared. For any cleared row, you have to move the squares in the row above the cleared row down into the cleared row. Hopefully that makes sense, but it's not that straight-forward.

If two rows were cleared, the squares in the row that is two rows up have to move down into this cleared row. That's why it has to count the number of cleared rows as it works its way up to the top. It counts them in the while loop. Although the number of cleared rows I counted so far is still less than the total number of cleared rows (nRows < rows.length) and the row above this row (r - nRows) was cleared to (rows[rows.length - nRows - 1]) increment nRows (nRows++). Remember that the rows[] array elements store the matrix row indices that were cleared, so if the row above this one needs to be cleared, it will be stored at the next index of the rows[] array, which is why this check works. As it moves up in rows, it moves the squares of rows that are nRows above this row down into this row.

For example if you clear rows 10 and 8, the squares in row 9 move down into row 10. But because row 8 was cleared, row 7 moves down into row 9, and then row 6 moves into row 8, row 5 into row 7, and so on. It also has to be careful near the top. What row moves down into row 0? It's the top row, so there are no rows above it to move down. These rows just have all their colors set to `null`. That's what the last `if` statement does. If this row index is greater than or equal to the number of rows cleared, there must be some actual rows still left to move down, but if this is row index 1, for example, and four lines were cleared, there aren't any more rows to fall down, so set the colors to `null`.

This `PlayArea`'s `run()` method is invoked from within the `introduceBlock (Block)` method:

```
public void introduceBlock(Block b) {
  if (block == null) {
    blockPos = new Point();
    block = b;
    blockPos.x = (getCols() - b.getSize()) / 2;
    blockPos.y = 1 - block.getSize();
    addBlock();
    repaint();
    blockDrop = new Thread(this);
    blockDrop.start();
  }
}
```

If this `PlayArea` doesn't already have a block (`block == null`), set `block` to the passed in `Block` parameter. Then center its position at the top (actually above the top), add the colors by calling `addBlock()`, show the colors by calling `repaint()`, and create a new thread using this `Runnable PlayArea`, and then start a-droppin' the block.

The *EventThread* Inner Class

The `handleBlockLanded()` method also takes care of setting up and dispatching the `EventThread`s. `EventThread` is an inner class that extends `Thread` and fires `PlayAreaEvents`. The reason why you fire them off in their own threads is because there is no reason to tie up the current thread (`blockDrop`) with calling the listeners' `PlayAreaEvent` handling methods. Who knows what they do and how long they will tie you up? Well, you do because you're writing the code for it eventually. It is definitely good practice to fire events off in their own threads so that the current thread is not taken over by any of the listeners to perform what could be enormous tasks. Nope, you'll just fire off a thread and then go about your business. Here is a listing of the `EventThread` inner class:

```
private class EventThread extends Thread {
  final static int BLOCK_LANDED = 0;
  int event;
  PlayAreaEvent pae;
```

```
protected EventThread (PlayAreaEvent pae, int e) {
  this.pae = pae;
  event = e;
}

public void run() {
  switch (event) {
    case BLOCK_LANDED:
      fireBlockLanded(pae); break;
  }
}
}
```

Its members are a PlayAreaEvent, pae, an integer that represents the type of event (called event), and a constant that represents the event is a block landed event (called BLOCK_LANDED). Because there is actually only one type of event, it wasn't necessary to use the two integer members, but consider how much easier it is to be able to handle multiple types of events now. Just create new constants that represent them and then check for them in the switch statement in the run() method. The constructor accepts the PlayAreaEvent and the integer event type. When the thread is started, it checks the event type, which actually has to be BLOCK_LANDED and calls fireBlockLanded(PlayAreaEvent) to fire of the event that it passes in as the parameter.

The handleBlockLanded() method that I just described in the previous section starts the thread:

```
(new EventThread(pae, EventThread.BLOCK_LANDED)).start();
```

It creates a new EventThread instance, which it doesn't name, that is, it doesn't store it in an instance variable. It passes pae, which is a PlayAreaEvent object that was created earlier, and specifies EventThread.BLOCK_LANDED as the event type. It invokes the start() method on this new EventThread. It does this all on one line. The handleBlockLanded() method sets up the pae variable like this:

```
pae = new PlayAreaEvent(this, nComplete, blockOut);
```

this is passed into the PlayAreaEvent constructor as the source of the PlayAreaEvent. nComplete, which is the number of rows completed as a result of the block landing, is passed as the second argument. It, in turn, passes blockOut, a boolean variable that indicates whether the block landed out of the PlayArea's area, as the third argument.

You saw that when the EventThread is started, it calls the fireBlockLanded(PlayAreaEvent) method, passing in the PlayAreaEvent object created within the handleBlocklanded() method. The fireBlockLanded(PlayAreaEvent) method just loops on the registered listeners and calls their blockLanded(PlayAreaEvent) methods. One more important thing to mention about the PlayArea class is that it overrides the BlockGrid's clear() method. The PlayArea class has more to worry about, such as the `blockDrop` thread, and it needs to be careful when it sets the `block` to `null` because there can be active threads moving the `block` around. Here is the code:

```
public void clear() {
  if (blockDrop != null && blockDrop.isAlive()) {
    stopRequest = true;
    blockDrop.interrupt();
    try {
      blockDrop.join();
    } catch (InterruptedException ie) {}
    block = null;
  }
  super.clear();
}
```

If the `blockDrop` thread is currently running, put in a `stopRequest`, which you saw earlier will break the thread out of its `while` loop. Then `interrupt()` the thread so it will see the stop request ASAP. Then, invoke `join()` on `blockDrop`, which causes the current thread to wait for `blockDrop` to die. Then it can finally set the `block` to `null` and rely on the superclass's `clear()` method to remove the matrix's colors.

Putting it All Together

You've looked at the `PlayArea` class, piece by piece; now, here is the full source code listing for `PlayArea.java`:

```
/*
 * PlayArea
 * A BlockGrid capable of dropping and moving blocks. When a block
 * is dropped users can move and rotate it using key commands.
 * There is only one block at a time, but old blocks are still painted
 * by not removing their colors after they land at the bottom
 */

import java.awt.*;
import java.awt.event.*;
import java.util.Vector;

public class PlayArea extends BlockGrid implements Runnable {
  //opposite move constants are negatives of each other
  protected final static int BLOCK_DOWN = 1, BLOCK_UP = -1,
                             BLOCK_RIGHT = 2, BLOCK_LEFT = -2,
                             BLOCK_CLOCKWISE = 3,  BLOCK_COUNTERCLOCKWISE = -3;
  protected Thread blockDrop;
  protected long dropPeriod;
  protected long fastDropPeriod;
  private long currentDropPeriod;
  protected boolean pressingDown, blockOut, stopRequest;
  protected Vector listeners;
```

```java
public PlayArea(int cols, int rows, int cellsize) {
  super(cols, rows, cellsize);
  pressingDown = blockOut = false;
  currentDropPeriod = dropPeriod = 1000;
  fastDropPeriod = 50;
  listeners = new Vector(0, 1);

  addKeyListener(new KeyAdapter() {
    public void keyPressed(KeyEvent ke) {
      if (ke.getKeyCode() == KeyEvent.VK_LEFT) {
        if (moveBlock(BLOCK_LEFT)) repaint();
      }
      else if (ke.getKeyCode() == KeyEvent.VK_RIGHT) {
        if (moveBlock(BLOCK_RIGHT)) repaint();
      }
      else if (ke.getKeyCode() == KeyEvent.VK_UP
                  || ke.getKeyCode() == KeyEvent.VK_X) {
        if (moveBlock(BLOCK_CLOCKWISE)) repaint();
      }
      else if (ke.getKeyCode() == KeyEvent.VK_CONTROL
                  || ke.getKeyCode() == KeyEvent.VK_Z)  {
        if (moveBlock(BLOCK_COUNTERCLOCKWISE)) repaint();
      }
      else if (!pressingDown && ke.getKeyCode() == KeyEvent.VK_DOWN) {
        pressingDown = true;
        currentDropPeriod = fastDropPeriod;
        blockDrop.interrupt(); //causes immediate effect
      }
    }

    public void keyReleased(KeyEvent ke) {
      if (ke.getKeyCode() == KeyEvent.VK_DOWN) {
        pressingDown = false;
        currentDropPeriod = dropPeriod;
      }
    }
  });
}

public void setDropPeriod(long dp) {
  dropPeriod = dp;
}

public long getDropPeriod() {
  return dropPeriod;
}

/*
 * Introduces a block to the playarea
 * The block is introduced at the top, centered
 * The last row of the block matrix is in the first row
 * of this matrix
 */
```

```java
public void introduceBlock(Block b) {
  if (block == null) {
    blockPos = new Point();
    block = b;
    blockPos.x = (getCols() - b.getSize()) / 2;
    blockPos.y = 1 - block.getSize();
    addBlock();
    repaint();
    blockDrop = new Thread(this);
    blockDrop.start();
  }
}

/* Overridden to kill thread and remove block */
public void clear() {
  if (blockDrop != null && blockDrop.isAlive()) {
    stopRequest = true;
    blockDrop.interrupt();
    try {
      blockDrop.join();
    } catch (InterruptedException ie) {}
    block = null;
  }
  super.clear();
}

/* Moves the current block down until it lands */
public void run() {
  stopRequest = false;
  //causes standard pause for new blocks even if pressingDown
  try {
    Thread.sleep (dropPeriod);
  } catch (InterruptedException ie) {}
  while (block != null && !stopRequest) {
    if (moveBlock(BLOCK_DOWN)) repaint();
    if (block != null) {
      try {
        Thread.sleep(currentDropPeriod);
      } catch (InterruptedException ie) {}
    }
  }
  if (!stopRequest) handleBlockLanded();
}

/* Inner Thread that fires events */
private class EventThread extends Thread {
  final static int BLOCK_LANDED = 0;
  int event;
  PlayAreaEvent pae;

  protected EventThread (PlayAreaEvent pae, int e) {
    this.pae = pae;
    event = e;
  }
```

```java
    public void run() {
      switch (event) {
        case BLOCK_LANDED:
          fireBlockLanded(pae); break;
      }
    }
  }


  /* method that animates row clearing */
  protected void rowClear (int[] rows) {
    Color[] flashColors = {Color.red, Color.green, Color.blue,
                           Color.white, Color.yellow, Color.magenta,
                           null};

    int nRows = 1;
    for (int f=0; f < flashColors.length; f++) {
      for (int c=0; c < getCols(); c++) {
        for (int r=0; r < rows.length; r++) {
          matrix[c][rows[r]] = flashColors[f];
        }
      }
      repaint();
      try {
        Thread.sleep(25);
      } catch (InterruptedException ie) {}
    }
    for (int c=0; c < getCols(); c++) {
      nRows = 1;
      for (int r = rows[rows.length - 1]; r >= 0; r--) {
        while (nRows < rows.length
                && r - nRows == rows[rows.length - nRows - 1]) {
          nRows++;
        }
        if (r >= nRows) matrix[c][r] = matrix[c][r - nRows];
        else matrix[c][r] = null;
      }
    }
    repaint();
  }

  /* Returns true if successful. If block movement causes block
   * to be out of bounds, movement is not performed, returning false;
   */
  protected synchronized boolean moveBlock(int movement) {
    boolean moved = true;
    if (block == null) return false;
    removeBlock();
    performMove(movement);
    if (blockOutOfBounds()) {
      performMove(-movement);
      if (movement == BLOCK_DOWN) {
        addBlock();
        blockOut = blockOutOfArea();
```

```
          block = null;
          return false;
        }
        moved = false;
      }
    addBlock();
    return moved;
  }

  private void performMove(int movement) {
    switch (movement) {
      case BLOCK_DOWN: blockPos.translate(0, 1); break;
      case BLOCK_UP: blockPos.translate(0, -1); break;
      case BLOCK_LEFT: blockPos.translate(-1, 0); break;
      case BLOCK_RIGHT: blockPos.translate(1, 0); break;
      case BLOCK_CLOCKWISE: block.rotateClockwise(); break;
      case BLOCK_COUNTERCLOCKWISE: block.rotateCounterClockwise(); break;
    }
  }
  private void handleBlockLanded() {
    PlayAreaEvent pae;
    int nComplete = getRows();
    boolean[] rows = new boolean[getRows()];
    for (int r=0; r < getRows(); r++) {
      rows[r] = true;
    }
    for (int c=0; c < getCols() && nComplete >= 0; c++) {
      for (int r=0; r < getRows(); r++) {
        if (matrix[c][r] == null && rows[r]) {
          rows[r] = false;
          nComplete--;
        }
      }
    }
    pae = new PlayAreaEvent(this, nComplete, blockOut);
    if (nComplete > 0) {
      int Rindex = 0;
      int[] rowsToClear = new int[nComplete];
      for (int r=0; r < getRows(); r++) {
        if (rows[r]) rowsToClear[Rindex++] = r;
      }
      rowClear(rowsToClear);
    }
    (new EventThread(pae, EventThread.BLOCK_LANDED)).start();
  }

  private void fireBlockLanded(PlayAreaEvent pae) {
    for (int l = 0; l < listeners.size(); l++) {
      ((PlayAreaListener)listeners.elementAt(l)).blockLanded(pae);
    }
  }
```

```
public void addPlayAreaListener(PlayAreaListener pal) {
  listeners.addElement(pal);
}

public void removePlayAreaListener(PlayAreaListener pal) {
  listeners.removeElement(pal);
}

/* Gives ability to gain focus and fire keyboard events */
public boolean isFocusTraversable() {
  return true;
}

}
```

There you are—the full source listing for PlayArea.java. Now you can test it and make sure it works the way it should. The PlayAreaTest class extends GUIFrame and implements the PlayAreaListener interface. It creates a Block object, called block, which you can introduce it to its PlayArea instance, called playarea, by clicking the provided button. PlayAreaTest constructs playarea with the arguments 10, 10, and 40, so the resulting area is 10 columns by 10 rows and each cell of the row is 40 by 40 pixels. When you click the button, it invokes playarea.introduceBlock(block) to make the block start falling into the PlayArea and then calls playarea.requestFocus() so that you don't have to click in the play area to gain keyboard control.

The status label is updated with what is going on. When you click the button, it states "Block Falling." When it lands, it tells you that the block landed, it tells you how many rows were cleared as a result, and it also tells you whether the block landed out of area. It gets this information by listening to PlayAreaEvents with the blockLanded(PlayAreaEvent) method it must implement. Here is the listing for PlayAreaTest.java:

```
/*
 * PlayAreaTest
 * Tests the PlayArea class
 */

import java.awt.*;
import java.awt.event.*;

public class PlayAreaTest extends GUIFrame
                          implements PlayAreaListener {
  PlayArea playarea;
  Label status;
  Block block;

  public PlayAreaTest() {
    super("PlayArea Test");
    playarea = new PlayArea(10, 10, 40);
```

```
    Point[] p = { new Point(1, 0), new Point(0, 1),
                  new Point(1, 1) };
    block = new Block(3, p, Color.white);
    playarea.addPlayAreaListener(this);
    add(playarea, BorderLayout.CENTER);

    status = new Label("", Label.CENTER);
    add(status, BorderLayout.NORTH);

    Button b = new Button("Gimme a Block!");
    b.addActionListener(new ActionListener() {
      public void actionPerformed(ActionEvent e) {
        playarea.introduceBlock(block);
        playarea.requestFocus();
        status.setText("Block Falling");
      }
    });
    add(b, BorderLayout.SOUTH);

    pack();
    setVisible(true);
  }

  public static void main(String args[]) {
    new PlayAreaTest();
  }

  public void blockLanded(PlayAreaEvent e) {
    String s = "Block Landed; ";
    s += "Rows = " + e.getRows();
    s += "; Out = " + e.isOutOfArea();
    status.setText(s);
  }

}
```

Figure 11.5 shows a possible test run of the PlayAreaTest application.

Creating the *ScoreInfoPanel* Class

The ScoreInfoPanel class keeps score of the Block Game. It displays the top score, the next block that will fall after the currently falling block lands, your current score, and the number of lines that you have cleared. It also displays the point values. You get one point per each block that lands, you get 100 points for each line that you clear, 300 if you clear two lines at once, 600 points for clearing three lines at once, and 1000 points for clearing four lines with a single block. You also get a 10,000 point bonus each time you clear four lines multiple times in a row (not necessarily with two successive blocks, but two successive times lines are cleared).

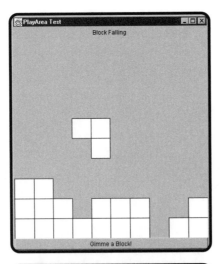

FIGURE 11.5

The `PlayAreaTest`
application tests
the `PlayArea`
class.

Reading and Writing Files

The classes that you need to use to read and write files are found in the `java.io`
package. Specifically, in this chapter, you use the `FileReader` and `FileWriter`
classes to read and write files. Further, you use the `BufferedReader` and
`BufferedWriter` classes, which use buffering to make reading and writing files
more efficient. Here is a quick example of a Java program that copies a file by
reading the files contents and writing it to a new file. The source code for `File-Copy.java` is:

```
/*
 * FileCopy
 * Demonstrates File I/O by copying a file
 * arg[0] - source filename
```

```
 * arg[1] - destination filename
 */

import java.io.*;

public class FileCopy {

  public static void main(String args[]) {
    BufferedReader reader;
    BufferedWriter writer;
    int c;
    if (args.length != 2) {
      System.out.println("Args are: <source> <destination>"
                          + "\n Nothing copied...");
      return;
    }
    try {
      //can cause FileNotFoundException
      reader = new BufferedReader(new FileReader(args[0]));
      //can cause IOException
      writer = new BufferedWriter(new FileWriter(args[1]));
      while((c = reader.read()) != -1) {
        writer.write(c);
      }
      //flushes and closes the stream
      writer.close();
    }
    catch (FileNotFoundException e404) {
      System.out.println("File " + args[0] + " not found.");
    }
    catch (IOException e) {
      System.out.println(e);
    }
  }

}
```

This application accepts two arguments; it accepts the original file path as the first argument and the path for the copy as the second argument. It declares a BufferedReader, reader, and a BufferedWriter, writer, which it uses to read and write the files. The reader is instantiated by passing in a new FileReader object. It passes args[0] to the constructor. The FileReader(String) constructor constructs a FileReader given the string name of the file it needs to read. This can cause a FileNotFoundException if the string argument is not a valid path to a file. That's why it is in a try catch and the FileNotFoundException is caught and tells the users that the file couldn't be found. Constructing the BufferedWriter instance works similarly. The FileWriter constructor is passed the name of the file that will be written and the FileWriter instance is passed to the Buffered-Writer constructor. This can cause an IOException. The while loop reads a single character at a time using the reader.read() method. If the end of the file (EOF) is reached, this method returns −1. So the while loop checks for this as its condition. Although each character read in is not −1, write that character to the writer buffer anyway. Invoking the writer.close() causes the buffer to be cleared, written to the file, and closed. Figure 11.6 shows one run of the FileCopy application.

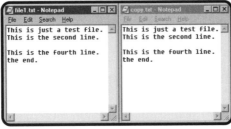

FIGURE 11.6

The FileCopy application copied the file1.txt file and saved the copy as copy.txt.

TRAP

Don't forget to call the close() method on the BufferedWriter. If you don't you won't get any actual output. There is also a method called flush() which flushes the buffer and writes it out to the file, but calling close() actually flushes the buffer before closing anyway.

Keeping Score

The ScoreInfoPanel class keeps score basically by keeping track of three integers: scoreValue keeps track of the current score, hiValue keeps track of the high score, and nLinesValue keeps track of the number of lines cleared.

The ScoreInfoPanel class also provides methods for modifying these values such as setScore(int), setHiScore(int), and setLines(int) for setting these values to the given int value. It also provides addToScore(int) and addToLines(int)

methods for adding the given `int` value to these values. Here is the source code
for `ScoreInfoPanel.java`:

```java
/*
 * ScoreInfoPanel
 * A Panel that shows the scoring info for a BlockGame
 * and shows the next block.
 */

import java.awt.*;
import java.io.*;
import java.text.NumberFormat;

public class ScoreInfoPanel extends Panel {
  protected Label scoreLabel = new Label("Score: "),
                  linesLabel = new Label("Lines: "),
                  score = new Label(),
                  hiLabel = new Label(),
                  lines = new Label(),
                  nextLabel = new Label("Next Block", Label.CENTER);
  protected int scoreValue = 0,
                hiValue = 0,
                nLinesValue = 0;
  protected BlockGrid nextBlockDisplay = new BlockGrid(6, 6, 10);
  public static int BLOCK = 1, ROW1 = 100, ROW2 = 300,
                    ROW3 = 600, ROW4 = 1000, ROW4BONUS = 10000;
  protected Label[] points = { new Label("Block = " + BLOCK + " points"),
                  new Label("1 Row = " + ROW1 + " points"),
                  new Label("2 Rows = " + ROW2 + " points"),
                  new Label("3 Rows = " + ROW3 + " points"),
                  new Label("4 Rows = " + ROW4 + " points"),
                  new Label("BONUS = " + ROW4BONUS + " points") };
  NumberFormat nf = NumberFormat.getInstance();
  Block block = null;

  public ScoreInfoPanel() {
    super();
    nf.setMinimumIntegerDigits(8); //pack in zeros
    nf.setGroupingUsed(false);     //no separators e.g. commas
    hiLabel.setForeground(Color.blue);
    readHiScore();
    nextBlockDisplay.setBackground(Color.black);
    nextLabel.setForeground(Color.blue);
    scoreLabel.setForeground(Color.blue);
    linesLabel.setForeground(Color.blue);
    setScore(0);
    score.setAlignment(Label.CENTER);
    score.setForeground(Color.green);
    score.setBackground(Color.black);
    score.setFont(new Font("Courier New", Font.BOLD, 12));
    setLines(0);
```

```
      lines.setAlignment(Label.CENTER);
      lines.setForeground(Color.red);
      lines.setBackground(Color.black);
      lines.setFont(new Font("Courier New", Font.BOLD, 12));
      GridBagLayout gridbag = new GridBagLayout();
      GridBagConstraints gbc = new GridBagConstraints();
      setLayout(gridbag);
      gbc.gridwidth = GridBagConstraints.REMAINDER;
      gbc.anchor = GridBagConstraints.CENTER;
      addComp(hiLabel, gridbag, gbc);
      addComp(nextBlockDisplay, gridbag, gbc);
      addComp(nextLabel, gridbag, gbc);
      gbc.anchor = GridBagConstraints.WEST;
      for (int p=0; p < points.length; p++) {
        addComp(points[p], gridbag, gbc);
      }
      addComp(scoreLabel, gridbag, gbc);
      gbc.anchor = GridBagConstraints.CENTER;
      addComp(score, gridbag, gbc);
      gbc.anchor = GridBagConstraints.WEST;
      addComp(linesLabel, gridbag, gbc);
      gbc.anchor = GridBagConstraints.CENTER;
      addComp(lines, gridbag, gbc);
   }

   protected void addComp(Component comp, GridBagLayout g,
                          GridBagConstraints c) {
     g.setConstraints(comp, c);
     add(comp);
   }

   protected void readHiScore() {
     try {
       BufferedReader r = new BufferedReader(new FileReader("hi.dat"));
       setHiScore(Integer.parseInt(r.readLine()));
       r.close();
     } catch (Exception e) { setHiScore(0); }
   }

   public void saveHiScore() {
     try {
       BufferedWriter w = new BufferedWriter(new FileWriter("hi.dat"));
       w.write(String.valueOf(hiValue));
       w.close();
     } catch (Exception e) {}
   }

   protected void setHiScore(int h) {
     hiValue = h;
     hiLabel.setText("High: " + nf.format(h));
   }
```

```
public void setScore(int s) {
  scoreValue = s;
  score.setText(nf.format(s));
  if (s > hiValue) setHiScore(s);
}

public void addToScore(int addValue) {
  scoreValue += addValue;
  setScore(scoreValue);
}

public void setLines(int l) {
  nLinesValue = l;
  lines.setText(nf.format(l));
}

public void addToLines(int addValue) {
  nLinesValue += addValue;
  setLines(nLinesValue);
}

public void showBlock(Block b) {
  if (block != null)
    nextBlockDisplay.removeBlock();
  block = b;
  nextBlockDisplay.setBlock(block);
  nextBlockDisplay.setBlockPos(new Point(1, 1));
  nextBlockDisplay.addBlock();
  nextBlockDisplay.repaint();
}

public Insets getInsets() {
  return new Insets(5, 5, 5, 5);
}

}
```

The ScoreInfoPanel uses labels to display its information, defined as follows:

- scoreLabel is the label for the current score
- score is the label for the actual numerical score
- linesLabel labels the number of lines
- lines is the label that displays the number of lines
- highLabel labels and displays the high score on one line
- nextLabel labels the box that shows the next block

nextBlockDisplay is a BlockGrid instance that displays the next block. The show-Block(Block) method can be called, and the given Block will be displayed in the nextBlockDisplay. The ScoreInfoPanel also provides some static constants that represent score values:

BLOCK   The score value for landing a block.

ROW1   The score value for clearing one line with a single block.

ROW2   The score value for clearing two lines with a single block.

ROW3   The score value for clearing three lines with a single block.

ROW4   The score value for clearing four lines with a single block.

BONUS   The score value for clearing four lines with a single block multiple times.

It reads and writes the high score using a file named hi.dat. These are the methods that do this:

```
protected void readHiScore() {
   try {
      BufferedReader r = new BufferedReader(new FileReader("hi.dat"));
      setHiScore(Integer.parseInt(r.readLine()));
      r.close();
   } catch (Exception e) { setHiScore(0); }
}

public void saveHiScore() {
   try {
      BufferedWriter w = new BufferedWriter(new FileWriter("hi.dat"));
      w.write(String.valueOf(hiValue));
      w.close();
   } catch (Exception e) {}
}
```

It works similarly to the FileCopy application, except the BufferedReader reads a whole line, which you actually did way back in Chapter 2, when you used a BufferedReader to read command-line input. It parses the string read in to an integer value by calling Integer.parseInt(r.readLine()). The readHiScore() method is not public because there is no reason for any other class to tell this class to read in the high score because it does it automatically in the constructor and keeps it up to date.

The saveHiScore() method, on the other hand, is public because you want to wait until the game is over before you save the score. You'll rely on the application program to tell you when that is. The BufferedWriter writes a whole string that represents the high score by calling w.write(String.valueOf(hiValue)). Everything else is pretty much straight-forward, such as laying out these components.

However, the use of the NumberFormat class needs some explanation. NumberFormat is part of the java.text package. It helps you format numbers. I created a new instance of a NumberFormat by calling NumberFormat.getInstance(). Number-Format is an abstract class, so it can't have a direct instance. getInstance() returns the default number format. There are other methods for getting other types of instances such as getCurrencyInstance() and getPercentInstance(). nf is the NumberFormat. Calling nf.setMinimumIntegerDigits(8) does exactly what you'd expect it to do based on the name of the method. It expresses integers using a minimum of eight digits. For example, 27 is expressed as 00000027. nf.setGroupingUsed(false) makes sure that no commas separate the pieces of the number (so 1000 doesn't use a comma like 1,000).

TRAP Running Block Game from the CD will not allow you to maintain a high score. You can't write a file onto the CD, so the high score won't get saved. The exception handling will cause this flaw to just be ignored. To save your high scores, either write your own copy, which you should be doing for learning purposes anyway, or copy the games files to your hard drive and run it from there.

Creating the Block Game Application

The Block Game application puts the PlayArea and ScoreInfoPanel classes together, along with a Play/Reset button so you can start a new game. The members it declares are as follows:

lastNLines	Holds the number of lines (rows) that were cleared the last time lines where cleared.
playarea	The PlayArea instance.
infoPanel	The ScoreInfoPanel instance.
resetButton	The button used for playing and resetting the game.
block	The current block that will be introduced to the PlayArea.
nextBlock	The block that will be introduced to the PlayArea after block lands.
I, L, O, R, S, T, and Z	Constants that represent the seven block shapes. I used the letter that looks most like the shape of the block.

The createBlock() method pumps out one of the seven blocks. It generates a random number and then uses a switch statement to generate the block based on that random number and then returns that block. The initialize() method sets score values to zero and creates a new block for nextBlock. The intro-duceNextBlock() method sets block to nextBlock, creates a new block for nextBlock, shows nextBlock in infoPanel, and calls playarea.introduce-Block(block) to make the block start falling into the PlayArea. The resetButton has an ActionListener that calls the playGame() method. This method calls initialize(), playarea.clear() (for clearing the PlayArea when the game is reset), playarea.requestFocus() (so the PlayArea will immediately accept keyboard commands), and introduceNextBlock() to get things rolling.

It adds an anonymous inner class to listen for PlayAreaEvents to the playarea instance. It checks for block landings. It adds the point values specified by the ScoreInfoPanel constants based on how many rows are cleared. After it adds the score it checks whether the block landed out of area by invoking the isOutO-fArea() method of the PlayAreaEvent class. If it isn't out of area, it introduces the next block into the PlayArea, if it is, the game is over and it calls infoPanel.saveHiScore() to write the high score back to the file. Here is the full source code listing for BlockGame.java:

```java
/*
 * Block Game
 * The actual Application Frame for the Block Game.
 */

import java.awt.*;
import java.awt.event.*;

public class BlockGame extends GUIFrame {
    protected int lastNLines;
    protected PlayArea playarea;
    protected ScoreInfoPanel infoPanel;
    protected Button resetButton;
    protected Block block, nextBlock;
    protected final static int I = 0,
                               L = 1,
                               O = 2,
                               R = 3,
                               S = 4,
                               T = 5,
                               Z = 6;

    public BlockGame() {
        super("Block Game");
        GridBagLayout gridbag = new GridBagLayout();
        GridBagConstraints constraints = new GridBagConstraints();
        setBackground(SystemColor.control);
        playarea = new PlayArea(10, 20, 20);
        setLayout(gridbag);
        playarea.setBackground(Color.black);
        constraints.gridheight = GridBagConstraints.REMAINDER;
        gridbag.setConstraints(playarea, constraints);
        add(playarea);
```

```
    infoPanel = new ScoreInfoPanel();
    constraints.anchor = GridBagConstraints.NORTH;
    constraints.gridheight = 1;
    constraints.gridwidth = GridBagConstraints.REMAINDER;
    gridbag.setConstraints(infoPanel, constraints);
    add(infoPanel);
    resetButton = new Button("Play/Reset");
    resetButton.addActionListener(new ActionListener() {
      public void actionPerformed(ActionEvent e) {
        playGame();
      }
    });
    constraints.gridwidth = constraints.gridheight = 1;
    gridbag.setConstraints(resetButton, constraints);
    add(resetButton);

    playarea.addPlayAreaListener(new PlayAreaListener() {
      public void blockLanded(PlayAreaEvent pae) {
        infoPanel.addToScore(ScoreInfoPanel.BLOCK);
        infoPanel.addToLines(pae.getRows());
        switch (pae.getRows()) {
          case 1:
            infoPanel.addToScore(ScoreInfoPanel.ROW1);
            break;
          case 2:
            infoPanel.addToScore(ScoreInfoPanel.ROW2);
            break;
          case 3:
            infoPanel.addToScore(ScoreInfoPanel.ROW3);
            break;
          case 4:
            infoPanel.addToScore(ScoreInfoPanel.ROW4);
            if (lastNLines == 4)
              infoPanel.addToScore(ScoreInfoPanel.ROW4BONUS);
            break;
        }
        lastNLines = pae.getRows() > 0 ? pae.getRows() : lastNLines;
        if (!pae.isOutOfArea()) introduceNextBlock();
        else infoPanel.saveHiScore();
      }
    });

    initialize();
    pack();
    setVisible(true);
  }

  public static void main(String args[]) {
    new BlockGame();
  }
```

```java
protected void initialize() {
  lastNLines = 0;
  infoPanel.setScore(0);
  infoPanel.setLines(0);
  block = createBlock();
  nextBlock = createBlock();
}

public void playGame() {
  initialize();
  playarea.clear();
  playarea.requestFocus();
  introduceNextBlock();
}

public void introduceNextBlock() {
  block = nextBlock;
  nextBlock = createBlock();
  infoPanel.showBlock(nextBlock);
  playarea.introduceBlock(block);
}

//randomly returns one of the seven blocks
protected Block createBlock() {
  Point[] squareCoords = new Point[4];
  int randB = (int) Math.floor(Math.random() * 7);
  int s;
  Color c;
  switch (randB) {
    case I:
      squareCoords[0] = new Point(2, 0);
      squareCoords[1] = new Point(2, 1);
      squareCoords[2] = new Point(2, 2);
      squareCoords[3] = new Point(2, 3);
      s = 4;
      c = Color.white;
      break;
    case L:
      squareCoords[0] = new Point(1, 0);
      squareCoords[1] = new Point(1, 1);
      squareCoords[2] = new Point(1, 2);
      squareCoords[3] = new Point(2, 2);
      s = 3;
      c = Color.blue;
      break;
    case O:
      squareCoords[0] = new Point(0, 0);
      squareCoords[1] = new Point(0, 1);
      squareCoords[2] = new Point(1, 0);
      squareCoords[3] = new Point(1, 1);
      s = 2;
      c = Color.cyan;
      break;
```

```
      case R:
        squareCoords[0] = new Point(1, 0);
        squareCoords[1] = new Point(2, 0);
        squareCoords[2] = new Point(1, 1);
        squareCoords[3] = new Point(1, 2);
        s = 3;
        c = Color.red;
        break;
      case S:
        squareCoords[0] = new Point(1, 1);
        squareCoords[1] = new Point(1, 2);
        squareCoords[2] = new Point(2, 0);
        squareCoords[3] = new Point(2, 1);
        s = 3;
        c = Color.yellow;
        break;
      case T:
        squareCoords[0] = new Point(0, 1);
        squareCoords[1] = new Point(1, 1);
        squareCoords[2] = new Point(1, 2);
        squareCoords[3] = new Point(2, 1);
        s = 3;
        c = Color.green;
        break;
      case Z:
        squareCoords[0] = new Point(1, 0);
        squareCoords[1] = new Point(1, 1);
        squareCoords[2] = new Point(2, 1);
        squareCoords[3] = new Point(2, 2);
        s = 3;
        c = Color.magenta;
        break;
      default :
        squareCoords = new Point[1];
        squareCoords[0] = new Point(0, 0);
        s = Block.MIN_SIZE;
        c = Color.orange;
    }
    return new Block(s, squareCoords, c);
  }
}
```

Summary

In this chapter, you wrote a larger scale project than in any of the preceding chapters. You learned how to create custom event-handling models. You learned about inner classes, including anonymous inner classes. You also learned some file I/O. In building the Block Game application and the classes associated with it, you used many of the concepts you learned in previous chapters. In the next chapter, you will learn how to create custom lightweight components, how to create your own custom packages, and also how to take advantage of the `javadoc` utility included with the Java SDK. You will apply this knowledge to building another big project, the MinePatrol game.

CHALLENGES

1. **Create a program that reads a file and writes a new file that is completely backwards.**

2. **Create some new block shapes in the Block Game to shake things up and give your game a twist of your own.**

3. **Rewrite the `ImageTest` application from Chapter 9, except this time, extend `GUIFrame` and override the `paint(Graphics)` method by making the `Canvas` an anonymous inner class.**

Creating Your Own Components and Packages

Up until this point, you've been either using classes from prede-fined packages included in the Java 1.3 SDK, or creating your own classes. In this chapter, you will build a package. You learn what lightweight components are and how to create them and build a package that includes three classes. It is a rather small package, but there's a lot of code involved. The source files are rather large because of how heavily commented they are. You're going to learn how to comment your code in such a way that you can run the javadoc utility to generate documentation for your packages. The main goals of this chapter include the following concepts:

- Declare packages

- Create lightweight components

- Create and extend abstract classes

- Use javadoc comments and run the javadoc tool

- Create the MinePatrol game by importing the custom packages

The Project: MinePatrol

This chapter's project is a game that is similar to Minesweeper, a game you might be familiar with. The game board opens up and presents you with a grid of buttons. The contents underneath the buttons are unknown until you left-click one of them. If there's a mine hidden under one of them, you will explode and die if you click it. If there isn't a mine directly in that cell, but there is one in close proximity, such as at least one of the surrounding eight cells, you will get an intensity reading that shows you how many mines surround that cell.

If there aren't any mines in close proximity, you can take more accurate readings and some of the surrounding cells will reveal themselves and show their intensity readings. In fact, all cells surrounding the clicked cell that are also empty will be revealed. None of the cells that contain mines will be revealed. Only cells that directly border an empty cell within a clear path of the cell you clicked are revealed. The object is to use the intensity readings as clues to determine where the mines are.

You can flag a cell, if you think there is a mine there, by right-clicking the cell. You can't click a cell with the left mouse button once its flagged. This prevents messy accidents. You can unflag a cell by right-clicking the cell again. You win the game by flagging all the mines and clearing the rest. The game also ends if you blow up. In either case, the entire board is revealed to you so you can see where you went wrong. Figure 12.1 shows this game in action.

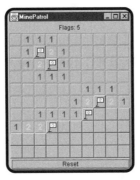

FIGURE 12.1

Here is the MinePatrol game. Let's see... is there a mine here? I don't think... KABOOM.

Creating Lightweight Components

AWT components are called *heavyweight* components because they have a native peer associated with them. This means that in order for your operating system to make use of the components, system-dependent calls are made (in the background, because Java is a system-independent language) to native API. *A native API (Application Programming Interface)* is a term that refers to the operating system's resident interface. Each component has its own representation depending on what operating system you're using. Each component is rendered in its own opaque window, which can be memory intensive. *Lightweight* components do not have a native peer. They represent themselves functionally and graphically. Basically, you create a lightweight component by overriding the Component class. That's it; that's all it takes.

The Swing Package

No, not *schwing*, Garth, *Swing*! Take your Ritalin. The Swing package (javax.swing) provides a set of lightweight components. Swing is included with the standard edition of the Java 2 platform. Its components are all Java code and don't have native peers. They work the same on all platforms. Although Swing is not fully covered by this book, you already have a head start. The concepts of the Swing components are similar to the concepts in the AWT package. Take the following code for instance:

```
/*
 * SwingTest
 * Demonstrates, very basically, how to use swing
 */

import javax.swing.*;
import java.awt.*;
import java.awt.event.*;

public class SwingTest extends JFrame {

  public SwingTest() {
    JLabel label = new JLabel("JLabel");
    JTextField tfield = new JTextField("JTextField", 15);
    JButton button = new JButton("JButton");
    getContentPane().setLayout(new FlowLayout());
    getContentPane().add(label);
    getContentPane().add(tfield);
    getContentPane().add(button);
    setDefaultCloseOperation(WindowConstants.DISPOSE_ON_CLOSE);
    addWindowListener(new WindowAdapter() {
      public void windowClosing(WindowEvent e) {
        System.exit(0);
      }
```

```
    });
    pack();
    setVisible(true);
  }

  public static void main(String args[]) {
    new SwingTest();
  }

}
```

You should pretty much be able to tell what is going on here just by reading the code because it is so similar to how the AWT works. The JFrame class inherits from Frame and exists to offer support for the Swing component architecture. The SwingTest class subclasses the JFrame class and adds a JLabel, a JTextField, and a JButton to itself. These three components are similar to the Label, TextField, and Button components found in the AWT, except for the fact that they are lightweight. Their appearance is different as well, as you can see in Figure 12.2. JFrames, unlike their Frame ancestors, have a method that allows for some window closing handling. I passed WindowConstants.DISPOSE_ON_CLOSE to the setDefaultCloseOperation(int) method. This causes the window to be disposed when you close the window. However, you still need to use a WindowListener if you want to exit the program when the window is closed.

FIGURE 12.2

Here are a few of Swing's lightweight components.

Creating Your Own Lightweight Components

There are four main steps to follow to create a useful lightweight component.

1. Extend the Component class.
2. Override paint(Graphics).
3. Call enableEvents(int).
4. Register appropriate listeners.

Extending the Component class is easy, just do it like this:

```
public class myLightWeight extends Component { ... }
```

Overriding the paint(Graphics) method is also simple enough; you've already done this countless times to modify the graphics of AWT components. The enableEvents(int) method enables the type of event specified by its given parameter. These parameters are specified as static constants in the AWTEvent class and some of them are listed in Table 12.1. If you need to review these event types, refer to Chapter 7, "Advanced GUI: Layout Managers and Event Handling."

These event types are enabled automatically when the appropriate listener is added, but the enableEvents(int) method should be called by subclasses of Component that want specific event types delivered to processEvent(AWTEvent) regardless of whether there is a registered listener. A lightweight button would want to do this, for example, to process mouse events so that its appearance changes somewhat when it is clicked. You don't need any registered listeners to do that; just call enableEvents(AWTEvent.MOUSE_EVENT_MASK) and handle the event in the processMouseEvent(MouseEvent) class. The generic processEvent (AWTEvent) calls whatever process method is appropriate to handle whatever the event type is. You will do this when you create the JPRButton3D lightweight component.

To register listeners, you can make use of the AWTEventMulticaster class, which implements thread-safe dispatching of AWT events. Here is an example of how to register ActionListeners with your component.

```
public class myLightWeight extends Component {
  ActionListener actionListener;
  ...
  public void addActionListener(ActionListener listener) {
    actionListener = AWTEventMulticaster.add(actionListener, listener);
  }
  ...
}
```

TABLE 12.1   AWTEVENT EVENT MASK CONSTANTS

Event Mask	Description
ACTION_EVENT_MASK	Selects action events.
ADJUSTMENT_EVENT_MASK	Selects adjustment events.
FOCUS_EVENT_MASK	Selects focus events.
ITEM_EVENT_MASK	Selects item events.
KEY_EVENT_MASK	Selects key events.
MOUSE_EVENT_MASK	Selects mouse events.
MOUSE_MOTION_EVENT_MASK	Selects mouse motion events.
TEXT_EVENT_MASK	Selects text events.
WINDOW_EVENT_MASK	Selects window events.

You declare an `ActionListener`—here it's named `actionListener`—and then provide the `addActionListener(ActionListener)` method. Inside of that method, you register the given listener with `actionListener` by calling `AWTEventMulti-caster.add(actionListener, listener)`, which adds the given `ActionListener` argument to your `actionListener` and returns the result, which you store right back into `actionListener`. The `AWTEventMulticaster` class itself implements `ActionListener` (as well as the other types of listener interfaces) and returns an instance of itself when you call the `add()` methods. Its `actionPerformed(Action-Event)` method invokes the `actionPerformed(ActionEvent)` method of all the `ActionListeners` that were registered in this way.

Preparing to Create the *jpr.lightweight* Package

The `jpr.lightweight` package has three classes, described as follows:

- The `JPRComponent3D` class represents a lightweight component. It has borders that can be drawn to make the `JPRComponent3D` appear to be raised above its container, sunk into the surface of its container, or flat (not raised or sunk). It is an abstract class.

- The `JPRRectComponent3D` class extends the `JPRComponent3D` class and defines its rectangular shape and therefore overrides the `paint(Graphics)` method to represent the component as a rectangular 3D shape. It is also an abstract class.

- The `JPRButton3D` class extends the `JPRRectComponent3D` class and encapsulates a rectangular button that changes its appearance based on its state—whether it is being clicked or whether it is enabled. It is not an abstract class. Ultimately, you will use the `JPRButton3D` class to represent the buttons of the MinePatrol game.

Before you create this package, you need to know a few things, such as how do you declare a package? What is an abstract class? How do you use the `javadoc` utility to generate documentation for packages? Who had Frankie Pentangeli killed? Who gave the order? All, well most, of these questions are answered in the next few sections.

Declaring Packages

When you create a Java source file, it consists of three main sections: the package declarations, the `import` statements, and the class definitions. The syntax for declaring a package is very straight-forward:

```
package jpr.lightweight;
```

The package keyword is followed by the package name. That's it. There is more to learn about package names, however. Package names imply directory structures, so the previous class file better be in a directory called jpr and then in a subdirectory called lightweight or you won't be able to import the class later.

 T R A P   Keep in mind, your CLASSPATH variable was discussed in Chapter 1, "Getting Started." In order for you to make your packages accessible, you either have to make the package directory structure relative to the current directory or you need to add the path of your package's parent directory to your CLASSPATH variable. In this case, a parent directory has access to the package if there is a directory named jpr in it and jpr has a subdirectory named lightweight in it that contains the class files for the classes that belong to the package. Here is an example:

CLASSPATH=.;C:\PACKAGES

In this instance, the jpr and lightweight subdirectory structure should be in the PACKAGES folder. Not having the CLASSPATH set also causes problems when compiling one source file from the package. To get around this, if you don't want to mess with your CLASSPATH variable, get yourself into the lightweight folder where the jpr.lightweight package source files will be and just compile them all at once like this:

javac *.java

Abstract Classes

Abstract classes are shells of classes that defer implementation to subclasses. For instance, let's say you have an abstract class, Automobile. You decide that all subclasses of Automobile need a drive() method. Each subclass of automobile drives differently; a moped doesn't drive anything like an 18-wheeler. The Automobile class has the abstract idea that all its subclasses need to override this method in order for it to make sense. The Automobile class itself has no use for it. Abstract classes cannot be instantiated, anyway. Subclasses must be defined and subclasses of Automobile can be considered Automobiles. You've used abstract classes before when you used event listener interfaces. All interfaces are implicitly abstract. Here's what the Automobile class might look like:

```java
public abstract class Automobile {
  public boolean driving;
  public abstract void drive();
  public boolean isDriving() {
    return driving;
  }
}
```

Notice that the `drive()` method is declared abstract. It has no body, and as you saw in the previous chapter, that's how you create an abstract method. Any non-abstract subclass of `Automobile` must provide the body for this method. Also notice that there is a non-abstract method here too: `isDriving()`. I put that there to show you that an abstract class can provide some actual implementation of its methods. Something as wide a concept as "is this `Automobile` driving?" should really be able to apply to most, if not all, subclasses of `Automobile`.

The *javadoc* Utility

The `javadoc` utility generates HTML documentation for your package classes. You can run the `javadoc` utility on individual class files or entire packages. You have to comment your code in a special way for this to work. Here is an example of a `javadoc` comment, also known as a *documentation comment*.

```
/**
 * This is a javadoc comment
 */
```

A `javadoc` comment starts off like a regular multi-line comment with a forward slash and an asterisk, but the second asterisk flags this comment as a `javadoc` comment. The other asterisks that precede each line are not required and are ignored to the extent that they will not be included directly into the documentation, but they do have meaning. White space that follows the asterisk is included in the documentation, so if you are formatting your comments in your source files and you want the formatting to translate into the documentation, keep the asterisks in. Because the documentation is written in HTML, HTML tags can be used within the `javadoc` comments:

```
/**
 * This is a <b>javadoc</b> comment
 */
```

The `<b>` and `</b>` tags surround text that should be bolded in HTML coding. `javadoc` also provides its own tags, which are described in Table 12.2.

Note also that the first sentence of each comment should be a summary comment; that is, it should explain, in short, what the rest of the following comments explain in detail because the first sentence creates summary sections of the generated documentation. So, these are the basics of using the `javadoc` utility, how do you actually generate the documentation? At your command prompt, type the `javadoc` command using the following syntax:

```
javadoc [options] [package-names] [source-files]
```

TABLE 12.2	JAVADOC **TAGS**	

Tag	Arguments	Description
@author	*author_name*	Specifies the author's name.
@deprecated	*deprecated_text*	Adds a comment that specifies that the code is deprecated.
{@link *package.name#member label*}	(appears in the braces)	Creates a hyperlink to the specified member's documentation and uses the given label.
@param	*parameter_name description*	Describes parameters of methods.
@throws	*exception description*	Generates a comment that specifies which exceptions the method throws (same as @exception).
@version	*version_text*	Generates a comment indicating the version you specify.

The only options you're going to use in this chapter are these:

- -d specifies which directory to put the documentation into.
- -author makes sure you know how to specify yourself as the author of your packages.
- -version shows you how to make the javadoc utility include the version you specify using the @version javadoc command.

The author and version information are left out by default even if the tags are in the source file's javadoc comments. A more real example is:

```
javadoc -d docs -author -version pkg.mypackage
```

This generates the documentation for a package named pkg.mypackage. The documentation will be placed in the docs directory (specified by the -d option) and will include the author and version information. There is actually much more information to learn about javadoc. This chapter only covers the basic essentials, so you'll have to refer to the tool documentation, which is included in the API documentation download package, to expand your knowledge from here. You know all you need to know for documenting the jpr.lightweight package.

Creating the *jpr.lightweight* Package

From this point on, this chapter gets a bit code heavy. The javadoc comments take up a lot of space, but you will see that the end result is well worth the effort. Not just so you have documentation for the jpr.lightweight package, but also because you will get a good feel for creating your own documentation while you copy the source files.

Creating the *JPRComponent3D* Class

Here is the source code listing for the first class you're going to create for the jpr.lightweight package, JPRComponent (by the way, jpr doesn't really stand for anything, they're just my initials).

```
package jpr.lightweight;
import java.awt.*;

/**
 * A LightWeight component whose borders can be drawn to
 * make itself look sunk, raised, or flat.
 * @author   Joseph P. Russell
 * @version 1.0
 */
public abstract class JPRComponent3D extends Component {
  /**
   * Indicates to draw this component flat (not raised or sunk).
   * An "etched" border will be drawn but will appear flat.
   */
  public final static int FLAT = 0;
  /**
   * Indicates to draw this component to appear raised from its parent.
   */
  public final static int RAISED = 1;
  /**
   * Indicates to draw this component to appear to be sunk into its
   * parent.
   */
  public final static int SUNK = 2;
  /**
   * The width of the edges.
   */
  protected int magnitude;
  //where magnitude is 1 and inner area is only one pixel:
  protected final static int ABSOLUTE_MIN_WIDTH = 5;
  protected final static int ABSOLUTE_MIN_HEIGHT = 5;
  protected int current_appearance;
  protected Color shadow, dkshadow, highlight, lthighlight;
  /**
   * The color to be used as the control color. This color will affect
   * the other colors used to make the component appear to be three
```

```java
 * dimensional. The default value is
 * <code>java.awt.SystemColor.control</code>.
 */
protected Color control;

/**
 * Gets the appearance of this <code>JPRComponent3D</code>.
 *
 * @return The appearance of this <code>JPRComponent3D</code>.
 */
public int getAppearance() {
  return current_appearance;
}

/**
 * Sets the magnitude for this <code>JPRComponent3D</code>.
 * It controls how deep or raised it looks.
 * @param thick The magnitude of projection.
 */
public void setMagnitude(int thick) {
  magnitude = thick > 0 ? thick : magnitude;
}

/**
 * Gets the magnitude of this <code>JPRComponent3D</code>.
 * @return The magnitude of this <code>JPRComponent3D</code>.
 */
public int getMagnitude() {
  return magnitude;
}

/**
 * Overrides <code>java.awt.Component.getMinimumSize</code> to
 * ensure room for at least one pixel in the center of the borders.
 * @return the minimum size, taking into account the magnitude and
 *   allows for at least one pixel in the center.
 */
public Dimension getMinimumSize() {
  int min_wh;
  min_wh = magnitude * 4 + 1;
  return new Dimension(min_wh, min_wh);
}

/**
 * Overrides <code>java.awt.Component.getPreferredSize()</code>
 * to return the current size.
 * @return the preferred size.
 */
public Dimension getPreferredSize() {
  return getSize();
}
```

```
/**
 * Returns <code>true</code>.
 * @return <code>true</code>.
 */
public boolean isLightweight() {
  return true;
}


/**
 * Sets the color to be used as the base color and also sets the
 * colors used for shading and lighting effects. If the parameter
 * is <code>java.awt.SystemColor.control</code>, then the shading
 * and lighting colors will be set to the colors defined in the
 * system. If it is any other color, then the shading and lighting
 * colors will be different shades of the given color.
 * @param base_color The color to be used as the base color.
 */
public void setControlColor(Color base_color) {
  if (base_color == null) return;
  control = base_color;
  if (base_color == SystemColor.control) {
    shadow = SystemColor.controlShadow;
    dkshadow = SystemColor.controlDkShadow;
    highlight = SystemColor.controlHighlight;
    lthighlight = SystemColor.controlLtHighlight;
  }
  else {
    shadow = base_color.darker().darker();
    dkshadow = shadow.darker().darker();
    highlight = base_color;
    lthighlight = highlight.brighter().brighter();
  }
}


/**
 * Sets the appearance of this <code>JPRComponent3D</code> to
 * the given style.
 * @param appearance.
 *    Appearances may be {@link #FLAT FLAT}, {@link #RAISED RAISED},
 *    or {@link #SUNK SUNK}.
 */
public void setAppearance(int appearance) {
  if (appearance != SUNK && appearance != FLAT
      && appearance != RAISED) current_appearance = FLAT;
  else current_appearance = appearance;
}


/**
 * Sets the color used for highlighting effects to the given color.
 * @param hl The color to be used for highlighting effects.
 */
public void setHighlightColor(Color hl) {
  if (hl != null) highlight = hl;
}
```

```
/**
 * Sets the color used for light highlighting effects to the
 * given color.
 * @param lhl The color to be used for light highlighting effects.
 */
public void setLtHighlightColor(Color lhl) {
  if (lhl != null) lthighlight = lhl;
}

/**
 * Sets the color used for shading effects to the given color.
 * @param shade The color to be used for shading effects.
 */
public void setShadowColor(Color shade) {
  if (shade != null) shadow = shade;
}

/**
 * Sets the color used for dark shading effects to the given color.
 * @param dkshade The color to be used for dark shading effects.
 */
public void setDkShadowColor(Color dkshade) {
  if (dkshade != null) dkshadow = dkshade;
}

/**
 * Gets the color used for the control color
 * @return The color used for the control color.
 */
public Color getControlColor() {
  return control;
}

/**
 * Gets the color used for highlighting effects.
 * @return The color used for highlighting effects.
 */
public Color getHighlightColor() {
  return highlight;
}

/**
 * Gets the color used for light highlighting effects.
 * @return The color used for light highlighting effects.
 */
public Color getLtHighlightColor() {
  return lthighlight;
}

/**
 * Gets the color used for shading effects.
 * @return the color used for shading effects.
 */
```

```java
  public Color getShadowColor() {
    return shadow;
  }

  /**
   * Gets the color used for dark shading effects.
   * @return the color used for dark shading effects.
   */
  public Color getDkShadowColor() {
    return dkshadow;
  }

  /**
   * Results in a call to {@link #paintFlat(Graphics) paintFlat},
   * {@link #paintRaised paintRaised(Graphics) paintRaised},
   * or {@link #paintSunk(Graphics) paintSunk}, depending on appearance.
   */
  public void paint(Graphics g) {
    switch (current_appearance) {
      case FLAT:
        paintFlat(g);
        break;
      case RAISED:
        paintRaised(g);
        break;
      case SUNK:
        paintSunk(g);
        break;
      }
  }

  /**
   * Paints this <code>JPRComponent3D</code>'s {@link #FLAT FLAT}
   * appearance.
   */
  public abstract void paintFlat(Graphics g);

  /**
   * Paints this <code>JPRComponent3D</code>'s {@link #RAISED RAISED}
   * appearance.
   */
  public abstract void paintRaised(Graphics g);

  /**
   * Paints this <code>JPRComponent3D</code>'s {@link #SUNK SUNK}
   * appearance.
   */
  public abstract void paintSunk(Graphics g);

}
```

The first thing to notice is the package declaration:

```
package jpr.lightweight;
```

Basically, all its members specify the current appearance of the JPRComponent3D object. RAISED, SUNK, and FLAT are static constants that describe how this JPRComponent3D should be painted. The different Color members actually render the JPRComponent3D. There are five of them. control is the basic control color. The other colors are based off of this color. There are two highlight colors, highlight and lthighlight, and two shadow colors shadow and dkshadow.

If these colors are all different shades of the same color, they can be used effectively to give the appearance of a three-dimensional component, but you can leave that up to subclasses of JPRComponent3D. This is an abstract class and doesn't define the methods paintRaised(Graphics), paintSunk(Graphics), or paint-Flat(Graphics). It just declares them abstract. Subclasses of this component can be any shape, so it is up to them to paint themselves. It does define the paint(Graphics) method, though. What it does is check the current_appearance variable to see if it's raised, sunk, or flat and calls the corresponding paint… method.

The get and set methods are fairly straight-forward. Other methods that need some explanation are isLightWeight(), which returns a boolean value, I just overrode it here to return true because this and its subclasses are lightweight components. The setControlColor(Color) method also needs a bit of an explanation. You see, if the parameter passed in to this method is SystemColor.control, it uses the following color scheme:

```
shadow = SystemColor.controlShadow;
dkshadow = SystemColor.controlDkShadow;
highlight = SystemColor.controlHighlight;
lthighlight = SystemColor.controlLtHighlight;
```

These colors define the colors that you have set for your operating system's GUI. As an example in Windows, if you right-click the desktop, go to Properties, and then Appearance, you can choose a color scheme for your GUI. You can even go as far as specifying your own custom scheme. So the SystemColor colors specify these colors and if you want to maintain the look of your operating system (at least as far as color is concerned), pass in SystemColor.control as the argument to this method. On the other hand, if a different color is passed in, it attempts to create appropriate highlighting and shadowing colors by making use of the brighter() and darker() methods of the Color class. If you don't like the defaults, you can just use the set… methods to explicitly set any colors.

Creating the *JPRRectComponent3D* Class

The JPRRectComponent3D class extends the JPRComponent3D class. It is also an abstract class, although it implements all the methods that were declared to be abstract in its superclass JPRComponent3D. The reason why it's still abstract is because it has no actual use other than to provide basic functionality for other components to expand on.

You can't do anything with a JPRRectComponent3D except for painting it graphically, so making it abstract here prevents any other classes from creating instances of this useless class; that is, useless to non-subclasses. It can come in handy for creating subclasses such as components that act like buttons, which appear raised until they are clicked and then they appear sunk and pop back up again after you release the mouse button.

Another good use is for a text field or text area component that appears sunk and possibly has a white background and a cursor in the inside and listens for key events. There is a good base for functionality that can be very useful and should be reusable, but is not very useful by itself. This is a perfect example of the usefulness of abstract classes. This is how robust, reusable, highly customizable packages are created in the real world. Here is the source code for JPRRectComponent3D.java:

```java
package jpr.lightweight;

import java.awt.*;

/**
 * A LightWeight 3D rectangular component.
 * @author  Joseph P. Russell
 * @version 1.0
 */
public abstract class JPRRectComponent3D extends JPRComponent3D {
  /**
   * Constructs a <code>JPRRectComponent3D</code> using all default
   * settings. The default appearance is
   * {@link #FLAT FLAT}, the default size is the
   * minimum size, and the default magnitude is <code>1</code>.
   */
  public JPRRectComponent3D() {
    this(ABSOLUTE_MIN_WIDTH, ABSOLUTE_MIN_HEIGHT, FLAT, 1);
  }

  /**
   * Constructs a <code>JPRRectComponent3D</code> with the given
   * dimensions. The default appearance is
   * {@link #FLAT FLAT} and the default magnitude is <code>1</code>.
   * @param wide the overall width
   * @param high the overall height
   */
```

```
public JPRRectComponent3D(int wide, int high) {
  this(wide, high, FLAT, 1);
}

/**
 * Constructs a <code>JPRRectComponent3D</code> with the given
 * appearance, using minimum size and a magnitude of <code>1</code>.
 * @param appearance The appearance.
 *    Appearances may be {@link #FLAT FLAT}, {@link #RAISED RAISED},
 *    or {@link #SUNK SUNK}.
 */
public JPRRectComponent3D(int appearance) {
  this(ABSOLUTE_MIN_WIDTH, ABSOLUTE_MIN_HEIGHT, appearance, 1);
}

/**
 * Constructs a <code>JPRRectComponent3D</code> with the given
 * dimensions and appearance. The default magnitude is <code>1</code>.
 * @param wide the overall width.
 * @param high the overall height.
 * @param appearance The appearance.
 *    Appearances may be {@link #FLAT FLAT}, {@link #RAISED RAISED},
 *    or {@link #SUNK SUNK}.
 */
public JPRRectComponent3D(int wide, int high, int appearance) {
  this(wide, high, appearance, 1);
}

/**
 * Constructs a <code>JPRRectComponent3D</code> with the given
 * dimensions, appearance, and magnitude.
 * @param wide the overall width.
 * @param high the overall height.
 * @param appearance The appearance.
 *    Appearances may be {@link #FLAT FLAT}, {@link #RAISED RAISED},
 *    or {@link #SUNK SUNK}.
 * @param border_magnitude The thickness of the border. The larger
 *    it is, the more deep or raised it appears. If the appearance is
 *    {@link #FLAT FLAT}, then it won't look deeper or higher, but it
 *    will have a thicker border. The actual pixel thickness is twice
 *    that of the magnitude since there are two different-colored
 *    rows of pixels around the border to enhance the three
 *    dimensional look.
 */
public JPRRectComponent3D(int wide, int high, int appearance,
                                   int border_magnitude) {
  super();
  if (wide < ABSOLUTE_MIN_WIDTH) wide = ABSOLUTE_MIN_WIDTH;
  if (high < ABSOLUTE_MIN_HEIGHT) high = ABSOLUTE_MIN_HEIGHT;
  setAppearance(appearance);
  setMagnitude(border_magnitude);
  setSize(wide, high);
  setControlColor(SystemColor.control);
```

```
      setBackground(SystemColor.control);
      setForeground(Color.black);
    }

    /**
     * Gets the size of the interior portion.
     * The interior portion is in the center, surrounded by the border.
     * @return The Dimension of the interior portion.
     */
    public Dimension getInteriorSize() {
      return new Dimension(getSize().width - (4 * magnitude),
                           getSize().height - (4 * magnitude));
    }

    public void paint(Graphics g) {
      g.setColor(getBackground());
      g.fillRect(0, 0, getSize().width, getSize().height);
      super.paint(g);
    }

    public void paintFlat(Graphics g) {
      g.setColor(lthighlight);
      g.fillRect(0, 0, getSize().width, getSize().height);
      g.setColor(shadow);
      g.fillRect(0, 0, magnitude, getSize().height);
      g.fillRect(magnitude, 0, getSize().width - magnitude, magnitude);
      for (int i = 0; i < magnitude; i++) {
        g.drawRect(magnitude * 2 + i, magnitude * 2 + i,
                   getInteriorSize().width, getInteriorSize().height);
      }
      g.setColor(getBackground());
      g.fillRect(magnitude * 2, magnitude * 2, getInteriorSize().width,
                 getInteriorSize().height);
    }

    public void paintRaised(Graphics g) {
      g.setColor(lthighlight);
      for (int i = 0; i < magnitude * 2; i++) {
        if (i == ((magnitude * 2) - 1)) g.setColor(highlight);
        g.drawLine(i, i, getSize().width - (i + 2), i);
        g.drawLine(i, 1+i, i, getSize().height - (i + 2));
      }

      g.setColor(dkshadow);
      for (int i = 0; i < magnitude * 2; i++) {
        if (i > 0) g.setColor(shadow);
        g.drawLine(i, getSize().height - (i + 1), getSize().width
                   - (i + 1), getSize().height - (i + 1));
        g.drawLine(getSize().width - (i + 1), i, getSize().width
                   - (i + 1), getSize().height - (i + 2));
      }
    }
```

```
public void paintSunk(Graphics g) {
    for (int i = 0; i < magnitude * 2; i++) {
        if (i == ((magnitude * 2) - 1)) g.setColor(dkshadow);
        else g.setColor(shadow);
        g.drawLine(i, i, getSize().width - (i + 2), i);
        g.drawLine(i, 1+i, i, getSize().height - (i + 2));
    }
    for (int i = 0; i < magnitude * 2; i++) {
        if (i == ((magnitude * 2) - 1)) g.setColor(highlight);
        else g.setColor(lthighlight);
        g.drawLine(getSize().width - (i + 1), i, getSize().width
                - (i + 1), getSize().height - (i + 2));
        g.drawLine(i, getSize().height - (i + 1), getSize().width
                - (i + 1), getSize().height - (i + 1));
    }
}

}
```

This class provides a good number of constructors for specifying its initial state. Other than that, the most significant code in this program is the implementations of the different paint… methods. The paint(Graphics) method is overridden to clear the background with the background color, and then it calls its superclass's paint(Graphics) method which just calls one of the three methods for rendering its current appearance.

The three methods can seem a bit complicated at first, but basically what they're doing is painting lines that make the appearance look three-dimensional and represent the state of being RAISED, SUNK, or FLAT. In general, highlighted colors on the top and left of the shapes and the darker shadow colors on the bottom and right make it appear to be raised and reversed, it appears to be sunk. The FLAT appearance is drawn so that the border around the JPRRectComponent3D appears to be etched and the surface appears to be at the same level as its container. The magnitude variable specifies the degree of dimension (how much it is raised or sunk, or how deep and wide the etched border is around the FLAT appearance).

Another thing it provides is the getInteriorSize() method, which returns a Dimension object that represents the size of the interior portion of the JPRRect-Component3D. It calculates this value by subtracting four times the magnitude from the width and the height because the magnitude is half the width of the border (so it can paint at least two colors given a magnitude of one). This means that the border takes up twice the width of the magnitude on all four sides of the JPRRectComponent3D.

Creating the *JPRButton3D* Class

The JPRButton3D class is the only non-abstract class that you're going to be defining for the jpr.lightweight package. It extends the JPRRectComponent class and adds functionality that makes it behave like a button. It is initially RAISED in appearance, but when you click it with your mouse it changes its appearance to SUNK and then back again to RAISED when the mouse button is released or when the mouse cursor exits the area of this JPRButton3D. It makes itself FLAT when it is disabled. Take a look at the source code:

```java
package jpr.lightweight;
import java.awt.*;
import java.awt.event.*;

/**
 * A lightweight 3D Button class that fires actions when clicked.
 * When it is enabled it appears {@link #RAISED RAISED}, when
 * it is pressed it appears {@link #SUNK SUNK}, and when it is
 * not enabled, it appears {@link #FLAT FLAT}.
 */
public class JPRButton3D extends JPRRectComponent3D {
  private boolean pressed;
  /**
   * This <code>JPRButton3D</code>'s <code>ActionListener</code>.
   */
  protected ActionListener actionListener;
  private String actionCommand;

  /**
   * Constructs a new <code>JPRButton3D</code> with minimum size
   */
  public JPRButton3D() {
    this(ABSOLUTE_MIN_WIDTH, ABSOLUTE_MIN_HEIGHT, 1);
  }

  /**
   * Constructs a new <code>JPRButton3D</code> with the given dimensions.
   * @param wide the width
   * @param high the height
   */
  public JPRButton3D(int wide, int high) {
    this(wide, high, 1);
  }

  /**
   * Constructs a new <code>JPRButton3D</code> with the given dimensions
   * and border magnitude.
   * @param wide the width
   * @param high the height
   * @param border_magnitude the border's magnitude
   */
```

```java
public JPRButton3D(int wide, int high, int border_magnitude) {
  super(wide, high, RAISED, border_magnitude);
  enableEvents(AWTEvent.MOUSE_EVENT_MASK);
}

public void processMouseEvent(MouseEvent e) {
  if (isEnabled() & e.getModifiers() == MouseEvent.BUTTON1_MASK) {
    switch(e.getID()) {
      case MouseEvent.MOUSE_PRESSED:
        pressed = true;
        current_appearance = SUNK;
        repaint();
        break;
      case MouseEvent.MOUSE_EXITED:
        if (pressed) {
          pressed = false;
          current_appearance = RAISED;
          repaint();
        }
        break;
      case MouseEvent.MOUSE_RELEASED:
        if (pressed) {
          current_appearance = RAISED;
          repaint();
          if (actionListener != null) {
            actionListener.actionPerformed(new ActionEvent(this,
              ActionEvent.ACTION_PERFORMED, actionCommand,
              e.getModifiers()));
          }
        }
        break;
    }
  }
  super.processMouseEvent(e);
}

/**
 * Adds the specified <code>ActionListener</code>
 * @param listener <code>ActionListener</code> to add
 */
public void addActionListener(ActionListener listener) {
  actionListener = AWTEventMulticaster.add(actionListener, listener);
}

/**
 * Removes the specified <code>ActionListener</code>
 * @param listener <code>ActionListener</code> to remove
 */
public void removeActionListener(ActionListener listener) {
  actionListener = AWTEventMulticaster.remove(actionListener,
                                              listener);
}
```

```
/**
 * Sets the action command associated with action events.
 * @param command The action command.
 */
public void setActionCommand(String command) {
  actionCommand = command;
}

/**
 * Gets the action command associated with action events.
 * @return the action command
 */
public String getActionCommand() {
  return actionCommand;
}

/**
 * Enables or disables this <code>JPRButton3D</code>.
 * @param b <code>true</code> to enable, <code>false</code> to disable
 */
public void setEnabled(boolean b) {
  if (b) current_appearance = RAISED;
  else current_appearance = FLAT;
  repaint();
  super.setEnabled(b);
}
}
```

This extension of JPRRectComponent3D is basically responsible for giving itself some life by supporting event handling. Here is how it accepts mouse events. First, in the constructor, it calls enableEvents(*AWTEvent.MOUSE_EVENT_MASK*) so that mouse interactions get processed by the processMouseEvent(*MouseEvent*) method automatically. The processMouseEvent(*MouseEvent*) method is pretty big, but what it does is fairly simple. Here's what it's doing:

First it puts the event's ID (e.getID()) into a switch statement if the mouse button is the left button and this JPRButton3D is enabled. The ID specifies what kind of mouse event occurred. If it's pressed, the processMouseEvent(*MouseEvent*) method sinks the button and repaints it. If the mouse cursor exits before the button is released, the processMouseEvent(*MouseEvent*) method just re-raises the button's appearance and forgets about it (doesn't fire any events). If the mouse is released on the button (and it was previously pressed down), the process-MouseEvent(*MouseEvent*) method raises it back up again and fires an Action-Event. It fires the event by constructing a new ActionListener event and passing it to the actionListener member which is created just like you saw in the section "Creating Your Own Lightweight Components," by using the AWTEventMulticaster class. So it calls:

```
actionListener.actionPerformed(new ActionEvent(this,
```

```
ActionEvent.ACTION_PERFORMED, actionCommand,
e.getModifiers()));
```

Which results in the `AWTEventMulticaster` informing all registered listeners of the event. It provides the `addActionListener(ActionListener)` and `removeActionListener(ActionListener)` methods for registering with the `AWTEventMulticaster`.

Generating the Documentation for *jpr.lightweight*

All that commenting is about to pay off. Now it's time to generate the documentation by using the `javadoc` utility. First make sure you're in the directory that contains the `jpr` subdirectory and that the `jpr` directory has the `lightweight` subdirectory in it, which contains the class files for the `java.lightweight` package. Also, before you do this, create a new subdirectory of the current directory called `jprdoc`. Now at the command prompt, type:

```
javadoc -d jprdoc -author -version jpr.lightweight
```

and watch what happens. The `javadoc` utility goes into action and pumps out HTML files. It puts them in the `jprdoc` directory. Figure 12.3 shows what your `javadoc` utility output should look like.

Now browse into the `jprdoc` directory and open the index.html file. You should see the documentation for all three classes: `JPRComponent3D`, `JPRRectComponent3D`, and `JPRButton3D`. Figure 12.4 shows the index.html documentation as it appears in my browser window. The index file has links to each of the three classes and when you click the link it brings to the page that document's details you specified using the `javadoc` comments.

FIGURE 12.3

The `javadoc` utility in action.

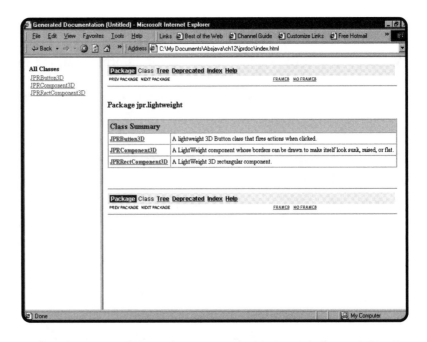

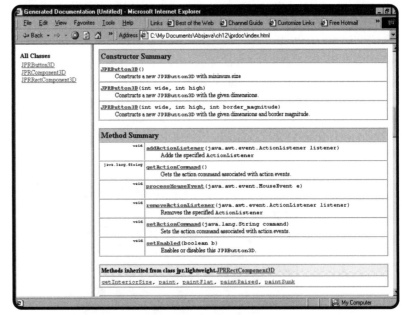

FIGURE 12.4

Clicking any of the links brings you to detailed information about the `jpr.lightweight` thing that you clicked.

Testing the *JPRButton3D* Class

Let's give the JPRButton3D class a whirl and make sure it works. The JPRButton3DTest class extends GUIFrame and implements ActionListener. It keeps track of four JPRButton3Ds in an array, b[]. It constructs the first button, b[0] passing no arguments to the constructor. This creates a tiny little button. The second button, b[1] constructs itself having dimensions 100 by 100 and a magnitude of 2. The third one is 100 by 50 and sets its action command to "Button 3".

Finally, the last JPRButton3D is disabled, all four of the buttons are added and it registers this as an action listener for all of them and then it shows itself. The actionPerformed(ActionEvent) method just prints the ActionEvent object, unless the button is the first, small, button, in which case it will also print Tiny Button and disables the second button. This is just there to show you that testing the source of the action event is working properly and also that setting a JPRButton3D to a disabled state will cause it to appear flat. Here is the source code listing:

```
/*
 * JPRButton3DTest
 * Tests the JPRButton3DTest class
 */

import java.awt.*;
import java.awt.event.*;
import jpr.lightweight.JPRButton3D;

public class JPRButton3DTest extends GUIFrame
                             implements ActionListener {
  JPRButton3D[] b;

  public JPRButton3DTest() {
    super("JPRButton3D Test");
    setLayout(new FlowLayout());
    b = new JPRButton3D[4];

    b[0] = new JPRButton3D();
    b[1] = new JPRButton3D(100, 100, 2);
    b[2] = new JPRButton3D(100, 50);
    b[2].setActionCommand("Button 3");
    b[3] = new JPRButton3D(100, 50);
    b[3].setEnabled(false);

    for (int i=0; i < b.length; i++) {
      b[i].addActionListener(this);
      add(b[i]);
    }

    pack();
    setVisible(true);
  }
```

```java
public static void main(String args[]) {
    new JPRButton3DTest();
}

public void actionPerformed(ActionEvent e) {
    System.out.println(e);
    if (e.getSource() == b[0]) {
        System.out.println("Tiny Button");
        b[1].setEnabled(false);
    }
}
}
```

Figure 12.5 shows a typical session. The MS-DOS prompt is showing in the background. The image on the top shows the second JPRButton3D before it is disabled and the image on the bottom shows it after it is disabled.

FIGURE 12.5

Yup, the buttons seem like they're working okay. Clicking them really looks like they're being pressed down!

Building the *MineCell* Classes

The classes that make up the functionality of the mine cells are the following:

- MineCell extends JPRButton3D.
- MineCellEvent encapsulates events that can be fired by MineCells.
- MineCellListener provides an interface for other classes to listen to Mine-CellEvents.

I'll start with the MineCellEvent class and then explain MineCellListener, and finally, MineCell.

The *MineCellEvent* Class

There are four types of events that MineCells can fire and are represented by the static constants REVEALED, FLAGGED, UNFLAGGED, and DETONATED. Mine cells are revealed when the player left-clicks it and doesn't blow up, which means there isn't a mine there. Flagged events occur when the player right-clicks a cell to mark it as containing a mine and unflagging occurs when the flag is removed by right-clicking the cell again.

When the player clicks a mine cell and blows up, it triggers a detonated event. The MineCellEvent constructor accepts two arguments. The first one is the object that triggered the event and the second one is the type of event that it triggered. MineCellEvent stores the type of event in its eventID member and returns that value when the getID() method is invoked. Here is the source code:

```
/*
 * MineCellEvent
 * Encapsulates events fired by MineCells
 */

public class MineCellEvent extends java.util.EventObject {
  protected int eventID;
  // event id constants
  public final static int REVEALED  = 0,
                          FLAGGED   = 1,
                          UNFLAGGED = 2,
                          DETONATED = 3;

  public MineCellEvent(Object source, int id) {
    super(source);
    eventID = id;
  }

  public int getID() {
    return eventID;
  }
}
```

The *MineCellListener* Interface

MineCellListener is an interface for listening to the four types of mine cell events. The four methods that correspond to these types of events are as follows:

mineCellRevealed(*MineCellEvent*)	Listens for when mine cells are revealed.
mineCellFlagged(*MineCellEvent*)	Listens for when mine cells are flagged.
mineCellUnflagged(*MineCellEvent*)	Listens for when mine cells are unflagged.
mineCellDetonated(*MineCellEvent*)	Listens for when mine cells are detonated.

As with most interfaces, the listing is extremely quick and to the point. Here it is:

```
/*
 * MineCellListener
 * Interface for listening for MineCellEvents
 */

public interface MineCellListener {
   public void mineCellRevealed(MineCellEvent e);
   public void mineCellFlagged(MineCellEvent e);
   public void mineCellUnflagged(MineCellEvent e);
   public void mineCellDetonated(MineCellEvent e);
}
```

The *MineCell* Class

This class is a subclass of JPRButton3D. In order to get access to the class you need to import it:

```
import jpr.lightweight.JPRButton3D;
```

The MineCell has an int member, called contents, which it uses to store one of ten values. It stores zero, which is specified by the EMPTY constant if there is no mine in this cell and there are no mines surrounding this cell. There is a maximum of eight cells that surround this cell. If any or all those cells have mines in them, contents stores the number of mines in cells that immediately surround this cell. If this cell has a mine in it, it indicates this fact by storing the number nine, which is specified by the MINE constant.

This class also has a ten-element array of colors, subscripted by the same possible values of the contents variable. colors[0] indicates the color of an empty mine that has been revealed in case you want to distinguish it from the other cells further (when cells are revealed, they are disabled and therefore appear flat). Colors stored at indices from 1 through 8 represent the colors of the numbers that are painted that indicate the number of mines that immediately surround the cells they reside in. The color stored at colors[MINE] is the color of the cell that is revealed with a detonated mine inside of it. It declares three images, flagImg, mineImg, and explodeImg, which store images that represent flags, mines, and explosions, respectively. These Image objects are static, so there is only one instance of each of them no matter how many instances of MineCell exist. The images are set by calling the static setImages(Image, Image, Image) method. listeners is a vector of MineCellListeners.

MineCell also declares an inner class, EventThread, which extends Thread and fires off MineCellEvents. Its constructor accepts a MineCellEvent parameter and the MineCellListener event method that it fires depends on the MineCellEvent ID:

```
protected class EventThread extends Thread {
  MineCellEvent e;

  EventThread(MineCellEvent mce) {
    e = mce;
  }

  public void run() {
    switch(e.getID()) {
      case MineCellEvent.REVEALED:
        for (int i=0; i < listeners.size(); i++) {
          ((MineCellListener)listeners.elementAt(i)).mineCellRevealed(e);
        }
        break;
      case MineCellEvent.FLAGGED:
        for (int i=0; i < listeners.size(); i++) {
          ((MineCellListener)listeners.elementAt(i)).mineCellFlagged(e);
        }
        break;
      case MineCellEvent.UNFLAGGED:
        for (int i=0; i < listeners.size(); i++) {
          ((MineCellListener)listeners.elementAt(i)).mineCellUnflagged(e);
        }
        break;
      case MineCellEvent.DETONATED:
        for (int i=0; i < listeners.size(); i++) {
          ((MineCellListener)listeners.elementAt(i)).mineCellDetonated(e);
        }
        break;
    }
  }
}
```

The MineCell class has an anonymous inner class that listens for its Action-Events. If an action event occurred, it means that someone clicked this cell. If there's no mine in here, it reveals the cell and dispatches a `MineCellEvent.REVEALED` event. If there is a mine in here, it sets the color to `col-ors[MINE]` and dispatches a `MineCellEvent.DETONATED` event. Another anonymous inner class listens for `MouseEvents`.

The superclass, `JPRButton3D`, doesn't do anything with right mouse clicks, but this `MouseAdapter` does. It either flags or unflags this cell based on whether the cell is already flagged and dispatches the corresponding event.

Another thing the `MineCell` class needed to take care of was to prevent action events from mine cells that are flagged. You don't want to let the player click a flagged cell and blow up, right? Nor do you want the cell to be animated. You want it to be concrete that if this cell is flagged, you can't click it with the left mouse button, period. To accomplish this, the `MineCell` class overrides the `processMouseEvent(MouseEvent)` method. If this cell is not flagged or if you're right-clicking it, just go ahead and let the `MouseEvent` pass, but if this cell is flagged and you're trying to left-click it, stop it dead in its tracks:

```java
public void processMouseEvent(MouseEvent e) {
  if (!flagged || e.getModifiers() == MouseEvent.BUTTON3_MASK)
    super.processMouseEvent(e);
}
```

Here is the full source code listing for `MineCell.java`:

```java
/*
 * MineCell
 * Defines one cell of the MinePatrol Game.
 */

import java.awt.*;
import java.awt.event.*;
import java.util.Vector;
import jpr.lightweight.JPRButton3D;

public class MineCell extends JPRButton3D {
  protected int contents;
  public final static int EMPTY = 0;
  public final static int MINE = 9;
  //These colors are indexed by the contents Color[EMPTY] is for
  //revealed cells and colors[MINE] is for detonated cells
  protected Color[] colors;
  protected boolean hidden, detonated, flagged;
  //acts as the background color when the cell becomes visible
  protected static Image flagImg, mineImg, explodeImg;
  protected Vector listeners;

  public MineCell() {
    this(EMPTY);
  }
```

```
public MineCell(int contains) {
  super();
  colors = new Color[] {getBackground(), Color.blue,
             Color.cyan, Color.green, Color.magenta, Color.yellow,
             Color.orange, Color.red, Color.black,
             Color.red.darker().darker()};
  setFont(new Font("Arial", Font.BOLD, 16));
  resetContents(contains);
  listeners = new Vector();
  addActionListener(new ActionListener() {
    public void actionPerformed(ActionEvent e) {
      MineCellEvent mce;

      if (flagged) return;
      if (contents < MINE) {
        setHidden(false);
        mce = new MineCellEvent(MineCell.this,
                                MineCellEvent.REVEALED);
      }
      else {
        detonated = true;
        setBackground(colors[MINE]);
        setControlColor(colors[MINE]);
        setHidden(false);
        mce = new MineCellEvent(MineCell.this,
                                MineCellEvent.DETONATED);
      }
      (new EventThread(mce)).start();
    }
  });

  addMouseListener(new MouseAdapter() {
    MineCellEvent mce;

    public void mousePressed(MouseEvent e) {
      if (e.getModifiers() == MouseEvent.BUTTON3_MASK && hidden) {
        if (flagged) {
          flagged = false;
          repaint();
          mce = new MineCellEvent(MineCell.this,
                                  MineCellEvent.UNFLAGGED);
        }
        else {
          flagged =  true;
          repaint();
          mce = new MineCellEvent(MineCell.this,
                                  MineCellEvent.FLAGGED);
        }
        (new EventThread(mce)).start();
      }
    }
  });
}
```

```
protected class EventThread extends Thread {
  MineCellEvent e;

  EventThread(MineCellEvent mce) {
    e = mce;
  }

  public void run() {
    switch(e.getID()) {
      case MineCellEvent.REVEALED:
        for (int i=0; i < listeners.size(); i++) {
          ((MineCellListener)listeners.elementAt(i)).mineCellRevealed(e);
        }
        break;
      case MineCellEvent.FLAGGED:
        for (int i=0; i < listeners.size(); i++) {
          ((MineCellListener)listeners.elementAt(i)).mineCellFlagged(e);
        }
        break;
      case MineCellEvent.UNFLAGGED:
        for (int i=0; i < listeners.size(); i++) {
          ((MineCellListener)listeners.elementAt(i)).mineCellUnflagged(e);
        }
        break;
      case MineCellEvent.DETONATED:
        for (int i=0; i < listeners.size(); i++) {
          ((MineCellListener)listeners.elementAt(i)).mineCellDetonated(e);
        }
        break;
    }
  }
}

public void setContents(int contains) {
  contents = contains >= EMPTY && contains <= MINE ? contains : EMPTY;
  setForeground(colors[contents]);
}

public void resetContents(int contains) {
  setContents(contains);
  setHidden(true);
  detonated = false;
}

public int getContents() {
  return contents;
}

public void setHidden(boolean h) {
  hidden = h;
  if (h) {
    setBackground(SystemColor.control);
    setControlColor(SystemColor.control);
  }
```

```
    else if (!detonated) {
      setBackground(colors[EMPTY]);
      setControlColor(colors[EMPTY]);
    }
    flagged = false;
    setEnabled(h);
    repaint();
}

public boolean isHidden() {
  return hidden;
}

public boolean isFlagged() {
  return flagged;
}

public static void setImages(Image f, Image m, Image e) {
  flagImg = f;
  mineImg = m;
  explodeImg = e;
}

public void paint(Graphics g) {
  super.paint(g);
  if (!hidden || flagged) drawContents(g);
}

protected void drawContents(Graphics g) {
  Image img = null;
  if (contents == MINE || flagged) {
    if (flagged) img = flagImg;
    else if (contents == MINE && detonated) img = explodeImg;
    else if (contents == MINE && !detonated) img = mineImg;
    if (img != null) {
      g.drawImage(img, (getSize().width - img.getWidth(this)) / 2,
                  (getSize().height - img.getHeight(this)) /2, this);
    }
  }
  else if (contents != EMPTY) {
    FontMetrics fm = g.getFontMetrics();
    g.setColor(getForeground());
    g.drawString(String.valueOf(contents),
      (getSize().width
      - fm.stringWidth(String.valueOf(contents))) / 2,
      (getSize().height + fm.getHeight()) / 2 - fm.getDescent());
  }
}

public void processMouseEvent(MouseEvent e) {
  if (!flagged || e.getModifiers() == MouseEvent.BUTTON3_MASK)
    super.processMouseEvent(e);
}
```

```
public void addMineCellListener(MineCellListener mcl) {
    listeners.addElement(mcl);
}

public void removeMineCellListener(MineCellListener mcl) {
    listeners.removeElement(mcl);
}

}
```

Testing the *MineCell* Class

The MineCellTest class constructs 12 MineCell instances in an array. When it constructs the array of MineCells it sets the contents of the array to the value of the subscript, so the MineCell at cells[0] has its contents set to 0 (MineCell.EMPTY), the MineCell at cells[1] has its contents set to 1, and so on. Because the indices of the array go higher than nine, the last three mines are set to nine, (Mine-Cell.MINE). MineCellTest also implements MineCellLisetener and adds itself as a listener of all the MineCells. Next it loads the images flag.gif, mine.gif, and explode.gif using MediaTracker and sets the images by calling MineCell.setImages(Image, Image, Image).

It implements the MineCellListener methods to notify you of what events are occurring by updating its label each time an event is heard. If a cell detonates, all the other cells are revealed too, so you can see the mine graphic in the other two cells that contain mines. You can see a run of this in Figure 12.6. Here is the source code:

```
/*
 * MineCellTest
 * Tests the MineCell class
 */

import java.awt.*;

public class MineCellTest extends GUIFrame
                          implements MineCellListener {
  MineCell[] cells;
  Label statusLabel;

  public MineCellTest() {
    super("MineCell Test");
    cells = new MineCell[12];
    Panel cellPanel = new Panel();
    cellPanel.setLayout(new GridLayout(3, 0));
    for (int i=0; i < cells.length; i++) {
      cells[i] = new MineCell(i < 10 ? i : 9);
      cells[i].addMineCellListener(this);
      cells[i].setSize(50, 50);
      cellPanel.add(cells[i]);
    }
```

```
      add(cellPanel, BorderLayout.CENTER);
      MediaTracker mt = new MediaTracker(this);
      Image[] imgs = {
        Toolkit.getDefaultToolkit().getImage("flag.gif"),
        Toolkit.getDefaultToolkit().getImage("mine.gif"),
        Toolkit.getDefaultToolkit().getImage("explode.gif") };

      for (int i=0; i < imgs.length; i++) {
        mt.addImage(imgs[i], i);
      }
      try {
        mt.waitForAll();
      } catch (InterruptedException e) {}
      MineCell.setImages(imgs[0], imgs[1], imgs[2]);
      statusLabel = new Label();
      add(statusLabel, BorderLayout.SOUTH);

      pack();
      setVisible(true);
    }

    public static void main(String args[]) {
      new MineCellTest();
    }

    public void mineCellRevealed(MineCellEvent e) {
      statusLabel.setText("Revealed");
    }

    public void mineCellFlagged(MineCellEvent e) {
      statusLabel.setText("Flagged");
    }

    public void mineCellUnflagged(MineCellEvent e) {
      statusLabel.setText("Unflagged");
    }

    public void mineCellDetonated(MineCellEvent e) {
      statusLabel.setText("Detonated");
      for (int i=0; i < cells.length; i++) {
        cells[i].setHidden(false);
      }
    }
  }
```

FIGURE 12.6

A test of the
MineCell class is
a success.

Creating the Mine Field Classes

Similar to the mine cell classes, the mine field classes consist of an event class, MineFieldEvent, a listener interface, MineFieldListener, and the MineField class itself.

The *MineFieldEvent* Class

There are four types of events that MineFields can trigger indicated by Mine-FieldEvent static constants, as follows:

- SOLVED is for when the entire field of mine cells is solved, such as when all the cells are either flagged or revealed and no one blew up.
- RANDOM indicates that the MineField was randomized, which means that the mines that are hidden within the mine field were rearranged randomly.
- The DETONATED constant indicates that one of the field's MineCell objects exploded.
- FLAG_COUNT_CHANGED occurs when the player flags or unflags a cell within the MineField.

The constructor accepts the object that triggered the thread and also the integer flag that indicates what type of event it fired. The eventID member holds this value and you can access its value by calling the getID() method. Here is the source code listing for MineFieldEvent.java:

```
/*
 * MineFieldEvent
 * Encapsulates events fired by MineFields
 */

public class MineFieldEvent extends java.util.EventObject {
  protected int eventID;
  // event id constants
  public final static int SOLVED = 0,
                          RANDOMIZED = 1,
                          DETONATED = 2,
                          FLAG_COUNT_CHANGED = 3;

  public MineFieldEvent(Object source, int id) {
    super(source);
    eventID = id;
  }

  public int getID() {
    return eventID;
  }
}
```

The *MineFieldListener* Interface

The MineFieldListener interface provides methods that correspond to the types of events that are defined in the MineFieldEvent class. There's not much to explain here, so I'll just list the short source code file:

```
/*
 * MineFieldListener
 * Interface for listening for MineFieldEvents
 */

public interface MineFieldListener {
  public void mineFieldSolved(MineFieldEvent e);
  public void mineFieldRandomized(MineFieldEvent e);
  public void mineFieldDetonated(MineFieldEvent e);
  public void mineFieldFlagCountChanged(MineFieldEvent e);
}
```

The *MineField* Class

The MineField class lays out a grid of MineCells, randomly places a set number of mines into the cells, and then listens for MineCellEvents. It also has an inner EventThread class that is uses to fire MineFieldEvents for all its listeners, which it keeps in a Vector. You know, the same model you've been using for custom event handling since the last chapter. It should be fresh in your mind from just reading the MineCell class which does the same kind of thing. The MineField class's members are declared as follows:

```
protected int rows, cols, mines, flagged, revealed;
protected AudioClip revealClip, flagClip, unflagClip, explodeClip;
protected MineCell[][] cells;
protected Hashtable pointIndex;
protected Vector listeners;
```

Its integers are rows and cols, which keep track of the number of rows and columns in this MineField, mines keeps track of the number of mines, flagged counts the number of cells that are flagged, and revealed counts the number of cells that are revealed. It also declares four AudioClip objects that play sounds. You can tell by their names when they are played. The cells[][] array is a two-dimensional array of MineCells that make up this MineField. The pointIndex object is a Hashtable. The Hashtable class is provided in the java.util package. It allows you to index an object by another object. The MineField class makes use of the Hashtable by storing the cells[][] indices as Point objects in the Hashtable stored by the MineCells that are stored at that point in the cells[][] array. It's a mouthful, eh? Here's what I'm talkin' bout, Willis.

Say that MineCell a is stored at cells[1][2]. Unlike the matrix[][] array of the PlayArea class from the previous chapter, this array stores by [row][column] because you don't need to mess around with the actual component (x, y) coordinates like you did for the BlockGame application. So MineCell a is at row 1, column 2 of the cells[][] array.

Conceptually, x coordinates move left to right, specifying the columns, and y coordinates move up and down, specifying the rows. The Point in the cells[][] array where the cell is stored is x=2, y=1. So I construct that point and store the Point into the Hashtable indexed by the MineCell a (cells[1][2] stores a and (Point)pointIndex.get(a) returns the point (2, 1)).

Why is this information useful, you ask? When a MineCell triggers an event you can get a reference to that MineCell by calling getSource(), but what is its position in the MineField? You don't know. You'd have to loop through every index of the cells[][] array and compare e.getSource() == cells[row][column] to find it. You need to know where it is because you have to start checking the cells around it to see if they can be revealed.

Remember from the beginning of the chapter that if you click an empty cell, all the surrounding empty cells are revealed and also any empty cells that surround those cells are revealed too, up until it reaches cells that have some sort of mine adjacent to them, those cells don't have their adjacent cells revealed. To make getting the location quick and painless, you just store the location and index it by the MineCell object it contains, and then you can get any MineCell's coordinates by checking the pointIndex Hashtable.

The pointIndex Hashtable is constructed by passing in its initial size, rows * cols. A hash table is a general computer science term that refers to mapping keys to values. In our case, we are mapping the MineCell object (the key) to its Point location (the value). A Hashtable stores a value by a key by calling the put(Object, Object) method. The first argument is the key and the second argument is the value. To retrieve the value based on its key, you then call the get(Object) method, passing in the key, and it returns the value. So in this case passing in the MineCell will return the Point object that stores where the given MineCell is positioned.

The randomizeField() method first loops on all the MineCells and sets their contents to MineCell.EMPTY. Then for each of the mines, it generates a random number based on the total number of cells. Because there is only one random number, the row is determined by dividing the random number, index, by the number of columns (if there are 10 columns and the random number is 11, 11/10 is 1, so it would be the second row, dividing by the number of rows would not necessarily be correct). The column number is the remainder (index % cols), so given the previous example, the column number would be 1, (the second column from the left). So once it has a row and a column figured out, it looks to see whether there is a mine there already (it wouldn't be for the first mine, but could be for subsequent mines). If not, it puts one there:

```
cells[index / cols][index % cols].resetContents(MineCell.MINE);
```

If there already is one there it just continuously generates new random numbers until it can find an index that is not occupied by a mine already. Here is the loop that does this:

```
for (int m=0; m < mines; m++) {
  do {
    index = rand.nextInt(rows * cols);
  }
  while (cells[index / cols][index % cols].getContents() != MineCell.EMPTY);
  cells[index / cols][index % cols].resetContents(MineCell.MINE);
}
```

After all the mines are set in place, the number clues are set. This is done by looping on each cell. For each cell, it counts the number of mines that are in the eight cells that surround it and sets the contents of the cell to that number. If there are zero, this results in MineCell.EMPTY which is equal to zero. Here is the code that accomplishes this feat:

```
protected void setNumberClues() {
   int nMines;
   for (int r=0; r < cells.length; r++) {
     for (int c=0; c < cells[r].length; c++) {
       if (cells[r][c].getContents() != MineCell.MINE) {
         nMines = 0;
         //count the number of mines surrounding this cell
         for (int dr = r - 1; dr <= r + 1; dr++) {
           //prevent ArrayIndexOutOfBoundsException
           //continue puts control back to the beginning of the loop
           if (dr < 0 || dr >= cells.length) continue;
           for (int dc = c - 1; dc <= c + 1; dc++) {
             if (dc < 0 || dc >= cells[dr].length) continue;
             if (cells[dr][dc].getContents() == MineCell.MINE) nMines++;
           }
         }
         cells[r][c].resetContents(nMines);
       }
     }
   }
}
```

You can see that the nested for loops iterate through all the cells and if the cell doesn't have a mine in it, it counts the number of mines that surround it. The dr and dc variables loop on the cells that are adjacent to this cell (a 3-by-3 cell grid area, actually). Every time it encounters a mine, it increments nMines, and then it sets the contents of this cell (the center cell of the 3-by-3 grid) to nMines. The continue statements return control to the beginning of the innermost loop in instances where an ArrayIndexOutOfBoundExceptions might occur, like the top-left cell. There is no cell to the left of or above this cell. Therefore, before it checks a cell that is out of the array's bounds, it just uses the continue statement to try the next cell instead. Take a look at Figure 12.7 to see how a center cell displays the number of mines that surround it when it is revealed.

FIGURE 12.7

The number 2 in the cell in the center of the boxed group of cells indicates that there are two mines adjacent to it.

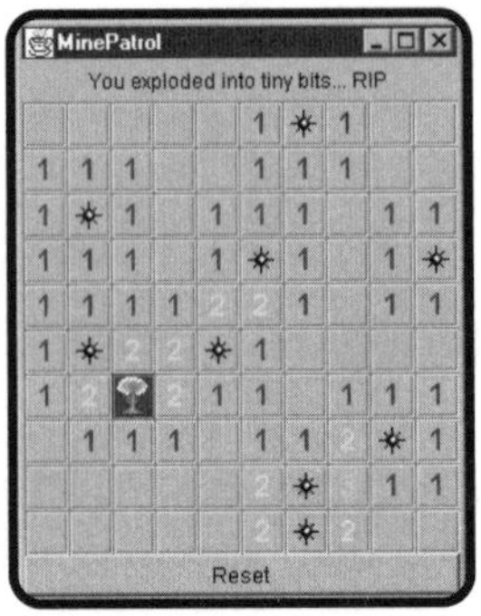

The MineCellListener interface methods are implemented to listen for Mine-CellEvents. When a MineCell is detonated, this MineField plays the explodeClip audio file, and then reveals all its cells by calling revealAll(), so that the user can see where he or she went wrong, and dispatches a MineFieldEvent.DETONATED event to its listeners.

When a MineCell is flagged, the mineCellFlagged(MineCellEvent) method is invoked. MineCells by themselves don't care how many flags you have left, because they are blind to the MineField you have them grouped together in. As far as the MineCell is concerned, as long as it is enabled, it can be flagged. The MineField needs to keep track of how many flags there are. The number of flags is the same as the number of mines. If the player tries to flag a MineCell after all his or her flags are gone, the MineField immediately clears the flag away by invoking setHidden(true) on the MineCell that triggered the event. This ensures that you don't flag the eleventh MineCell when you only have ten flags to use.

If there are enough flags left, though, the cell remains flagged, the flagClip audio file is played. Also, if a MineCell is flagged or unflagged a MineField-Event.FLAG_COUNT_CHANGED event is fired for its listeners to handle and the flagged variable is incremented or decremented accordingly.

The mineCellRevealed(MineCellEvent) method plays the revealClip audio file, increments the revealed variable, and calls the showSafeArea(MineCell) method if the revealed MineCell is empty. The showSafeArea(MineCell) method uses the following algorithm to determine which cells should be revealed:

1. It starts off by revealing all the eight cells that immediately surround this cell (if they haven't already been revealed, even if it's flagged). Any empty cell should have all its surrounding cells revealed. A cell that has any value other than `MineCell.EMTPY` should not automatically have any of the hidden cells that surround it revealed. See Figure 12.8 for a visual of how this should work.

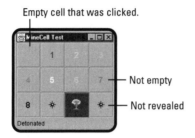

Empty cell that was clicked.

FIGURE 12.8

This shows how every empty cell adjacent to the clicked cell was revealed. Recursively, any newly revealed empty cell had its adjacent cells revealed as well.

Not empty

Not revealed

2. As it reveals the cells that surround the original cell, if one of the newly revealed cells is also empty, it should have its safe area revealed as well, so from this `showSafeArea(MineCell)` method, it recalls itself, passing in the newly revealed cell to have its surrounding safe area revealed.

    When a method calls itself, it is called a recursive method. This can be dangerous. The compiler checks for obvious infinite loops, but when you call a method from within itself, it can get very confusing to keep track of what is going on. This recursive method is very careful to not cause an infinite loop. It doesn't attempt to clear mine cells that are already revealed, and it immediately reveals the current cell if it needs to be, so ultimately it will run out of cells to reveal and the loop will terminate.

3. You should also note that this is where the `pointIndex Hashtable` object is most useful. The parameter to the `showSafeArea(MineCell)` method is the cell that needs to have its adjacent cells cleared, but all you have is an object reference, where this `MineCell` is in the `cells[][]` array. Because you set up the `pointIndex` member earlier, getting this point is as easy as invoking the `get(Object)` method: `(Point)pointIndex.get(start)`, which returns the indices for the `MineCell`.

Any time a `MineCell` is flagged or revealed, the `MineField` checks whether it has been solved by calling the `checkIfSolved()` method. Checking whether the `MineField` is solved is very simple. If the number of flagged cells plus the number of revealed cells is equal to the total number of cells, the `MineField` must be solved.

The number of flags that you have is equal to the number of mines that are in the MineField. So if all the cells that are left over are flagged, they must all be mines. Mission accomplished.

Here is the full source code listing for MineField.java

```java
/*
 * MineField
 * Maintains a grid of MineCells
 */

import java.awt.*;
import java.util.*;
import java.applet.AudioClip;

public class MineField extends Panel
                            implements MineCellListener {
  protected int rows, cols, mines, flagged, revealed;
  protected AudioClip revealClip, flagClip, unflagClip, explodeClip;
  protected MineCell[][] cells;
  //keeps track of MineCell indices
  protected Hashtable pointIndex;
  protected Vector listeners;

  public MineField(int nRows, int nCols, int nMines) {
    rows = nRows > 0 ? nRows : 1;
    cols = nCols > 0 ? nCols : 1;
    cells = new MineCell[rows][cols];
    mines = nMines >= 0 && nMines < rows * cols ? nMines : 1;
    pointIndex = new Hashtable(rows * cols);
    setLayout(new GridLayout(rows, cols));
    for (int r=0; r < cells.length; r++) {
      for (int c=0; c < cells[r].length; c++) {
        cells[r][c] = new MineCell();
        cells[r][c].addMineCellListener(this);
        //Points use (x, y) coordinates so x=c and y=r
        pointIndex.put(cells[r][c], new Point(c, r));
        cells[r][c].setSize(25, 25);
        add(cells[r][c]);
      }
    }
    listeners = new Vector();
    randomizeField(false);
  }

  protected void randomizeField(boolean fireEvent) {
    Random rand = new Random();
    int index;
    //initialize empty
    for (int r=0; r < cells.length; r++) {
      for (int c=0; c < cells[r].length; c++) {
        cells[r][c].resetContents(MineCell.EMPTY);
      }
    }
```

```
      //randomly place all mines
      for (int m=0; m < mines; m++) {
        do {
          index = rand.nextInt(rows * cols);
        }
        while (cells[index / cols][index % cols].getContents() != MineCell.EMPTY);
        cells[index / cols][index % cols].resetContents(MineCell.MINE);
      }
      setNumberClues();
      flagged = revealed = 0;
      //does not fire flagCountChanged, only mineFieldRandomized
      if (fireEvent) (new EventThread(new MineFieldEvent(this,
                          MineFieldEvent.RANDOMIZED))).start();
  }

  public void randomize() {
    randomizeField(true);
  }

  public int getFlagCount() {
    return flagged;
  }

  public int getMineCount() {
    return mines;
  }

  //counts and sets the number of mines surrounding each cell
  protected void setNumberClues() {
    int nMines;
    for (int r=0; r < cells.length; r++) {
      for (int c=0; c < cells[r].length; c++) {
        if (cells[r][c].getContents() != MineCell.MINE) {
          nMines = 0;
          //count the number of mines surrounding this cell
          for (int dr = r - 1; dr <= r + 1; dr++) {
            //prevent ArrayIndexOutOfBoundsException
            //continue puts control back to the beginning of the loop
            if (dr < 0 || dr >= cells.length) continue;
            for (int dc = c - 1; dc <= c + 1; dc++) {
              if (dc < 0 || dc >= cells[dr].length) continue;
              if (cells[dr][dc].getContents() == MineCell.MINE) nMines++;
            }
          }
          cells[r][c].resetContents(nMines);
        }
      }
    }
  }

  protected class EventThread extends Thread {
    MineFieldEvent e;
```

```
        EventThread(MineFieldEvent mfe) {
          e = mfe;
        }

        public void run() {
          switch(e.getID()) {
            case MineFieldEvent.SOLVED:
              for (int i=0; i < listeners.size(); i++) {
                ((MineFieldListener)listeners.elementAt(i)).mineFieldSolved(e);
              }
              break;
            case MineFieldEvent.RANDOMIZED:
              for (int i=0; i < listeners.size(); i++) {
                ((MineFieldListener)listeners.elementAt(i)).mineFieldRandomized(e);
              }
              break;
            case MineFieldEvent.DETONATED:
              for (int i=0; i < listeners.size(); i++) {
                ((MineFieldListener)listeners.elementAt(i)).mineFieldDetonated(e);
              }
              break;
            case MineFieldEvent.FLAG_COUNT_CHANGED:
              for (int i=0; i < listeners.size(); i++) {

((MineFieldListener)listeners.elementAt(i)).mineFieldFlagCountChanged(e);
              }
              break;
          }
        }
      }


      public void setImages(Image f, Image m, Image e) {
        MineCell.setImages(f, m, e);
      }

      public void setAudioClips(AudioClip r, AudioClip f, AudioClip u,
                                AudioClip e) {
        revealClip = r; flagClip = f; unflagClip = u; explodeClip = e;
      }

      /* Reveals areas mine-free minecells */
      protected void showSafeArea(MineCell start) {
        //get the point index for the starting cell
        Point p = (Point)pointIndex.get(start);
        for (int r = p.y - 1; r <= p.y + 1; r++) {
          if (r < 0 || r >= cells.length) continue;
          for (int c = p.x - 1; c <= p.x + 1; c++) {
            if (c < 0 || c >= cells[r].length || !cells[r][c].isHidden())
              continue;
            if (cells[r][c].isFlagged()) {
              flagged--;
```

```
          (new EventThread(new MineFieldEvent(this,
                         MineFieldEvent.FLAG_COUNT_CHANGED))).start();
        }
        cells[r][c].setHidden(false);
        revealed++;
        if (cells[r][c].getContents() == MineCell.EMPTY)
          showSafeArea(cells[r][c]);
      }
    }
  }

  protected void checkIfSolved() {
    if (flagged + revealed == rows * cols) {
      //solved if we get here.
      revealAll();
    (new EventThread(new MineFieldEvent(this,
                         MineFieldEvent.SOLVED))).start();
    }
  }

  public void revealAll() {
    for (int r=0; r < cells.length; r++) {
      for (int c=0; c < cells.length; c++) {
        cells[r][c].setHidden(false);
      }
    }
  }

  public void mineCellRevealed(MineCellEvent e) {
    if (revealClip != null) revealClip.play();
    revealed++;
    if (((MineCell)e.getSource()).getContents() == MineCell.EMPTY)
      showSafeArea((MineCell)e.getSource());
    checkIfSolved();
  }

  public void mineCellDetonated(MineCellEvent e) {
    //game over show all
    if (explodeClip != null) explodeClip.play();
    revealAll();
    (new EventThread(new MineFieldEvent(this,
                         MineFieldEvent.DETONATED))).start();
  }

  public void mineCellFlagged(MineCellEvent e) {
    if (flagged >= mines) {
      ((MineCell)e.getSource()).setHidden(true);
      return;
    }
    if (flagClip != null) flagClip.play();
    flagged++;
    (new EventThread(new MineFieldEvent(this,
                         MineFieldEvent.FLAG_COUNT_CHANGED))).start();
```

```
      checkIfSolved();
    }

    public void mineCellUnflagged(MineCellEvent e) {
      if (unflagClip != null) unflagClip.play();
      flagged--;
      (new EventThread(new MineFieldEvent(this,
                           MineFieldEvent.FLAG_COUNT_CHANGED))).start();
    }

    public void addMineFieldListener(MineFieldListener mfl) {
      listeners.addElement(mfl);
    }

    public void removeMineFieldListener(MineFieldListener mfl) {
      listeners.removeElement(mfl);
    }

}
```

Creating the *MinePatrol* Application

You've already done the hard part. You wrote all the classes necessary to support this project. Now all you need to do is create an application that makes use of them. That's what the MinePatrol class does. It is responsible for loading the media files—the sounds and the animation and passing them to the MineCell object, as well as including the MineField and handling its MineFieldEvents. Its members are mineField, its MineField object, resetButton, a button that lets you reset the game, and flagCountLabel, a label that displays the number of flags you have left.

The reset button just calls the MineField's randomize() method to reset all the MineCells. The MineFieldListener interface methods update the flagCountLabel any time the number of flags left changes. This label also displays a message when the player blows up or when he or she wins the game. The source code listing for MinePatrol is as follows:

```
/*
 * MinePatrol
 * The MinePatrol Game Driver
 */

import java.awt.*;
import java.awt.event.*;
import java.applet.Applet;
import java.net.URL;
import java.net.MalformedURLException;

public class MinePatrol extends GUIFrame
                        implements MineFieldListener, ActionListener {
```

```java
  protected MineField minefield;
  protected Button resetButton;
  protected Label flagCountLabel;

  public MinePatrol() {
    super("MinePatrol");
    minefield = new MineField(10, 10, 10);
    minefield.addMineFieldListener(this);
    add(minefield, BorderLayout.CENTER);
    MediaTracker mt = new MediaTracker(this);
    Image[] imgs = {
      Toolkit.getDefaultToolkit().getImage("flag.gif"),
      Toolkit.getDefaultToolkit().getImage("mine.gif"),
      Toolkit.getDefaultToolkit().getImage("explode.gif") };

    for (int i=0; i < imgs.length; i++) {
      mt.addImage(imgs[i], i);
    }
    try {
      mt.waitForAll();
    } catch (InterruptedException e) {}
    minefield.setImages(imgs[0], imgs[1], imgs[2]);
    try {
      minefield.setAudioClips(
        Applet.newAudioClip(new URL("file:reveal.wav")),
        Applet.newAudioClip(new URL("file:flag.wav")),
        Applet.newAudioClip(new URL("file:unflag.wav")),
        Applet.newAudioClip(new URL("file:explode.wav")));
    } catch (MalformedURLException e) {}

    flagCountLabel = new Label("Flags: 10", Label.CENTER);
    add(flagCountLabel, BorderLayout.NORTH);
    resetButton = new Button("Reset");
    resetButton.addActionListener(this);
    add(resetButton, BorderLayout.SOUTH);
    pack();
    setVisible(true);
  }

  public static void main(String args[]) {
    new MinePatrol();
  }

  public void mineFieldSolved(MineFieldEvent e) {
    flagCountLabel.setText("You Win!");
  }

  public void mineFieldRandomized(MineFieldEvent e) {
    flagCountLabel.setText("Flags: " + minefield.getMineCount());
  }

  public void mineFieldDetonated(MineFieldEvent e) {
    flagCountLabel.setText("You exploded into tiny bits... RIP");
  }
```

```
public void mineFieldFlagCountChanged(MineFieldEvent e) {
   flagCountLabel.setText("Flags: "
     + (minefield.getMineCount() - minefield.getFlagCount()));
}

public void actionPerformed(ActionEvent e) {
   minefield.randomize();
}

}
```

Summary

In this chapter, you learned how to create lightweight components. You learned that lightweight components are components that don't have an associated native peer and are defined using Java-only code. You also learned how to declare packages and how to use the `javadoc` utility to document your code. Finally, you imported the `jpr.lightweight` package and extended it to create the `MinePatrol` game.

That's it. You've just finished the final chapter! You learned a lot in this book. From Chapter 1, "Getting Started," where you learned how to install the Java SDK and wrote your first program, `HelloWorld`, and progressively reading through more challenging chapters, up to and including this advanced chapter, you've learned a great deal about the Java language. At this point, you should be ready to develop your own projects using the Java language, or if you love to learn as much as I do, you can pick up a more advanced Java book and be able to follow it. Wherever your life takes you, I wish you good luck!

The stars appear every night in the sky. All is well.

CHALLENGES

1. Extend the `JPRButton3D` class to create a button that displays a label just like the AWT `Button` class you're so familiar with by now. As an extra test, override the `isFocusTraversable()` method so that your button class can be traversed and make sure you paint some special graphic to make it obvious when your button has focus.

2. Add functionality to the `MinePatrol` game so that you can specify different numbers of rows, columns, and/or mines each time you run it, either by accepting command-line arguments or by providing some menu options.

A

Using the CD-ROM

To take advantage of the goodies on the CD-ROM, first insert the CD into your CD-ROM drive. If your drive is configured to automatically execute the CD-ROM, it will open automatically. If nothing happens automatically when you insert the CD, you can run it manually by opening the start_here.html document located on the CD's root directory. For example, if your CD-ROM drive is labeled D, you can find it at D:\start_here.html.

You will be presented with the license agreement and notice of limited warranty. Read that information, and then Click I Agree to continue to the welcome page. This page presents you with four options, Java SDK, Source Code, Web Links, and Programs. You can also click the Prima Tech logo on the bottom left of the screen to visit their Web site at http://www.prima-tech.com.

Java SDK

Click on the Java SDK button to get to this page. From this page, you can run the installation file, which will install Java SDK, version 1.3.1. There are different files depending on which operating system you have. Look for the file that is right for your operating system. If you have any Windows version, look under the Microsoft section. If you are using Linux, look under the Linux x86 section. If you want to install the SDK on a Solaris machine, look under the Solaris SPARC/x86 section. You can find the instructions for installing and setting up the SDK for your system in Chapter 1, "Getting Started."

You can also find the Java Documentation installation here. You can either install the documentation on your system or browse it online on Sun's Web site by using the URL **http://java.sun.com/j2se/1.3/docs/**.

Source Code

All of the source code of the examples in this book can be found on the CD-ROM. Click on the Source Code button to get to the source code page. The source code and class files are organized under their respective chapters. Each chapter gives you the option to either browse or download the files. If you chose to download, click the Download button. The download file is in ZIP format, so you will need an unzip tool, such as Winzip (included on the CD-ROM), to unpack the files into the local directory of your choosing. If you choose to browse the files without saving them to your local disk, click Explore. A new window will open up that contains the files associated with that chapter. The file extension for the source code is .java. You can open this file with any text editor since it is a straight text file.

It is still possible to run the example programs without installing them locally. To do this, you need to open up a shell (command prompt) and change to the class file directory. For example, if you're using Windows and your CD-ROM drive letter is D, to run the `HelloWorld` example from Chapter 1, you need to change to the directory D:\Source Code\Chapter 1\. Next, you need to run the `java` command on the program. (Note: you can only do this after you've installed the SDK.) For example, this is what you type at your command prompt to run the `HelloWorld` application: **`java HelloWorld`**.

Web Links

The Web Links section includes links to some useful Internet sites. To get to this section, simply click the Web Links button. The links you will find there are:

Sun Java	This takes you directly to Sun's Java Web site. (**http://java.sun.com**).
Sun Microsystems	This takes you to Sun's main Web site. Sun Microsystems is the innovator behind Java technology. (**http://www.sun.com**).
Sun Educational Services	Here you can learn how to further your Java education and become a Sun-certified Java programmer! (**http://suned.sun.com**).
East Coast Games	A site written by programmers that you can use as a resource for your video game programming endeavors. (**http://www.east-coastgames.com**).
NetBeans	NetBeans is an open source integrated development environment (IDE) that you can download and use to facilitate your Java application programming projects (**http://www.net-beans.org**).

Programs

This section includes some programs that you can install and use on your system. To get to this section, click on the Programs button. For installation instructions, visit the Web site link, which is under the program name listing on this page. The programs are:

Cool Edit Pro	This is a demo version of a very cool audio editing program.
The GIMP	The GIMP is a powerful image-editing tool. Just install it and thank me later. It rocks.
Internet Explorer 5.5	Microsoft's very popular Internet browser. You can install this latest version and run the applet examples from the book with it.
Winzip 8.0	Winzip is a great tool for packaging and unpacking file archives.

Java Language Summary

Reserved Words

The following list included Java's reserved words, also known as key-words. You cannot use them to name identifiers.

abstract	default	if	private	this
boolean	do	implements	protected	throw
break	double	import	public	throws
byte	else	instanceof	return	transient
case	extends	int	short	try
catch	final	interface	static	void
char	finally	long	strictfp	volatile
class	float	native	super	while
const	for	new	switch	
continue	goto	package	synchronized	

The boolean literals true and false, and the null literal, although not technically keywords, cannot be used as identifiers either.

Primitive Data Types

Type	Number of Bits
boolean	1
byte	8
short	16
char	16
int	32
float	32
long	64
double	64

Ranges for Integral Types

Type	Minimum	Maximum
byte	-2^7	$2^7 - 1$
short	-2^{15}	$2^{15} - 1$
int	-2^{31}	$2^{31} - 1$
long	-2^{63}	$2^{63} - 1$
char	0	$2^{16} - 1$

Floating-Point Constants

```
Float.NEGATIVE_INFINITY
Float.POSITIVE_INFINITY
Float.NaN
Double.NEGATIVE_INFINITY
Double.POSITIVE_INFINITY
Double.NaN
```

NaN stands for "not a number" and represents values of undefined operations such as 0.0 / 0.0.

Comments

There are three types of comments used in Java (single line, multi-line, and javadoc).

This is a single line comment example:

```
// this is a single line comment
```

This is a multi-line comment example:

```
/* this is a multi-line
   comment */
```

This is a javadoc comment example:

```
/**
 * This is a javadoc comment
 */
```

Literals

Literals are used in Java to represent values that are of the primitive, String, or null types in source code. The following sections summarize their syntaxes. Anything within square braces ([and]) is optional and the bar character (|) separates different options. For example, [+|-] means the code can include +, -, or neither (because they are within square brackets).

Integer Literals

Integer literals can be expressed in octal (base 8), decimal (base 10), or hexadecimal (base 16). Octal digits can be any digits from 0 to 7. Decimal digits can be any digits ranging from 0 to 9. Hexadecimal digits can be any digit ranging from 0 to 9 and also any letter (case-insensitive) from A to F. A=10, B=11, C=12, D=13, E=14, F=15. The syntax for an integer literal is:

```
[+|-][0[X|x]]number[L|l]
```

Example	Description
67	int literal having value 67
+67	int literal having value 67
-67	negative int literal having value –67
012	octal int literal having value 10

-0X27C   hexadecimal int literal having value −636

1234567890L long literal having value 1,234,567,890

-0XBEL   hexadecimal long literal having value -190

Floating-Point Literals

A floating-point literal can be either a float or a double. The syntax for a floating-point number is:

`[+|-]number.number[[+|-]Eexponent|[+|-]eexponent][F|D|f|d]`

Example	Description
-10.	double literal having value -10.0
+.01	double literal having value 0.01
1.23	double literal having value 1.23
1.23d	double literal having value 1.23
1.23f	float literal having value 1.23
2E4	double literal having value 20,000.0 (2×10^4)
-133e-2F	float literal having value -1.33 (-133×10^{-2})

Boolean Literals

Boolean literals must be either true or false.

Character Literals

A character literal is a single character or escape sequence enclosed in single quotes. The data type of a character literal is always char. A Unicode character escape sequence is in the form \unnnn, where *nnnn* is the hexadecimal representation of the character. The syntax for a character literal is (exactly one character or escape sequence must appear within the single quotes):

`'character|escape_sequence'`

Example	Description
'a'	char literal a
'$'	char literal $
'\u003F'	char literal ?
'\''	char literal ' (single quote)
'\"'	char literal " (double quote)

'\b'	char literal for backspace
'\f'	char literal for form-feed
'\n'	char literal for new line
'\r'	char literal for carriage return
'\t'	char literal for tab
'\\'	char literal for backslash (\)

String Literals

A string literal consists of a string of characters and/or escape sequences within double quotes. The data type is always String. The syntax for a String literal is:

`"[characters&|escape_sequences]"`

Example	Description
""	The empty string
"Abc"	String literal Abc
"\"Java\""	String literal "Java"
"C:\\My Documents\\myfile.txt"	String literal C:\My Documents\myfile.txt

Null Literal

The null literal is null.

Operators

In the following table, arg refers to any variable or value. Some operators only take certain types of arguments. For example, ! only works on Boolean types.

Type	Syntax	Description
Unary	+arg, -arg	Sign (positive or negative)
	++variable	Prefix increment
	variable++	Postfix increment
	--variable	Prefix decrement
	variable--	Postfix decrement
	!arg	Boolean compliment (Not)
	~arg	Bitwise inversion
	(type)arg	Cast

Arithmetic	`arg + arg`	Addition
	`arg - arg`	Subtraction
	`arg * arg`	Multiplication
	`arg / arg`	Division
	`arg % arg`	Modulus
Shift	`arg >> arg`	Left shift
	`arg >> arg`	Right shift
	`arg >>> arg`	Unsigned right shift
Comparison	`arg < arg`	Less than
	`arg > arg`	Greater than
	`arg <= arg`	Less than or equal to
	`arg >= arg`	Greater than or equal to
	`arg == arg`	Equal to
	`arg != arg`	Not equal to
	`arg instanceof` `    class`	Instance of
Bitwise	`arg & arg`	Bitwise AND
	`arg | arg`	Bitwise OR
	`arg ^ arg`	Bitwise XOR
Logical	`arg && arg`	Logical AND
	`arg || arg`	Logical OR

Ternary	`condition ?`
	`    val_if_true :`
	`    val_if_false`
		Conditional operator

Assignment Operators

Assignment operators store a value into a variable. This section covers the operators that included the equals sign (=), however, the increment (++) and decrement (--) operators perform assignments as well. The assignment operator can be just the equals sign or the equals sign followed by an additional operator (although the combination of the two constitutes one single operator). The syntax for the assignment operator is:

```
variable =[op] arg
```

If = is combined with another operator, the operation is logically equivalent to:

```
variable = variable op arg
```

The following are all assignment operators:

=		+=	-=	*=	/=	&=	|=	^=	%=	<<=
>>=		>>>=								

Loops

Name	Syntax
for loop	`for([init, init, …];[condition];[update, update, …]) { body }`
while loop	`while(condition) { body }`
do loop	`do { body } while (condition);`

Break and Continue

The break and continue statements redirect the flow of loops. break takes control out of the loop and continue returns control to the top of the loop.

Conditionals

The conditional statements are if, switch, and also the Ternary operator described in the "Operators" section. The syntax for the if conditional is (the square brackets [] indicate that the else if and else statements are optional and are not part of the syntax):

```
if (condition) {
  statements_condition_true;
}
[else if (other_condition) {
  statements_other_condition_true;
}, …]
[else {
  statements_no_condition_true;
}]
```

The syntax for the switch conditional is:

```
switch (test) {
  case value: [statements_test_equals_value] [break;]
  ...
  [default: [statements_test_equals_no_case_value]
}
```

Try... Catch Blocks

Try... catch blocks are used for exception handling. Here is the syntax:

```
try {
  statements_that_might_cause_an_exception;
} catch (exception_type exception_variable_name) {
  [statements_that_execute_if_exception_is_caught]
}
```

Class Definition

The syntax for defining a class follows:

```
[package package_name;]
[[import Imported_class_or_package;] ...]
[access_modifier] class class_name [extends super_class_name] [implements
implemented_Interface, ...] {
  [class_definition]
}
```

Class Modifiers

Modifier	Description
public	Access modifier
final	Class cannot be subclassed
abstract	Must be subclassed (cannot be instantiated)

Constructor Definition

The syntax for a constructor is as follows. The first line of the constructor body must be either an explicit call to the superclass's constructor using super(), an implied call to the superclass's no-arg constructor, or a call to another constructor within this class using this():

```
[access_modifier] class_name([arg, …]) { [constructor_body] }
```

Variable Declaration

The syntax for declaring a variable is as follows:

```
[access_modifier] [modifier, ...] type variable_name [ = initial_value];
```

Variable Modifiers

Modifier(s)	Description
public protected private	Access modifiers
static	Indicates this is a class variable
final	Indicates a constant
transient	Indicates a variable that cannot be serialized
volatile	Indicates that variable may be modified asynchronously

Method Definition

The syntax for defining a method is as follows. Unless the return type is void, the last executable statement of any logical path of execution within the method must be a return statement that returns a value of type *return_type*:

```
[access_modifier] [modifier, …] return_type method_name([arg, …]) [throws
exception, …] { [body] }
```

Method Modifiers

Modifier(s)	Definition
public protected private	Access modifiers
static	Indicates this is a class method
final	Indicates that this method cannot be over-ridden
abstract	Indicates the body must be defined in a subclass

native	Indicates the method body is defined outside of Java in a native library
synchronized	Indicates that, at most, only one thread can have control of this method at any given time

Index

492

Index

498

Index